DISCARD

E99.C9 H34 2004
NRG
33663003691439
The invention of the Cre
Nation, 1670-1763

D1499120

DISC

DATE DUE

MAR 2 4 2006	
SEP 1 7 2011	
JUN 2 7 2012	

BRODART, CO.   Cat. No. 23-221-003

*The Invention of
the Creek Nation,
1670–1763*

INDIANS OF THE SOUTHEAST

SERIES EDITORS

Michael D. Green
University of North Carolina

Theda Perdue
University of North Carolina

ADVISORY EDITORS

Leland Ferguson
University of South Carolina

Mary Young
University of Rochester

The Invention of
the Creek Nation,
1670–1763

STEVEN C. HAHN

University of Nebraska Press
Lincoln and London

Portions of chapters 2 and 3 previously appeared in
The Transformation of the Southeastern Indians, 1540–1760,
edited by Robbie Ethridge and Charles Hudson
(Jackson: University Press of Mississippi, 2002), 79–114.

© 2004 by the Board of Regents of the University of Nebraska
All rights reserved
Manufactured in the United States of America
∞

Library of Congress Cataloging-in-Publication Data
Hahn, Steven C., 1968–
The invention of the Creek Nation, 1670–1763 / Steven C. Hahn.
p. cm.—(Indians of the Southeast)
Includes bibliographical references and index.
ISBN 0-8032-2414-1 (cloth : alk. paper)
1. Creek Nation—History.   2. Creek Indians—First contact
with Europeans.   3. Creek Indians—Politics and
government.   4. Creek Indians—Government relations.
5. Oglethorpe, James Edward, 1696–1785—Relations with
Creek Indians.   6. Tomo-chi-chi, d. 1739.   I. Title.   II. Series.
E99.C9H34 2004
975.004'97385–dc22
2003026821

Library Services
Austin Community College
Austin, Texas

To Erin and Luke

Contents

Map

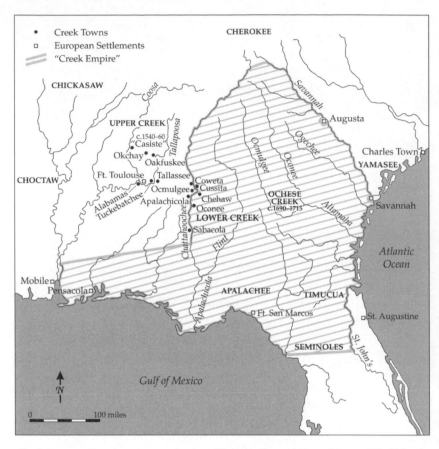

Creek Country. Based on map previously published in Braund, Deerskins and Duffels, *10.*

Acknowledgments

Though my name alone appears on the cover of this book and I will assume full responsibility for its virtues and shortcomings, I want to extend my sincere thanks to the many people and institutions that made this work possible. The book began several years ago as my doctoral dissertation at Emory University. For four years Emory University financed my graduate studies and was most generous in awarding me additional funds to attend conferences and conduct research outside of the Atlanta area. Emory University, in conjunction with the Andrew W. Mellon Foundation, provided to me a fifth year of funding as a Southern Studies Fellow. While I was in graduate school, the American Philosophical Society was kind enough to honor me with a Phillips Fund Grant for Native American Research. In addition the William L. Clements Library in Ann Arbor, Michigan, rewarded me with a Price Visiting Research Fellowship. The generosity of those two institutions enabled me to conduct research in Michigan, Florida, and South Carolina that proved instrumental in completing the dissertation.

It has been my great fortune to experience the generosity of yet other institutions since completing my graduate work. The Huntington Library of San Marino, California, awarded me with a W. M. Keck Fellowship that allowed me to work in residence there for an entire month. My employer, St. Olaf College of Northfield, Minnesota, awarded me a Summer Faculty Development Grant that permitted me to conduct subsequent research in South Carolina toward the completion of the book manuscript.

Of greater importance to me have been the many individuals who have contributed, knowingly or not, to the content of these pages. I begin with my dissertation advisor John Juricek, who has had a hand in this project since its inception. His scholarly insight, moral support, and patience continue to inspire me. It is my hope that this book will justify all of his hard work on my behalf. My dissertation committee members Michael Bellesiles and John Worth deserve thanks for their learned criticism and for the enthusiasm they showed for my work as it progressed. I extend a particular note of thanks to John Worth for allowing me to use his private collection of Spanish documents. This book would not have been possible without his generosity and inspiration. Bruce Chappell of the P. K. Yonge Library of Florida History in Gainesville, Florida, John Dann of the Clements Library, and Roy Ritchie of the Huntington Library deserve thanks for making my stay at their respective institutions a most pleasant and rewarding experience.

More recently, the editorial staff at the University of Nebraska Press has played an all-important role in shaping the content of the book and the mind of the man behind it. I wish to express my thanks to both the anonymous reviewers and the press staff: their criticisms have made me (I hope) a better historian. Most of all I want to thank Michael Green for his devotion to this project. The intellectual energy he contributed to it went above and beyond the call of duty, as it was his hand that helped me to transform a once-unwieldy dissertation into the book that you now hold. To my colleagues and students at St. Olaf: thank you for your support, understanding, and for making me a better scholar and person.

Finally, I want to thank my family for giving me the strength to endure the agony and the ecstasy of writing history. My parents John and Barbara and my brother Keith have given their unconditional love and support for my work. My children Erin and Luke don't yet know much about the content of these pages, but their smiles, hugs, and kisses have contributed in more ways than one to the author's well-being. Above all they have taught me that life's most valuable lessons are not to be read in books. I therefore dedicate this work to them in the hope that they may one day read it and learn from me. Last, but certainly not least, none of this would be possible without the love and support of Mary, my wife and best friend, whom I cannot begin to thank enough just for loving me, even when the rigors of my professional life have made me less than lovable.

Series Editors' Introduction

When English colonists first coined the term "Creek Confederacy," they were trying to make political sense of a group of Indians that was very important to them but one that they did not understand very well. Uncomfortable with an Indian political culture that did not incorporate ideas of leadership, executive enforcement power, legislative authority, a centralist political structure, or national identity that conformed to English usage and assumptions, the colonists repeatedly felt the need to impose those ideas. Scattered villages became tribes and nations, clan elders became chiefs and kings, and sometimes local chiefs became emperors. The idea of "confederacy" for the Creeks reflected the observation by the English that a large number of towns located in present Georgia and Alabama seemed to have a great deal in common and periodically acted in concert. Too big and too complex to be a tribe or a nation, the English thought "confederacy" fit a Creek political reality that they believed was both organized and chaotic.

Students of Creek history have long been frustrated by the term confederacy, even as they have agreed that on some levels it is more accurate than not. The Creeks were organized in autonomous towns, each with a separate history, and their primary political loyalties were to those towns. They had no perception of a Creek national identity and even today that idea rests lightly among many Creek people in Oklahoma. But Creek towns usually had friendly relations with one another, they cooperated in joint endeavors, and they formed alliances against enemies. Hard pressed to come up with a better term, scholars have perpetuated the idea of a Creek Confederacy in countless publications.

In this book Steven C. Hahn challenges the idea of a Creek confederacy. He argues that thinking about confederacy forces us to think about the political relations between towns, which were episodic, contingent, and confusing. "Nation," on the other hand, shifts our attention on the one hand to the land and a national domain and on the other to relations with outsiders. Nation, Hahn argues, gives the Creek problem a concreteness that "confederacy" and "alliance" cannot. This, then, is Hahn's history of the creation of the Creek Nation. Focusing on the period from 1670 to 1763, Hahn centers his story on the town of Coweta and its chiefs. In particular he foregrounds what he calls the "Coweta Resolution," the foreign policy of play-off diplomacy that empowered Coweta and laid the groundwork for Creek nationhood.

Based on exhaustive research in English, Spanish, and French sources that is analyzed within a culturally sensitive framework, and written with a graceful hand, this book will take its place as an important interpretation of a critical period in Creek history. We welcome it to the list of volumes in the Indians of the Southeast Series.

Michael D. Green
Theda Purdue

Introduction:
The Question of the
"Creek Confederacy"

In times of calamity, it has been said, any rumor is believable. Calamitous indeed were the rumors circulating among the Creek Indians in the final year of the Great War for Empire, Britain and France's climactic struggle for supremacy on the American continent. Unsubstantiated reports indicated that British troops were gathering for a great assault on the French towns of New Orleans and Mobile, "with a view, from thence, to attempt the extirpation of the Creeks."[1] Others feared the English had not been entirely forthcoming about their true war aims, causing one experienced Creek headman to surmise that "the white people intend to take all their lands."[2] The arrival of British troops at the Spanish post of Pensacola, Florida, scared others into believing that "the English were to surround the Indians and punish them," the ultimate goal being "to make them tame."[3] So startling was the rumor of the French defeat in the north that the Creeks sent a party to Canada just "to see if it was true."[4]

But if calamitous times make it possible to believe what cannot be proven, the Creeks were wise enough to know that rumors often contain a seed of truth. By the summer of 1763 word had begun to spread among the Creeks that Britain, France, and Spain had finally settled on a peace agreement, penned on February 10, 1763, in Paris. There the victorious British forced France and Spain to cede their North American possessions to King George, potentially leaving the Creeks exposed to British encirclement.[5] Sensing that rumor had turned to prophesy, many Creeks responded to this news with horror and indignation. "We have advice from Augusta," reported the *South Carolina Gazette* on June 4,

1763, "that the Creeks have been informed the French and Spaniards are to evacuate all they possess on this side of the river Mississippi, and do not seem to relish the news; that they declare they will not suffer them to depart." The Creeks insisted, the report continued, "that in case the French and Spaniards should be taken from them, we have noe right to possess the lands that were never given to us, and they will oppose all our attempt that way."[6]

Although the Creeks could do little more than watch as British troops marched into the fortresses that had once belonged to the Catholic monarchies, they resisted the transfer of power in various direct and indirect ways. At the former Spanish posts of St. Augustine and Pensacola, Creek chiefs haggled with British officers to fix precise boundaries between British and Creek lands. Eager to vent their frustrations against all outsiders, Creek warriors began killing an occasional Choctaw and Cherokee to punish those two nations for what the Creeks perceived as their support for the British. Creek warriors also murdered several British traders as the transfer of power was taking place, as if to demonstrate to British officials that they would not succumb easily to British encroachment.[7] The Treaty of Paris may have concluded the war between the European powers, but it did little to pacify the Creeks, who were quickly earning a reputation as the "least friendly" Indian nation in the entire Southeast.[8] "Never," it was observed, had the Creeks been "so audacious as lately."[9]

To bring the Creeks and their Indian neighbors to more peaceful terms, the newly appointed superintendent of Indian Affairs, John Stuart, invited the Indians and the governors of the southern British colonies to a grand "congress," scheduled to take place in November 1763 at Augusta, Georgia. At Augusta, Stuart succeeded in convincing representatives of the five Southern Indian nations—the Creeks, Cherokees, Chickasaws, Choctaws, and Catawbas—to sign a peace treaty, commonly known as the Treaty of Augusta. In an attempt to pacify the land-hungry British, the Creeks agreed to cede a portion of their hunting grounds to the colony of Georgia, foreshadowing the infamous Removal of the 1830s.[10]

Hailed in the colonies as a stroke of diplomatic genius, the Treaty of Augusta nevertheless exposed the problems—as they were understood in the colonies—inherent in conducting Indian affairs. The main problem was that the headmen who signed the treaty on behalf of the "upper and lower Creek nation" may have had no authority to cede the nation's land. As a Chickasaw headman warned British officials, "Nothing done here will be confirmed by the absent [Creek] leaders, in comparison of whom the present chiefs are inconsiderable."[11] Many important chiefs, it was argued, had absented themselves in protest, thereby calling into question the legality of the land cession and the nature of Creek political leadership, if not the very definition of the "Creek Nation."

In this book I tell the political history of the Creek Indians, the native inhabitants of the region of the Chattahoochee, Coosa, and Tallapoosa Rivers, which span the present-day states of Georgia and Alabama. The time frame chosen for this study—1670 to 1763—reflects my belief that the period beginning with the establishment of Charles Town, South Carolina, and ending with the Treaty of Paris should be considered a distinct epoch in Creek political history; it is identified here as the South's Imperial Era. With the rise of English and, later, French colonies to challenge the long-established Spanish colony of Florida, the American South became a theater of imperial struggle. The Creeks' territory abutted the lands claimed by each of the three European powers, and at times the Creeks found themselves thrust onto center stage and forced to improvise new political strategies and institutions to meet new challenges.[12]

If it would at first appear that these circumstances led to the swift demise of the Creeks, scholars have long recognized that, to the contrary, the Creeks fared rather well in the early eighteenth century. Writing in 1928, the influential historian Verner Crane dubbed the Creeks the "custodians of the wilderness balance of power in the South," in recognition of the Creeks' policy of "neutrality," which enabled them to play the British off against the Spanish and French.[13] While most scholars concur that the policy of "neutrality" was the centerpiece of Creek foreign policy, few have sought to understand precisely how and when the Creeks put this policy into practice or how neutrality became enshrined as a Creek tradition. Furthermore, because of the decentralized nature of political power among the Creeks, we cannot be sure if the Creeks consciously pursued neutrality as a policy, or if it came about accidentally as the de facto result of various Creek political factions acting in their own interests.[14]

In an attempt to answer such lingering questions, I have consulted not only the paper trails of the respective British colonies but also the underutilized archives of Spanish Florida and, to a lesser extent, French

Louisiana, in an attempt to "triangulate" Creek diplomatic activity. I will demonstrate that the Creeks, reeling from the effects of the Yamasee War of 1715, first formally articulated this policy of neutrality in 1718 in the Creek town of Coweta. Over time the "Coweta Resolution," as I have called it here, became the political wisdom of much of the Creek Nation, acquiring the sanctity of tradition among later generations.

By demonstrating the evolution of Creek "neutrality" policy in this way, I hope the reader will gain a better appreciation of Creek perspectives on European colonialism. The Creeks believed that their political autonomy was best preserved in the context of imperial competition and feared the arrival of a day when one of the European powers would gain the upper hand. Therefore, from the Creek perspective the Treaty of Paris of 1763 was a radical shift in the political dynamics of the region that brought to an abrupt end a style of politics that had been two generations in the making. Little wonder, then, that the Creeks recoiled in horror upon learning the articles of the Peace of Paris and behaved in a manner befitting their reputation as the "least friendly" Indians.

The subject under scrutiny here—politics—may at first glance appear to be an uncomfortable fit in an ethnohistorical study. As defined by James Axtell, ethnohistory is best thought of as "the use of historical and ethnological methods and materials to gain knowledge of the nature and causes of change in a culture defined by ethnological concepts and categories." Succinctly put, ethnohistorical studies utilize culture as the central category of analysis, with great attention paid to the patterns of meanings, values, and norms shared by a society and the symbolic expression and transmission thereof.[15] Political history, in contrast, tilts toward a more chronological, event-driven approach, and emphasizes questions of realpolitik rather than questions of cultural change. The goal of this work is to apply the insights of ethnohistory to some of the more traditional concerns of political history and to embed Creek political action in the broader context of Creek culture. In the end I hope the reader will discern new Creek perspectives on familiar events and gain insight into the culturally specific political motives of the Creeks and their leaders.

Increasingly, historians have come to recognize the benefits of what might be dubbed "ethnopolitical" history. Three general points of emphasis are discernable as products of the ethnopolitical approach as it pertains to Native Americans. The first is the importance of kinship as the basis of Native American political concepts and practices. Kinship not only served as the bond among Native Americans but applied more abstractly to their relationship with Europeans. The Creeks incorporated Europeans into their social and political circles when necessary, subjecting them to rules of reciprocity, giving the Native Americans leverage over traders and colonial governors alike. The second major point emphasized in such works is that broad tribal distinctions such as "Creek," "Ojibwe," or "Sioux" fail to capture the political complexity of loosely organized tribal peoples. For this reason scholars have rightly begun to turn their attention to smaller political units, discovering in the process that local political concerns and loyalties often superseded loyalties to an imagined "tribe." Third, ethnopolitical histories tend to examine in greater detail the roles of individual Indian leaders, who had motives, desires, and goals that sometimes placed them at odds with their own people. Thus, Indian leaders emerge not simply as stock representatives of their tribe or victims of grand historical processes but as complex characters forced to make difficult decisions in a morally ambiguous world.[16]

In this light Creek peoples are better understood not as a nation in the modern sense but as an extended family united by bonds of clan affiliation, marriage, and ritually prescribed friendships. "Creek politics," then, might be considered something of a misnomer, because I devote much attention to smaller political units and networks, the concerns of which often superseded the concerns of the broader "Creek Nation." Where possible, I discuss the political careers of individual Creek leaders to demonstrate the various ways those in positions of authority chose to respond to pressures exerted by the colonists and their peers back home.

The evolution of the Creeks' ambiguous political organization, which scholars deem the "Creek Confederacy," is a recurring theme in this discussion. I explore the longstanding scholarly debate over the timing of the Confederacy's emergence, which has yet fully to be resolved. Was the Creek Confederacy an ancient political arrangement that "coalesced" by the turn of the eighteenth century, as many notable historians and anthropologists have argued? Or did the Confederacy emerge slowly over the course of the eighteenth century in response to the European presence in the Southeast? Is "confederacy" even an appropriate term, or did the Creeks' political organization consist of a series of shifting alliances of kin groups for which we have no good descriptive language?[17]

The use of the term "confederacy" in reference to the Creeks began

in the late eighteenth century with the publication of several important accounts of the southern Indians. Among the most important of
these works was James Adair's *History of the American Indians*, published
in 1775, and William Bartram's *Travels*, first published in 1791, both of
which assumed the existence of the "Muskogee" or "Creek Confederacy." Adair, who lived among the Indians for more than thirty years,
believed that the Muskogee Confederacy became powerful due to an
"artful policy" of incorporating the remnants of other tribes. William
Bartram, who made several excursions through Creek country in the
1770s, habitually referred to the Creeks as a confederacy, while also
noting their linguistic and ethnic heterogeneity.[18]

Like Adair and Bartram, historians and anthropologists working in
the twentieth century described the Creeks as a multi-ethnic confederacy but generally neglected to subject its formation to rigorous historical
scrutiny. John Swanton, the eminent anthropologist who wrote exten-
sively on the Creeks in the early part of the twentieth century, viewed
Creek history through the lens of the "ethnographic present," a method
of observation many anthropologists have used to analyze the "savage" cultures that persisted well into the twentieth century. Though
useful for analyzing the cultural practices of small-scale societies, the
ethnographic present fails to place these cultures in an historical framework. Swanton's voluminous works, which remain classics in the field
of ethnography, nevertheless insufficiently question the Confederacy's
purported emergence.[19]

Among the first to consider the Creek Confederacy from an historical
standpoint was the foremost scholar of the southern frontier, Verner
Crane. In an influential 1913 article, Crane argued that the Confederacy arose around the time of the Yamasee War of 1715. In support of
his thesis Crane noted that Carolina traders and government officials
began to refer to their Indian allies then living on the Ocmulgee River
as the "Ochese Creek Indians," which they then shortened to "Creek
Indians" by the time of the Yamasee War. When the "Creek Indians"
returned to their old homes on the Chattahoochee in 1716, Carolina
officials continued to use the "Creek" moniker and began applying it
to the linguistically and culturally similar peoples living farther west,
on the Coosa and Tallapoosa Rivers. The name stuck, and Carolina, and
later Georgia, officials would continue to refer to the Creeks as a single
nation composed of two distinct divisions: the Lower Creeks, who lived

on the Chattahoochee River, and the Upper Creeks, who lived on the Coosa and Tallapoosa Rivers.[20]

While scholars continue to describe the Creeks as a confederacy that emerged some time during the "long" eighteenth century, most have rightly become somewhat uncomfortable assigning a specific date to its emergence. Moreover, scholars justifiably tend to use equivocal modifiers that raise doubts about the existence of a confederacy, if not the very utility of the term. Ironically, the first scholar to study the Creeks, Albert Gatschet, recommended in 1884 abandoning the term "confederacy" in favor of "war-confederacy," "war league," or "symmachy."[21] Subsequent scholars have generally refused to adopt Gatschet's equally vague terminology but have nevertheless stressed the decentralized nature of the Confederacy. Kathryn Braund, for example, labels the Confederacy "an anomaly of unity and division," and further qualifies it as "loosely structured" and "ill-defined."[22] In a similar vein, Michael Green describes the Confederacy as a "loosely organized alliance of independent and autonomous tribes" that gradually "evolved into a nation."[23] Likewise, scholars who have most recently written about the Creeks describe the Confederacy variously as "loose," a "loose defensive and offensive alliance," "shifting and diverse," "emerging," or "not a perfect confederation" but one that was "subject to frequent disunity."[24]

How, then, does one explain the rise of a Confederacy so ill-defined that it appears to divest the term of any useful meaning? The strategy employed here will be not to assume the Confederacy's pre-existence but to investigate explicitly the historical dimensions of confederacy building. Confederation, William Fenton reminds us, was not an event but a "process" requiring decades if not centuries.[25] As a process, then, I will not depict the making of the Creek Confederacy through any single event but through a series of what shall be termed "acts of confederation"—episodes of common action requiring broad-based planning and leadership. This is not to suggest that individual acts of confederation inevitably led to the creation of a Creek Confederacy. The persistence of local, kinship-based political units made the Confederacy subject to oscillating periods of decline and renewal, fission, fusion, and factionalism.[26]

Moreover, I will draw a sharp distinction between the distinctly political act of "confederation" and "ethnogenesis," which is the emergence of a particular ethnic group's awareness of its own distinctiveness based

upon perceived similarities in language, folk practices, and mythic traditions.[27] As the following pages will attest, an ethnic group's awareness
of its own distinct identity may be a precondition for political confederation. But political affiliation and ethnicity do not coincide so neatly
in many cases, particularly in Creek country, where political sentiments
could unite persons of different ethnicity and yet divide blood relatives.

So as to assess better the ways in which Creek political culture did
change, I will abandon the search for the elusive "Creek Confederacy"
in favor of an investigation into the origins of Creek "nationhood."
The concept of nationhood is defined here as the drawing of territorial
boundaries, the creation of institutions of national leadership, and the
invention of ideologies that legitimize the existence thereof. These categories of analysis are preferable because they offer more precise means
by which to assess the historical and cultural dimensions of political
change.[28] Not incidental to this process, of course, was the influence
of Europeans, whose territorial, economic, and imperial ambitions required the Creeks to adopt new territory-based concepts of nationhood
and national leadership in defense of their own political autonomy.

In particular, British colonial practices, by way of trade, land acquisition, and the creation of British-sponsored "chiefs," were the stimuli
that inched the Creeks toward this new concept of nationhood. This is
not to say, however, that the British imposed nationhood entirely upon
the Creeks. Some Creek leaders began making innovative territorial
claims of their own after the establishment of the colony of Georgia
in 1733. By claiming absolute authority over recently conquered territory, the Creeks themselves participated in the invention of a territory-
based Creek Nation, as distinguished from the small, traditional kinship
groups that lived on the three rivers in Creek country. Certain Creek
leaders, eager to aggrandize their own political authority, attempted
at times to place themselves at the head of this new political entity,
thus establishing a precedent for national leadership. The Creek town
of Coweta appears to have figured prominently in this enterprise, and
its chiefs can be credited as the first to offer the vision of a "Creek
Nation" and an ideological and historical defense—albeit a contested
one—for their right to exercise authority over it. The South's Imperial
Era, then, did not witness the rise of a monolithic Creek Confederacy. But
it saw the invention of an entirely new, ambiguous political concept—
the territory-based Creek Nation—which both Creeks and Europeans
worked to define and control.[29]

A Final Note on Spelling and Terminology

Because British, Spanish, and French officials often spelled Creek towns in a variety of creative ways, I have adopted the most common English spellings to minimize confusion and facilitate (I hope) readability. Spanish and British officials also often spelled Creek names and titles differently. Generally this work will use the most common English spellings, except for the few individuals who appear more often in the Spanish archival materials. I have also edited many of the egregious anachronisms to reflect modern practices in spelling, capitalization, and grammar. I retain some of those anachronisms in an attempt to preserve some of the characteristics of seventeenth- and eighteenth-century language.

It should be further noted that I use the term "Creek" with some reluctance because this group was a heterogeneous, diverse people that generally lacked a concept of "Creekness." But, in an effort to demonstrate the gradual processes of nation building, I avoid employing the term "Creek Confederacy" when discussing the Creeks' mysterious political arrangements. Instead, I have chosen to adopt terms more suitable to each specific period in question, such as "Apalachicolas," "Ocheses," "Lower Creeks," or "Upper Creeks." I use the term "confederacy" or "confederation" in the lowercase to differentiate these ad hoc political arrangements from the scholarly notion of the "Creek Confederacy." Last, in an attempt to differentiate the Creek peoples from the political or legal entity known to the British as the "Creek Nation," I refer to the Creeks collectively as a "nation" using the lowercase.[30] The term "nation," derived from the Latin root *natus*, means "to be born"; its derivative noun, *natio*, can be used as a synonym for "tribe," a concept that the Creeks themselves undoubtedly understood.[31]

CHAPTER ONE

Tall Coweta

Derived from the Muskogee verb *vyetv*—"to go"—"Coweta" seems an apt label for a wandering people.[1] As Creek oral traditions have it, before time began the Cowetas' ancestors emerged from a hole in the ground somewhere to the west. After emerging from this sacred portal, which the Creeks called the mouth of the ground, these ancestors became eastward travelers, making a generations-long journey that eventually brought them to the banks of the Chattahoochee River, which divides the present-day states of Georgia and Alabama. In fact as in legend, archaeological and documentary evidence supports the notion that the people who would one day be called Cowetas had relocated to the Chattahoochee after a series of stops farther west, on the Tallapoosa and Coosa Rivers.

The Cowetas, however, do not appear to have been the leaders of this eastward migration, but rather its followers. As it was told, the Cowetas were but one of several peoples "who had anciently lived together in the west" in territory that became "so evil that they could find nothing pure in the world except the Sun." Looking for a pure world in which to live, these peoples "determined to travel eastward to find the place from whence it [the Sun] came." The first to find the Sun were called the Chickasaws, in honor of their achievement in finding it first. The Chickasaws in turn called the second body of people "Kohasita," or "See the Sun," from which is derived the town's name, Cussita. A third party, trailing the others, "had some difficulty in passing a brier thicket and were left a long distance behind." For this reason both of the advance parties began calling the stragglers Ko-aoita, or "those that are following us."[2]

Many Creek stories likewise attest to Coweta's inauspicious origins. The preceding story, for one, relates that at one point on the long march, the advancing Cussita warriors had built a town on the east bank of a small river, leaving their women and children behind as the warriors continued east. The Cowetas—trailing, as usual—arrived on the opposite bank of the river, then sent word to the defenseless Cussitas that they intended to kill them "because the Cussita warriors had not waited to have them join in the expedition." By way of a magic pebble, a Cussita woman was able to warn the absent warriors of the Cowetas' hostile intentions. The Cussita warriors then "retraced their steps, cut switches, and, passing over to the Coweta warriors, whipped them severely."[3] Not only had they deserved this punishment for their unmanly threats against the Cussita "noncombatants," but the Cowetas' weakness made it possible to bring them into line using mere switches. In a similar vein, Albert Gatschet, an influential anthropologist of the nineteenth century, recorded one legendary incident whereby the Cussitas herded together the Coweta warriors, built a large fire, and, to humiliate them, "made them dance, pushing them down into the fire so that they jumped over it to escape." After subjecting the Cowetas to the flames the Cussitas then took sticks and "beat them on the front parts of their calves, and they cut off their ears." Adding salt to fresh wounds, the Cussitas continued to play tricks on the Cowetas, making them wear "strings of dog excrement on their necks."[4]

The Cussitas, in fact, take credit for bestowing on Coweta its government, its rituals, even its very name. According to legend, the Cussitas acted as lawgivers, instructing the Cowetas in the rules prohibiting adultery and the punishments awaiting those who broke the rules. The Cussitas then built two mounds for their own protection, telling the Cowetas, "you must sit down and watch." The Cussitas also claim to have elected the first chief of the Cowetas, a member of the Fish clan. "And there," it was said, "they made a tribe of the Cowetas." Once they had organized as a tribe the Cussitas prepared the ritual black drink (*asi*) and instructed the Cowetas to drink it every morning while sitting on the top of two hollow mounds. This, it was argued, permanently established the Cowetas as a tribe. Once established, the new "tribe" needed a name, and the Cussitas obliged: since, as the story goes, the Coweta tribe "came afterward," the Cussitas determined that "the tribe shall be named Awita, and it was so named."[5]

If Creek oral traditions make the Cowetas' beginnings appear rather humble, those same traditions inform us that the Cowetas experienced a rather remarkable rise in influence and esteem. One tale includes an episode in which the Cussitas, advancing east, left the Cowetas behind to "take charge" of their sacred "great mound." After the Cussitas had departed, "the Cowetas made medicine and went inside the mound to purify themselves" when a Cherokee war party came to attack. To the surprise of the Cherokees, "Coweta warriors poured out from the bowels of the earth, and they [the Cherokees] were defeated with great slaughter." This event, it was said, caused all the Creeks to look upon Coweta as "the great war town" among the Creek Nation.[6]

In addition to Cussita, other Creek towns preserve in their oral traditions a similar sense that the Cowetas had served as their protectors in the remote past. Take, for example, the town of Tuckebatchee, once located on the Tallapoosa River in central Alabama. According to John Swanton, the Tuckebatchees preserve the memory of being a "small, persecuted people whom the Cowetas agreed to defend and protect." Fulotkee, one of Swanton's Creek informants, related a story in which two Creek warriors appeared "out of the northwest," running and whooping, and causing the "earth to quake and [making] echoes in every direction." As people flocked to watch the two warriors, lightning flashed from the north, and thunder came from the southwest. The people sent four men to investigate, and they found that people levitating had caused the disturbances. Several of the levitating men—all Tuckebatchees—followed the four men back to their town. The men of the two towns said, "We have seen each other's power; let us unite." "The Cowetas," it was determined, "will be the leaders."[7] And so it was that with the passage of time Coweta earned distinction as one of four great "foundation towns" of the Creek confederation—along with Cussita, Abika, and Tuckebatchee. In honor of this distinction, later generations of Creeks commonly referred to Coweta in ritual contexts as "Coweta mahma'yagi," or "Tall Coweta."[8]

Considering the problems inherent in using oral tradition as a guide to ancient history, we should be skeptical of some of the details of the Creeks' stories regarding Coweta's origins. The nature of such evidence likely will never enable us to verify the objective "truth" of the narratives. Still, as a whole, Creek oral traditions appear to articulate two basic truths about Coweta's early history: it was not an ancient town by Creek (or by anyone else's) standards but an upstart community of migrants who followed in the footsteps of others in search of a better life; and, despite its humble beginnings, it did emerge as a leading town among the Creek peoples. Two questions, then, must necessarily concern us here: When did this change to a leadership position happen? And, How did it happen?

Like many Southeastern peoples, the Creeks generally held in high regard the towns that had been founded in the remote past. Quite frequently they called these older establishments "mother towns" as a token of honor and respect. Other factors could create this respect, too. Towns with a large population, for instance, seem to have been held in high regard due to their potential military strength. And it did not hurt that the Creeks generally interpreted a town's vitality as a sign that its people—particularly its leaders—had somehow garnered the favor of the spirits, which might have enabled that town to prosper and grow.

Given, however, that it was a relatively new town, and possibly one with a small population, Coweta appears not to have conformed to the normal criteria befitting an influential ancient town. It is thus necessary to seek a better explanation for Coweta's apparent rise. Coweta likely did not emerge as an independent political unit until the late seventeenth century, a time that saw great changes in the political context of the southern interior. The principal impetus for this change was the creation of the colonies of Spanish Florida and, even more important, England's Carolina Colony established in 1670. Coweta was able to rise in influence primarily because it, above all other towns, developed strategic alliances with the English colonists and their Indian allies. Not only did the Cowetas use the English alliance to bring a regular trade to the Chattahoochee region, but they were able to secure the one trade item that afforded them a measure of protection against their enemies— guns. Coweta was the product of a decidedly new world and its fate was inextricably tied to that world. In addition, no town did more to help forge the emerging Creek Nation.

Out of the Mississippian

Coweta, like most Southeastern Indian towns of the historic era, rose out of the ashes of an earlier civilization that appeared in the region, usually referred to as the Mississippian culture. The Mississippian way of life emerged after 900 A.D. in the wake of an agricultural revolution involving the intensification of corn agriculture. Essential to this concentration on corn agriculture was a corresponding period of global warming, known as the Medieval Optimum (900–1350 A.D.), that led to longer growing seasons and greater agricultural productivity. Mississippian cultures appear to have evolved first in the Mississippi River basin, most likely at the well-known site of Cahokia, Illinois. Over several centuries Mississippian culture then spread to other areas of the American South, as evidenced by the region-wide proliferation of certain symbolic artistic motifs and a regional dependency on the culture's staple crop, corn.

An important point to emphasize is that many of the tribal confederacies of the post–Invasion period—the Creeks, Cherokees, Chickasaws, and Choctaws, for example—did not yet exist in a form recognizable to people of the late seventeenth and eighteenth centuries. Mississippian societies instead are best thought of as a series of regionally circumscribed and politically and socially stratified polities called chiefdoms by most anthropologists. Mississippian chiefdoms, however, came in a variety of sizes and types, making it difficult to characterize any one form as "typical." On one end of the spectrum, the great chiefdom that emerged at Cahokia, Illinois, appears to have been home to more than twenty thousand souls and its chief may have held sway over a territory beyond the confines of Cahokia itself. On the other end of the spectrum, groups such as the Florida Timucuans organized themselves into much smaller chiefdoms of a few thousand at most and adopted Mississippian cultural motifs only selectively.[9]

If we were forced to draw a composite sketch of the average Southeastern chiefdom, however, suffice it to say that most chiefdoms were multicommunity polities typically consisting of clusters of eight towns located on the margins of a river or large creek. Each town probably held no more than one hundred individual habitations, and the population of the chiefdom as a whole rarely, if ever, exceeded five thousand persons. The maximum radius of these chiefdoms appears to have been twelve and one-half miles, a size that is thought to have facilitated the cohesiveness of the chiefdom. A chief, it has been argued, could have walked the length of such a polity in a single day, thereby enabling him to maintain face-to-face contact with his people.[10]

Documentary and archaeological evidence clearly suggests that the early chiefdoms were hierarchical societies. At the top of the hierarchical political structure was the chief, who ruled over his own village and the outlying villages that comprised his chiefdom. Southeastern Indian chiefs appear to have been the objects of divine worship and were thought to be the earthly representatives of the Indians' principal deity, the Sun. The chiefs enjoyed many privileges that their fellow townspeople did not, including the right to command warriors and the right to appropriate tribute—in the form of deerskins, corn, or meat—the latter of which freed them from the burden of earning their keep by the sweat of their own brows.

Whereas the right to command warriors or tribute can be seen as a chief's material basis for power, the ideological basis for that power derived in part from the chief's ability to demonstrate his or her connectedness to the world outside the village or chiefdom. One way Southeastern chiefs demonstrated their connectedness was by acquiring and displaying exotic trade goods of foreign manufacture, the procurement of which the chiefs appear to have monopolized. Analyses of Mississippian-era burial grounds, for instance, reveal that chiefs and their families received different treatment in death—much as they are assumed to have received in life. Chiefly burials contain a disproportionate amount of exotic goods, such as monolithic ceremonial axes, carved shell gorgets, and bracelets and gorgets made of hammered copper.[11] In contrast, the burials of individuals thought to be "commoners" contain few, if any, such items.

The quintessential artifacts of the prehistoric chiefdoms, though, are the earthen platform mounds, which to this day can be found scattered throughout the Southeast. Evidence suggests that the mounds represented the "navel of the world" from which sprang the town's (if not the entire chiefdom's) people sometime in the remote mythical past. Scholars are convinced that Southeastern Indians built these mounds in successive stages, most likely during periodic episodes of rebuilding that occurred when new chiefs were installed as rulers.[12] Stratigraphic profiles suggest, moreover, a certain degree of political stability, as each phase of rebuilding (or "capping," as it is called) indicates the transmission of power from one generation to the next.[13] A mound likewise served as a literal symbol of the chief's elevated status, as his or her private dwellings and other sacred buildings were routinely built on the summit of such earthworks.

In ritual life, too, Mississippian peoples exalted their chiefs above the commoners. Southeastern peoples who met the first Spanish explorers in the sixteenth century often greeted the newcomers by performing a traditional procession ritual designed to invoke the grandeur of the chief. When Hernando de Soto first entered the town of Coosa in 1540, for example, the people there carried their chief on a litter draped in white cloth, passing him above their heads as they sang and played flutes. The chief of Coosa, moreover, dressed in a way that separated him from his people, wearing a mantel made of the rare marten fur and a crown fashioned from white feathers, the latter a symbol of peace.[14]

The invasion of Europeans in the sixteenth century brought marked change to the American South and to the Mississippian culture that had been several centuries in the making. Spanish explorers, some of whom had participated in earlier Spanish conquests in South and Central America, conducted three *entradas* into the southern interior: The first was led by Hernando de Soto in 1539; two later incursions were led by Tristan de Luna, in 1562, and by Juan Pardo, in 1568–69. Scholarly opinion remains divided, however, as to the lingering effects of these incursions. Some have argued that Spanish soldiers and their animals were the first to bring communicable diseases to the region, causing the chiefdoms to collapse within the space of a generation. Others believe this interpretation is somewhat lacking, due to the fact that the children tended to serve as carriers for disease microbes but obviously played no role in the *entradas*. Moreover, some evidence suggests that the Mississippian way of life had already declined significantly with the onset of the Little Ice Age (c. 1350), noting the collapse of important mound centers such as Cahokia and Moundville, Alabama, a full two centuries before the first Europeans arrived. Others have argued that diseases likely spread at a slower pace than had first been imagined, making it simply a "problematic" factor of sixteenth century aboriginal depopulation. In specific areas, however, the Spaniards wreaked destruction that may have precipitated the collapse of particular polities. De Soto, for example, appears to have utterly destroyed the town of Mabila in central Alabama, likely breaking up the fragile military coalition put together by Tascalusa, the paramount chief of the nearby town of Atahachi, who it appears never recovered the breadth of his authority.[15]

There can be little doubt, though, that in the American South, Spain's establishment of St. Augustine, Florida, in 1565 ushered in a new era in Indian life. Once the Spaniards possessed a permanent base on the Florida coast, they soon began to extend their reach into remoter regions, primarily through the efforts of Franciscan missionaries. Over the course of the first half of the seventeenth century, the Franciscans established Catholic missions among the Timucuans of central Florida, the Guales and Mocamas of the Georgia coast, and, eventually, the Apalachees of the Florida panhandle. Tens of thousands of Indians received instruction in the Catholic faith through this mission network, and the demands of the contract labor arrangement known as *repartimiento*, while oppressive in many respects, introduced to the Indians many new skills in construction and ranching. The Spaniards introduced a wide array of natural products to the Southern Indians as well, ranging from peaches to cattle. With the Europeans, of course, came trade goods, and it appears that a small but brisk trade in beads, brass pendants, and iron implements developed between the Florida missions and Indians in the southern interior by the mid-seventeenth century.[16]

As trade in the interior increased and as the missions proliferated, so too did communicable diseases. Lacking natural immunity to diseases such as smallpox, influenza, measles, and whooping cough, Native populations declined rapidly in many quarters of the American South. Startling population losses occurred among the missionized groups. Among the Timucuans a series of plagues that occurred between 1614 and 1617 are thought to have reduced the population by half. Diseases wreaked havoc among the nonmission interior groups as well. For example, the Coosa River valley in northern Georgia and Alabama experienced a remarkable population loss, resulting in the demise of the once-powerful Coosa chiefdom, the survivors of which eventually became concentrated into a single town.[17]

These dwindling populations of the Deep South interior, which had begun to procure a growing supply of trade goods from Spanish Florida, were inviting targets for predatory bands of Indians bent upon acquiring slaves and booty. One such band, the Chiscas, appear to have left their homes in the Appalachian Mountains in the early seventeenth century to prey upon the sedentary mission Indians living on the northern frontier of Florida.[18] A similar predatory group, the Westos, a small group of Erie refugees allied with the Virginia slave traders, first appeared on the scene in the late 1650s, capturing people living as far south as the middle Chattahoochee River and earning a terrifying reputation among Southern Indians as "man-eaters."

The combined push factors of disease and slave raiding unleashed a complex series of population migrations, as weakened tribes aligned themselves with others to gain strength in numbers. The lure of the Spanish trade likely also served as a pull factor in these migrations, drawing people out from the interior and closer to Florida so as to partake of that trade.[19]

The profound effects of these historical phenomena can be seen in the steady decline of the hierarchical Mississippian societies. To understand how this occurred, it is first necessary to examine the status of the chieftainship, which appears to have diminished significantly in the one hundred years following the Spanish *entradas* of the mid-sixteenth century. As the populations began to decline due to disease, the chiefs lost their ability to command the labor that was necessary for building public works projects and fighting wars. The corresponding labor shortage made it next to impossible for the chiefdoms to grow and harvest the corn surpluses that the chiefs had traditionally redistributed in times of need and had used to support their military and priestly hierarchies. Disease and population losses must have undermined the chief's religious authority as well; as the inability of his or her priests to ward off disease microbes would have revealed the impotence of his "medicine" and called into question the spiritual union that chiefs worked so hard to maintain. Furthermore, as trade goods from Spanish Florida became more commonplace, the chiefs must have relinquished—willingly or unwillingly—their presumed monopoly over rare and exotic items that at one time had been used to display their connectedness to powers outside of their chiefdoms.

Perhaps the most conspicuous evidence of the decline of the chieftaincy is the rather abrupt decrease in platform mound construction. Platform mounds, a primary characteristic of Indian towns before the Spanish invasions, all but ceased to be built a generation or two after 1540. Also gone were the many ceremonial items that chiefs used to display their largess, such as copper breastplates, ceremonial axes, and pottery, much of which was inscribed with iconography thought to have been associated with the mysteries of chieftainship. Indian burials tell a similar tale of the chiefs' declining status. Whereas the burials of what are presumed to have been chiefs and their families once contained a disproportionate amount of exotic trade items, trade goods found in seventeenth-century burials—derived from Spanish Florida—appear to have been distributed more equally among the population. It is worth noting that the ideological underpinnings of the chieftainship also waned during this period. For example, myths concerning the ancient southeastern Indian ball game (*pelota* to the Spanish), gradually de-emphasized chiefly rivalries and began to place greater importance on intertown rivalries.[20]

Out of the ashes of the Mississippian societies emerged new coalescent societies that proved better suited to changing world conditions. The Chattahoochee, Coosa, and Tallapoosa River valleys each served as points of coalescence, drawing refugees from nearby river systems. Archaeologist Vernon J. Knight has identified three loci as important points of population concentration. Knight argues that the middle Chattahoochee River valley, the lower Coosa River, and the lower Tallapoosa River attracted displaced peoples from various quarters and may have even sustained town populations similar or equal to the size of Mississippian villages. These loci, of course, continued to be important population centers and eventually became the epicenter of the Creek Nation.[21]

Though it is easy to imagine that displaced peoples seeking to mitigate the effects of disease and slave raiding would have been drawn together by a mutual interest in survival, the coalescence of stable societies and governments also requires that certain problems be solved. Consider, for example, the problem of leadership. If two peoples—each led by a different "chief"—sought to form a new town, how would they determine which chief would rule? Assuming that the two factions were equal in number, could a system be arranged whereby each would have a say in political matters? Might there not also have existed other individuals who commanded a sizable following? Could these others usurp the chief's authority when it suited their needs? On a similar note, who determined when peace was the goal? Who organized war parties?

Other problems presented themselves as well. When remnant populations of different towns came together to form a new unit, what would the new group call itself? Moreover, since it can be assumed that disparate groups held a diverse array of ritual practices, how did the people determine which rituals to follow? Given that Southeastern Indians believed that many of their rituals were important to cultivating spiritual favors, rituals were probably a matter of the utmost importance. At planting time, who was to plan the work that had to be done? Which agricultural fields were to be used, and by whom? Who should oversee the building of public structures? In short, how could the interests of the many be harmonized?

Given the need to solve such important problems, it should come as no surprise that the historic "Creek" culture that emerged from this revolutionary period was tailored to solve the kinds of social and political problems that coalescent peoples faced. In the process, the ancestral Creeks created new rituals, new beliefs, and new social forms. This is not to say, however, that the emergent Creek culture was entirely unrelated to the Mississippian culture that preceded it. Rather, it appears that as the hierarchical superstructure of the chiefdoms became impossible to maintain, the emergent Creeks came to rely more on the social substructure of the Mississippian culture. As a result, the historic Creeks, like other Southeastern Indian groups of the historic period, forged a culture that de-emphasized the cult of the chief and emphasized the balance and harmony of the group.[22]

One of the most important changes that came out of the Mississippian collapse was the enhanced importance of individual towns. Any understanding of Creek political life, in fact, must begin with an understanding of the towns, since the towns were, and for a very long time continued to be, the most important political unit among the Creeks. Creek towns were essentially autonomous political entities, each with its own political hierarchy and free to make independent political decisions. For individual Creeks, the town (*talwa*) was the principal source of one's political identity. The Creeks euphemistically described the town as comprising a people of "one fire," thus linking their outlook to the perpetual deity, the Sun.[23]

Public architecture in the towns also reflected the emphasis that the historic Creeks placed upon group harmony. In contrast to the elevated role of the Mississippian platform mound, the Creeks began to build ceremonial town squares enclosed by four buildings. This arrangement conformed to the Creeks' sense of the cosmic order as represented artistically, architecturally, and in myth as the four cardinal directions. The chief's building, usually situated to the west, was often decorated with pictographs invoking the memory of past accomplishments, of the ancestors, or of the connected clan groups in that town. The chief's building also served as a storage space for sacred ritual paraphernalia, a kind of *sanctum sanctorum* that preserved the purity of the ritual objects. Unlike the platform mound, the town square was a more accessible public and ritual space that, according to one leading historian, had "taken over" and "communalized" much of the symbolism and practice once associated with the mound.[24]

Creek towns, though politically autonomous, did not exist in a vacuum. The needs of defense and resource management required that individual towns find the institutional and ritual means by which to forge alliances and mediate disputes. Individual Creek towns were known, for example, to enter into officially sanctioned "friendships" that may have required them to assist each other in times of war. Creek towns also regularly adopted individuals from other towns who served as ambassadors and were charged with carrying "talks" between the two. In some Creek towns this adoptive ritual appears to have become somewhat fixed in the institution of the *fani mico*, or "Squirrel King," often regarded as a town's official ambassador. At times two or more Creek towns deputized an individual, often a chief, who was expected to act in the interests of the whole.[25]

This emphasis on group harmony, of course, was also manifest in the sociopolitical organization and rituals of each Creek town. The most conspicuous evidence for this can be found in the Creeks' dualistic political structure, which featured two political hierarchies, one civil and the other military. The Creeks' dual system of government reflected their more general dualistic view of the natural world, which they described using an array of metaphors that connoted opposing principles: male-female, old-young, and peace-war. The Creeks, like most Southern Indians, represented this dualistic view of the universe using the colors white and red. White signified peace, age, wisdom, and deliberation. Red, in contrast, represented war, youth, passion, and bold action.[26]

The Creeks applied the principle of dualism when they formed their political communities and institutions. For instance, the Creeks appear to have organized their several matrilineal clans into two exogamous, matrilineal moieties, one designated as "white" and the other "red." Within the individual Creek towns, clans that traced their descent to the founding family were imagined to be the original "owners" of the town square; they were assigned a "white" designation and called *hathagalgi*. Secondary lineages assumed the position as the town's *tchilockalgi*, or "red" faction.[27]

The choice of the term *tchilockalgi* in reference to secondary clans is yet another indication that the Creek culture of the historic period was likely a product of the coalescence of disparate groups. The Muskogee word *tchilocki* translates more accurately as "people of another speech," no doubt a reflection of the Muskogees' past experiences of incorporating outsiders. *Tchilocki* can also be translated as "foreigners," perhaps an indication of past experience in adopting foreigners into the town social and political hierarchies.[28]

Members of "white" lineages typically held civil offices, which were probably passed to successive generations through the maternal line. Such offices included but were not limited to the town chief (*mico*), subordinate clan chiefs (the *mikalgi*), and the town "second men" (the *heni-hagalgi*) who advised the chief and could even assume political control in extreme circumstances. Civil officers controlled the town's internal affairs, playing a prominent role in planning and overseeing town rituals, adjudicating internal disputes, establishing the planting and harvest schedule, and maintaining tribal lore and tradition.

Complementing this civil order was a military hierarchy that drew its membership from both moieties but probably reserved top military posts for principal members of the "red" lineages. Whereas a town's civil hierarchy was generally thought to have been filled according to prescribed rules of inheritance, the military hierarchy was more of a meritocracy and was open to any person of distinction who had proved himself in war. Young men first entered this hierarchy by taking an enemy scalp, a feat that earned them distinction as a common warrior or *tasikaya*. Warriors who had proved themselves in battle numerous times and had taken a requisite number of enemy scalps (at least three) earned additional distinction as an *imathla*. Higher still on the warrior hierarchy were the *tastanagalgi*, who were honored with that office only after earning the respect of their peers as great warriors. In addition to these general warrior classes, each town had a number of war leaders, the head of which was usually designated *tastanagi thlucco* (literally "big warrior").[29]

This dual political and social structure was not unique to the Creeks, nor was it unique to Southeastern Indians. It is therefore plausible to suggest that dualism was a cultural norm of great antiquity in Native North America.[30] Still, the degree to which the Creeks applied the concept of dualism to their social and political structure suggests that it served some purpose in the past. As the cult of the Mississippian chiefs waned and as new groups coalesced, this dual structure was expanded to delegate political authority to recently incorporated groups, potentially giving every inhabitant (or every male inhabitant, at least) some say in village affairs.

Delegating at least some local authority to secondary clans was not only the politically expedient thing to do but may have been necessary due to the fact that Creek clans were exogamous (meaning those reckoned to be members of the same matrilineal clan and other closely affiliated clans of the same moiety were prohibited from intermarrying). The problem was that a single clan under the direction of an appointed "chief" tended to be responsible for founding new communities. The practice may have fostered cohesiveness, but it necessarily left a town's founders without suitable marriage partners. To recruit members of nonaffiliated clans with whom the town's founders could intermarry, political power had to be shared.

The most astute English observers of Indian customs indeed recognized this power-sharing arrangement. Thomas Nairne, South Carolina's leading Indian agent and a skillful observer of Indian customs, noted that Indian chiefs who established new communities tended to share power rather than erect petty "patriarchies" of followers from within their own clans. Nairne believed it impossible that small-scale societies could be founded "by any other way than by agreement." As a hypothetical example, Nairne imagined that a charismatic chief might attract followers from within his own clan, but that the need for marriage partners mitigated against the monopolization of political power. Nairne wrote of such hypothetical chiefs:

> Now he would never carry out his collony, as a Patriarch, for suppose his fameily [clan] be [ever] so numerous and willing to obey him, yet they could not inter marry. Thus suppose a savage of the ogilisa fameily inclining to Erect a petty monarchy and hath 50 men and as many woman of the same neme, willing to forward the project, he can never bring his designes to perfections, unless he can procure as many Lyslalas or others to accompany him, that according to their constant practice the men of that family may take wives out of this, and the woman out of this, husband out of that, which can't be done unless their fathers Brothers or the like marry them, and consequently never so small a society be formed but by consent of a willing people.[31]

Nairne's portrait of the Creek towns as small-scale communities of consensus is confirmed by his characterization of the Creek chief, or *mico*: "Nothing can be farther from absolute monarchy," Nairne wrote, adding that "[o]ne can hardly perceive that they have a king, at all," and that it was all but impossible to distinguish the *mico* "by their garb and fashion, which in nothing differs from the rest." As to their governing power—where the word "governing" is something of an exaggeration— Nairne among others noted that Creek *mikalgi* rarely made decisions unilaterally unless deputized by their people to do so. Creek chiefs, moreover, did not possess the authority to command warriors into battle against their will and could not always prohibit individuals or small groups from fighting against their enemies. Nor were they generally given the authority to carry out corporal or capital punishment, except perhaps during times of war or for other serious matters. Creek leaders relied instead upon the art of persuasion to convince others to abide by their directions, which led them to apply the arts of oratory and sometimes ridicule as forms of peer pressure. As force could not be used as a coercive mechanism, Creek individuals were in some sense "free" to pursue their own political or economic interests, which in turn served the needs of a coalescent society that frowned upon concentrated political authority.[32]

The need to harmonize group interests also manifested itself in Creek rituals. The most important ritual among the Creeks was *poskita* (literally "to fast"), or busk, an annual celebration that usually occurred in late July or early August just as the green corn was beginning to ripen. Busk typically lasted between four and eight days and involved several days of fasting and dancing, culminating in a grand feast. Though on one level busk served as a means of thanking the spirits for the year's corn crop, it also served an important social function as well. Creeks used the opportunity of busk to renew alliances and to forgive past disputes, even murder. Symbolically, one of the most important busk rituals was the ceremonial snuffing out of the town's perpetual fire and the kindling of a new one. The making of a new fire commonly occurred after the end of the fasting period, typically on the fourth day. After the old fire had been extinguished, a "priest," often dressed in white (the symbol of peace), kindled a new fire in the town square. Once the fire was kindled, the priest or his deputies took fire to each homestead, where a new fire was rekindled in every hearth. The ritual reaffirmed the association between fire and the Sun as the giver of life, but the means by which it was kindled and distributed reinforced the message of communality.[33]

Daily rituals conducted in the town square similarly emphasized group harmony. In Creek towns the men commonly gathered each morning to discuss town affairs and to conduct business of a public nature. Before doing so, however, the men imbibed the sacred ritual drink made from the leaves of the yaupon holly. The leaves, once parched over a fire, were steeped in a large cauldron of hot water, giving the ritual tea a distinctive black color. The "Black drink," as the Europeans called it, was called the "White drink" by the Creeks since the brew was thought to purify and establish peaceful relations between and among the individuals who drank it. Once the drink was brewed, a priest or, more commonly, a deputy put in charge of the tea, dipped out a portion of the drink from the cauldron and served it to each man in the town square using a ceremonial cup made from a sea shell or gourd. The drink distributors served the town *mico* and foreign dignitaries first and then passed the cup to each person in the town square according to his rank. Though the distribution of the drink reaffirmed the town's political hierarchy, the fact that each man was allowed to partake of the sacred beverage underscores the rather egalitarian political structure of the village and the need for harmony.[34]

Just as the towns and their associated rituals became more important in historic Creek culture, the Mississippian collapse appears to have led to the elaboration of the clan system. The Creeks reckoned kinship according to matrilineal rules, whereby a child assumed the clan affiliation of his or her mother. In a matrilineal system the child's biological father was not looked upon as a "blood" relative and played less of a role in preparing his child for adulthood. Young Creek boys were instead often prepared for adulthood by their mothers' brothers—clan uncles—who gave instruction, meted out discipline, and likely educated the youngster in the tales of his ancestors' exploits. A Creek girl likewise would have been instructed in female responsibilities by her mother, her related aunts, and other female clan-kin.

Clan affiliation was of utmost importance to the Creeks because clan membership gave an individual his or her identity, determined who that person could marry, dictated ceremonial obligations, and, in the case of male clan members, determined who he was obliged to defend or revenge in times of war. Because Creeks typically labored together in small kinship units, clan membership determined which agricultural fields one could cultivate and influenced the makeup of hunting parties. And because the Creeks typically invested individual clans with particular political titles—which clans guarded as a kind of property—clan affiliation often determined which political offices an individual was eligible to hold throughout the course of his or her life.

As was typical in many clan-based Native American societies, the language of kinship was the central idiom by which the Creeks expressed their reciprocal relationships to each other and to outsiders. The language of kinship tended to serve the interests of group harmony and balance, which in practice meant that clan relatives were expected to share food, go to war on each other's behalf, and assist in building houses, rearing children, planting crops, and helping with every mundane detail of existence. Thus to call someone a brother or sister was more than a symbolic mark of respect; the language used by the Creeks served to remind individuals of their responsibilities to each other and to stifle greed and selfishness.[35]

Kinship was an elastic system that not only applied to blood-kin but could be applied more abstractly to outsiders, so as to oblige outsiders to act as good kin should act. Creek towns, for example, used kinship terminology in reference to each other, in a sense making the Creek Nation an extended family. Older towns were often referred to as "grandfather," "grandmother," or "mother" towns. Correspondingly, satellite towns that had separated from older established towns often identified themselves as "daughter" or "grandchild" towns. Other Indian nations, it appears, could be designated as "grandfathers" or "brothers" according to the existence of a perceived relationship. After the arrival of Europeans, the Creeks made kinship the basis of their relationships with the traders, who quite literally became "kin" by marrying into the villages, and to government officials, who became fictive "brothers" or "fathers" when it was convenient to name them so.[36] The Cowetas were among the first to make such a connection with English traders when the foreigners descended into the Chattahoochee River valley in the late seventeenth century.

Coweta's Origins

The first clues concerning Coweta's origins and its relationship to other peoples come from the chronicles of Hernando de Soto's southward march through the Coosa River valley in the fall of 1540. Having reached Coosa in August, during October de Soto and his men passed through several towns, the names of which suggest close connection to historic Creek towns: Tuasi [Towassa], Ulibahali, and Tallassee. Traveling south from Tallassee, de Soto's men passed through a town called Casiste, which was likely the ancestral beginnings of the historic Lower Creek town of Cussita, from which sprang the Cowetas at a much later date.

In 1540 Casiste appears to have been situated on the lower Coosa River, possibly near present-day Sylacauga, Alabama. De Soto's chroniclers depicted Casiste as a pretty village located near a stream, though they did not regard it as an important political center. Clues suggest, moreover, that the town may have owed allegiance to one or more larger villages. In fact, Casiste may have been situated at a political frontier; it seems to have been subject to Tallassee, the larger village farther north. Shortly before de Soto's arrival Casiste may have fallen under the influence of Tascalusa, the chief of Atahachi, whose village was located south of the confluence of the Coosa and Tallapoosa Rivers. De Soto's chroniclers neither single it out as particularly important, nor identify it as particularly poor, so perhaps Casiste had something of a "middling" status at the time.[37]

De Soto's *entrada* did not cause the people of Casiste to immediately abandon their position on the lower Coosa River, however. Twenty years later Spanish explorer Tristan de Luna passed through the same territory in an attempt to establish a Spanish colony at Coosa. While en route north up the Coosa River, de Luna's chroniclers made passing mention of a town called "Caxiti," the inhabitants of which, like most others on the river, had fled to the woods in an attempt to avoid the Spanish army. As was the case twenty years earlier, Caxiti appears not to have been a place of great importance in comparison to Nanipacana to the south and Coosa to the north.[38]

Unfortunately for the modern historian, one hundred years passed before any other Europeans ventured into the Coosa River valley, making it difficult to trace the movements of the Casiste people. As a consequence, the century between de Luna's *entrada* and renewed European interest in the region in the 1670s constitute something of a "lost" period in Casiste's history. Cussita's oral traditions, however, provide some clues as to subsequent shifts in population. The Cussita migration legend, first handed down to Georgia officials in 1735, related that after a stay among the Coosas, the Cussitas migrated to an area known to them as Collasa-hutche. Spanish accounts dating to the late seventeenth century suggest, moreover, that the Cussitas and the Cowetas—by then living on the Chattahoochee River—retained some connection to the Colossa territory and may have used it as a refuge.[39] As to the precise location of "Colossa," the most likely spot was the lower course of the Tallapoosa River, perhaps near the town of Muccolassee.[40]

The Cussitas relocated yet again from Colossa to the Chattahoochee River, most likely under duress because, as it was said, while at Colossa the Cussitas "had no corn" and lived on "roots and fishes." Archaeological evidence suggests that a substantial shift in material culture occurred on the Chattahoochee between 1550 and 1650, a time archaeologists called the "Stewart Phase." For evidence of this population shift archaeologists point to the appearance on the Chattahoochee of diverse types of pottery, much of it resembling pottery found among groups to the west and north. Also noteworthy was the appearance of a new type of arrow point—the Guntersville—that cannot be found in earlier archaeological sequences. In sum, these shifts in material culture seem to indicate that a kind of cultural blending occurred prior to the mid–seventeenth century due to the influx of people not indigenous to the Chattahoochee River valley.[41]

While the archaeological evidence may generally indicate that the Cussita migration occurred at some point over the course of a century, the nature of the evidence does not provide much precision in affixing a specific date to that migration. Documentary evidence, however, confirms that Cussita was established on the Chattahoochee no later than 1662, when Spanish officials in Florida sent two detachments of soldiers into the Chattahoochee valley in search of a predatory band of Westos. When interviewed years later about that expedition, one soldier who took part in that exercise, Nicolas Ramirez, named Casiste as the northernmost town on the Chattahoochee.[42]

But what of Coweta? Had Coweta been established by 1662 we could expect Ramirez to have mentioned it among the towns that later appeared on the northern frontier of the Apalachicola province. If Ramirez was not in error, then, it is plausible to suggest that the source population of the Cowetas remained on the Tallapoosa River or were living as one people among the Cussitas and had not yet emerged as an independent political entity. Evidence strongly suggests that the Cowetas emerged only in the early 1670s, when Florida officials began hearing reports of people pouring into the Chattahoochee valley to evade Westo attacks and to request missionaries.[43] By the fall of 1674 the English adventurer Henry Woodward entered the Westo town of Hickahauga near the falls of the Savannah River. There he received reports that to the west there lived, among others, the "Cowatoe" Indians—making Woodward's account the first to mention the town of Coweta specifically by name. The Catholic bishop of Cuba, who just a few months later conducted a survey of the existing and potential Florida Indian missions, included Coweta among the towns on the Chattahoochee River's northern frontier, thus verifying the reports Woodward had received from his Westo informants.[44]

In summary, historians can trace Coweta's origins obliquely to the "Casiste" people Hernando de Soto encountered on the lower Coosa River in 1540. The Casistes likely remained there for at least another generation, since de Luna's accounts confirm Casiste's presence at approximately the same location. Sometime after 1560 the Casistes ventured east to the nearby Tallapoosa River and began living at a place remembered only as "Colossa," which was likely near the confluence of the Tallapoosa and Coosa Rivers. Then, sometime prior to 1662 the Casistes migrated east to the Chattahoochee River, ensconcing themselves on the northern frontier of the domain of the indigenous Apalachicolas. The Cowetas emerged between 1662 and 1674, likely due to a later migration of people or the amalgamation of Casiste. Thus we may say with some certainty that Coweta's establishment coincided approximately with the establishment of South Carolina in 1670, in a sense making both groups new "colonies."

Coweta's Rise to Power

While the Cowetas later presented themselves as traditionally the most "ancient" and the most powerful town on the Chattahoochee River (and were able to convince many Europeans in the process), in 1674 little indicated that such a future lay in store for them. They were, after all, an immigrant, Muskogee-speaking people who had only recently positioned themselves on the northern frontier of the Apalachicola province. At the time Apalachicola consisted of at least eight towns of Hitchiti-speaking peoples who likely were indigenous to the region. Political power was concentrated on the southern margins of the province and was reflected in the Spanish tendency to use the name of the leading town in reference to all polities of the river system—hence the Spanish term "province of Apalachicola." As the town of Apalachicola and its chiefs had had more contact with the Spanish in Apalachee, Apalachicola chiefs were in a position to use European alliances to their advantage. The town of Sabacola, also located on the southern margins of the Apalachicola province, may have held great sway. Its chief, for example, may have become a Catholic convert, cementing an alliance with the Spanish that earned him recognition as the "grand cacique" of that province.[45] Moreover, the Cowetas' position on the northern frontier of the province left them disproportionately exposed to the attacks of the Westos, who had been ravaging the Chattahoochee valley since 1659.[46]

But rise to power Coweta did, due to the convergence of historical circumstances that made it well-positioned to thrive in the new political climate of the late seventeenth century. Some of this influence might be explained in strictly "native" terms. As the size of an ancient village often played some role in determining its political prowess in relation to other villages, perhaps the size of the Coweta population exceeded others and made the town a force to be reckoned with and an ally to be courted. Perhaps the Cowetas had established a martial reputation for themselves, fighting Westo or Cherokee intruders and earning distinction in battles that are lost to historians. Most probable, however, is that Coweta rose to power by making strategic alliances with others, creating a far-flung political network that no other town in the region could match.

When considering Coweta's strategic alliances it should first be mentioned that Coweta's peripatetic maneuvers prior to the 1670s likely served as an advantage in making contact with other Native peoples in the region. In sharing their origins on the Coosa River, it is plausible to suggest that the Cowetas and Cussitas retained at least a few contacts—by way of marriage, diplomacy, or kinship—with those who had chosen not to migrate. Furthermore, having perhaps recently been settled on the lower Tallapoosa River, the Cowetas undoubtedly retained close connections to the communities established there. Evidence of this connection can be found in the Cowetas' hunting, trading, and sharing intelligence with the Tallassees, Atasis, Tuckebatchees, and other "Tallapoosa" groups. Coweta's regional influence, then, might have been built upon a strictly Native network, as the wandering group with historic links to those in the west began spinning webs of influence that predated permanent European influence.[47]

By the 1670s, though, both the Spanish and the English began to establish regular and sustained contact with the inhabitants of the Chattahoochee River, ushering in a new era of politics. The Spanish, who had maintained a presence in Apalachee since the 1630s, first gained direct influence in the Chattahoochee interior in the early 1670s, inviting the region's inhabitants to migrate south toward Apalachee to establish new mission towns. At first a good number of people appear to have accepted the Spanish offer. As a result, the "Apalachicolas," as the Spanish referred to them, established two mission towns—Sabacola and Sabacola el Grande—on the southern frontier of the Apalachicola province before the year 1675 drew to a close. Spain's influence among the Apalachicolas, then, appeared to be on the rise on the eve of English contact.[48]

As it concerned Coweta, the founding of South Carolina in 1670 proved to be a pivotal event in the town's history. The origins of the Carolina colony can be traced to the restoration of the Stuart monarchy in 1660, which came after nearly a decade of parliamentary rule under

Oliver Cromwell. Called to the throne from his home in exile in France, Charles Stuart (King Charles II) owed a considerable political debt to his loyalist allies in England who had worked diligently with Parliament to replace England under Stuart rule. To repay these debts, on May 23, 1663, Charles issued a colonial charter to a group of seven supporters (commonly referred to as lords proprietors) for land that lay between the thirty-sixth and thirty-first parallels, known to posterity as "Carolina." Settled in 1670, at its inception Carolina was—like most proprietary colonies—a money-making enterprise intended to enrich the lords proprietors as well as the kingdom itself. The king's charter, for example, exempted Carolina Colony from most trade restrictions and duties to encourage economic activities as various as mining, whaling, and wine and silk production. Most important, the king's charter also encouraged the proprietors to "trade with the natives," thereby setting Carolina on a course of economic interaction with neighboring Indian groups.[49]

Initially, at least, the Cowetas and other Indian peoples likely viewed the establishment of the new English colony favorably, as the trade regime that emerged there offered new and perhaps better opportunities than did Spain's mission system. Spain's contract labor arrangement of *repartimiento*, for instance, demanded that each spring and fall Indian chiefs send several of their men to work for the presidio in St. Augustine, thus depleting the town of a few of their most able-bodied people at the critical planting and harvesting seasons. Mission life, too, required that Indians make cultural adjustments so as to conform to the expectations of the Franciscan friars, who forbade Indians to hold traditional dances, pressured the chiefs to abandon the common practice of polygamy, and required everyone to attune their daily schedules to the mission bell's calls to prayer. The English, on the other hand, being motivated by profits, initially demanded little more of the Indians than the opportunity to trade their European wares for furs and skins, a sort of "live and let live" approach to Indian relations that at first made the English appear as a better alternative.[50]

It is not known precisely when or how the Carolinians and Cowetas became aware of each other's presence. Evidence strongly suggests that the English became apprised of the Chattahoochee peoples by word of mouth through rumors suggesting that the "Cussitaws," as they were known, were a "powerful nation" living on land that contained freshwater pearls and silver.[51] These rumors, in turn, appear to have led proprietor Anthony Ashley Cooper (who was later named the first earl of Shaftesbury), to order Dr. Henry Woodward to explore the interior in May 1674.

Shaftesbury's decision to send Dr. Woodward for the task was a wise one, for there was no one in Carolina who could match Woodward's knowledge of the Indians or the southern backcountry. Woodward, a London surgeon, first came to Carolina in 1666 during Robert Sandford's reconnaissance mission of the coast near Port Royal. When Sandford's party weighed anchor to return to England, Woodward voluntarily stayed with the Indians at Port Royal and spent several months learning their languages and customs. Soon thereafter Woodward fell into the hands of the Spanish, who detained him at St. Augustine. Woodward escaped from prison in 1668 when an English buccaneer named William Searle attacked the city and released all English prisoners then in Spanish custody. Upon his eventual return to Carolina in 1670, Woodward immediately became a valuable asset to the proprietors, who regularly employed his services for exploration and discovery.[52] According to all accounts, Woodward was an astute student of Indian culture and customs and was said to have known five different Indian languages.[53]

The opportunity to fulfill Shaftesbury's orders eventually came in October 1674, when ten Westo Indians approached Shaftesbury's St. Giles plantations, asking for trade. Woodward accompanied the Westos to their town on the Savannah River, received an honorary welcome from the town's inhabitants, and cemented the short-lived English-Westo alliance. Woodward, moreover, used this opportunity to "view the adjacent part of the country" and acquire information about other Indian peoples living in the deep interior. Woodward learned, for instance, that the Westos had been fighting wars against the "Cowatoe" and "Cussitaw" people who lived farther west. The Westos, moreover, gave to Woodward a young Indian boy taken from the "falls of that river" who likely served Woodward best as an informant, giving him the information he would have needed to make discoveries of other Indian people.[54]

Soon after Woodward's initial voyage, vague reports of Englishmen traveling through the interior Indian provinces began to reach the leery Spanish officials at St. Augustine, which hints at the possibility that Woodward had garnered enough information from the Westos and his Indian servant to penetrate successfully into the deep interior of the region. On May 23 an Indian woman who had escaped from Westo slave raiders arrived in St. Augustine to report to the governor that the Carolinians had entered into an alliance with the Westos and that together they planned to attack the Christian Indian provinces of Timucua and Apalachee that summer. The woman also claimed that a mysterious English settlement existed somewhere in the interior, five days' travel from Apalachee.[55] Since Spanish officials generally believed the Westo settlements to be a thirty-day march from Apalachee, the woman was probably describing the intrusion of English traders into the heart of the Chattahoochee River valley.[56]

It is evident from later sources that in the year or two following his Westo voyage, Woodward likely reached the town of Cussita and forged a multilateral peace agreement between the Carolinians, the Westos, and the "Cussetoes." In January of 1677 the lords proprietors issued a statement acknowledging "the discovery of the country of the Westoes and the Cussatoes . . . hath been made at the charge of the Earl of Shaftesbury . . . and by the industry and hazard of Doctor Woodward." The proprietors further asserted that the Westos and "Cussetoes" were both fierce, warlike nations that were now "at peace" with the Carolinians. Their loyalty, the proprietors assumed, would offer the fledgling colony a measure of protection from the Spaniards at St. Augustine.[57]

However beneficial it may have been to the Carolinians, the peace undoubtedly served the "Cussetoes'" own political and military interests. Peace would have been an achievement in and of itself, for the English-mediated truce ended a generation of fighting against the Westos. Most important, however, it appears Woodward achieved this truce by promising to open up trade, as evidenced by the lords proprietors' assertion that it was "absolutely necessary that the trade be carried on with those nations that so they may be supply'd with commodities according to agreement made with them by which rewards a firm and lasting peace shall be continued, and we become necessary and useful to them."[58]

While it is reasonable to suspect that the "Cussetoes" eagerly sought to acquire a "necessary and useful" ally, they were sadly disappointed, as English contact with the inhabitants of the Chattahoochee valley was infrequent at best. A Spanish report of English intrusions in the interior in the fall of 1678 is the only piece of evidence citing English activity in the region before the summer of 1685.[59] Furthermore, it is not entirely clear that all parties on the Chattahoochee were equally enamored of the English, for the Apalachicolas living farther south continued to court Spanish influence. In the waning months of 1678, Governor Hita Salazar

remained optimistic about establishing Spanish influence on the Chattahoochee, reporting that the Apalachicolas continued to trade regularly
with the Apalachees and were still "desiring a priest."[60]

This is not to say, however, that the alliance with the English and
Westos came to naught. To the contrary, evidence suggests that the
Cowetas remained in continual contact with the well-armed Westos,
who may have begun living periodically in Coweta and other Chattahoochee villages. As the Westos' principal allies, the Cowetas were able
to use the relationship to their advantage and turned Westo firepower
against groups farther south that continued to entertain Spanish invita-
tions to become a part of the mission system.

The crucial turning point came in the fall of 1679 when the chief of
Coweta used the threat of Westo firepower to oust Franciscan missionaries who had come to the town of Apalachicola. The episode began on
October 31, 1679, when Hita Salazar ordered the Franciscan *difinidor* of
Florida, Jacinto de Barreda, to convert the "pagan" Indians surrounding Apalachee so as to stem the rising tide of English influence in the
region.[61] Days later Barreda sent the resident friar at the Sabacola Mission, Fr. Juan Ocon, and two other clergymen to Apalachicola, where the
local population received them with open arms. Three days later, however, "other Indians" from nearby towns arrived in Apalachicola and
convinced the chief to denounce the missionaries and to order them to
return to Apalachee. Hita Salazar later blamed the "Chief of Coweta" for
instigating the friars' expulsion, as he appeared to have been steadfastly
against "becoming Christians." The Cowetas and other like-minded
allies, it was learned, had been in frequent communication with the
Chichimecos (the Westos) and had threatened to "set the Chichimecos
against them [the friars]" if they did not leave when asked.[62]

The expulsion of the friars in the fall of 1679 thus appears to coincide with an observable shift in the region's political dynamics, with
Coweta and its northern allies temporarily gaining the upper hand over
Apalachicola. We should be careful, however, not to assume that the
chief of Coweta had entirely consolidated his authority, for the Spanish
did not yet recognize him as a "grand cacique" and scant evidence suggests that he was known as "emperor," as he would be in later years.
Still, Florida officials began to take note of the Coweta chief's rising
influence and had clearly singled him out as the leader of a faction that
was ill-disposed toward Catholic and Spanish influence.

Another abrupt shift in regional politics occurred in the waning months of 1680, when a cabal of private planters and Indian slave traders initiated a short but destructive war against the Westos, leaving perhaps as few as fifty Westos alive. The action, which infuriated the lords proprietors back in London, was defended as a reprisal against the Westos for killing several Englishmen and Indians allied to Carolina. Other evidence indicates, however, that these up-and-coming traders had financial motives for eradicating the Westos and were jealous of the proprietors' monopoly of the Westo trade. Their jealousy in turn prompted the private traders to do away with the Westos and employ another renegade Indian group, the Savannahs, as slave raiders, enabling the traders to profit from the sale of human chattel.[63]

Back in Coweta the Westo war became an immediate concern when the surviving Westos fled to Coweta for protection. Choosing Coweta as a site of refuge makes sense, given that the Westos had been communicating amicably with Coweta and other northern Apalachicola towns for more than five years. Though it is likely we will never know the horror stories of the Westo migrants, their tragic tales must have caused the Cowetas to become leery of the English. Consequently, the Cowetas immediately initiated an attempt to mend their relationship with the Spanish. In the spring of 1681 the chief of Coweta sent his "son" to the Christian town of Sabacola to inform the Spaniards of the Carolinians' hostility and to report to the friar in residence that "many Chichimecos had come to live in the town of Coweta."[64]

Beyond Coweta, news of the Westos' apparent destruction also caused the Apalachicolas and other allied towns to renew contact with the Spanish in Florida. In the fall of 1680, nearly a year after the initial expulsion of the friars from Apalachicola, the chief of Sabacola traveled to St. Augustine to invite soldiers and missionaries to Coweta.[65] As could be expected, Spanish officials responded enthusiastically to the invitation and sent a detachment of twelve soldiers and two friars under the leadership of Capt. Andres Perez into Apalachicola territory sometime in late summer 1681.[66] Relations soured briefly, however, when word arrived that a party of Apalachicolas entered Apalachee territory and killed two Christian Indians. More Spanish soldiers were then sent from Apalachee to Apalachicola—too many, it appears—which caused the Apalachicolas to turn against the missionaries and forced the missionaries to flee "at the risk of their lives."[67] Gov. Juan Marquez Cabrera soon sent word to the chief of Apalachicola that he would pardon the murderers if the chiefs under his jurisdiction would come to St. Augustine to render obedience to the Spanish king. If the chief chose not to comply, Marquez threatened to send the entire Apalachee garrison to the chief's town to "force them to do it." If they came of their own free will, he promised to do them no harm.[68]

Seeking to avoid a military confrontation, five chiefs from Apalachicola arrived in St. Augustine on September 19, 1681, just as the governor had requested. Upon their arrival Marquez asked them why they allowed their "vassals" to commit hostilities upon the Christian Indians, and why, "when they went to apprehend the aggressors . . . they had become altered and demonstrated as if they wanted to kill the soldiers and the missionaries?"[69]

The identities of the chiefs and their responses to the governor's question reveals much about the inner workings of Apalachicola politics as well as prevailing attitudes among the Apalachicolas toward the Spanish mission system. The group consisted of the chief of Apalachicola and four subordinate chiefs from "all of the towns under his jurisdiction." Evidently the chief of Apalachicola was still regarded as having authority greater than the others, but he claimed leadership over only Apalachicola and four other towns (presumably indigenous towns in the southern part of the province). Regardless of the leadership he claimed, the chief of Apalachicola had little control over the population there, as can be seen in his argument to the governor that he could do little to prevent attacks on Christian Indians: "they cannot remedy them, because the perpetrators are bandits and fugitives who go about the woods without recognizing or being subjected to their caciques, and [they] cannot help it."[70]

Seeking to deflect further the responsibility for their peoples' behavior, the five chiefs argued that the chief of Coweta was to blame for the recent mischief, since he was "the chief one to whom all render vassalage."[71] This statement stands as the first extant reference that the chief of Coweta was the head of the entire province, suggesting that his ascent was of a recent vintage. The statement also suggests that the political consolidation of the Apalachicola "province," like the chief of Coweta's recently conceived authority, was still considered a work in progress.

The governor's later description of the chief of Coweta suggests that the chief derived much of his new-found authority from his association with the Westos and, indirectly, with the English. Governor Marquez described the chief of Coweta as the "most feared" of all the chiefs, emphasizing that his lands touched upon the lands of the "Chichimecos [Westos] and other provinces that touch upon the lands of the Englishmen." Of course what made the Westos such an important ally was the fact that they were armed, causing Marquez to note that "they have firearms which they have taken away from the English on some occasions."[72] The recent influx into Coweta of Westo refugees and the Westos' acquisition of firearms had apparently bolstered Coweta's influence in the region.

While it is easy to dismiss the Apalachicola chief's words as an attempt to shift blame for the conflict upon the chief of Coweta, Marquez was convinced that the real center of power on the Chattahoochee was not Apalachicola but rather the upstart Coweta. In recognition of the new power dynamic, Marquez pleaded in earnest with his Indian visitors to invite the chief of Coweta to visit St. Augustine in person so as to establish a real truce.[73] Once invited, the chief of Coweta readily accepted and soon prepared to make the long journey. Traveling south into Apalachee territory, the chief of Coweta and his party arrived in Bacuqua, the residence of the Franciscan *provincial* of Apalachee, Fray Rodrigo de la Barrera, during the first week of December 1681.

In Bacuqua, Fray Barrera interviewed the chief of Coweta, then penned a letter to the governor summarizing his opinion of the enigmatic chief. Contrary to circulating opinions, Fray Barrera found the chief receptive to Christianity: "I found false all of the accusations against him. The facts are so contrary that he states he will not refuse admittance to the priests. And it is true, sir governor, that it is within your power that he should admit them or not, according to the reception you offer him."[74] Evidently the chief of Coweta was anxious to see what kind of reception he could get from the Spaniards before deciding how best to confront missionization efforts.

In addition to claiming that the chief of Coweta was receptive to mission proselytizing, Fray Barrera also made several grandiose assumptions about the chief's power that the chief himself later denied. According to Barrera, the chief of Coweta "lorded" over sixty-six towns, including the towns of the Apalachicola province as well as far-away towns such as Chiaha and Chicassa. Convert the chief of Coweta to Christianity, he argued, and the rest would follow.[75]

Bearing Fray Barrera's letter in his own hands, the chief of Coweta made his way across Florida and arrived in St. Augustine on January 1, 1682. The next day Marquez summoned the chief and his retinue and explained the contents of the letter. According to Marquez, "they answered with consternation that they had not come to request priests, but on the summons from his Grace." What they really wanted, Marquez wrote, "was to confirm the peace which he had offered them. And . . . for no other purpose."[76] In addition to denying that he had wanted priests, the chief of Coweta "flatly denied" that he had authority over sixty-six towns, claiming a mere nine towns under his jurisdiction.[77]

Perplexed by the chief of Coweta's denials, Marquez ordered a second interview, perhaps to verify that the chief had understood the letter's contents correctly. The chief confirmed his earlier statements and added that "the reason for their coming was that his vassals had come to see the governor and had told him about the great reception they had . . . and as they had pledged allegiance to his Majesty, they had come to see his grace, as [he] was a person representing the king."[78]

Again the chief denied that he presided over the fabled "sixty-six towns," but during his second interview he claimed that there were eleven towns under his dominion, "which are those comprising the province of Apalachicola." For the second time in one day the chief of Coweta affirmed that he presided over the entire province, lending credence to the Apalachicolas' previous assertions that the Coweta chief was the one "to whom all render vassalage." Curiously, the chief's "dominion" seems to have increased from nine to eleven towns in the course of a single day. This discrepancy, though minor in some ways (and perhaps reflecting a mis-translation), nevertheless hints that the chief may have been trying to consolidate his authority, therefore making him unsure, to an extent, of the size or loyalty of his "dominion."

While the exchange between the governor and the chief of Coweta betrays the cultural misunderstandings that often occurred between Europeans and Indians, the remarks of both the Coweta chief and the Apalachicola chief suggest that the Mississippian collapse was incomplete, and that the Apalachicola province bore the form, if not the substance, of a multicommunity "chiefdom." It is evident, for example, that late-seventeenth-century chiefs believed that individual towns, though independent to a great extent, were ranked according to their perceived antiquity or influence. Perhaps due to his town's antiquity, the Apalachicola chief claimed authority over five towns, including his own. But even he appears to have deferred to the chief of Coweta when it came time to issue a final word to Marquez concerning the offer of peace and priests. The chief of Coweta's own "dominion" further suggests a "chiefdom" level of political concentration since it consisted of nine to eleven towns all located on the same river. Thus it appears that even in the wake of catastrophic population losses and a denuded cult of the chief, political traditions of the past still habituated the late-seventeenth-century inhabitants of the Chattahoochee River and caused them to look upon their riverine populations as part of a broader political community. The "chief" of the most influential town was a source of superior authority, at least as it pertained to external affairs.

Fray Barrera rightly understood that the Cowetas possessed some serious misgivings about the Florida mission system and feared losing their independence—which would become an all-too-familiar theme in the coming years. As neighbors to and trading partners of the Apalachees, the residents of the Chattahoochee had observed the mission system's effects on their southern neighbors for two generations. The chief of Coweta was not unaware of the toll that the *repartimiento* labor draft had taken on the population. He also might have witnessed the growing presence of the Spanish military and the expansion of cattle ranches and wheat plantations, both of which undercut traditional Apalachee political authority and encroached upon the Apalachees' traditional economy. For these reasons, Fray Barrera urged Governor Marquez to convince the Coweta chief that, "it [missionization] will be different from the Appalachians; they would not be taken from their lands to work in the presidio to dig or build. On the contrary, they will be aided in everything possible, and will not be deprived of their right as natural lords."[79]

Whatever their misgivings about the Spaniards, the chiefs of Coweta and other towns continued to renew the peace through the alliance for several more years, indicating that the precipitous demise of the Westos still burned fresh in their memories. The chiefs of Coweta and Apalachicola (or their representatives) appear to have made at least two more journeys to St. Augustine, one in 1684 and another in 1685, to renew their pledge of friendship and allegiance to the king of Spain. In 1686, as hostilities erupted between the Spanish and the Apalachicolas, Governor Marquez lamented the fact that the chiefs of Coweta and Apalachicola had "for two years entered the government to render obedience." Furthermore, the chief of Colone and his "vassals" also journeyed to St. Augustine in 1685 to render obedience to the Spanish king.[80] As late as 1685, then, the Cowetas' political allegiances were anything but certain and their eventual turn toward the English was not inevitable.

Pleading Ignorance

Whereas the occasional presence of English explorers and Westo warriors had begun to draw the entire Apalachicola province into the orbit
of international intrigue, the eventual arrival of English traders on the
Chattahoochee River drew them more directly into the brewing imperial
rivalry between Spain and England. An accelerated phase of the imperial struggle effectively began in the summer of 1685, when a group of
English traders led by Henry Woodward made their way to the Chattahoochee River to establish the trade that had been promised to the
"Cussetoes" a decade earlier.

The intrusion of English traders, though anticipated and welcomed
by the people living on the Chattahoochee, raised the ire of the Spanish,
who believed that by trading with the English the "Apalachicolas" had
violated their pledge of "obedience" to the king of Spain. Fearful that
the intrusion of these traders might enable the English to make their
own claims to Apalachicola territory, the governor of Florida ordered
his lieutenant of Apalachee, Antonio Matheos, to lead two expeditions
to Apalachicola in September 1685 and January 1686 to capture the English traders and restore the Indians to their proper "obedience."[81] The
Apalachicolas, however, did very little to assist Matheos and later admitted that they had fled their towns, hid the English traders, and "pleaded
ignorance" as to their whereabouts.[82] In retaliation, Matheos burned the
four "most guilty" towns, an act that caused a generations-long breach
between the Apalachicolas and Spain.

Though Matheos appeared capable of discriminating between the
"most guilty" and the "less guilty" towns, it should be emphasized that
the entire Apalachicola province was complicit in welcoming the English
traders and thwarting Matheos's attempts to catch them. The most conspicuous evidence for the regional dimension of the plot was the fact that
the inhabitants of every town fled to the woods upon hearing of Matheos's approach. Matheos's own accounts verify that the Apalachicolas
had spied on the Spanish and tipped off their northern neighbors about
his arrival. Moreover, the traders were welcomed with open arms in
towns such as Osuche, whose inhabitants even compelled the traders
to help them build their council house after Matheos left briefly in the
fall of 1685. Matheos also discerned that the inhabitants of the entire
province had assisted in the construction of a fort north of the province,
which had been erected for the traders' protection.[83]

Matheos was correct in assuming that resistance centered in the four northernmost towns in Apalachicola: Casiste, Colone, Tasquique, and Coweta. After burning the towns Matheos justified his actions on the grounds that the four towns were "from other places," and had only recently come into existence and remained politically distinct from their neighbors to the south.[84] These four northern towns continued their close contact with the Tallapoosa peoples living farther west. The Tallapoosas themselves later verified that they had close contact with the Chattahoochee peoples, admitting to one Spanish officer that many Tallapoosa people had ventured to the Chattahoochee to establish towns but had recently returned in the wake of Matheos's invasions.[85]

The Cowetas and their "guilty" counterparts had already established Indian and European networks linking them to the coast that were meant to serve as a kind of pipeline for facilitating trade. The Cowetas had close connections to the Westos, who roamed frequently and appear to have traded on the outskirts of the Carolina settlements, perhaps even after their supposed destruction in 1680. Furthermore, in 1683 pirates fell upon a coalesced Indian group living on the Georgia coast known as the Yamasees, causing a great many of them to flee to Coweta and Cussita for safety. The Yamasees appear to have lived in the vicinity of Coweta and Cussita for nearly two years before returning once again to the coast to settle in the vicinity of Stuart's Town, a Scottish colony established in January 1685 at Port Royal.[86]

While most historians tend to credit Henry Woodward for bringing trade to the Chattahoochee region, an emphasis on the heroic actions of the English tends to neglect the Indians' own initiatives in establishing this important commercial relationship. If we reverse our perspective and see these events through the eyes of the people living on the Chattahoochee, it appears that the Cowetas and the Cussitas actually used their already established communication network to invite Woodward and other English traders into their territory. In fact, evidence indicates that within the space of three months the Cowetas communicated their desire to trade with the two leading colonists at Stuart's Town, Lord Cardross and William Dunlop. Dunlop, writing to one of the colony's patrons back in Scotland, reported in March 1685 that the colonists were planning "a method for correspondence and treade with Cuita and Cussita nations of Indians," indicating that the two towns in particular had made contact by word of mouth. The Cowetas and Cussitas, moreover, had made it known that they wanted little to do with the Spanish so as to encourage the Scots and the English, causing Dunlop to argue that the

Cowetas and the Cussitas had "for severally yeirs left off any Comercie with the Spanirds."[87]

News of the Scots' plans soon reached the ears of Henry Woodward who, after a long sabbatical in England, had recently returned to Charles Town armed with a proprietary commission to explore the "undiscovered" western frontier.[88] As the recipient of a one-fifth share of the profits derived from the western Indian trade, Woodward clearly viewed the Scots' pretensions as a threat to his economic interests.[89] To preempt the Stuart's Town trade, Woodward hastily departed from Charles Town in late April with his own supply of trade goods.[90] After being briefly detained by the Scots at Stuart's Town, Woodward made the acquaintance of a Yamasee headman named Niquisaya, who had connections to the interior and may have even lived in the vicinity of Coweta and Cussita between 1683 and 1685.[91] Making Niquisaya's acquaintance proved beneficial, for the headman volunteered to guide Woodward to the Chattahoochee and offered his own people as burdeners. Soon after (probably sometime in June), Woodward and Niquisaya in addition to seven or eight other traders and approximately fifty Yamasee burdeners, departed Stuart's Town and made their way to the Chattahoochee.[92]

Woodward's party reached the Chattahoochee region sometime that summer, possibly arriving first in Coweta—which may not have been an accident, since both the Cowetas and the Cussitas were mentioned by name as specific targets of the Scottish traders. Most important, the traders' arrival in Coweta had lasting significance because later it enabled the Cowetas to make the claim of being "the first" to open the trading path to Charles Town. Opening the path gave the Cowetas a privileged voice in Anglo-Creek relations, following the common practice in Native North America to defer to particular towns or clans that had prior claim to the European trade, at least when it came time to negotiate prices, treaties, and other pressing matters.[93] The Cowetas also would have had the first opportunity to adopt traders into their kinship networks, in effect forcing the traders to conduct trade in a way that benefited Coweta's leaders. In this sense being "first" enabled particular towns or clans to serve as caretakers of the English alliance, giving them a privileged voice in any national affairs that pertained to the English.

The Creeks appear to have regarded Coweta's role as particularly important (more so than the English did), and subsequent generations continued to remember the Cowetas as being "the first." Malatchi, Coweta's preeminent leader in the 1740s, on one occasion defended his right to speak on behalf of the Creek Nation, arguing that his "father" had been "the first to accept English traders" into their towns.[94] In 1774, nearly a century after the events in question, a Creek leader named Emistisiguo defended the antiquity of the trade path connecting the Creeks to Charles Town by remembering being taught by his forefathers that "the Cowetas were the first who opened the path."[95] Thus it appears that Creek oral traditions—in Coweta and elsewhere—retained the vague memory of Coweta's historical role in opening the path to Carolina.

Later events also attest to the probability that Coweta and the other "most guilty" northern towns played a significant role in ushering in the trade. That summer, for instance, Henry Woodward ordered the construction of two edifices that served as centers for trade: one a "block house" built near Coweta and the other, a palisade, erected several miles north of Tasquique, the northernmost village on the Chattahoochee. It should be emphasized that the locations of these two edifices likely was not chosen accidentally, but they probably were built on land "given" to the English by specific chiefs. The fact that the two edifices arose in the north near Coweta likely reflects the growing intimacy between the four towns and the traders.[96]

As further evidence of this growing intimacy, Matheos's letters describing his activities during that fall reveal that a man named "Quiair" —probably the chief of Coweta—gave in marriage an unnamed "niece" to none other than "the leader" of the English traders, most likely Henry Woodward.[97] By giving his "niece" to Henry Woodward the Coweta chief sought to draw the English leader into the web of kinship relations that conferred important rights and obligations on both parties in a mutually beneficial way. Thomas Nairne described the method by which several generations of Anglo-Scotch traders could "procure kindred" in Creek country: "Its the easiest thing in the world," Nairne wrote, "to procure kindred among the Indians, It's but taking a mistress of such a name, and he has at once relations in each Village . . . and if in travelling he acquaints them with what fameily he is incorporated into, those of that name treat, and wait on him as their kinsman."[98] Conversely, the Indian "family" into which the English trader was incorporated would have expected something in return: perhaps gifts, a preferential trade agreement, or the promise of military assistance should their people go to war.

Considered in that light, the reported marriage between the chief of

Coweta's niece and Woodward was of particular importance. According to the Creeks' matrilineal system, the chief's niece was his blood relation, making Woodward himself a surrogate member of Coweta's ruling clan. Such a connection would have conferred immediate benefits to Woodward, for it is likely that prior to his marriage he first had to procure the consent of the Coweta rulers before he could travel freely through the territory, conduct trade, and erect trading posts. The Coweta elites, of course, figured to gain certain advantages as well, for their link to Woodward gave them privileged access to the traders and provided them with a critical link to the new political power base emerging on the Ashley and Cooper Rivers.

As the events unfolded over the next several months, Matheos compiled a long list of incriminating evidence that implicated the chief of Coweta and chiefs from the other three northern towns as the leading conspirators in the effort to hide the English traders, suggesting that the chief of Coweta wielded authority over the entire province. The virtually complete abandonment of the towns after Matheos's arrival at Talispasle, the southernmost town on the Chattahoochee, for instance, indicates that the towns were acting in unison under the chief's direction. One woman caught by Matheos even revealed that the chief of Coweta had issued a death threat against anyone who revealed the location of the hidden traders. Other evidence indicates that the chief of Coweta was himself directing counterespionage efforts by placing Westo, Yamasee, and Apalachicola sentinels at various places along Apalachicola's southern frontier.[99]

The arrival of Matheos and his several hundred Apalachee warriors and Spanish soldiers may have caused a crisis—albeit, a brief one—in the Coweta chief's leadership. His policy of defending and hiding the traders had placed all the villages directly in danger, since Matheos had issued repeated threats to burn the towns and confiscate the corn. Good chiefs, of course, were supposed to protect their people, evade confrontations when possible, and avoid unnecessary loss of life and property. These dangers, arguably caused by the Coweta chief's actions, may have caused others to question his reputation as the one "to whom all render vassalage."

The individual most likely to call that reputation into question was Pentocolo, the chief of Apalachicola who had prior links to the Spanish and the Apalachees and whose people might have resented being endangered by the policy of a chief from a "different" place. During the course of Matheos's two rampages through the region, Pentocolo emerged as the principal mediator, traveling frequently with Matheos to divert him and protect the villages. Though Matheos was prone to dismissing Pentocolo as a mere "spy" for the chief of Coweta, Pentocolo's behavior suggests a certain reluctance to defer entirely to the Coweta chief. On occasion Pentocolo himself cast blame on the four northern towns, arguing during an initial interview that "he was not sure," but he had heard rumors that two Englishmen were "in Casiste, two at Tasquiqui, and two at Colone," with another forty traders expected any day. Furthermore, during the interim between Matheos's two incursions, Pentocolo traveled to Apalachee with Acalaque, the chief of Achito, in an apparent attempt to mend their relationship with the Spanish. During the interviews (which took place in Apalachee that winter), Pentocolo disclosed little as to the whereabouts of the English traders but did not prevent Acalaque from revealing their presence in Casiste.[100]

The most glaring evidence for the growing breach between the southern Apalachicola towns and the four northern towns affiliated with Coweta came during Matheos's second incursion. In January 1686 Matheos spent several weeks in the abandoned town of Coweta, all the while urging Pentocolo (who was traveling with him) to summon the chiefs in the region to a talk. Towns that chose to ignore these instructions, Matheos warned, would be burned. After several weeks of pleading Pentocolo was able to gather only eight chiefs, all from the southern towns, giving further evidence that the Coweta chief's authority—if it existed in the first place—was not absolute. The assembled southern delegation blamed the "four agitators" for forcing them to admit the traders; the chief of Osuche argued that they "had not wished to meet in friendship with the English, as they had always repulsed them . . . and could not receive a pass in their towns." Accordingly, all eight of the southern chiefs submitted quietly in "obedience" to Matheos, causing him to burn only the four "most guilty" towns of Cussita, Colone, Tasquiqui, and, of course, Coweta.[101]

In this way Pentocolo and the other chiefs effectively stigmatized the four northern towns and in the process spared their own towns from the flames. Furthermore, the burning of the four towns may have served as a dramatic reminder of the dangers of the chief of Coweta's policies, causing yet another crisis in his leadership. To continue their new alliance with the English, the four northern chiefs would have been required to demonstrate the alliance's tangible benefits and convince the Apalachicolas that the English were worthy allies. It appears that the chiefs of Coweta and Cussita, together with the English, spent much of the next several months trying to regain the confidence of the southern towns. That May, an Apalachee spy working for Matheos reported that one Englishman and forty-five Yamasees had come to the town of Apalachicola bearing twenty-six guns and an assortment of machetes and other trade items. It was an important gesture, particularly because they were given as a "gift . . . from the governor of Carolina," who had apparently become apprised of the importance of gift-giving as a token of friendship. Perhaps aware that the destruction of the four towns had made the English appear weak, the English ambassador made the bold claim that the English were soon to attack St. Augustine with one hundred ships and asked the Apalachicolas to assist with a coordinated land attack.[102]

The gesture, it appears, was not enough. The Apalachicolas were already indebted to the traders for some "slaves" taken at some point months earlier. By way of the chief of Tama, a mission village located on the outskirts of Apalachee, Matheos learned of a "mutiny" against the traders in Apalachicola for not having done enough to defend the Apalachicolas against their enemy, the Chiscas, who had killed twelve of their men that summer. The Apalachicolas considered the act as a breach in kinship etiquette, since friends and brothers were required to protect each other in times of need. In retaliation the Apalachicolas threatened to withhold food from the traders, as if to remind them of the reciprocal nature of their relationship.

To head off a crisis, Henry Woodward, though nursing a snakebite he had received somewhere "in the woods," came into the town and gave cloth and beads to Pentocolo, the Apalachicola chief. Pentocolo in turn distributed the gifts among the other chiefs and repeated Woodward's promise that greater things lay in the future. Through the gift distribution Woodward signified the traders' intention of behaving as good kinsmen and enhanced the chiefs' ability, quite literally, to "deliver the goods," effectively supporting the chiefs' authority. In early August 1686, Woodward, in the company of 150 Indian burdeners and a chief from each town, left for Charles Town, carrying loads so as to "spite the Chiscas."[103]

From that point on the chiefs of Coweta and Cussita continued to lead the people of the Chattahoochee River valley on a political and eco-

nomic course facing east toward the new colony at Carolina. As Antonio Matheos apparently recognized after he burnt their towns, the
Cowetas and Cussitas followed through on their repeated hints that
they might "go with the English" and had "no intention of remaining"
on the Chattahoochee.[104] That the Cowetas and Cussitas led the push
eastward signifies that some remarkable reconfigurations in the region's
political dynamics had occurred. In allying themselves with the English
at this important juncture, the Cowetas and Cussitas, people from "other
places," had taken effective control of Apalachicola's foreign relations.
Coweta, once known as "those who are following us," was to be a town
of followers no longer; its chief would emerge as "the one to whom all
render vassalage," and together they became caretakers of the growing
Anglo-Creek alliance.

CHAPTER TWO

Enemigos

On April 1, 1688, more than two years after Antonio Matheos reduced four Apalachicola towns to ashes, the newly installed governor of Florida, Don Diego de Quiroga y Losada, exclaimed that "it was a great act of God that they [the Apalachicolas] have not united with the enemies of St. George [Charles Town] to revenge their grievances."[1] Rarely have colonial governors written such tragically shortsighted words, for soon after the pronouncement the Apalachicolas and a diverse group of like-minded Indian peoples emigrated en masse to new homes in the heart of Georgia—earning for themselves a new name, the Ochese Creek Indians, in the process—and conducted a twenty-year war against the missions and presidios of Florida. In the course of this protracted war the Ocheses and their allies virtually exterminated Florida's aboriginal population, reduced La Florida to a shell of its former self, and earned among Florida officials the well-deserved appellation *enemigos* (enemies).

Most historians portray this war as only a part of the larger struggle between Britain and Spain called Queen Anne's War (1702–1713), and reduce the multifaceted quest for power in the Southeast—fought primarily by Indians—to a contest between Europeans.[2] Although one cannot dismiss the importance of this imperial rivalry, it must be recognized that the Ocheses did not share the imperialist ambitions of South Carolina officials. Rather, their struggle against Florida began as an act of revenge against Spain's Christian Indian allies, who made convenient targets for a generation of Ochese slave catchers. Thanks in part to the new military technology—the gun—that they exchanged for their human prisoners, the Ocheses and their allies became the most powerful and militaristic Indians of the Southeast. Gradually, particularly in the years following the collapse of the Spanish missions in 1705, the slaving wars against Christian Indians evolved into an imperial war, when Carolina traders began encouraging the Ocheses to escalate their attacks on those living in the remaining Spanish and French possessions. Threatened with becoming Carolina's mercenaries, some Ocheses came to recognize that their rise to power compromised their political and economic autonomy and sowed the seeds of discontent—and, eventually, revolt—against the Carolina regime.

The Flight to Ochese Creek

The Apalachicolas' flight to Ochese Creek, completed in the spring of 1691, should be considered a pivotal event in Creek history primarily because many of the Creeks remember it that way. As the Philadelphia naturalist William Bartram related more than eighty years after the fact, the Creeks regarded the Okmulgee old fields as "remarkable for being the first town or settlement, when they sat down (as they term it) or established themselves, after their immigration from the west . . . their original native country."[3] The Creeks did not remain permanently at Ochese Creek, but one generation's presence there established a perpetual spiritual link to that territory. James Adair, for one, claimed that his Creek acquaintances frequently heard "at the dawn of morning, the usual noise of Indians singing their religious notes, and dancing, as if going down to the river to purify themselves and then returning to the old town-house." Adair, who camped at Ochese Creek on numerous occasions, never heard the Creek spirits singing, which the Creeks attributed to Adair's being "an obdurate infidel in that way."[4] Though the eighteenth-century Creeks were unable to make a believer out of Adair, modern historians should recognize more than a grain of truth in this enduring Creek oral tradition, for in many ways the Creeks became a new people living in a new kind of world during their years on Ochese Creek.

Though in the long view the Indians' flight to Ochese Creek was rooted in the *entradas* orchestrated by Antonio Matheos several years earlier, the more immediate cause of the exodus can be tied to the recent construction of a Spanish fort on the Chattahoochee River. The fort, completed in December 1689 and garrisoned with Spanish soldiers and Apalachee militia, was designed to "prevent the trespassing of the said

English," who were rumored to be operating on the Chattahoochee.[5] Although it is not known how the Apalachicolas initially reacted to the arrival of the Spanish that fall, they seem to have acquiesced peacefully to Spanish intrusion. By December 21, Capt. Enrique Primo de Ribera boastfully reported that the Spanish had constructed a modest-sized fort in the vicinity of Coweta and had met "with little disagreement" from the local inhabitants.[6]

The Apalachicolas' apparently peaceful reception of the Spanish garrison, however, was only a ruse. Behind the scenes the Apalachicolas were busy making plans to relocate. Leading the way in this enterprise were the chiefs of Coweta and Cussita, who ordered the reconstruction of their towns at Ochese a year prior to the general exodus. In April 1690 a Scottish trader named John Stewart related that another trader had returned from his time among the Cowetas with twenty-eight hundred deerskins and the chiefs of Coweta and Cusseta in tow: "[H]e's brought the Coweta and Cusheda K[ings] here with him," he wrote, "[w]ho have now return'd loaded with presents: they have being 2500 fighting men, deserted the Spanish protection and com'd and setl'd 10 days Jurnay nerer us to Injoy the English frier protection."[7] Stewart's letter does not make clear who boasted of the twenty-five hundred fighting men but the impression must have been fostered by the two chiefs, who may have wished to make their widespread influence known.

Though the chiefs of Coweta and Cussita led the way in establishing new towns in the spring of 1690, evidence suggests that the majority of residents on the Chattahoochee River did not flee until a year later. Curiously, Spanish officials in Apalachee and St. Augustine, who usually were apprised of most events that occurred on the Chattahoochee, knew nothing about the construction of the two new towns despite the fact that Captain Primo de Ribera and a twenty-man garrison remained at the Apalachicola fort throughout the winter and early spring. The garrison's new commander, Don Faviano de Angelo, did not suspect that the Apalachicolas were up to anything when he met with them on various occasions in May 1690. Indeed, at those meetings the Apalachicolas convinced de Angelo that they had renounced the English; they were rewarded with a supply of corn, which the Apalachicolas likely put to use in sowing their new fields at Ochese.[8]

The majority of the Apalachicolas remained in their traditional homes on the Chattahoochee, and the exodus was completed only by September 1691 when the governor ordered Primo de Ribera, who had returned as commander, to abandon the fort in Apalachicola. The governor justified the move on the grounds that the English were "aggregated with the Indian towns on the Uchise River," an unmistakable reference to a tributary of the Ocmulgee River that the English called Ochese Creek.[9]

Although this demographic readjustment began with the wholesale relocation of the Apalachicola towns on the Ocmulgee and Oconee Rivers, it is important to emphasize that people from a variety of locations made a similar exodus to Ochese.[10] Ochese Creek, then, was not simply the new home of the Cowetas, the Cussitas, and the Apalachicolas but was a locus of settlement that attracted a variety of Indian groups fleeing Spanish aggression and participating in Carolina's burgeoning trade in deerskins and Indian slaves. Bearing in mind these incentives, the flight to Ochese should be seen as a patently political act made in a self-conscious attempt to achieve that particular end.

Among the first to accompany the Apalachicolas to their new homes were the Sabacolas, a group then living in the mission town located near the confluence of the Chattahoochee and Flint Rivers. In 1689 Sabacola was home to approximately thirty families and at one time boasted a Christian population of thirty individuals, including the head chief and five "sons" of the leading *heniha*, or second man. Some Christians appear even to have chosen Spanish soldiers to serve as godparents to their children, while others served Antonio Matheos as spies against their kin to the north. By the spring of 1692 Fr. Jacinto Barreda, the provincial head of the Apalachee missions, reported that the inhabitants of Sabacola had entirely "depopulated" their town after being solicited "by the Apalachicola people of the same nation."[11] When circumstances forced them to choose between the Spanish or their Apalachicola kin, the Sabacolas decided to throw in their lot with the people they still regarded as their own.

Joining the Sabacolas were a conspicuous number of people from the Tallapoosa River towns. That such a course of action was taken by peoples not directly affected by the recent Spanish invasions certainly attests to the lure of the Carolina trade. It also suggests that the leaders of the migration—Coweta and Cussita—continued to hold some sway over certain closely allied Tallapoosa towns. Cartographic and documentary evidence indicates that at least some portion of three separate towns—Tuckebatchee, Atasi, and Tallassee—chose to relocate to Ochese Creek during those years.[12]

Once the Cowetas, the Cussitas, and their neighbors had established new homes and had commenced trading regularly with the Carolina traders, Ochese Creek served as a magnet for a variety of other Southeastern Indian peoples seeking to benefit from the English trade. In the ensuing years Ochese Creek and other interior regions filled with remnant bands of Cherokee-speaking people from the Tennessee River such as the Hogologes, as well as a northern branch of the Westos, the Rickahechrians, who had been living among the Mohawks in New York.[13] Joining in the exodus were the Yamasee-speaking Chehaws and Tamas, the latter of whom fled their mission in Apalachee to escape the persecution of the Franciscan friars and Spanish military authorities.[14] In sum, Ochese Creek became home to a mixed multitude divided by language and ethnicity but sharing the common goal of enjoying the benefits of the Carolina trade alliance.

A War for Slaves and Vengeance

From Ochese Creek and other surrounding territories a diverse array of Indian groups (hereafter referred to as "Ocheses") commenced a protracted war against Spanish Florida that occupied both for the better part of twenty years. But this generation-long conflict should not be considered as a single war carried out against the Spanish. Rather, it was a series of smaller wars, each fought against a distinctly different enemy to further the advancement of a different goal. The first phase of the war began in the summer of 1691, just a few short months after the general exodus to Ochese Creek. The Ocheses engaged in the early series of conflicts both as a means of acquiring prisoners for the lucrative slave trade and to enact revenge against Florida's Christianized Indian population, whom the Ocheses apparently blamed for harboring the Spanish and whose sedentary, unarmed populations made easy prey for gun-bearing Ochese warriors.

Neither warfare nor slavery were new to the Ocheses who, like most Southeastern Indian groups, for many years (undoubtedly for centuries) had engaged in the practice of acquiring slaves during times of war. Southeastern Indians traditionally believed warfare possessed a spiritual dimension because many acts of war appear to have been carried out to exact blood revenge for a slain kinsperson, whose spirit, it was thought, would not rest nor depart peacefully to the land of the dead until the blood of the offending party had been shed. Responsibility for organizing a war party primarily fell to the victim's clan-kin, many of whom continued to partake in the rituals of mourning—

sexual abstinence or hair shearing, as dictated by one's relationship to the deceased—until a successful war party returned with an enemy scalp and restored a state of balance between the dead and the living. At times, however, war parties returned not with scalps but with prisoners, many of whom were ritually tortured and executed to satisfy the requirements of blood vengeance. Though ritual executions of this sort were not uncommon, grieving families often spared the life of a prisoner and forced the captive to live and work for the family as one of its "slaves." Though these subordinates lacked clan connections, they were not chattel commodities subject to the frequent physical abuse that slaves in the English dominions received. In fact, many such slaves of the Indians appear to have been ritually adopted into their host families, eventually marrying and becoming full members of the clan and surrounding community. Through institutional mechanisms the captured slaves served to replace—both physically and spiritually—those who had died at the hands of an enemy.[15]

By at least the middle of the seventeenth century, and especially after the establishment of Carolina in 1670, the context in which Indian slavery was practiced began to change as profit-seeking merchants in Charles Town sought to acquire Indian slaves to work on the plantations or to sell abroad. Through the burgeoning slave market the Indian prisoners destined to become slaves also became commodities, a status they shared with imported African slaves. The Ocheses themselves figured to profit handsomely by selling their war captives, since each sold slave could earn a gun and perhaps some gunpowder, shot, and a few clothes. Thus, beginning especially in the 1690s, a vicious cycle that drew the Ocheses increasingly into the world of guns, warfare, and slavery had begun.

The Ocheses launched their first series of attacks just a few short months after the exodus, when a group comprised of "Uchises, Yamasees, and Englishmen" from Carolina descended upon the Timucuan town of San Juan de Guacara, located on the Suwanee River in north-central Florida, to kill and enslave its residents, who could scarcely defend themselves against the well-armed aggressor. The onslaught proved to be simply the first (and most dramatic) of many blows struck against the Florida missions in the ensuing months, as other mission provinces soon suffered the same intrusion of guerrilla-style bands of Ocheses and other warriors. In Apalachee, Father Barreda, the head of the Apalachee missions, reported a series of attacks on other towns during the fall of 1691 and stressed the danger that the roaming bands of "heathen" Indians posed to his missions. The most substantial such assault came sometime before April 1692 when a "bloodthirsty" party of *enemigos* entered the Chacato town of San Carlos on the Apalachicola River, killing or taking captive many of the resident Indian population. Two summers later, in 1694, a party of Sabacolas, Apalachicolas, and Tiquipaches returned to San Carlos to finish the destruction they had begun two years earlier. Spanish officials continued to lament unspecified "infestations" of Ochese war parties as 1694 drew to a close.[16]

Though it is difficult to probe their motives, ample evidence suggests that the Ocheses conducted their wars in a way that may have had little to do with appeasing the spirits of slain kin. Rather, the scale and ferocity with which such campaigns were carried out indicate that both profit and the desire to acquire firearms were equally important catalysts. Reports indicated, for instance, that the party that attacked the Timucuan mission of San Juan de Guacara had killed a number of its inhabitants, enslaving as many of the survivors as possible. Likewise, the pattern of violence against San Carlos de Chacatos Mission betrays similar actions, as one report indicated that five persons had been killed while more than forty had been detained as prisoners and sold into slavery.

By directing their attacks against small unfortified missions and carrying away rather large numbers of prisoners, the Ocheses and their allies employed a strategy that ensured success and profit. Spanish officials often lamented that the Ocheses secured their prisoners specifically to acquire muskets, and it was believed that this desire helped to explain the ferocity of the attacks and the large number of people detained as prisoners. Indeed, by the turn of the eighteenth century the possession of a firearm had become a distinguishing cultural marker that set groups such as the Ocheses and Yamasees apart from the Indians of Florida and elsewhere. By acquiring firearms the Ocheses further solidified their growing power over other Indian groups, particularly the Apalachees, who appear to have been their ultimate target. A deposition taken from an old Chacato woman prisoner who had escaped and had courageously made her way back to St. Augustine, indicates that this was in fact the case. According to the records of her interview, "the said enemies told her that they seized them [the Chacato prisoners] to sell them to the English for muskets in order to come together to begin one day against the Spanish and Apalachees."[17]

Extant recordings of these events indicate that the attackers specifically targeted Christian Indians, perhaps because they blamed those converts for allowing the Spanish to gain influence in their corner of the world. We may therefore speculate with some assuredness that the attackers intended, in part, to cleanse the land of its Catholic stain. For example, the victims of the raid on San Carlos de Chacatos in 1694 were described as "forty-two Christians," and Spanish officials writing to inform the governor of the guerrilla-style attacks in Apalachee described the events as "murders of Christians." Moreover, when Florida officials organized a war party in the fall of 1694 to seek punishment of the Ocheses, the officials specifically instructed their officers to recruit Christian Apalachees, a telling sign that suggests the Christian Indians had suffered disproportionately.[18]

The symbols of Christianity likewise came under direct attack, as Ochese war parties sought to eradicate churches, convents, and all accouterments of the faith. The attackers who destroyed San Juan de Guacara set fire to the church, the convent, and the rest of the town. One band of attackers, said to consist of warriors from Atasi and Tuckebatchee, entered the San Carlos old town and, finding it depopulated, proceeded to break apart the crosses, the church, and the convent. Witnesses to this act of destruction later reported overhearing the pillagers say that they destroyed the church, crosses, and convent "because the Spanish esteem such things."[19]

In many respects the destruction of Catholic buildings and other symbols of the faith conforms to ancient warfare practices found in the Southeast. Mississippian-era warriors, for example, specifically targeted ceremonial platform mounds and looted the chief's house of the sacred ritual paraphernalia so important to invoking the mysteries of the chieftaincy. It was believed that this tactic lessened the spiritual efficacy of a rival chief. Archaeologists have discerned that the Mississippian peoples built palisades and earthworks specifically to protect their sacred ceremonial items, including the chief himself. In this light the plunder of things and places Catholic was an old tactic turned against a new foe: remove the spiritual underpinnings that sustain a people and conquest follows.[20]

As attacks on the mission provinces escalated, the Spanish and Apalachees naturally stepped up efforts to defend themselves by fortifying several of the Apalachee missions and by organizing war parties. One such war party, comprised of four hundred Apalachee warriors and seven Spanish soldiers, set out in November 1694 to root out and capture two or three Englishmen and a single Frenchman rumored to be leading Ochese war parties from the old towns on the Chattahoochee. Instead they found the old towns depopulated and burned, causing them to redirect their attacks toward the newly established towns at Ochese Creek, where they captured at least fifty people and stole an estimated eight hundred pesos worth of trade goods and deerskins.[21]

Though some historians portray these struggles as a part of the imperial struggle between Spain and England, it is reasonable to suggest that quite the opposite may have been true: that the Indians were using the Europeans to advance their own interests, threatening to draw Spain and England—officially at peace—into an unwanted colonial war. To avoid such a catastrophe, both Gov. John Archdale of Carolina and Gov. Laureano de Torres y Ayala of Florida began corresponding regularly in 1695, partly to defend their territorial aspirations and partly to reverse the escalation of violence that had taken place over the previous three and one-half years. On one occasion Governor Archdale even coerced the Yamasees into returning four Christian Indian prisoners they had taken as war booty. Both governors repeatedly issued orders to their respective Indian allies to refrain from fighting.[22]

The correspondence generated during this flurry of cooperative activity suggests that the Ocheses and their allies were very much in control of their own military and political affairs. Archdale, who struggled diligently to exert some control over the military actions of the Ochese Indians, admitted to his counterpart in Florida the difficulty of doing so:

> *I have taken care for the future, by sending an Express to command them, that they do not commit any Acts of Hostility on any of your Indians, and do expect there be given the like Orders to your vassals: And surely you cannot be ignorant of the Temper of the Indians as well as my self, how hard a matter it is to keep them from taking Revenge for any Injuries received, to the third and fourth Generation; making personal Murders often times National Quarrels; notwithstanding which I hope to prevent it for the future, being that they live in great Obedience to our Government; but if they should happen to do any small Mischief to each other, I desire you not to send any more White Persons amongst them, least you thereby make the Quarrel National.*[23]

As Archdale observed, English and Spanish officials alike struggled to both understand and control "their" respective Indian populations. In Indian country, however, the rivalry between the two imperial powers did not translate so neatly. In the months following the Apalachicolas' flight to Ochese Creek, for instance, religious officials in Apalachee complained that a significant number of their flock had begun "fleeing to the woods" to live with their supposed enemies to the north. It had become clear to the Spanish that many of the Apalachees had fled in order to avoid attending mass or to evade the work assignments that the friars and soldiers compelled them to carry out.[24] As a further sign that the Apalachees were conspiring with the enemy, Spanish officials complained frequently that several Apalachee towns on the northern frontier—Escambe, Bacuqua, and Patale, in particular—continued to trade with "heathens" (undoubtedly the Ocheses and their allies). Others, moreover, maintained ties through intermarriage.[25]

Just as not all Apalachees were at war with the heathens, evidence indicates that at least a few of the Indian groups associated with the eighteenth-century "Creek Confederacy" did not choose to fight alongside the *enemigos*. For example, though some of the Alabamas and Tavasas appear to have relocated close to and participated in the wars of the Ocheses, some significant elements of these two groups remained reluctant to break with the Spanish.[26] In the fall of 1694 an Indian runner arrived in Apalachee in the name of the chiefs of Alabama and Tavasa to advise the lieutenant that they had become "afflicted" and "disconsoled" because the Indians of Tuckebatchee, Atasi, and a few other towns continued to "threaten them every day with death because they did not want to secure the partiality of the English." In defiance of their northern and eastern neighbors, these Alabamas and Tavasas requested that Spanish troops be sent to their towns to guarantee their safety.[27]

It is evident, then, that the war of the early 1690s cannot be described as a war between the Ocheses and Apalachees or between "English Indians" and "Spanish Indians." Nor did the war necessarily unify every tribe or town into a loosely knit Creek Confederacy. Some evidence suggests that in the war's initial stages, lines may have been drawn between traditional Indian groups—whom the Spanish called pagans—and other Indian groups that lived in a more Christian manner. But even an antagonism between pagan and Christian fails to fully explain the dynamics of the war. On the contrary, two generations of trade between the Apalachee and Apalachicolas had allowed bonds of friendship and kinship to develop and unite the Christians and pagans in Florida and Apalachicola, respectively. The Christian Chacatos, for example, who suffered some of the enemies' fiercest attacks, just a decade earlier were known to have many relatives in Apalachicola and some even joined the exodus to Ochese Creek.[28] Furthermore, there appears to have been some kind of affinal bond between Quiair (who was probably the chief of Coweta) and the chief of the Apalachee town of San Luis de Talimali (who Spanish officials described as a relative of Quiair's).[29] In later years an influential Coweta warrior, Chipacasi (Seepeycoffee), claimed that his mother was a Christian Apalachee, which supports the idea that distinguishing between Christian and pagan is an oversimplification.[30]

Given the permeable boundaries between supposedly hostile Indian groups, it is not be surprising to learn that the Apalachicolas and Apalachees possessed enough common ground to initiate a truce at the turn of the eighteenth century. The Apalachees were steered toward this truce after the construction of the San Luis blockhouse in March of 1698, which resulted in an oppressive influx of Spanish troops and caused some Apalachees to flee to the woods.[31] Eventually these repeated excursions by the Spanish stimulated informal efforts between the two groups to renew peace by the beginning of the year 1700.[32] Spurred on by these informal parleys, the Ocheses and Apalachees reached a more formal peace accord the following winter. The individual responsible for initiating the accord, Hafuluque, was a *heniha* ("second man") from the town of Apalachicola who, in conjunction with several other principal chiefs from Apalachicola, made a formal peace agreement with the Apalachees sometime before February 1701.[33]

Although Spanish officials continued to fear that the Ocheses might prejudice the Apalachees against them, evidence suggests that by the turn of the eighteenth century the promise of English trade, coupled with the aggressive policies of the Spanish regime, had steered the Apalachees and Ochese Creek immigrants toward a tentative but apparently sincere detente. Events brewing in Europe, however, soon placed the Indian-initiated truce in jeopardy when Spaniards and Englishmen found it beneficial to exploit preexisting grudges.

A Vacant Throne in Europe

As the world became more interconnected through exploration, colonization, and imperial rivalry, events in Europe had a marked effect on aboriginal populations in almost every quarter of the world. Ochese Creek was no exception. One such event occurred in 1700 when Charles II, the last Hapsburg king to rule Spain, died without leaving an heir to the throne. Austrian Hapsburgs, who wished to see the Spanish crown remain in the family, sought to elevate the dead king's nephew to the Spanish throne. King Louis XIV of France, seeking to aggrandize the Bourbon family, asserted that his grandson Phillip, Charles's grand-nephew, had an equal if not greater claim to the throne and had Phillip installed in 1701. Fearing that Phillip might one day unite Spain and France, in May 1702 England, Holland, and Austria together declared war on France and Spain, thereby initiating the War of Spanish Succession. The war, fueled by unresolved land disputes between England and Spain that had existed since 1670, spilled over into the American Southeast and evolved into a conflict known in America as Queen Anne's War.[34]

The French complicated matters further still when they initiated their own colonial projects in the Southeast as the seventeenth century drew to a close. In 1698, fearing English encroachment in the Mississippi valley, Louis XIV of France consented to the establishment of a new colony, dubbed "Louisiana" in his honor. The colony's first governor, Sieur d'Iberville, conducted three voyages between 1698 and 1702 that led to the establishment of the first French forts in the Gulf region. In the spring of 1699 d'Iberville and his men completed the construction of Fort Maurepas near present-day Biloxi, Mississippi, and by 1702 they had constructed other forts on the Mississippi River and on Mobile Bay.[35] The Carolinians, fearing a repeat of the ravages the French had precipitated against English colonists in Massachusetts and Connecticut in the 1690s, rightfully began to fear French and Spanish encirclement.[36]

In peacetime, Carolina officials such as John Archdale believed it was in their best interests to restrain the militaristic impulses of their Indian allies. In times of war, however, those same officials found it useful to promote Indian warfare in order to weaken and destroy Spanish Florida and, later, French Louisiana. The Carolinians had come to believe that their colony's survival depended on setting their Indians against Spanish and French Indians by exploiting preexisting grudges.

Given that the Ocheses and the Apalachees were momentarily on peaceful terms, it might have been difficult to provoke an Indian war if events brewing in Indian country in the summer of 1701 had not created a fertile ground for it. In August, Governor Zuñiga of Florida seized Hafuluque, the Apalachicola man responsible for making peace with the Apalachees, and imprisoned him in the governor's quarters in St. Augustine. Zuñiga accused Hafuluque of setting a fire in the vicinity of LaChua in north-central Florida. Hafuluque pleaded innocent to the charges, accusing the *usinjulo* ("beloved son of the chief" of Apalachicola) and two other warriors for the offense. On August 5, 1701, Hafuluque successfully pleaded for his release, but Governor Zuñiga warned him that he would be "punished with all rigor" should he dare to return to Florida.[37]

Governor Zuñiga's rough handling of the very man who had restored peace appears to have prompted the Ocheses to initiate a new round of violence against the Florida missions the following year. On May 20, 1702, one hundred Apalachicola warriors attacked Santa Fe, the garrisoned Timucuan town located along the *camino real* in north-central Florida. The initial battle lasted approximately three hours, at which point the attacking party retreated to the woods after failing to capture the stronghold. The retreat prompted the garrison's commander, Juan Ruiz de Canizares, to pursue the attackers for six leagues into the woods before the Apalachicolas ambushed his small party and killed Canizares, two other Spanish soldiers, and ten Timucuan warriors.[38]

It was no accident that the Apalachicolas chose to attack Santa Fe. As the home of a Spanish garrison, the blow struck against the mission village was not only intended to rid the area of its Spanish military presence—which likely played a role in Hafuluque's seizure and arrest as well—but also constituted a symbolic attack on the Spanish regime itself. According to one eyewitness who was present in the town of Achito (Hitchiti) when the victorious war party returned home, the attackers had taken many scalps and looted the town, taking a chest of clothing, some silver vessels, and an unspecified quantity of nails. The victors reported that they had burned the church and a house inhabited by a white woman. Such acts of destruction suggest that the attack on Santa Fe, like prior attacks on San Juan and San Carlos, was intended to send a message to the Spaniards and their Timucuan hosts.[39]

The Santa Fe attack set off a new round of violence between the Ocheses and the Apalachees, who had been at peace for more than a year. The violence spread because the Santa Fe garrison, which relied upon Indian auxiliaries to compensate for its small number of Spanish soldiers, included a few Apalachees and Chacatos who had killed two Apalachicola warriors during the battle. One eyewitness reported that when the war party returned to Achito, the townspeople burned a Timucuan prisoner to death "in revenge for the killing of two of their men by the Chacatos and the Apalachees."[40] That the Ocheses chose to kill a Timucuan man as a sign of revenge against the Apalachees and

Chacatos was no accident, for evidence suggests that the Ocheses may have considered all Christian Indians as a single, monolithic threat.

After the attack on Santa Fe, relations between the Ocheses and their Apalachee neighbors soured further, and in July and August Spanish officials once again began to make references to unspecified atrocities. One event that gained the particular notice of Spanish officials occurred around the time of the Santa Fe attack, when four Apalachee men traveled to the town of Apalachicola to conduct trade. The Apalachee traders, brazenly disobeying a Spanish prohibition on such trade expeditions, attempted to trade a few of their horses for Apalachicola firearms. The Apalachicolas, loath to give up their firearms to Spanish Indians, refused to make the deal and proceeded to seize and "sacrifice" three of the four men "in a cruel and inhuman manner" (one escaped). Though Spanish officials were prone to exaggerate Indian cruelty in their written reports, the manner in which the Apalachees died suggests that the Apalachicolas executed them in a ritualistic manner to avenge the deaths of slain kin.[41]

To South Carolina government officials the renewal of hostilities in Indian country was a fortuitous turn of events. Since war was breaking out in Europe almost simultaneously, the rupture provided an opportunity for the Carolinians to forge an alliance with Indians who had a similar vested interest in weakening or destroying La Florida. When unofficial news of war in Europe reached Charles Town in August of 1702, Gov. James Moore immediately proposed an attack against St. Augustine that ultimately ended in failure later that fall. The colony's general assembly debated Moore's proposals for several days; on August 26 the assembly officially proclaimed war against Florida and began to busy itself with war preparations.[42]

Meanwhile, as Carolina prepared for war, Governor Moore penned a boastful letter to the Ocheses in which he described Carolina's plans to destroy St. Augustine. Moore did not intend for his own people to hear the letter's message; rather, he tailored his words to the Ocheses, whose assistance he sought. Soon after the declaration of war, Moore gave the letter to one Anthony Dodsworth, a captain in the South Carolina militia, who traveled to Ochese Creek to read its contents to the Indians. Although the letter no longer exists, evidence suggests that Moore and Dodsworth sought to enlist the Ocheses' assistance by using language that portrayed the war as a struggle against Christian Indians rather than as a conflict between European monarchs.

According to an eyewitness on hand to hear Dodsworth read the letter to the Indians, the English offered "to depopulate the villages of Bacucua and Escambe, as well as Timucua, and carry off the women." "The next Spring," Dodsworth added, "there will be sent another party to capture the village of San Luis and do likewise to the others in the province." Kindling the animosity that many Ocheses held for the Christian Indians, Moore's letter portrayed the conflict as a struggle against the Christians and stated that "by this [method] the Christians will be exterminated from these parts." To add further luster to the plan, Moore boasted that the English would do their part by sending "as many as one hundred large vessels" against St. Augustine, a commitment that must have impressed the Ocheses. Finally, to convince them of the plan's feasibility, Moore argued in a distinct Indian idiom that the "the Spanish force is weak and [the men] are not valiant, nor [as well] supplied with arms or ammunition as they [the Ocheses] are."[43]

Dodsworth reiterated the contents of the letter at various times during his stay among the Ocheses and convinced them to call a council of war, which was probably held in September 1702. The war council, said to comprise "all of the towns of the province," rather quickly agreed to Governor Moore's proposals. The war resolution, for example, reiterated Moore's proposals almost verbatim, suggesting that the Ochese leaders and South Carolina's governor were of like minds.

But they were not. Whereas Moore and other like-minded Carolina imperialists wanted to eliminate the Spanish and French from the Southeast to make way for British expansion into the Gulf of Mexico and Mississippi valley, the Ocheses had their own competing ambitions: not to aggrandize Carolina but rather to "exterminate the Spaniards and Christian Indians from the land, leaving *themselves* masters of it" [emphasis added].[44] Clearly the Ocheses were not fighting Queen Anne's War. Instead, their struggle was a war of retribution against the Hispanic and Christian menace, the fruits of which they intended to expropriate for themselves.

Soon after the council ended the Ocheses constructed two palisades, one in Coweta and the other elsewhere, using a tactic some Indian groups employed on occasion to shelter their women and children.[45] Later that fall, either in late September or early October, Anthony Dodsworth and a small party of Englishmen assembled more than five hundred Ochese warriors to carry out their agreed-upon war plans. The war party set out from the town of Achito (located on the Ocmulgee River's lower course), crossed central Georgia, and descended the Flint River. At the same time an Apalachee war party that had formed to avenge themselves against their enemies left San Luis and met Dodsworth and his men somewhere on the Flint River's lower course.[46] The Ocheses, who were well armed with English weapons, routed the Apalachee war party in an ambush, killing perhaps half of the men and carrying away many scalps.[47]

Although the proposed spring attack on San Luis did not transpire as planned, by the fall of 1703 both the Carolina government and the Ocheses began planning for a final assault on Apalachee. On September 6 a committee wrote orders for Governor Moore to "go to the assistance of the Covetaw and other friendly Indians . . . to attack the Apalachees," wording that suggests that the English were not merely instigating or promoting an imperial war but rather were actively seeking to insert themselves into an ongoing war among Indians.[48] To assure their allies' success, the assembly members agreed to send a "present" of firearms and munitions to their Indian allies.

In late December 1703, Col. James Moore assembled 50 Carolina volunteers and perhaps as many as 1,000 Indian warriors at Ocmulgee, the Indian town that harbored a permanent English trading post. From there Moore's party advanced into Apalachee, and on the morning of January 14 the throng approached the church at Ayubale, which the Spanish garrison had converted into a makeshift fort. Just as Moore and his men reached the defensive structure, Apalachee warriors began firing arrows at the exposed English and Indian war party and forced them to take shelter behind the mud walls of the Ayubale council house. Moore and his men eventually overran the Apalachee stronghold by breaking down the church doors and setting fire to the church and fort. After two hours of fighting the English and their Indian allies succeeded in capturing approximately 170 persons, including the resident friar.[49]

The next morning, to put a stop to the invasion, the lieutenant in charge of Apalachee assembled a force consisting of 23 Spanish soldiers and 400 Apalachee warriors. The joint Spanish-Apalachee army soon met the English-led party in a pitched battle near the garrison town of San Luis. Once again Moore's army routed the Apalachees, killing 6 Spaniards and 200 Apalachee warriors and taking a like number as prisoners. Moore did not stop there, however, for once the Apalachees in the field were defeated, he and his men set fire to San Luis's town, church, and fort and forced its residents to flee to a safer location.[50]

In the days following the destruction of Ayubale and San Luis, Moore and his forces traveled through the Apalachee province seeking the submission of the remaining towns, most of which were unable to defend themselves. Moore concluded separate peace agreements with the chiefs of each successive town and, according to Moore, some surrendered without conditions, suggesting that the fate of the inhabitants lay in the hands of the English and Ochese conquerors. Many of these people probably comprised the 1,300 slaves taken back to Charles Town that spring. In contrast, Moore offered a conditional peace arrangement to the inhabitants of certain other towns, guaranteeing "freedom of Persons and Goods" to any chiefs who would agree to relocate their people in Carolina territory and "subject themselves to our Governments." A greater number of the Apalachee towns appear to have been offered and accepted Moore's more lenient terms, because at least three entire towns and the majority of four others relocated to the Savannah River and settled among the Ochese conquerors themselves. Given that a conspicuous minority of Moore's men were rebel Apalachees who had joined the Ocheses, the conquest could be called an Apalachee exodus. By the end of January, Moore and the Ocheses had reduced all of Apalachee into two enclaves of Catholic Apalachees, putting the mission system in a "feeble and low position" that posed little threat to the Carolina regime or to the Ocheses.[51]

With all of Apalachee (except San Luis and the town of Ivitachuco) destroyed, the Ochese Creek Indians had in a few short days made themselves the virtual masters of north Florida. The only remaining task was to eliminate the vestiges of the mission system that remained in both Timucua and Apalachee. To make their mastery complete and to fulfill the aims stated in their war resolutions, in June 1704 approximately 600 Ochese warriors and 50 rebel Apalachees—acting without the knowledge or permission of Charles Town officials—attacked the two remaining towns of San Luis and Ivitachuco. They forced a portion of the two towns' inhabitants to flee to an asylum in Timucua named Abosaya, a few to the new Spanish presidio at Pensacola, and some to Mobile. In the summer of 1705 a group of Ochese warriors, led by the "captain" of Cussita and by the *cacique* and *heniha* of Ocmulgee, began attacking the refugees at Abosaya, looting and plundering the former mission provinces and stealing cattle, horses, and pigs as they traveled along the *camino real*. Through a series of attacks in August and September of 1705 and May of the following year, the Ocheses and their

English auxiliaries had turned the once-populous Indian missions of La Florida into a barren wasteland and had put an end to Florida's world of mission bells, friars, and Spanish soldiers.[52]

A War for Empire

The year 1705 witnessed an important shift in the relations between the Ocheses and Carolina officials. Whereas the Ocheses were fighting to accomplish distinctly Ochese goals prior to 1705, the Carolinians had yet to accomplish their own goal of eradicating the Spanish and French posts from the region. Carolina officials and traders sought to turn their Indian allies into subservient auxiliaries, thereby asserting their own role as leaders in a war for empire rather than as followers in an Indian war of revenge. The Ocheses, in debt to the Carolina traders, found themselves obliged to assist the Carolinians but their reluctance to carry the war to its logical conclusion shows their divergence from the imperialist ambitions of the Carolinians.

To succeed in their enterprise the Carolina imperialists first had to secure the services of the Ocheses and their allies, whose warriors had succeeded so magnificently in reducing Florida to ashes. In August of 1705 Carolina's new governor, Nathaniel Johnston, appointed one Daniel Henchman to draw up a written agreement with the "Ochese Nation" and their allies. On August 15 Henchman met with a large group of Indians at Coweta, where they ratified a treaty that formalized their de facto military alliance. The agreement, entitled "The Humble Submission of Several, Kings, Princes, Generals, etc. to the Crown of England," was the first Anglo-Creek treaty of its kind and its creation began a tradition that flourished throughout the eighteenth century.[53]

Like most Indian treaties that followed, the 1705 treaty was written in a way that belies its function as a tool for imperialism.[54] In an attempt to bring order to the tribal political systems that appeared "anarchicall" to the Europeans, the treaty aggrandized the Indians' political institutions, likening the Coweta council house to a European court and applying titles of nobility such as king and prince to the Indian leaders. To reinforce the hoped-for deference of the Indians, the treaty included a phrase in which the Indians acknowledged that "our protection depends upon the English, and [we] return our greatest thanks for the continual goodness and happiness we enjoy under them." An oath of loyalty to Queen Anne was included in the treaty's wording, as well as a promise to "give a total rout" to the Spanish and French, who the Ocheses declared would not be allowed to "settle themselves hereafter in any of our territories or Dominions, nor within reach of our arms."

Records do not show whether or not the two interpreters present— the traders John Musgrove and John Jones—explained the contents of the treaty to the twelve Indian leaders who signed it "in the name of the rest." In all likelihood they did not, for the pledges of fidelity and allegiance bore a striking resemblance to Spanish attempts to enforce a strict obedience that had alienated the Apalachicolas in the 1680s. Arguably the English treaty sought to impose an even stricter form of obedience, because not only did it seek to limit the Indians' contact with the Spanish and French but it called upon the signers to conduct a total war against the two nations. Only time would tell if the Ocheses and their allies would agree to serve the British as mercenaries in their imperial war.

Despite the fact that the treaty was written by and for the obvious political purposes of Englishmen, Indian leaders may have signed the treaty for their own political intentions, making the document essentially "Native" in some important ways. For one, the published treaty was the tangible result of a ritual event conducted in the Coweta council house. Contrary to the opinions of various English leaders, gatherings such as these were never anarchical but followed a distinct pattern that emphasized the Indians' own sense of order and hierarchy. Because this particular gathering involved a diverse group of leaders from a variety of nations—including the Ocheses, the Alabamas, the Tallapoosas, and the Abikas—the treaty signing forced the Native leaders to imagine themselves, even if only briefly, as one people and to invent a suitable hierarchy for the whole.

Leading the list of treaty signers was the "king" of the Cowetas, referred to by his war title, *hoboyetly*. Here marks the first extant reference to the man the English eventually called Brims, the "emperor" who became one of the most important Creek leaders in the first half of the eighteenth century.[55] As the "king" of the host town that had been accorded special status beginning in the late 1670s, one would expect his name to appear first on the list. It is significant, however, that many who signed the document after him did so in the name of towns that were not a part of the old Apalachicola province over which Brims's Coweta predecessors had exercised region-wide influence. Could this particular event, then, have signified Brims's rise as a man of influence over a wider area? Perhaps.

From the many towns that Henchman, Musgrove, and Jones could have selected to sign the treaty first, they chose Coweta, undoubtedly a reflection of Coweta's continued influence over the Tallapoosas and Abikas. It also suggests that the ties of kinship established a generation earlier between the chief of Coweta and Henry Woodward remained intact and continued to bind Coweta to Carolina. That the Ocheses chose to build a palisade to protect Coweta in 1702 at the outbreak of the war suggests the town held a place of political, if not spiritual, importance.[56]

But the striking feature of the "Humble Submission's" language is the tendency to describe the Indian nations using the plural rather than the singular. Assuming, then, that Henchman's words to some extent reflect the Indians' input, the Ocheses and their allies did not consider themselves components of a single confederacy but rather as an allied yet individually provincial group. Each chief who signed the treaty— Brims included—did so as the representative of a single town or five distinct Indian "nations": the Ocheses, Haritamau (Altamaha or Yamasee), Talliboose (Tallapoosa), Holbamah (Alabama), and Abecaw (Abika).[57] Neither Brims nor Henchman made any indication of a centralizing political innovation among the Indians.

Also telling, especially as it pertained to the extent of Brims's influence, was the absence of a representative from Apalachicola, though it was once thought to be the most influential town on the Chattahoochee River. While the Apalachicolas undoubtedly supported the English war effort, some evidence indicates that the Apalachicolas operated outside the reach of Brims's authority. Furthermore, the fact that the Apalachicolas were willing to move their own town to a remote location on the Savannah River sometime before 1708 indicates the Apalachicolas' inclination to act independently.

Although the treaty of 1705 may have succeeded in creating a fleeting sense of political order among the various Indian towns, it ultimately failed to turn the Ocheses and their neighbors into the malleable military allies that the English so desperately desired. Consequently, by 1706 English traders occasionally began to resort to more coercive methods to stimulate the militaristic impulses of the Indians. Throughout 1706, for example, the trader John Musgrove incited the Indians living on Ochese Creek to go to war at his whim, invoking the governor's name as the source of his authority. The Indians who endured Musgrove's belligerent presence somehow made his threatening behavior known to the governor, who summoned Musgrove to appear before the Carolina

Assembly in November to explain his actions. Musgrove naturally denied the charges and the assembly voted not to punish him.[58] The fact that the Indians chose to issue a complaint to the governor rather than to blindly follow Musgrove to war illustrates the fact that it took more than a written agreement to convince the Ocheses and their allies to "rout" the Spanish and French or any of either's Indian allies.

This is not to say, however, that the attacks against the Spanish ceased. In the coming years the Ocheses, Alabamas, Tallapoosas, and Abikas began a war of attrition against the Spanish presidio of Pensacola that had been constructed in 1698 to defend Spanish territorial claims along the Gulf of Mexico. The first attacks commenced in the summer of 1706 when a band of "heathen" Indians attacked the fort, capturing several Indians and Spanish soldiers and burning the nearby Indian homes to the ground. According to the viceroy of New Spain, after capturing the prisoners the "heathens . . . [made] martyrs out of them" by burning them at the stake (which suggests that their executions were a part of a ritual punishment in revenge for past Spanish wrongdoing).[59] Attacks against Pensacola resumed the following May, when "Talapuzes, Apicas, and Aybamos" warriors waylaid a contingent of fourteen Spanish soldiers cutting wood near the fort. The attackers killed the leader of the group, then captured the other thirteen and carried them to Charles Town for a monetary reward. Similar hit-and-run attacks occurred throughout the late summer and fall of 1707.[60] By 1712 Pensacola had suffered so many small-scale attacks and was in such an impoverished state that Spanish officials seriously considered abandoning the fort.[61]

If the Ocheses and their neighbors displayed any hesitancy to destroy Pensacola, however, they displayed even more reluctance to dislodge the French from Mobile, despite the encouragement of Carolina traders and government officials. English plans to redirect their own war effort toward the French possessions essentially began on October 27, 1707, when the South Carolina Assembly received word that the French at Mobile and their Indian allies were plotting a surprise attack against Charles Town.[62] The ominous news naturally alarmed Carolina officials, whose persistent fears of French encirclement prompted them to mount a counteroffensive. Within two weeks the assembly resolved to "fall on the French at once" and named Thomas Nairne, an Indian trader and veteran of the wars against Florida, as commander in chief of an attack on Mobile. Carolina officials recognized, of course, that this type of campaign could not succeed without the help of Indian allies, so the assembly appointed Thomas Welch, an Indian trader with considerable experience on the far western frontier, to recruit Indian warriors for the expedition. The assembly set aside one hundred pounds local currency to purchase presents for the Indian warriors as an inducement to fight.[63]

In either late December 1707 or early January 1708, Nairne, Welch, and several other traders set forth from Charles Town to secure the allegiance of their Indian allies and to recruit more to their cause. In the course of his wanderings that winter and spring, Nairne penned a series of letters to Carolina officials that remained unknown to modern historians until the mid 1980s.[64] Since that time Nairne's letters have become a staple for scholars studying Southeastern Indians because they are rich in ethnographic detail, describing the governmental structure, beliefs, and certain ritual practices of the Ocheses, the Tallapoosas, and the Chickasaws. Nairne's letters, teeming with descriptions of Indian culture, could therefore rightly be called one of the first ethnographic works in the British Southeast.

It is important to remember that Nairne's real mission was not ethnography but rather to convince the Indians to carry out a total war against the French. As Nairne put it, his purpose was "to fall down from the Tallapoosas against the French with a fleet of 80 canoes manned with 500 Indians and 1,000 by land, 15 English on the one part and 30 on the other."[65] To make the Indians more responsive to British commands he knew it would be necessary to investigate and insert British influence into the Indians' own governmental and military command structures. For example, in the opening remarks of one letter, Nairne claimed that the Indian government was akin to "a petty republic" and described each *mico* (chief) as "only [the] heads of small townships." Curiously, however, at the Town of Oakfuskee, Nairne delivered a war commission to Cossittee, the Oakfuskee captain, and named him "the head of all the Tallapoosas." Nairne also gave Cossittee a blank commission that allowed him to choose a deputy. In doing so Nairne sought to alter the Indian political customs he had so richly described, concentrating Indian authority under a single figurehead. Since Oakfuskee, Cossittee's home, was an Abika town and thought to be politically distinct from the Tallapoosas located downriver, Nairne's attempt to make Cossittee the "head of all the Tallapoosas" constituted an attempt to unify two distinct Indian provinces.[66]

Cossittee and his unnamed deputy were more than willing to accept their commissions, but they knew that a mere piece of paper delivered by an Englishmen did not give them authority to command people from other towns much less people from their own town. Moreover, the Tallapoosas, like other Southeastern Indians, believed that political power possessed a spiritual dimension that required the aspiring chief to be ritually cleansed before accepting office. Failure to perform such rituals exposed the chief—and, by extension, his people—to the witchery of others and could result in misfortune for the people as a whole.

Neither Cossittee nor his deputy dared accept Nairne's commissions until the proper purification ceremonies had been performed. In an attempt to make their new offices seem legitimate, Cossittee's people orchestrated an impromptu coronation ceremony that was said to be "always heretofore used by his nation in investing their chiefs." The ceremony was not entirely traditional, however, for three important reasons. First, the Tallapoosas, like many Southeastern Indian groups, usually bestowed new titles and offices upon their leaders during busk, the green corn ceremony usually held in July. The coronation ceremony took place in January, hardly the time for rituals of such importance. Second, the ceremony did not bestow on the two men a traditional Indian office but alien English war commissions. Last, Nairne and his men appear to have played a small role in the ceremony by saluting and wishing the chiefs "joy" after the proper rituals had been performed, thereby making this particular coronation a frontier invention rather than an entirely ancient tradition.[67]

Nairne and his fellow Carolinians sought to remake Native political institutions somewhat in a European image. In the conclusion to his letter Nairne candidly expressed his reasons for inquiring into the nature of Native political systems: "their Government . . . tho mean, is much better than none at all. I shall some what improve it, by getting them gradually to introduce punishments." By introducing punishments, Nairne hoped to concentrate coercive authority in the persons who possessed English commissions, thereby bridging the gap between English and Native political systems. Nairne hoped that these new coercive powers would encourage his commissioned Indian chiefs to steer their people away from hunting and toward carrying out a total war against the French and their allies.[68]

Despite Nairne's attempts to drum up support for an offensive against Mobile, he could never stimulate the kind of zeal seen in the Ocheses' war against the Apalachees. For instance, the Tallapoosas refrained from initiating hostilities against Mobile for more than a year, a telling sign of their hesitance. Not until May 1709 did an army of six or seven hundred "English Indians"—most likely the Alabamas or Tallapoosas—descend the Alabama River toward Mobile to launch an assault on France's Indian allies, the Tahomes and Mobiles, located there. When French reinforcements arrived to head off the attack, the war party fled immediately, abandoning their canoes in the process. A French counterattack resulted in the death of thirty-five English Indians and the capture of five others. Though small war parties occasionally returned—presumably seeking revenge for the dead—the kind of sustained assault that Nairne had hoped for failed to occur. Jean-Baptiste Le Moyne de Bienville, the acting commandant at Mobile, described the attacks as "large bands that accomplish almost nothing," indicating that the Tallapoosas and Alabamas were content to capture merely a few Indian prisoners without conducting an outright assault on Mobile itself.[69]

Regardless of the obvious failures of the Mobile scheme, Carolina officials continued their attempts to bind their Indian allies more firmly to the English interest when the threat of French attacks demanded military action. In June 1711, for instance, rumors began to circulate that the Chickasaws, who had fought for and traded with Carolina for more than a decade, had formed a league or "conjunction" with France's most powerful Indian allies, the Choctaws.[70] Fearing a joint French–Choctaw–Chickasaw attack, the Carolina Assembly hastened to form an expeditionary force of nearly two thousand Indians led by the veteran traders Theophilus Hastings and Thomas Welch.[71]

To carry out the expedition the Carolina Assembly relied upon their familiar method of distributing presents—one pound of gunpowder and two pounds of musket balls—to each of the warriors and their chiefs. Additionally, the assembly granted the war party five hundred pounds of swann shot, four thousand gun flints, and some red paint—an item with which Southeastern warriors adorned themselves before going into battle—all of which were to be equally divided.[72] Recognizing that the planned attack required the commitment of the chiefs, the assembly gave seven recognized headmen "good coats [and] hatts" to mark the chiefs' authority to command in the name of the English. Singled out among all other Ochese chiefs was Brims, who received an English war commission that described him as their emperor.

By Indian standards Brims, of course, was no emperor, and the commission that named him as such reflects the Eurocentric practice of using European terms in reference to Indian leaders. Still, Brims's acceptance of the commission—and the tacit acceptance displayed by the other chiefs—indicates Brims's exceptional political authority. From an Ochese standpoint the commissioning might have meant that Brims came from a great family, that is, a clan of ancient origins with a large population scattered through many of the Ochese, Tallapoosa, and Abika towns. Brims's town of origin—Coweta—which had been "the first" to establish commercial and kin relationships with the Carolina traders, may have contributed to this designation as well. Given the importance that Southeastern Indians placed on ability, one may further surmise that Brims's countrymen regarded him as a man of wisdom. And, keeping in mind the high regard the Indians of that region placed upon martial qualities, Brims's skills as a warrior (if not his commanding physical presence) also set him apart.

If not as an emperor in the European sense of the term, how, then, might Brims have regarded himself? Since the Muskogee language Brims spoke did not at that time have a word (or an office, for that matter) equivalent to emperor, Brims likely regarded himself as a *mico thlucco*, or a "big chief" to whom others were supposed to defer in times of war, in diplomacy, and in other serious matters. Related to his people by way of a complex web of kinship, and conditioned to accept traditional rules governing such relationships, Brims would have had little reason to make political innovations or employ political tactics that did not conform to the expectations of his people. While trade, warfare, and imperial rivalry presented new opportunities for certain individuals to capitalize politically, to be accepted by his people as a great man necessarily required Brims to employ traditional means to achieve such regional influence.

While Brims's clan connections, town affiliation, and personal attributes positioned him to become a man of influence according to the norms of Ochese society, his accretion of wider regional authority demanded something more. As anthropologist Marshal Sahlins argues, in societies that lack proscribed systems of rank, tribal "big men" utilized the connection between gifts and rank to launch their careers. Bestowing gifts to potential followers, Sahlins adds, effectively places the recipients in an equivocal social position—in debt—that obliges them to return the favor in accordance with the norms of reciprocity common in kinship-based societies. In this way economic imbalance establishes political inequality, as the big man may call upon unrequited debts to make claims on his followers. Big men typically distribute such gifts in politically useful ways, first by cultivating a small core of followers drawn from among his own kin and then by spinning wider webs of influence by giving gifts or providing favors to persons less closely related. This system of calculated generosity enables the big man to establish what anthropologist Bronislaw Malinowski calls a "fund of power," giving him leverage on others' economic production or, in times of war, their military assistance. Ideally, successful big men present gifts publicly in a ritual manner. Moreover, it behooves the aspiring big man to reinforce his relationships periodically so as to maintain the differential economic and political relationship.[73]

In this light, the manner in which the Carolina Assembly distributed presents to the Ocheses in 1711 appears to conform to the strategy of calculated generosity that buttressed not only Carolina's claims upon the Ocheses but also Brims's claims upon the loyalty of his subordinate chiefs and their followers. For example, as the war commission appears to have singled him out as emperor, Brims likely had positioned himself as the titular recipient of the exceptionally large gift from the Carolina government. As such Brims must have assumed responsibility for naming the seven headmen who received the good coats and hats, thereby placing them in debt to him. We may then assume that the seven chiefs, acting on Brims's behalf, distributed the swan shot, gunpowder, and paint to the warriors and created a chain of debt that connected the warriors to the headmen and the headmen to Brims. The catch, of course, was that though it appears to have given Brims some leverage over his own people, this strategy of providing gifts ultimately indebted Brims to the Carolina regime.

In the short run Brims's and the Carolinians' strategies appear to have been successful. That fall, Hastings and Brims together led a 1,300–man force of Ochese warriors against the Choctaw towns. Although many of the Choctaws escaped, their party succeeded in killing 80 persons and capturing another 130. They also burned four hundred houses and plantations that the Choctaws had abandoned during the raids.

Despite these apparent successes, Hastings did not possess full control over Brims and Brims's warriors. The Indians, for example, began their assault before Hastings had issued his command to attack, which spoiled the element of surprise and rendered the expedition less successful than it might have been. Had his own Indian allies been "more governable," Hastings believed, that the Choctaws would have "met with a fatal blow."[74]

The expedition against the Choctaws, however, was not the last time that the Ocheses came to Carolina's assistance. In the fall of 1711 a war broke out between the Tuscaroras (inhabitants of the Neuse River and its tributaries) and the North Carolina colonists. Almost immediately the South Carolina Assembly sent a largely Catawba and Yamasee army led by John Barnwell to put down the uprising. Though Barnwell's army scored some victories, they failed to subdue the Tuscaroras which made further military action a necessity.

The following fall, in 1712, the South Carolina Assembly sent another expedition into North Carolina to end the Tuscarora war once and for all. The Ocheses were obliged to join in the fray, lured by free gifts of ammunition and a handsome compensation for each scalp taken.[75] Using these familiar incentives, the traders undoubtedly convinced some of the Ocheses to join the fall attack, and it is likely that Ochese men comprised a considerable part of James Moore's company.[76] Moore's men, said to be composed of "four hundred Indians of several nations," fought admirably at first and helped the English overrun the rebels' Nohoroco fort, sustaining heavy casualties in the process.

But the Ocheses' actions in the battle's aftermath suggest that they had gone to war for obligatory reasons only. Soon after taking the fort, more than half of Moore's men fled and quickly returned to South Carolina "to sell their captives as slaves."[77] For a majority of the Ocheses, then, the expedition against the Tuscaroras was not a war of extermination but a war of opportunity. Their immediate goal was not to pave the way for Carolina expansion but to acquire slaves which, by the end of Queen Anne's War in 1713, remained the Indians' only compelling reason to fight on England's behalf.

Carolina Imperialism and the Seeds of Discontent

In the years following the migration to Ochese Creek, English military assistance allowed the diverse Ocheses to score major victories against the Spanish missions. The Ocheses essentially used the English alliance as a means to a particular end. Permitting English traders to enter their towns and become a permanent part of the landscape had seemed like a good compromise—perhaps even a liberating development—at a time when Spanish missionaries and soldiers threatened their freedom. As

Queen Anne's War progressed, however, this symbiotic relationship underwent a near-complete reversal as the English began using Indians for their own imperialist purposes. In the course of this reversal the Ocheses and their Indian allies witnessed a number of disturbing developments that strained their relationship with the English.

Discontent began to simmer among the Ocheses and their allies when the intrusion of the Carolina trade regime wrought tremendous changes in the Indian political economy. Prior to the European intrusion into the Southeast, the ancestral Ochese economy was isolated from the general economic currents that had begun to draw together disparate parts of the world— Europe, Asia, and Africa-into a nascent capitalist system. Until the late seventeenth century the Ocheses' ancestors practiced small-scale agriculture (based primarily on the production of corn, beans, and squash) and supplemented it by hunting game animals. The Ochese economies remained local in nature, and surplus production was limited to the corn reserves and deerskins that commoners reserved as tribute for chiefs.[78]

Once English traders ensconced themselves in their towns, the Ocheses began regularly exchanging deerskins and Indian slaves for European manufactures. Contemporaries described the Ocheses and their neighbors as people who "consumed a lot of goods," and it is evident that a kind of "consumer revolution" had commenced within the span of a generation.[79] Although documentary evidence of this trade is sparse, archaeological evidence reveals that the Ocheses traded with the English for a variety of utilitarian goods such as guns, knives, scissors, needles, axes, and hoes. Decorative items that the Spaniards commonly traded in the previous century—such as bells and beads—also remained popular, particularly for the adornment of clothes. With the prevalence of English-made cloth most Indian clothing began to take on a more European appearance in the years following the exodus to Ochese Creek.[80]

With regular access to the English traders, the Ocheses were quickly becoming the South's wealthiest Indians, at least as it pertained to the acquisition of European trade goods. As a consequence, the Ochese economy began to assume a distinctly colonial appearance. By definition, a colonial economy is a peripheral usually rural or agrarian one that provides raw materials to manufacturing centers in core capitalist regions. Because raw materials comprise the bulk of the exports in such regions, profits are small due to an overemphasis on resource extraction that consequently tends to stunt economic diversification and growth. Core capitalist regions, in contrast, possess the ability to take raw materials and turn them into finished manufactured goods then sell the finished goods at high profits to domestic and foreign markets, including the peripheral regions from which the raw materials originated. The very structure of a colonial economy guarantees that the greatest rewards from raw materials go to core regions, rendering the peripheries dependent on consumer goods produced elsewhere and triggering price fluctuations on the world market.[81]

As a "poor" agricultural society, the Ocheses had little choice but to provide the English with their only salable commodities—agricultural produce, furs, and Indian slaves—in order to participate in the burgeoning trans-Atlantic economy. Yet the acquisition of guns, powder, and cloth—especially obtained from traders willing to extend credit—eventually made the Creeks dependent upon European technology and severely indebted to English traders.[82] It is significant, for example, that Thomas Nairne's ethnographic description of the Tallapoosas included a discussion on debt. According to Nairne, in addition to their more traditional duties, Tallapoosa chiefs also played a role in "haranguing" people to pay their debts to the English so as not to suffer the "ill effects." Likewise, the Carolina Assembly's repeated attempts to curb the traders' practice of trading on trust (a seventeenth-century English term equivalent to the modern-day "credit") illustrates that carrying debt had become a way of life among the Ocheses. By 1711 the Ochese Creek Indians were collectively in debt for 100,000 deerskins or approximately 250 deerskins (several years' work) per Indian man.[83] The Ocheses likely incurred much of this debt by purchasing liquor on credit, a practice that many authorities in South Carolina tried but failed to stop.[84]

Although the deerskin trade has received the most attention from scholars who study the Southeastern Indians' economy, the trade in Indian slaves was likely more responsible for drawing the Ocheses and others into a dependent role vis-à-vis the English in the Atlantic marketplace. Because traders were willing to pay a high price for Indian slaves, the practice of trading on credit had dire consequences. When the supply of slaves was plentiful the Ocheses were generally able to satisfy their English creditors; when the Spanish missions—the principal source for Indian slaves—collapsed at the turn of the eighteenth century, the Ocheses and other slave raiders were forced to search for new sources for their human commodity. Consequently, Ochese warriors began making slave raids against the Choctaws and other Indians groups living in the basins of the Mississippi–Tombigbee Rivers to the west. Spanish and English sources alike attest to the fact that Ochese warriors made excursions into the Florida Keys in search of slaves. Evidence further suggests that the Ocheses participated in the Tuscarora war primarily to cover slave debts.[85]

By the end of the first decade of the eighteenth century the combination of debt and slave trading created a variety of problems within Ochese society, both among Indians and between Indians and English traders. One of the principal problems with amassing debts, particularly for a people who traditionally held notions of communal property, was that indebted individuals sometimes sought to call upon the traditional notion of property to meet their personal obligations. For instance, on June 12, 1712, the newly created Indian Trade Commission of South Carolina heard the complaint of a Chehaw man named Tuskenaw who argued that while he was off to war, the town of Cussita stole two of his Indian slaves to cover their influential war captain's debt. After ordering the slaves to be returned to the said Tuskenaw, the commission mandated that "towns or relations" should not be responsible for individual debts, thereby enforcing new rules of individual property ownership on a people who clearly retained collective practices. This is not to say, however, that notions of individual property were entirely unwelcome among the Ocheses. Clearly Tuskenaw and others like him stood to gain from the enforcement of the new rules, and in this sense traditions concerning property remained a contested issue within Indian societies.

A further problem related to amassing debt stemmed from the fact that many of the Ocheses' so-called slaves constituted an important component of the local social fabric. For centuries Southeastern Indians had practiced a form of slavery through which prisoners of war were integrated into their captors' families, either as laborers of uncertain social status or quite commonly as ritually adopted members of the family. The English slave trade, which defined these persons as chattel property, strained the ancient practice when debts accrued. In Tuskenaw's case the two Indian slaves for which he sought redress—both of whom were Apalachee captive women—were not chattel but were related to him by way of marriage. One, named Toolodeha, was Tuskenaw's wife; the other was his mother-in-law.[86]

Such internal disputes among the Indians may have signified that something was rotten about the English trade regime. But it was the emerging conflict between Indians and English trader-creditors that ultimately led the Ocheses and their neighbors to conclude that they might become slaves themselves if debts continued to mount. Since the beginning of the slave trade Carolina officials lamented the abuses that traders committed against Indians who were supposed to be their allies. By the turn of the eighteenth century, complaints of trader abuses became so common that the Carolina Assembly deemed it necessary to set up a special commission to regulate the trade in 1707.[87]

While trader abuses, such as beatings, whippings, and the molestation of women, clearly drew the ire of the Ocheses, the real problems began in the waning years of Queen Anne's War. By that time the Ocheses had become so indebted that English traders began taking away Ocheses' Apalachee slaves when they were unable to acquire slaves by other means. However, the Apalachees were not chattel but, as in Tuskenaw's case, relatives of many of the Ocheses. By enslaving the Apalachees, then, English traders were in effect enslaving the Ocheses' own people.[88]

When English traders threatened to enslave the Ocheses themselves if they could not meet their debts, the specter of slavery loomed large in the minds of the people who had zealously enslaved others for more than a generation. By 1715 English-speaking Indian slaves who had escaped from Carolina plantations began to spread rumors, perhaps true to a certain extent, that the English traders were considering a plan to enslave the Ocheses and force them to cede their ancient lands. When the Indian agents John Wright and Thomas Nairne conducted a census of the Indians in the spring of 1715, the Ocheses and many of their neighbors viewed this intrusive action as a first step toward their enslavement.[89]

Adding to the fear of slavery was the fact that during Queen Anne's War the English traders played a dual role as military commanders. Traders such as John Musgrove and John Cochrane led numerous expeditions against Spanish missions and forts and incited the Indians to go to war against other Indians in order to obtain slaves to cover their debts. In this way the presence of English traders in the Indian towns began to assume the appearance of a military occupation. According to Spanish soldiers from Pensacola, whom English-allied Indians captured and dragged to Charles Town for a reward, the entire Southeast, from Ochese Creek to the Alabama River system, was a militarized zone. For instance, several soldiers interviewed by Spanish officials upon their return to St. Augustine in January 1710 claimed that each Indian town had at least one resident English "lieutenant" who gave gifts of powder and shot and traded for furs. Some towns, such as Tallassee on the Tallapoosa River, had two English lieutenants, and others appear to have been the headquarters for more important English officials. Tuckebatchee, for example, harbored a man named Captain Chanchon (perhaps the trader John Cochrane) who commanded sixteen subordinates.[90] At Tiguale, the southernmost Tallapoosa town, John Musgrove was said to command three other English lieutenants.[91] Although it is not certain whether or not these traders were actually commissioned officers in the Carolina militia, it is significant that to their Spanish prisoners they appeared to be. Such evidence indicates that the English traders were not merely humble merchants plying their wares but were the militaristic taproots of an increasingly aggressive British empire.

Even as they fought against the Spanish and French and their Indian allies, the Ocheses began to recognize that the English regime had trapped them in an oppressive spiral of warfare, debt, and more warfare. For this reason Carolina's Indian allies began to look upon the Spanish and French not as a threat but as potential allies and trade partners. For example, in 1707, while transporting a Spanish soldier named Juan Gabriel de Vargas to Charles Town for a monetary reward, a party of Tallapoosa warriors asked the Spanish prisoner, "if they were to go to the Spanish with a white flag, if they would have peace with them, and if so, would they sell them powder and bullets?"[92] Vargas, hoping to earn their good favor, responded in the affirmative which prompted the English traders privy to the conversation to separate the Tallapoosa warriors from the Spaniard and send them to an undisclosed location in Charles Town.

The Ocheses and their allies also looked to the struggling French outpost at Mobile for relief by sending overtures of peace to the French commander, Bienville, stationed there, word of which appears to have reached King Louis XIV no later than July 1709.[93] The leaders in this enterprise appear to have been the Alabamas, who continued to make peace overtures for several more years before agreeing, as did the Abikas and other nations of Carolina, to an official truce with Bienville in March 1712.[94]

By 1715 the political fortunes of the Ocheses and their neighbors had come full circle. In the 1680s they had resisted Spanish efforts to make them a part of La Florida and had fled to the English traders to avoid the missionaries and soldiers who threatened them with a particular form of enslavement. As the Ocheses became slave raiders themselves, however, the demand for Indian slaves, increasing debt, and the militarization of their society threatened them with a more immediate form of slavery from which they would be compelled to flee once again. By making tentative peaceful overtures to the Spanish and French, the Ocheses and their neighbors embarked upon a strategy to escape this new form of slavery and reconstitute their relationship with their belligerent English "allies."

CHAPTER THREE

A New World Order

The spring of 1715 was a trying time for Brims, the Coweta "emperor" and most influential leader of the Ochese Creek Indians. For several years Brims had looked on in silence as his people gradually became more indebted to English traders, who regularly subjected them to physical abuse, threatened to enslave their women and children, and hinted that they might appropriate their ancient lands. But that fateful spring, a time when Brims should have been preparing to plant corn, a rude awakening turned his thoughts to war: his most-esteemed kinsman, the *usinjulo* of Coweta, died at the hands of an unscrupulous trader. Tellingly, it was rumored that the trader made the *usinjulo* pay the ultimate price for a mere "accounting mistake," undoubtedly a debt dispute. As the *usinjulo* was a blood relative, his murder demanded that Brims not only seek revenge but directly confront the series of problems that had compromised the lives and independence of his people. Painfully aware that the time had come to put a stop to the traders' abuses, Brims sent runners into the villages of the many Carolina-allied Indians to inquire if they too had suffered and to propose terminating their relationships with Carolina—by force, if necessary. Brims's runners, traveling from village to village, collected the pledges of 161 towns—encoded in three fathom-long knotted strands of deer hide—to join Brims's insurrection.

Brims summoned the tribes to a meeting at Pocotalico, a village of the Yamasees, who had suffered disproportionately from the traders' abuses and who were clamoring for war. Brims shrewdly recognized that to fight the Carolinians at this stage might bring further disaster, and proposed an alternative plan to urge the Carolina government to remove the bad traders from their villages and replace them with a kinder, gentler sort. To restructure their debt, Brims proposed paying the Carolinians little by little in corn, oil, and livestock taken from the Spanish presidios, since these items could be obtained much easier than Indian slaves, the supply of which had diminished during recent years.[1]

News of the Pocatalico meeting reached the ears of a few traders, who quickly alerted Carolina officials that the Creek Indians were planning to cut off the English. In a few short days several traders, including Thomas Nairne, South Carolina's Indian agent, arrived in Pocotalico to address the Indians' concerns. To the Carolinians this seemed like good policy and the Indians at Pocotalico put their calls for vengeance in check, treating their guests amicably on the night of April 14, shaking their hands and sharing a few drinks. While the traders slept, several of the chiefs conferred to discuss the best course of action. Some Yamasee chiefs wanted to kill the traders, but Brims believed it might be better to bide their time.[2]

Fortuitously, a lone Indian woman arrived at Pocotalico in the pre-dawn hours of April 15, Good Friday. The woman, wife of a trader and conversant in English, warned the Yamasee chiefs that the Englishmen had come to Pocotalico "to inquire into the cause of the meeting." In other words, to spy. The unwelcome news caused the Yamasee chiefs to rouse their warriors, raise the war whoop, and begin firing their flint-locks indiscriminately at the traders, torturing those who had managed to survive the initial volley. The warriors reserved a disproportionate amount of their wrath for Nairne, who they burned repeatedly for several days before putting him to death. With this bold stroke Carolina's former Indians allies sparked a smoldering frontier conflict that with the passage of time became known as the Yamasee War.[3]

Few single events in the early history of the Southeast have captured the attention or the imagination of historians as the Yamasee War has.[4] And rightly so, since that conflict irreversibly transformed the lives of many of the region's Indian participants. The Yamasees, who bore the brunt of the fighting, quickly abandoned their towns near Port Royal for safer territory in Spanish Florida. By doing so they put an immediate end to the trade in slaves and deerskins that, though seductively profitable at first, had enmeshed them in an onerous debt payable only in English blood. Rather than return to Carolina when given the opportunity years later, the Yamasees chose to remain with the Spanish and eke out a marginal existence as dependent clients of La Florida.[5] Likewise, in South Carolina the war led to a variety of reforms in frontier defense and trade that guided wary South Carolinians for many generations. It also stimulated a revolution in South Carolina's government, prompting the colony's principal inhabitants to remove the proprietary regime and place themselves under royal control and protection.[6]

Historians have long known that the Creeks played an important role in the Yamasee War, and few dispute the finding that it produced a revolution in "forest diplomacy" that enabled the Creeks to carve a niche for themselves in the interstices of three European empires. Whether or not the Creeks were the accidental beneficiaries or the actual creators of this environment is an unresolved issue. Many prominent historians have argued, for example, that Creek foreign policy was the brainchild of Brims, who persuaded his people to remain neutral in European conflicts.[7] More recent revisionist interpretations explain Creek neutrality was an accidental byproduct of political factionalism that precluded the formation of a consistent foreign policy within the nation. Factionalism, so the argument goes, only produces the appearance of neutrality.[8]

Historians have hitherto failed to reach a consensus on Creek neutrality primarily because they view the Yamasee War through a distinctly Yamasee lens. The war against Carolina was a prolonged, bloody military conflict against a much-hated enemy that among the Yamasees left little or no room for ambiguity. For the Creeks, in contrast, the three years following the initial massacre at Pocotalico led to more diplomacy than warfare, which raises questions as to the degree to which we may call this a war in the strict sense of the term. If warfare is simply "a continuation of politics by other means" (as some shrewd minds have argued), then politics merits equal if not greater attention. Yet Creek neutrality was no mere accident, as revisionists have argued, but a clearly articulated political strategy carefully crafted by Brims that reflected the Creeks' growing awareness of their precarious place in the Atlantic world.[9]

Beyond Pocotalico: Overtures to the Catholic Powers

Hostilities that began on Good Friday of 1715 by the Yamasees at Pocotalico sparked a frontier conflict that involved a majority of the Southeast's Indian nations and caused many others to speculate that the conspiracy was of continental proportions.[10] There can be little doubt that many warriors from the towns customarily associated with the Creek Confederacy joined the Yamasees and their allies by pillaging Carolina farmsteads and by "knocking in the head" a majority of the traders in their midst. Some Creeks seized the opportunity to loot and plunder the plantations near Port Royal during the first twenty-four hours of chaos and bloodshed.[11] Evidence indicates that a group of Cowetas made the long trek west and killed two traders living among the Chickasaws, who at best may have been lukewarm participants in the uprising. Small Creek war parties continued to threaten the inhabitants of St. Paul's Parish in the fall and winter months of 1716–1717, long after fighting had died down in many other quarters.[12] Though we cannot be sure who among the Creeks did the fighting, it is likely participants included Chislacaliche, the leader of an anti-English faction from Apalachicola, and Chigelli of Coweta, who later admitted that he had done his own share of fighting during those troubled times.[13]

Despite evidence of Creek belligerence, one cannot wade through the correspondence of Carolina officials without sensing that the Creeks exhibited less enthusiasm for combat than their allies, the Yamasees, Apalachees, or Cheraws. When hostilities began in South Carolina, those present noted that on occasion Creek warriors merely attached themselves to Yamasees who, most agreed, had dealt the "first blow."[14] In fact, Anglican missionary Gideon Johnson noted that many Creeks and even some of the Yamasees "were against the war all along."[15] Brims later blamed the Yamasees for dragging his people into the conflict.[16]

One plausible explanation for this relative disinclination to fight was that Creek leaders, and Brims in particular, chose to establish diplomatic links to the local Catholic powers and to assert control over the revolt, which the Yamasees appear to have begun prematurely. Undoubtedly apprised of the recent contact made with the Spanish in Florida, Brims wasted no time in sending to St. Augustine four emissaries, who arrived in a small boat on May 27, 1715. On board was Alonsso, a leading Yamasee chief and Christian Indian known as "the *mico* and governor of the town of Ocuti of Tama.". Accompanying Alonsso was Gabriel, an "infidel" son of a baptized Yamasee chief. In addition to these two Yamasee leaders the group included Istopoyole, the chief of Nicunapa, and Yfallaquisca or Brave Dog, the war captain of Satiquicha; both Indians hailed from "the province of Apalachecole."[17]

The day after they arrived, the four Indians met with the governor in his private quarters. Brave Dog was the first to step forward to speak, stating that they had come on behalf of the "Grand Cacique of Coweta" and for "[Chislacaliche], the Governor and Mico General of Cusa," who together had been given authority to speak for "all the *caciques* and *micos* of the towns of all the provinces."[18] That Brave Dog claimed to be carrying the talk of two rather than one chief is a curious point that can be analyzed from several different angles. First, Brave Dog's inclusion of Chislacaliche hints that Brims was not fully in control of the towns he claimed, but shared power with a staunchly pro-Spanish leader that had attracted a large zealous following. Second, by assuming a shared diplomatic posture before the Spanish, the two Indians had constructed a dual governing structure consistent with their own dualistic notions of political hierarchy. Brims, referred to as *cacique*, may have been posing as the chief entrusted with negotiating peace. Chislacaliche, who was more commonly referred to as "general," may have represented the war faction of the ad hoc interethnic alliance.

Brave Dog explained that they had come to renew their obedience to the king of Spain and displayed the eight knotted fathom-long strands of deerskin that represented the 161 towns that had joined the alliance.[19] After placing the knotted strands ceremoniously in the hands of the governor, Brave Dog described in minute detail the reasons why the Indians had turned against the English, explaining their debt problems, the traders' abuses, Brims's call to meet at Pocotalico, and the events that took place the morning of April 15. In an expression of his people's more immediate concerns, Brave Dog begged the governor for trade goods, food, and other necessities that his people were sorely lacking. Most important, perhaps, Brave Dog asked permission to relocate the Yamasees near the Spanish presidio; the governor enthusiastically agreed.

Confident that the relatively weak Catholic powers would be happy to accept their peaceful overtures, the Creek peoples continued to court the leaders of St. Augustine, Pensacola, and Mobile throughout that summer and fall. While Brims and Chislacaliche took the lead in establishing contact with St. Augustine, the Tallapoosas initiated diplomatic contact with Pensacola. That May, Tallapoosa emissaries invited the captain of the Pensacola garrison to a parley at the "seat of the Talapuses." After this initial round of talks, twenty Tallapoosas accompanied the Pensacola captain and his men on their return to Pensacola, arriving on May 25 to inform the garrison that the "said nations had taken up arms against the English."[20]

In the wake of the Tallapoosas' diplomatic initiatives with Pensacola, Brims launched contact with that same garrison by way of an intermediary, Tickhonabe, the "principal Indian" of Tallassee. That Brims chose to rely on Tickhonabe as his Tallapoosa messenger suggests not only the existence of a close historical connection between the Cowetas and Tallassees but also that Brims may have had considerable influence in that town. Tickhonabe bore at least one son who later claimed Coweta as his hometown, indicating, perhaps, that Tickhonabe had married a Coweta woman. Tickhonabe, we may therefore assume, was well known to Brims and the Coweta leadership, making him a natural for the mediating assignment.

On July 7, Tickhonabe visited the Pensacola garrison accompanied by forty other chiefs and war captains of the said nations. Brims, seeking to make his own voice heard there, sent with the Tallassee headman three Spanish soldiers whom the Cowetas had previously detained as prisoners. Brims's magnanimous display undoubtedly pleased the Pensacola captain, Salinas Varona, who returned the favor by distributing powder, ball, shirts, cloth, and hats to the chiefs. These gifts were not incidental to the peace process. As generations of colonial governors had come to understand, Indians considered the exchange of gifts—not mere words—to be the truest sign of peace, symbolizing mutual obligations to treat one another as one would treat a friend or brother. "From that day," remarked the governor, "there has been no lack of parties coming and going as was effected by the principal chiefs of the Tequipache and Talapuche nations." On September 30, 1715, the chiefs of the Tuckebatchee and Tallapoosa nations again arrived at Pensacola to renew the peace which, characteristically, the Spaniards interpreted as obedience.[21]

Meanwhile, the Alabamas took the lead in establishing an alliance with the French at Mobile. The Alabamas had previously brokered a truce with the French and lived in close proximity to Mobile, making them likely candidates to initiate diplomacy with the French. In June of 1715 some small parties of Alabamas began drifting into Mobile, "coming here to trade," as Bienville put it, foreshadowing the shift in political allegiance that was soon to occur. The Alabamas soon invited the French to send soldiers into their territory, obliging Bienville to respond, which he did by sending seven French soldiers into Alabama territory.[22] In September Bienville boasted that the seven men had returned safely with the chiefs of several other Indian nations including the Abikas, Tallapoosas, and Cowetas, a sign that the Indians were coordinating their diplomatic efforts.

As with the diplomatic overtures made in Pensacola, the Indians shrewdly used white prisoners as tools of diplomacy. The entourage that arrived in Mobile that September, for instance, turned over to the French two prisoners—a man and a woman taken from Carolina—who were detained briefly in Mobile and later returned by ship to Charles Town. After handing over the pair the chiefs implored Bienville to send French traders into their nations. Bienville, hoping to convince the Indians that they would find "the same advantages with us that they had with the English," promised to "trade with them for their produce and pelts" and intentionally neglected to mention Indian slaves (which had indebted them to the English in the first place). Aware that the Indians expected to receive gifts from the French, Bienville distributed a few presents, sending the chiefs home "very pleased and satisfied."[23]

Though Brims did not personally attend any of these meetings, he undoubtedly made his voice heard whenever the representatives of the 161 towns met with a foreign leader. It is not possible to track with any certainty Brims's movements during this episode, but it is likely that he returned to his town at Ochese Creek to see to the safety of the women and children and to confer with his allies to send representatives (and prisoners) to the Catholic outposts. By September, though, Brims appeared in person at St. Augustine, undoubtedly to renew the peace that had been initiated in his name in May. Accompanying Brims were the chiefs of Casista and Tasquiqi, "and another ten *caciques, micos,* and *usinjulos*" (presumably subordinate Ochese headmen). Strangely, Brims's visit did not generate the amount of paperwork that Brave Dog's visit had generated in May, which may suggest a rather brief and unceremonious stay.[24]

Given the time that it generally took to traverse the Southern landscape in the early eighteenth century, events indicate that the leaders of the Ocheses, Tallapoosas, Abikas, and Alabamas were equally, if not more, preoccupied with diplomacy than with warfare during the spring and summer of 1715. As winter approached, however, both the Creeks and the Carolinians resumed war plans, and each planned to court the Cherokees to come to their assistance.

New Enemies: The Cherokees

One of the great ironies of the Yamasee War was that in its aftermath the Creeks began a decades-long period of detente with the English, yet gained a new Indian enemy, the Cherokees, against whom they conducted an on-again-off-again war that lasted the better part of four decades. Though later generations of Creeks tended to characterize the Cherokees as their ancient enemies, this antagonism was in reality of more recent origin. These peoples had fought together during the slave wars of the previous decades and operated a trade network that linked the Gulf Coast to Virginia.[25] Thus the traditional enmity that later existed in the eighteenth century appears to have been kindled during the era of the Yamasee War.

On the eve of the conflict the Cherokees undoubtedly suffered from the traders' belligerence and shared in the grave concerns articulated by Brims at Pocotalico. Additionally, in the months preceding the Pocotalico massacre, a few disgruntled Cherokee traders began circulating rumors that the Carolina government planned to make war on the Cherokees. These combined influences undoubtedly compelled at least a few Cherokees to join in the initial attacks on Carolina's outlying settlements. Several of the Cherokee leaders, however, hesitated to carry out a war against the English, prompting them to protect the traders living in their towns. Eight Cherokee leaders, hoping to remain at peace, ventured to Charles Town in October and promised peace and military assistance to the government so as to keep open the trading paths to their towns. That December the Carolina government responded in kind by sending three hundred men, under the leadership of Maurice Moore and George Chicken, into Cherokee country to recruit warriors to fight against Carolina's Indian enemies.[26]

Though it has been argued that the Carolinians sought to recruit a Cherokee army specifically to fight the Creeks, it is quite clear that the Carolina government believed the "northward Indians" posed the more immediate threat. Arriving in the Cherokee town of Tugaloo on December 30, Chicken learned from the mouth of Conjuror, the chief there, that the Creeks had accepted a flag of truce sent to them and had promised to come to Tugaloo in fourteen days to talk peace with the English. The Creeks promised to return to the English a white woman taken from the Carolina settlements. Brims, meanwhile, showed that he too was willing to exercise restraint. While trailing Moore's army up the Savannah River, Brims had repeatedly ordered his men to refrain from attacking despite the fact that they could have killed several of Moore's men. Indeed, on January 5 a Cherokee man who had recently come from the Creeks informed Colonel Chicken that "the whole talk of the [Creek] Kings and head men was for a peace with the white men and would accept the first message that came from any of them for peace." Thus the stage appears to have been set for a round of peace negotiations brokered by the Cherokees.[27]

All was not well between the Creeks and the Cherokees, however, particularly in the Cherokee town of Chota, which was clamoring for war. Problems appear to have begun weeks earlier in the nearby town of Cusauwaichee, whose chief, Cherry Heague, had placed two white men under his protection and kept them alive until he thought all was over. Believing they would be safe, Cherry Heague went out hunting only to find upon his return that two Abika men had slipped into his town and killed the two white men. As the Creeks probably lamented later, the murder of the two white men was a costly mistake. To kill the friends of a chief—in his own town—was likely seen as a direct attack on the Cherokees, who undoubtedly accepted, even if only temporarily, an obligation to defend and protect them as kin. As the Cherokees saw it, the murder of the two white men called for blood revenge and required them to spill Creek blood to atone for the murders.

Sometime during the final week of January a Creek delegation ventured to Tugaloo for a fateful meeting that the Creeks and the Carolinians remembered differently. A decade later Chigelly of Coweta recounted that the Creek delegation, which undoubtedly included a few Cowetas, had come to talk about establishing peace with the English. Though Chigelly was prone to gloss over evidence that suggested otherwise, the Creek delegation may in fact have had peaceful intentions. One member of the Creek delegation was a Coweta man known as "Hastings's Friend," a name he had earned in recognition of the solemn, ritualized friendship he had established with Theophilus Hastings, a trader and militia colonel who happened to be in Cherokee country at the time. Thus the Cowetas may have intended to use this man as a go-between to reestablish ties to the English. As the English and Cherokees remembered it, however, the Creek delegation came with warlike intentions, imploring the Cherokees to turn on the English and kill the white men roaming in the vicinity. Sensing that it was in their best interest to support the English, the Cherokees instead turned on the Creeks.[28]

Though we cannot be entirely sure of the Creeks' intentions, something caused the Cherokees in Tugaloo to kill or capture the entire Creek delegation. As George Chicken reported on January 27, that day the Cherokees had killed eleven men outright and taken two men prisoner. One of the prisoners, Hastings's Friend, was shot later that evening, while the other "was given to the white men to be shot." For three days the Cherokees and English waylaid the paths leading south to root out Brims's large war party rumored to be in the vicinity of Tugaloo. Finding that Brims's men had broken camp and scattered themselves in the woods, the English and Cherokees ceased their mission. The Carolina government, hesitant to commit its troops to a difficult and costly back-country war, opted to send to the Cherokees two hundred guns with powder and bullets to let them carry on the fight.[29]

As the Creeks saw it, the fact that the English had decided to embrace the Cherokees and provide them with firearms at this critical juncture was evidence of an alliance or conspiracy between the two. For safety reasons the Indians living on Ochese Creek decided to return to their ancient homes on the Chattahoochee. Rather than fighting, the Ochese migrants spent the spring of 1716 starting over: building houses, planting crops, and felling trees. As with earlier migrations, the Creeks probably timed this move in order to assure adequate preparation for the spring planting season that customarily took place in April or May.[30]

The appearance of a joint Cherokee-English alliance also caused the Ocheses to step up their efforts to compel the Catholic powers to make good on their promises to provide military assistance. Chislacaliche, who had recently relocated his people to the Sabacola old town at the confluence of the Flint and Chattahoochee Rivers, appears to have taken the lead in this effort. Arriving in St. Augustine in July, Chislacaliche implored Florida's new governor, Don Pedro de Olivera y Fullana, to send a Spanish envoy into Creek country to renew their friendship and distribute presents. Olivera y Fullana, hoping to use the occasion to convince the rest of the Creeks to follow Chislacaliche and relocate to Florida, sent retired lieutenant Diego Peña and four soldiers to the reconstructed towns on the Chattahoochee.[31]

On August 4, 1716, Peña and his companions left St. Augustine and arrived on the Chattahoochee on September 13, making him the first Spaniard to travel the course of that river—willingly, at least—in more than twenty years. In the course of his travels Peña kept a diary that provides a first glimpse of the repopulation activities of the old Apalachicola province.[32] Much of the surroundings that Peña observed bore a striking resemblance to the Apalachicola that Antonio Matheos had encountered a generation earlier. But Peña's diary also indicates that much had changed in the ensuing years. Perhaps in recognition of those changes, the Spanish and the Indians themselves appear to have rarely if ever

again referred to the province as Apalachicola, while the British preferred to call the Chattahoochee peoples the Lower Creeks.

The British adoption of the term "Creeks" occurred gradually over the
first decades of the eighteenth century. In their search for a convenient
label by which to describe the Indian peoples on the frontier, sometime
around the turn of the century Carolina officials adopted term "Ochese
Creek Indians" in reference to the mixed multitude that inhabited the
Ocmulgee and Oconee River basins. Eventually Carolina traders and
government officials simplified this term even further, and the first references to "Creek Indians" began to appear in English documents as
early as 1706.[33] At that time, though, Carolina officials and traders used
the term only sparingly in reference to the Indians living in the vicinity
of the Ocmulgee and Oconee Rivers. After the Yamasee War, Carolina
officials began to use "Creek Indians" with more frequency, adding the
prefix "Lower" in reference to the Chattahoochee peoples and "Upper"
in reference to the peoples of the Coosa and Tallapoosa Rivers. In time the
terms Upper and Lower Creeks stuck and gained wide currency among
the British, who continued to use the terms throughout the colonial era.

Taken at face value, the invention of such terms may appear as a
benign effort on the part of the Carolinians to simplify the diversity
that existed within Indian country. But the practice of naming Indian
peoples often only reflected the political goals and vantage points of
the people who were assigning such names. Curiously, the Spanish at
that time tended to use the indigenous term "Uchises" in reference to
the Chattahoochee peoples, opting to refer to their countrypersons to
the west as Tuckebatchees or Tallapoosas. For their part, the Creeks
tended to distinguish three major divisions within their "nation": the
Cowetas or Uchises; the Tallapoosas; and the Abikas. Thus, Carolina's
tendency to apply the Creek moniker to the former Ocheses and to other
related Indian peoples on the Coosa and Tallapoosa Rivers may have
been inextricably tied to British efforts to centralize and control a variety of small-scale Indian polities that often defied their control and
description.[34]

However imprecise and reflective of English imperial ambitions, the
new terminology can be justified on the grounds that the struggle against
British hegemony was a central theme in Creek history. As contact with
the British increased, so too did the use of the Creek name; the Creeks
may have used such imprecise terms themselves when explaining their

political organization to unfamiliar British officials. From a historical perspective, the use of the new terminology permits us to recognize that, though similar to earlier configurations, the Creek divisions reconstituted after the Yamasee War were not entirely the same as the Indian provinces that existed in the late seventeenth century.

Take, for example, the Chattahoochee River villages as Diego Peña observed them in 1716. In some respects Peña's diary indicates a basic reconstruction of the old Apalachicola province, which consisted of ten villages. Sabacola, Peña found, had been resurrected on the southern frontier of the province, the same relative position it had occupied before 1691. Apalachicola likewise appears on the southern margins just north of Sabacola. Coweta, Cussita, and Tuskegee [Tasquique], three of the four "most guilty" northern towns encountered by Matheos in 1685, appear again on the northern frontier of the province in roughly their same relative positions.

But Peña also found evidence that indicates the province was somewhat in a state of flux. One of the southernmost towns—Talispasle—had entirely ceased to exist. Other towns that originated among the Coosas and Tallapoosas to the west, such as Colone, appear to have joined with the Upper Creeks. Tuskegee, which was present on the Chattahoochee in 1716, soon relocated among the Upper Creeks as well. Osuche, which Peña failed to notice, eventually reemerged as one of the so-called point towns of the Lower Creeks but had not, as of yet, been rebuilt.

Most important, Peña recognized that this new Lower Creek province had become increasingly multiethnic, a sign of extensive contact with other Indian nations during the previous decades. South of Sabacola, for instance, Peña found scattered dwellings belonging to Christian Apalachees, many of whom had undoubtedly participated in the Yamasee revolt and had attached themselves to the Ocheses for reasons of security. Most noteworthy was the town of Uchi, a foreign people perhaps of northern origin who spoke a distinct language for which few interpreters could be found. Tellingly, Peña observed other foreigners, such as Afalayas, Timucuans, and Mocamans, scattered throughout the villages, all of whom had suffered recent Ochese attacks. Presumably these foreigners were living among the host population as adopted family members or slaves.[35] Peña likewise noted the ubiquitous presence of Yamasees, who had likely intermarried and remained with the host population.

By commencing diplomatic activities that September, Peña and the

Lower Creek chiefs expected to use the occasion to fulfill certain military and political goals. The Spanish, of course, hoped not only to secure the Creeks' "obedience" but also to entice them to relocate their villages back at the Apalachee old fields. The Creek chiefs, who had made the bold move to break with the English and place their peoples under the protection of the Catholic empires, needed a conspicuous show of support from the Spanish to solidify their own authority. Protecting the people and seeing to it that their needs were met were, after all, the chief's responsibility. Failure to succeed at this would have inevitably cost the Creek chiefs their influence.

Arriving in Apalachicola on September 28, Peña called all of the chiefs of the province to the town square to distribute presents and ask them to relocate to Apalachee. Peña began by distributing in ceremonious fashion unspecified arms and munitions, a gift of the king of Spain. Shrewdly, Peña placed these items in the hands of the "*cassiques*," who in turn distributed the arms to the warriors in an orderly manner. This ritualized transfer of the guns and ammunition clearly was intended to demonstrate the chiefs' command over the warriors and served to dramatize the military hierarchies of each village. Brims, the most conspicuous of the chiefs, used the occasion to remind the Spanish—and perhaps his own people—that he was the one "to whom all render obedience," pledging the loyalty of "seven provinces which are subject to his order and authority." Brims did not specify which of the seven provinces were his, but the fact that he made such a bold statement in the Apalachicola town square suggests that his influence extended to the southern extremity of the Lower Creek province. Moreover, after hinting that he held sway among the Tallapoosas, Brims immediately sent a runner to invite the Tallapoosas into the alliance and assured Peña that "all who come would be pleased and contented."[36]

However happy the Lower Creek chiefs might have been to see Peña, a substantial number of the Cowetas appear to have bristled when confronted with the prospect of a unilateral Spanish alliance. Several days later Peña observed that "many women abound," noting that more than 130 women loyal to the English had gathered together with 30 men to demonstrate their pro-English sympathies. Aware that many had escaped, Peña predicted that "all will flee to the English."[37]

The fact that women were conspicuous in fomenting pro-English factionalism suggests that women may have had a particular incentive to restore relations with Carolina. While most historians tend to emphasize the important role of guns, powder, and shot in colonial trade, such myopia obscures the fact that the women had their own needs as well, determined, of course, by the nature of women's work as traditionally defined in Indian society. Among their many important duties, Creek women bore responsibility for making clothing for themselves and their families; they increasingly relied upon English woolens and sewing implements to do so. One cannot help but venture to guess, then, that by the fall of 1716, after suffering nearly eighteen months without English trade goods, Indian women had begun clamoring for the things that made their tasks easier: cloth, scissors, thimbles, and awls. Because the English could supply wool cloth to Indians more efficiently and more cheaply than their competitors, cloth intimately bound the Indians to the Carolina trade regime and made the consumer demands of Indian women one of the critical links between the two groups.[38]

Thus, although the Creek leaders of the early eighteenth century commonly excluded their women from official political talks, women had their own ways of exerting political influence. In fact, by the turn of the eighteenth century Creek women had earned the reputation as particularly influential. Thomas Nairne, writing in 1708, observed that the Chickasaws ridiculed the Ochese men "for their indulgence of the fair sex."[39] Important as they were to the domestic economy, the Coweta women appear emboldened enough to challenge the chief and catalyze a new effort to restore peaceful relations with Carolina.

Overtures to the English: The Birth of Multilateral Diplomacy

That the women of Coweta were bold enough to snub Brims's diplomatic overtures to the Spanish undoubtedly pressured the Coweta chief to chart a new diplomatic course as the year 1717 approached. Pulling Brims in one direction were the women of Coweta who sought to repair their shattered relationship with the English. Conversely, Brims's close allies and mouthpieces in St. Augustine, such as Chislacaliche, Adrian the Apalachee chief, and his younger kinsman Chipacasi, continued to court the Spanish and French. In the coming year, while groping for a diplomatic solution that might balance the interests of both groups, Brims chose to restore contact with the English and simultaneously encouraged his people to renew their friendships with the Catholic powers. Thus the year 1717 witnessed the birth of a multilateral diplomacy that shaped Creek politics for generations to come.

It should be stressed, however, that the Creek Indians understood politics a bit differently than did the leaders of the European nations, whose own state-centered political traditions had conditioned them to assume that the Indians ought to pursue a unified foreign policy and declare themselves either friends or enemies of the respective European nations. But even an Indian leader as influential as Brims could not forge a unified foreign policy—provided that he had wanted to do so in the first place—largely thanks to the nature of his own political traditions. Rooted in kinship, the culture of Creek diplomacy placed greater emphasis on reciprocal relationships between particular people and was inherently parochial rather than state-centered. Thus, for Brims the challenge was not so much to forge a unified foreign policy but to allow the constituent interests in his nation the freedom to cultivate their own personal political networks or factions. Factionalism, then, was encouraged rather than discouraged.

The problem, however, was that Creek political factionalism could at times spin out of control and threaten to set the nation against itself and, in the process, undermine Brims's authority. To counteract this centrifugal tendency, Brims sought to assert a measure of control over the various factions by using his own kin—both men and women— to cultivate alliances with the various European powers. In this way Brims could be sure that his own voice would resonate in Carolina, St. Augustine, Pensacola, and Mobile, and in effect give him a monopoly over Creek international diplomacy.

Just as Peña's earlier observations had foreshadowed, the scarcity of trade goods had compelled the Creeks to make tentative peace proposals with the English, "not out of love," argued Carolina's agent in London, Richard Beresford, "but [a] want to be supplied."[40] Diplomatic overtures commenced in February 1717 when a Creek envoy making its way to the Savannah River happened upon Theophilus Hastings, commander of the newly established Savannah Fort. Two months later two Creek warriors arrived at the Savannah fort, bringing two English captives who had been given up for dead.[41] Brims, it was rumored, may not have initiated this contact, but it later became apparent that he approved of it.[42]

In response to these friendly overtures, in April or early May the Carolina Assembly sent a veteran Indian trader named John Jones to Coweta, where he received a warm welcome from Brims and the ruler's retinue, thereby putting to rest the rumor that Brims may not have supported the initial peace overtures. Jones's presence on the Chattahoochee River that spring was significant because not only was he the first Englishman to visit the Creeks since the Pocotalico massacre, he was the very man whose mistreatment of the Creeks may have touched off the war in the first place. Jones's voyage, then, may have been intended— and perceived by the Indians—as an attempt to bring some sort of closure to a bad episode in the English-Creek mutual history.[43] Upon Jones's return, both the Creeks and the English proposed to meet again in June to make their peace official.[44]

The Creeks' peace advance toward the English, however, appears to have been only one of several such initiatives undertaken at precisely the same time. That February, for example, a delegation of seven Creek chiefs under the leadership of Tickhonabe of Tallassee boarded a Spanish ship in Pensacola harbor bound for Veracruz. From Veracruz the chiefs ventured to Mexico City to "render obedience" before the viceroy of New Spain, the Marquis de Valero. Though we know little about what occurred at Valero's court, evidence shows that Tickhonabe was baptized, with Viceroy Valero serving as godfather. Furthermore, we know that Tickhonabe's delegation made their peaceful demonstrations in behalf of the great *cacique* of Coweta, that is, Brims. Such evidence suggests not only that Brims exercised some authority over the town of Tallassee, but that he had approved—perhaps even initiated—the voyage to Mexico.[45]

For Brims to exercise full control over Creek diplomacy, though, it was not enough to send his favorite Tallapoosa envoy to New Spain. He sought to exert further control over his nation's diplomatic maneuvers by employing his kinsman Chipacasi as the principle negotiator with the Spanish in Florida and with the French at Mobile. Chipacasi, regarded by the Spanish as the *usinjulo* of Coweta, had previously established contact with Spanish officials who, though erroneously believing him to be Brims's "son," recognized the pair's close kinship connection. Thus, Chipacasi proved to be an appropriate choice to convey Brims's messages to Spanish officials.

Brims and Chipacasi first set to work that spring to convince the Spanish to build a new fort and trading house in Apalachee, which was to serve the Creeks as a source of military support and trade. Departing Coweta sometime in March, Chipacasi finally arrived on the outskirts of St. Augustine on April 2. After two days of waiting, Chipacasi and his delegation, described as "157 heathen Indians, who have come from different provinces," entered St. Augustine on April 4 to conduct peace rituals and discuss Brims's plans.[46]

Although the Spanish typically interpreted these ritual demonstrations as a sign of obedience, a closer analysis of the proceedings suggests that the Creeks had somewhat different goals in mind. Specifically, by using a variety of symbolic acts and the language of kinship, it is clear that Chipacasi sought to forge a fictitious—though, for political purposes, a very real—kinship relationship to the Spanish governor if not to the king of Spain himself. By committing to this relationship Chipacasi intended to oblige the Spanish to reciprocate by building the fort and trading house in Apalachee and by distributing presents.

The meeting began at nine o'clock that morning. Seven cannons fired a salute as the Indians strolled toward the presidio, flanked on either side by the Spanish infantry as they passed through the fort's southern gate. As the English did in later years, this display of martial prowess was clearly intended to awe the Indians into a more submissive state of mind. But the Creek Indians were not so easily awed and they sought to impress the Spanish with their own military prowess, thereby making the encounter a meeting of equals.

Drawing upon a customary ritual, Chipacasi's delegation of 157 men proceeded into the fort in a formation that emphasized their own glorious military traditions. At the head of this procession were two warriors with reputations for being strong and valiant. Both came into the fort yelling and dancing, striking rehearsed poses that appeared "antick" to the Spaniards on hand to watch. Though the Spaniards appeared somewhat puzzled by the strange dance, it is evident that the Indians' performance was intended to instill a sense of awe in the Spanish and to cultivate their respect as equals by trumpeting their peoples' past military achievements. Behind the two warrior-dancers came several others playing flutes, rattles, and drums, which together produced the cadence by which the rest of the delegation marched in military formation.

Though Southeastern Indian chiefs and head warriors dressed and often acted in ways that did little to distinguish them from their inferiors, in ritual contexts the chiefs often assumed symbolic trappings of authority. Among the 157 men, 4 stood out as the leaders of this delegation: Chipacasi or the *usinjulo* of Coweta; Chislacaliche, the Uchise chief; Adrian, the chief of Bacuqua of the Apalachees; and Tatepique of the Tallapoosas. The Spanish noted that the chiefs made themselves conspicuous by dressing in the Spanish fashion, wearing sombreros and carrying silver-tipped canes.[47] By assuming the trappings of Spanish gentility, the four chiefs undoubtedly sought to make their own people recognize their important station. Exotic goods such as these, which for centuries chiefs had used to symbolically reinforce their authority, demonstrated a connection to the world beyond the village. Foreign diplomacy was, after all, a type of esoteric knowledge to which the chiefs and leading warriors had differential access over and above the commoners. By dressing specifically in the Spanish fashion the four chiefs meant to signify that they had symbolically transformed themselves into Spaniards. Only by doing so could they convince the Spanish governor to treat them with the respect due to brothers and fellow subjects of the king of Spain.

After exchanging initial salutations, Chipacasi and the four chiefs entered the governor's quarters. Chipacasi immediately seized center stage and delivered a speech filled with the kind of stock phrases that gave Indian oratory its ritualistic character. Chipacasi began by emphasizing the Indian nations' unity under Brims, much as Brave Dog had done nearly two years before. "Their coming," one observer noted, "was by arrangement of his [Chipacasi's] father, the great *cacique* of the province of Cabetta," who had ordered them to "renew obedience . . . according to their usage."[48] Though absent, Brims's kinsman made sure that his "father's" voice would be heard unambiguously in St. Augustine.

While the Creeks' recent alliance with the Spaniards was not yet two years old, Chipacasi demonstrated that he and his people desired to turn back the clock, so to speak, to a semi-mythical time in the not-so-remote past when the Spaniards and Apalachicolas had been on friendlier terms. Chipacasi claimed, for example, that their declaration of obedience "had come down from ancient tradition, being passed down from one generation to another from time immemorial." Clearly Chipacasi was drawing upon his people's oral traditions, which had preserved the memory of the obedience rendered to past Spanish governors. Chipacasi assured the governor that the memory of this past would remain burned in the memories of future generations as well, stating that his people would repeat "word for word and term for term" the meaning of their obedience to "their sons and descendants."[49]

Though many of the ceremonies and speeches clearly drew upon conventional Indian practices, rituals conducted between Europeans and Indians often required innovation. Only by making imaginative use of their own familiar rituals could the Spanish and Indians create a middle ground of meaning to bridge the two disparate belief systems. The

Indian chiefs had done their part by dressing as Spaniards. Acting governor Juan de Ayala Escobar, in turn, did his part, first by hugging Chipacasi when he had finished speaking. Then, drawing upon the European custom of toasting to the health of kings, Ayala ordered some drinks for his Indian companions and together they toasted to the king of Spain's health. To reciprocate and to show his respect for the Indians' supreme political leader, Governor Ayala toasted the chief of Coweta, which spurred all in attendance to imitate.

After sharing drinks, the Indians performed a rather lengthy, musical goodwill ceremony, said to be ancient in origin. To conclude, two Indian warriors danced around the room and sat at Ayala's feet, while another man placed a crown of feathers on the governor's head. The crown, according to the Indian man in charge of its care, was of ancient origin and a symbol of a chief's authority. Ayala optimistically interpreted this act as a sign of submission and obedience to the king, which they pledged would endure "until the end of the world."[50] It might be said, however, that by placing a chief's crown on Ayala, the Indians had symbolically transformed the Spanish governor into an Indian chief, thus obliging him—as every good Indian chief was compelled—to look after the interests of his people.

Two days passed before talks resumed. Having made Governor Ayala a chief, the time was now right to discuss "the rest that the Great Cacique of Coweta had charged them to do" but with far less pomp and ceremony than displayed at the first meeting.[51] Taking center stage again was Chipacasi who, accompanied by the three other chiefs, began by reiterating all the familiar promises of perpetual obedience to the Spanish. Documents make it quite clear that Chipacasi did not consider his people to be subjects of a foreign king. Rather, he used the language of kinship to emphasize that theirs was a relationship between friends and brothers. Chipacasi's choice of words, moreover, was no accident, for by establishing themselves as brothers he sought to impose Creek rules of kinship on the governor, which demanded reciprocity, not subjection. Chipacasi's flattering display of obedience was likely a ploy to oblige Ayala to comply with Chipacasi's demands.

To make Ayala further obliged to the Creeks, Chipacasi promised to maintain friendship with only the king of Spain and pledged that they would be willing to lose their lives in defense of the Spaniards.[52] By proclaiming his people's willingness to fight to the death for the Spanish, Chipacasi forced Ayala to make a similar promise to reciprocate lest

Ayala appear a half-hearted ally or brother. Ayala responded by stating that "he esteemed highly the loyalty and obedience, which he was offering to our king and lord," and offered, in return, "reciprocally the same thing that he was promising in their defense, as this presidio had always done." Embellishing further, Ayala pleaded that Spanish colonization had always been carried out for the good of Indians, arguing that "this presidio . . . [had] been established by His Catholic Majesty for the objective of supporting all the natives of all these provinces and for their conversion."[53]

While it is clear that Chipacasi explicitly sought military assistance, Ayala knew that his Indian guests also expected to receive gifts in return. Unfortunately, the governor found himself momentarily short on gifts and had to apologetically explain the role that the *situado* played in the Spanish empire: "For the presents which they needed at the present moment he was sending a *situado*-agent to the Kingdom of New Spain [Mexico], sending him to obtain everything which might be needed."[54] It would not be the last time that Spanish governors would have to explain to their putative Indian allies the Spanish empire's bureaucratic inefficiencies. The Creeks themselves came to learn that the *situado* could not always be relied upon, which in the long run undermined the Spanish-Creek alliance.[55]

Chipacasi, having listened to Ayala's firm promises, concluded his speech by stating that "from this day on they would not have nor recognize any other father." Chipacasi's choice of words was not an accidental slip into a familiar metaphor. By likening the king of Spain to a father, Chipacasi sought to instill further in Ayala's mind that the two men—both "children" of the king—were, in effect, brothers. Likewise, in the Creek matrilineal social system, fathers played a role that differed from the stern patriarchs that were the cultural norm in Europe. In Creek society a man's uncle (his mother's brother) commonly played the role of disciplinarian and was likely to pass along the traditions and history of the clan to which both nephew and uncle belonged. Creek fathers did not shoulder these responsibilities and played a more indulgent role as protectors and gift-givers. Chipacasi, by likening the king of Spain to a father, sought to oblige Ayala to play a more indulgent role, protecting and giving gifts to the Creeks.[56]

Chipacasi concluded his remarks by flattering the governor with predictions that the Creeks would one day convert to Catholicism. Chislacaliche then spoke up, bluntly eliminating from his oratory the ritual flattery that characterized earlier speeches. Chislacaliche reminded Ayala, for example, that on an earlier occasion, one of his predecessors had promised to place a garrison somewhere amongst them. Chislacaliche then explained to Ayala that he had passed along this information to Brims in Coweta, who "received it with great pleasure and desired that it be established." Chislacaliche was there, he explained, "to bring [the matter] up again."[57]

In response Ayala promised to "do it all" and inquired as to where they should build the proposed fort. In chorus-like fashion all four chiefs replied that they wanted it built on "the Guacara River in the province of Apalachee about two leagues distant from the port of San Marcos . . . where a fort was located in former times, because it was close to the sea and to the spot frequented by the vessels from Havana in order to trade with the Spaniards as they had done formerly."[58] Because their answer appears to have been rehearsed, the chiefs probably had discussed this matter on previous occasions, perhaps in consultation with Brims. More telling still was the Indians' knowledge of trade in Spanish Florida. Havana had been the origin and principal destination of the ships stationed in San Marcos de Apalachee prior to 1704. The Indians' decision to place the fort where it had been located so that they could trade with the Spaniards, "as they had done formerly," further indicates that they wished to improve their trade prospects with Spain and reverse the decline of La Florida.

Before departing later that day Ayala's four Indian guests made one last request for weapons and munitions, which they claimed to need to defend themselves against their Cherokee enemies. Ayala consented and, in a show of Spain's magnanimity, presented the Indians with 154 muskets as well as two pounds of powder and three pounds of ball for each man. As an added bonus, Ayala gave them another one hundred pounds of powder and a like measure of balls to stock the forts they had reportedly built "to shelter and protect their women and children during enemy attacks."[59] Chipacasi's delegation remained in the vicinity of St. Augustine for another week or so and departed unceremoniously on April 18, 1717.[60]

Adding another wrinkle to the peace initiatives with Spain was the establishment of a French fort at the confluence of the Coosa and Tallapoosa Rivers, named Fort Toulouse, erected in July 1717. Though the French had vaguely entertained the idea of building a fort in the interior for several years prior to the Yamasee War, the Indians' break with the

English appears to have caused French officials in Mobile to seriously entertain such a notion by January 1716. The Alabamas, with their close contacts to the French, may have first given their consent to the project. Later generations of Creek leaders asserted, however, that the lands upon which the fort was built belonged to the Tallapoosas. The French and the Alabamas had set up residence there only with the permission of the Tallapoosa chiefs. The Tallapoosas, moreover, believed that they had given the French usufruct rights to use the land rather than own it, an important distinction that the Tallapoosas maintained—and defended— when the French departed the region in 1763. Tellingly, the fact that both the Upper and Lower Creeks steadfastly shunned repeated offers from the English to dismantle the French fort suggests that the nation in general had also granted its approval. For his part, Brims, influential among the Tallapoosas, must have also lent tacit support to the project.[61]

That Brims chose to engage in diplomacy simultaneously with the three European powers suggests that the peace initiatives directed at Carolina in 1717 were not intended to reestablish the status quo as it existed in 1715. Quite the contrary. Rather than return to the Carolina fold as pawns of the British empire, the Creeks sought to cultivate a multilateral—and competitive—political environment. They hoped to use the circumstances to their advantage, drawing the English into a strictly commercial relationship while using their alliances with Spain and France to thwart Carolina's imperial and territorial ambitions.

Seen in this light, the Creeks considered it desirable to shore up their relationships with the two Catholic powers before rushing prematurely into an alliance with the English. Not only did they haggle with the Carolinians over the location of the proposed meeting—refusing to proceed any farther than the Savannah River—but they stalled when it came time to ratify earlier peace proposals. Rather than sending the 200 warriors that Carolina officials expected, on June 6 a lone Indian named Boocatee arrived at the Savannah fort to deliver an apologetic yet firm message: though his people desired peace they could not come "before the corn is ripe," an evident attempt to delay peace proceedings until midsummer or beyond. Though eager to right matters between themselves and the English, Boocatee sternly refused to cease hostilities with other Indian nations with whom the Creeks were at war. "As for the Cherokees and Catawbas," he added, "they will have no peace with them."[62]

When considered from the perspective of Creek politics, the Creeks' reluctance to commit to peace with the Carolina government reflects not a failure on their part to negotiate but a need to restore peace on terms that made sense to them culturally. Creek politics were intensely personal and founded on the basis of kinship; "Carolina" was an abstraction that Creek leaders found difficult to understand. To them peace could only be established between individuals operating within a reciprocal relationship of trust and respect. Though frequently blinded to the Indians' political ways, Carolina officials, probably with the assistance of the traders, came to recognize this personal dimension of Creek politics. For this reason the Carolina Assembly continually employed former traders known to be well-liked by the Creek Indians—such as Theophilus Hastings, Charlesworth Glover, and Matthew Smallwood—to arrange peace negotiations. Most influential among this group was Capt. John Musgrove, whom Carolina officials singled out as much respected by the Creeks (perhaps because he had a Creek wife and son). Because of these personal ties, Musgrove played a pivotal personal role in bringing the two sides to peace. [63]

Most important to the peace process, however, was a young girl named Coosaponakeesa, the daughter of Indian trader Edward Griffin. Her mother was Brims's sister, which by Creek matrilineal rules made her a clan kinswoman to Coweta's "emperor" and related headmen. As Coosaponakeesa later recounted, she was born in Coweta town on the Ocmulgee River and lived there until reaching "about the age of seven years." Her father, seeking to Anglicize her and breed her in the "principles of Christianity," brought her to the English settlement of Pon Pon that was then located on Carolina's southwestern frontier. Coosaponakeesa was in Pon Pon when the Yamasee War broke out, effectively caught between two peoples and two cultures at war. [64]

Early on in the peace negotiations with the Creeks, it appears that Musgrove and the Carolina assembly recognized Coosaponakeesa as politically useful to them. Though there is no direct evidence indicating as much, circumstantial evidence suggests that Musgrove wanted to conduct peace negotiations "with some of their headmen" specifically at Pon Pon where their relative Coosaponakeesa lived. [65] When the Creeks' reluctance to come so far into the Carolina settlements became apparent, however, Musgrove organized and outfitted a trade expedition bound for the Chattahoochee. Coosaponakeesa herself was never explicit as to her movements during this time, but we may imagine that she accompanied Musgrove to the Chattahoochee that summer. If not, it is clear that Coosaponakeesa was there in spirit.

Col. John Musgrove and trader Theophilus Hastings, who had been deputized by the Carolina government "to proceed to the Creek Indians," set forth on a formal mission of trade and diplomacy that June.[66] Musgrove's party of "twelve Englishmen and a negro" arrived in the waning days of July. Stopping first at the newly built Cussita town on the eastern side of the river, Musgrove and his men found that the locals wanted nothing to do with them and had indicated so when they raised a red flag in the town square—an unmistakable symbol of war. Musgrove decided to cross the river and proceed to Coweta.

At Coweta the leaders of the so-called pro-English "malcontents" gave Musgrove's party a hearty reception. Diego Peña, the Spanish officer then making his way toward Coweta, learned from informants that "all the malcontents rejoiced over their arrival." Given that months before Peña had noted that the vast majority of the malcontents were women, we may assume that the Coweta women played an important role in organizing the joyful reception.

Indeed. Singled out among the malcontents was a woman Peña referred to as the "Chieftainess Qua." While it is often assumed that Qua was Brims's wife, a chief's wife could not make claim to such a distinction due to the fact that she would not have been her husband's blood relative according to matrilineal rules. It may therefore be argued that Qua was Brims's eldest sister, making her the leading female authority of Coweta's ruling clan. Though the eighteenth-century Creeks generally did not honor their women as chieftainesses, such distinctions were commonly made throughout the Mississippian world and even in the seventeenth century among missionized peoples on the Georgia coast.[67] Qua's apparently elevated status, therefore, may be evidence of a vestigial practice whereby a woman of the ruling clan could be—and, in the past, were—recognized as chieftainess or, at the very least, a woman of influence.

Qua's actions suggest that she exercised a certain amount of authority in Coweta. At a time when Brims remained aloof, Qua boldly greeted Musgrove's party in the town square. As Peña's informants described it, she "opened her arms and with wailing and sighs celebrated their arrival." By doing so Qua necessarily pressured Brims and other Coweta headmen to accept the traders and make good on earlier promises to restore peace. Her exceptional display of emotion suggests, moreover, a personal connection to Musgrove or a member of his party. It would therefore not be implausible to suggest that Coosaponakeesa was in tow and that Qua was her mother or a closely related aunt of the same clan.

While Europeans tended to depict European-Indian diplomacy strictly as man's work, it is clear that Qua and Coosaponakeesa embodied the personal connection between Brims and Musgrove that the Creeks understood as a precondition for peace. As Peña later learned, it was then that "the leader of the English [was given] the daughter of the chief as wife." What Peña misunderstood, though, was that Coosaponakeesa was not Brims's daughter, but was the daughter of one of Brims's sisters, perhaps Qua herself. Nor was Coosaponakeesa given in marriage directly to Musgrove. Rather, it appears that she was betrothed to Musgrove's son Johnny by a Creek woman; they eventually wed when Coosaponakeesa became of marriageable age. An exchange of gifts completed the ceremony, with Musgrove bequeathing his wares to Brims and the Creeks giving Musgrove more than fifty deerskins, two horses, and an unspecified number of slaves.[68]

Clearly Brims, and possibly Musgrove as well, regarded the betrothal of Coosaponakeesa to Musgrove the younger as the critical episode that effectively bound the groups together according to the rules of kinship reciprocity. Diego Peña was made aware of the betrothal in absentia, being informed that Musgrove had placed his entire cache of trade goods, including "fine clothes, ribbons, beads, [and] two fine saddles" in Brims's personal storehouse. In return the English were allowed free access in Coweta, suggesting that intimate personal connections had been made. As Peña wrote, "[to] all this I give credence, for the reason that from the public house, where the English were housed, to that of the chief, is no more than fifty steps." "The said English," he added, could be observed "loitering with much laxity." So intimate were they, it was rumored that Musgrove's men and the Coweta women were entertaining each other's carnal desires, prompting Peña to speculate that the English "instigated a thousand indecencies which I will not bring to the attention of Your Lordship [Gov. Olivera y Fullana of Florida] because of their lewdness."[69]

Thus, through the exchange of presents and the marriage of the chief's "daughter" to the English leader, the Cowetas and the English had already cemented their relationship by the time Diego Peña arrived on the Chattahoochee in early September 1717. When a Sabacola headman informed him that "twelve Englishmen and a negro" were in the province, Peña grew increasingly distrustful of Brims and knew that he would have to work hard to cultivate Creek support for the Spanish.

Upon reaching Coweta on September 9, Peña first won an audience with Brims by presenting him with a plumed hat, dress coat, and stockings (all gifts from the governor of Florida). Brims, though undoubtedly pleased to accept Peña's gifts, was forced to listen as Peña scolded him for entertaining the Englishmen contrary to his promise of unilateral obedience to the king of Spain. Brims, seeking to deflect Peña's animosity, denied his complicity in the matter, stating that the English had come of their own free will to buy some horses.[70] Undeterred, Peña continued to press the Coweta chief, asking him to explain why he had so willingly let the enemy move about freely in his town while Peña was detained for several days in Sabacola. To this round of questioning Brims bowed his head and began to cry.

Brims may have been shedding crocodile tears for, after a short pause, he regained his composure and uttered words that summarized his growing conviction that the efforts of the Spanish and English to enforce a strict obedience upon his people was having a harmful effect: "He replied to me," wrote Peña, "that I was as white as were (the English) and that I should reach an agreement with the said English."[71] Historians have rightly seized upon Brims's words to demonstrate Brims's growing neutralist convictions.[72] But Brims's utterance goes much deeper than that; it suggests that the Indians were apprised of the peace accord signed by Spain and England in Utrecht in 1713. By urging Peña to reach an agreement, Brims was essentially telling the Europeans to abide by their own terms of peace and leave his people alone. Brims wanted no return to the military conflicts of Queen Anne's War, but instead a simmering detente under which his people might stand a chance of surviving.

The next morning the Lower Creek chiefs met with Peña in the Coweta town square, as Brims had requested the previous day. By agreeing to meet with Peña, Brims was clearly trying to placate the pro-Spanish interest and demonstrate to the pro-English malcontents that together they should steer a more neutralist course. By trying to please everyone, however, Brims appears to have succeeded in pleasing no one. The pro-English malcontents, for example, protested by refusing to attend the gathering, opting instead to secret away the English traders into Tallapoosa territory.[73] As a result, they were not on hand to receive Peña's gifts of cloth, ribbons, beads, knives, gunpowder, and rum.[74] Nor had Brims done enough to placate the pro-Spanish chiefs, particularly his kinsman Chipacasi. Chipacasi and his supporters openly mocked Brims's neutralist policies by bestowing the kiss of peace repeatedly upon Peña and personally distributing Peña's presents in the Coweta square. Brims, Chipacasi, and the Apalachee chief Adrian quarreled later that day, "of a character," Peña reported, "which became very serious." Chipacasi, it appears, sought permission to hand over to Peña the English traders (who were in hiding), while Brims wanted to keep them safe. That evening Chipacasi warned Peña not to trust Brims: "He [Brims] had two words," warned Chipacasi, "one he would say to me [Peña] and the other remain in his head."[75]

Sensing that Peña's presence was having an ill effect, the following day Chipacasi recommended that Peña "should get on the road" to avoid potential conflict with the malcontents. Yet regardless of how much Peña feared the malcontents, he remained determined to court Brims's favor by asking him to recommend a proper place to build the new Spanish fort in Apalachee. Brims, still committed to the restoration of Spanish influence in Apalachee, recommended that Peña send fifty men into the villages that were "most oppressed" and begged Peña to write letters of friendship to the commanders of Pensacola and Mobile. Chipacasi, continually wary of Brims's mixed motives, vowed to "give his life for the Spaniards" and hinted that it might be necessary to make war upon his "father" (Brims) if no agreement could be reached.[76]

Though Chipacasi was likely exaggerating the course of action that he might have taken against his kinsman, Peña's visit undoubtedly exposed the problems inherent in simultaneously conducting diplomacy with more than one European nation, particularly when his own relatives— Qua and Chipacasi—stood at opposite ends of the political spectrum. Brims, perhaps sensing that he was losing control over the diplomatic course he had initiated, tried to reassert control over the peace process through other means. First he sent his "second son," Ouletta, to Charles Town to make peace with Carolina's governing officials. Then he ordered Chipacasi once again to travel to Mobile, Pensacola, and St. Augustine to assure their leaders of his good faith and to certify that the Spanish built the fort as promised. By using his kinsmen as envoys, Brims ensured that his voice resonated in every European outpost in the Southeast and that his deputies, when they returned home, would be obliged to answer to him.

After Peña's hasty departure in mid-September, Brims wasted no time in appointing Ouletta and ten other men to proceed to Carolina. To guarantee Ouletta's safety, Brims appears to have detained Theo Hastings, who remained in Coweta as Brims's "slave." Col. John Musgrove, Brims's new son-in-law, escorted Ouletta's entourage to Charles Town, appearing there on November 6, 1717.

Ouletta's arrival, deemed an unmistakable sign of goodwill in Charles Town, prompted the Carolina Commons House of Assembly to officially open the trading path to Creek country the next day.[77] In the week that followed, the Indian and English parties hammered out several articles of peace and friendship that reflected their mutual desire to safeguard against future violence. Given that English and Indian notions of crime, punishment, and justice often diverged, it should come as no surprise that the negotiating parties devised a hybrid justice mechanism representing a middle ground between English and Indian ways. For their part the Creeks promised to shelter English traders in their white or beloved towns, which according to Creek custom were charged with harboring such threatened persons. They agreed to hand over anyone accused of murdering an Englishman so that that person could be punished according to the dictates of the English justice system.[78]

The Creeks, though, remembered the 1717 articles of friendship in quite a different way, reflecting their persistent concern over English encroachment on their hunting grounds. To address this potential source of dispute, the Creeks demanded that the Carolina government prohibit all English settlement south of the Savannah River. Later generations of English colonists conveniently tried to ignore this provision, particularly after the establishment of Georgia in 1733. Subsequent generations of Creeks, however, preserved the condition in their oral history, and by the middle of the eighteenth century the Carolinians' promise not to settle south of the Savannah River was common knowledge in Creek country.[79]

The Creeks' firm determination to prohibit English settlements south of the Savannah may indicate that by the time of the Yamasee War it had become obvious to Indian leaders that this new colony—Carolina— was somehow different from the atrophied colonies of the Spanish and French. By 1717 Indians would have observed that English traders had established contact with tribes west of the Mississippi, a clear indication of the trade regime's expansionist capabilities. Likewise, by 1717 Creeks and their neighbors had already witnessed the proliferation of rice plantations and the corresponding boom in English and especially African populations in the years following 1710.[80] The Creeks may have noticed that the now-vacant Yamasee lands were currently being surveyed and sold to aspiring English planters, an ominous sign of English expansion that continued throughout the century.[81]

While the Creeks viewed the articles of 1717 as a potential check against English encroachment, it appears that Ouletta's primary intent was to secure the release of several Coweta prisoners held in Cherokee country. Though English documents are largely silent about this transfer of prisoners, evidence suggests that traders such as Musgrove, Hastings, and Glover worked behind the scenes to secure the safe release of the prisoners. Given that the restoration of missing kindred—both the dead and the living—to their proper place was essential to restoring peace, Ouletta and Brims likely did not consider this element as only incidental to the peace process.

While Carolina officials believed that the agreement reached in Charles Town that November brought the "late warr" between themselves and the Creeks to an official end, Spanish sources indicate that the Indians saw nothing final in the agreement. However important the 1717 "treaty" between the Creeks and Carolina might have been for the development of the British empire's "Southern Frontier," the agreement represents at best only half the story.[82] Unbeknownst to officials in Charles Town, just as Ouletta and his men were making protestations of good faith to the English, Chipacasi was arriving in St. Augustine to again request that they build a fort in Apalachee.

Brims's decision to send Chipacasi to St. Augustine at the precise time that he sent Ouletta to Charles Town appears to have been intentionally designed to cultivate further the rivalry between the Spanish and the English and, perhaps more important, to assert control over the peace process. Brims likely knew that both Adrian and Chislacaliche had accompanied Peña on his return to St. Augustine. Both men remained there for three months waiting for the arrival of the ship carrying the *situado*. They hoped that when the *situado* arrived—if it did arrive—Governor Ayala would use those funds as promised to buy presents for the Indians and build the store and fort in Apalachee. Brims, aware that his recent friendly overtures to the English traders had alienated Peña, needed to make amends with the Spanish in order to guarantee that the Spanish would go forward with their plans to build the fort.

Fortunately, Brims's friends and neighbors in Cussita appear to have worked hard to rehabilitate his reputation in St. Augustine, thus preparing the way for Chipacasi's imminent arrival. Leading this effort was Sunicha, a "principal [man] of Casista," who with eleven of his own men arrived in St. Augustine on December 18 to explain that Brims was not the English sympathizer that Peña had made him out to be. A recent dispute with the English traders, Sunicha explained, had caused Brims to reassess his position and proclaim "he did not want a union with them." Sunicha, moreover, was quick to point out that the Creeks still held a grudge against the English for providing the Cherokees with arms and ammunition, thus making them complicit in the Cherokees' war against the Creeks. Sunicha boldly concluded that the entire province had raised the red flag against the English and sought only an alliance with Spain—a serious level of hyperbole indeed, given that Brims's own kinsman was in Charles Town and that his "daughter" was betrothed to an Englishman's son.[83]

Two days later, on December 20, Chipacasi arrived in St. Augustine after conducting diplomatic missions in Mobile and Pensacola to plead, yet again, with the Spanish governor to erect the proposed Apalachee fort. Like Sunicha, Chipacasi sought to mask the divisions within his own society, stating that he had come to speak not merely on his own behalf but on behalf of the entire province, "in the voice of his father and the great General Chislacaliche and in the name of the rest of the *caciques* and principales of the Province of Apalachicola . . . . together with the *cacique* Adrian." By linking his "father" to the most conspicuous leaders of the Spanish faction, Chipacasi restored Brims as the head of the Spanish-allied Indian confederation. It was a ploy that reaped great dividends, for the *situado* had in fact arrived on November 30. Ayala, convinced of Brims's sincerity, soon issued formal orders to begin construction of the long-anticipated Apalachee fort.[84]

The Coweta Resolution: The Invention of Neutrality

As the year 1717 came to a close, Creek leaders had accomplished two important goals: the reestablishment of the English trade and the planned erection of a Spanish fort in Apalachee. But this success was not carried out in a methodical manner, as evidenced by the development of contentious factions within Creek society and the apparent indecisiveness of its most prestigious leader, Brims. While it is tempting and to some extent justified to conclude that pro-Spanish and pro-English factions within Creek society were competing for the sentiments of the whole, underlying Creek foreign diplomacy at the time was a mistrust of all Europeans. Particular circumstances—the construction of a French fort among the Alabamas, occasional promises of a Spanish fort in Apalachee, the arrival of an English trading party, and the eventual ratification of a peace agreement—caused differing political sentiments to ebb and flow and produced the indecisiveness inherent to the period. Only in the opening months of 1718 did events unfold in a way that permitted Brims's people to conceive of neutrality as a viable solution to their peculiar diplomatic problems.

The year began with the arrival of a Spanish sloop at Santa Maria de Galve, the fort that guarded the shallow blue waters of Pensacola Bay. Aboard the ship were the seven chiefs who had recently made the voyage to Mexico City. On hand to receive their countrymen were numerous parties of "Cavetas and Talapuces," who convinced Gov. Don José de Torres to reciprocate by sending a Spanish official to their villages "to ratify the peace treaty and reaffirm the loyalty promised the King and their friendship promised the Spanish." In compliance with the Indians' request, the governor dispatched an adjutant, Don Juan Fernández de la Orta, and four members of the garrison to conduct this diplomatic mission.[85]

Orta's party departed from Santa Maria de Galve on January 24 and arrived at Tiguale, the southernmost Tallapoosa town, on February 26. Awaiting Orta's party was none other than "Emperor" Brims and his subordinate chiefs. On that day Brims conducted the usual ceremonies to renew the peace, complete with the solemn processions and accompanying merriment witnessed in St. Augustine the previous April. The fact that Brims would take the lead in conducting ceremonies in a town square other than his own suggests that his influence may have extended beyond Coweta, perhaps even to the Tallapoosa towns. The town square, after all, was the epicenter and symbol of the local *mico*'s power. That the *mico* of Tiguale deferred to Brims to conduct the ceremonies suggests that, when it came to matters of Spanish diplomacy, Brims was to be heard first.

Though Brims and his entourage welcomed the Spanish with ceremonies of friendship, Orta made a few diplomatic mistakes that cost him the valuable support he had received from the Coweta leaders. First he proposed that the Creeks should relocate their villages in the vicinity of Pensacola, suggesting that by doing so the chiefs might, under Spanish influence, "wield greater authority and become richer than the common people."[86] Such an offer likely appealed little to the Creek chiefs, or even to Brims, who knew that their people would never consent to such sub-jugation. Brims, in fact, responded coldly to the offer, stating only that he would "give answer later" on the subject.[87]

As if Orta had not already done enough to chill Brims's celebratory mood, Orta stumbled again by interceding in the Indians' own internal affairs in a way that challenged both Brims's and Chipacasi's political authority. Soon after discussing his kingdom's plans to relocate the In-dians to Pensacola, Orta explained that in Mexico City, the Marquis de Valero had appointed Tickhonabe, the Tallassee war captain, as "camp-master general (*maestro de campo*) over all the nations that were subject to the Emperor of Coweta." Tickhonabe had been honored with the title, Orta explained, "so that he might prevail on the emperor to hand over . . . whatever Christian slaves, Apalaches, or others who might be in his domain." In short, Tickhonabe was aggrandized specifically to exert pressure on Brims to release the slaves that had been living among his people (likely adopted relatives, spouses, or in-laws). Though the assembled Creeks promised to return the slaves, the fact that the meet-ing adjourned shortly thereafter suggests that the Creeks were hesitant to do so, just as the English traders had seen a few years earlier.

If Brims considered Tickhonabe to be a threat, however, his kinsman Chipacasi appears to have been most disturbed by Tickhonabe's eleva-tion to campmaster general. As Chipacasi explained to Orta at a private meeting held later that night, with the "acclamation of all the nations" Brims had named him, not Tickhonabe, to assume the office of *cacique*. Chipacasi added that he had refrained from exercising his authority, wishing instead to await the return of the delegation from Mexico City. Chipacasi went on to explain that "he was to assume office the following day," but that Tickhonabe's recent elevation to high office, presumably as Brims's second in command (Brims, recall, was named "generalissimo"), seriously placed his own status in jeopardy. In an effort to convince Orta that he was the true heir to Brims, Chipacasi explained that he had been given "the baton of Captain general" previously at St. Augustine, long before Tickhonabe. Moreover, sensing that Tickhonabe's new status as a Christian might have given him political leverage, Chipacasi explained that "he did not consider himself an infidel" because not only was his mother a "Christian woman from Apalache," but also because he himself was married to "another woman of the same nation and religion."

On the following day the Indians assembled under Brims's leadership conducted a ceremony in Tiguale that ritually dramatized the chain of command in their nation, much to the benefit of Chipacasi, who appears to have convinced the Spanish as well as the Indians to recognize his authority over Tickhonabe. As Orta explained, Chipacasi on that day "assumed office in the manner arranged by the Indians, and with as much formality as possible." Chipacasi, hoping to demonstrate before Orta his widespread support, asked his chiefs to state publicly what their stand would be in case of war. Much to Chipacasi's satisfaction, the assembled chiefs replied that "in any circumstance or occasion they would follow whomever he [Chipacasi] followed and go wherever he went."

Having established both Brims's and Chipacasi's authority, it was necessary nevertheless for Orta to acknowledge Tickhonabe's influence and honor him with an exalted yet subordinate title. In a ceremony soon after, Orta read the Marquis de Valero's investiture of Tickhonabe as campmaster general. But, to dramatize before the crowd that Chipacasi was in fact second in command, Orta placed Tickhonabe's *baton* in the hand of Chipacasi. Orta, of course, was well aware that this act dramatized Chipacasi's authority over Tickhonabe. "Making it clear that Chipacasi was second in command after the emperor," Orta explained, "he [Chipacasi] handed him [Tickhonabe] the rod of office, so that Tickhonabe might receive it from his hand, in the name of the King." Tickhonabe, then, was not to be Brims's successor, but "lord of the Tallapoosas."

It was probably no coincidence, then, that Brims chose to go with Tickhonabe to Tallassee (Tickhonabe's village), to celebrate the arrival of the new "lord of the Tallapoosas." Once again Brims appears to have conducted ceremonies in yet another Tallapoosa town, a likely sign that the close historic connection between the Tallassees and the Cowetas gave him some authoritative voice even as it pertained to the investiture of one of its leading warriors to a high office. But, while Brims was celebrating in Tallassee, a runner from Coweta arrived with the startling news that greatly influenced the shape of Creek diplomacy: thirty Englishmen had just arrived in Cussita seeking an audience with Brims. Startled by the size of the English delegation and unsure of their intentions, Brims and his companions first considered expelling or even killing them. Instead, Brims decided to return to their homes on the Chattahoochee, "to find out what the English were trying to do" before taking such a rash action. Brims and his entourage promptly set out for Coweta on the final day of February, arriving home on the Chattahoochee on the morning of

March 3, 1718. Shrewdly, Brims had convinced Orta to accompany him on this particular trek to prove to the English traders that he had friends and defenders in Spain and, as Orta appears to have believed, to cast them out. Once in Coweta, Brims sent a runner to the neighboring town of Cussita, where the Englishmen had been forcibly detained since their arrival, to inquire into the purpose of their visit.[88]

Brims's runner returned the same afternoon bearing the good news that their leader, John Musgrove, had returned from Charles Town with the eleven-man delegation sent to ratify the peace treaty several months ago. If that was not proof enough that the English had peaceful intentions, Musgrove had also secured the release of an unspecified number of "Cavetas prisoners" that the Cherokees had taken in war. This good news prompted Brims and his associates to reassess their initial (possibly feigned) hostility toward the English, thus paving the way for a lasting peace.[89]

The following day John Musgrove led an English delegation into the town of Coweta bearing a familiar white flag of peace. Musgrove, the likeliest Englishman to ratify the peace, broke a knife to dramatically symbolize that Carolina wished to end its war against Brims's people. Chipacasi, in turn, took out two arrows, one of which he broke to symbolize in Indian fashion that their war against the English was now over. The other arrow, however, he kept intact, laying upon it a blood-stained knife to signify that they remained at war with the Cherokees. Chipacasi then issued a stern warning to Musgrove: if the English aided their enemy in violation of the peace, without hesitation they would wage war against them as well.[90]

The symbolic display of the weapons between two men who had recently become relatives by marriage—not the so-called treaty of 1717—officially brought to a close a year of on-again, off-again peace negotiations with the English. Thus the Creeks and English could now turn their attention toward a matter of mutual interest: trade. So eager were the Creeks to resume trade that they quickly dispensed their entire cache of deerskins in a single day, paying five deerskins for a single yard of cloth. Orta, who observed the bartering in progress, humbly concluded that "had the English brought a greater quantity of goods, it would have gone just the same."[91]

Meanwhile, a French officer arrived in Coweta bearing even more good news: three vessels from France had arrived in Mobile, "loaded with exquisite objects" that the commander wished to dispense to

Chipacasi and his people. The French officer, a member of the garrison at the newly established Alabama fort, invited Chipacasi to visit Bienville at Mobile in order to smoke a peace pipe and receive gifts.[92] With the arrival of the French officer that day, the town of Coweta found itself as the host of representatives of all three competing European powers. On the one hand the situation might have been an ideal scenario for Brims, who could demonstrate before the English, French, and Spanish emissaries his impressive ability to maintain ties to their respective rivals. On the other hand, the arrival of envoys from the three European nations could threaten to inflame the same factional disputes that Peña's and Musgrove's arrival had triggered just months before—perhaps with even more serious consequences, because Brims now had two kinsmen with ties to different European powers. It would be necessary to foster the kind of political environment that would allow them to sustain or renew these friendships. The simultaneous arrival of the Europeans failed to spark a factional uprising, and instead sparked a discussion on foreign policy that had lasting influence on Creek diplomacy for generations to come.

In the week that followed the Europeans' arrival, Brims called a general meeting (*junta general*) of all the Indian nations in the town of Coweta. The purpose of the meeting was to decide once and for all how to resolve the competing demands of the English, Spanish, and French for the affections of his people. It is not known exactly who was invited or who attended this particular meeting, though circumstantial evidence suggests that all or most of the Lower Creek chiefs (eleven total) were involved.[93] Moreover, Brims's recent journey west hints that a number of Tallapoosas were also on hand.

It is abundantly clear, however, who did not attend the meeting: Chislacaliche, the great warrior who at one time rivaled Brims in authority and influence. Rather than remain in Coweta, Chislacaliche departed south toward Apalachee in order to meet with José Primo de Ribera, who had just arrived at the Tomole old fields to commence construction on the new Apalachee fort for which the Creeks had so assiduously lobbied. On March 18, while Ribera and his men were busy cutting wood, Chislacaliche and twenty other men arrived to warn Ribera that an important general meeting was about to take place. Chislacaliche wanted Ribera to return to signal to the others "the resolution that they did not want their [the English] friendship."[94] Sensing that his presence might influence the outcome of the meeting, Ribera left the fort's construction in the hands of a subordinate and departed with Chislacaliche that same day. After traveling three days, Ribera and company arrived in the town of Sabacola, where they chose to rest. Meanwhile, the chiefs assembled at Coweta, several leagues to the north, were deliberating about the future course of diplomacy with the three European nations.[95]

Had the native inhabitants of Creek country been a literate people in the early eighteenth century, and had they measured the passage of time according to the Gregorian calendar, it is probable that March 23, 1718, would have gone down as a proverbial red-letter day in the annals of Creek history. On that day a large delegation of chiefs from surrounding territories assembled in the council house of Coweta to discuss the proper course of action to take regarding their European neighbors. Should they submit solely to Spanish authority in accordance to the obedience they had sworn repeatedly in St. Augustine and Pensacola? Or, conversely, should they admit the English traders into their towns? Could they somehow simultaneously satisfy both powers? And what about the French? Where did they figure in in the imperial struggle for their affection and loyalty?

Undoubtedly the persons assembled in Coweta discussed these and many other questions pertaining to the Europeans. Although the Creeks had nearly one year of experience with triple-nation diplomacy upon which to draw, evidence indicates that they also drew upon the advice of outsiders when crafting their diplomatic positions. The Iroquois may have been one of those foreign groups, because Seneca and Mohawk diplomats began descending upon the Chattahoochee in the spring of 1717 to forge their own anti-Cherokee alliance. Although we will probably never know the tenor of their discussions with their Creek hosts, the fact that the initial peace overtures to the English occurred at the precise time of their visit suggests an Iroquois influence on the foreign policy decisions of Brims and his associates.

Specifically, the Iroquois would have been able to warn the Creeks of the dangers of siding too closely with one European power, and the apparent benefits of neutrality. They would have been able to relate, for example, how they themselves had been drawn into an alliance with the English in New York in 1676, when Gov. Edmund Andros employed Iroquois warriors to put down an uprising of Wampanoag Indians, a fight known as King Phillip's War. The Iroquois diplomats could have told their Creek hosts how the alliance proved beneficial at first but had soured over the course of the 1680s and 1690s as the English drew them into an imperial conflict between England and France known as King William's War (1689–1697). They would have been able to relate further how the war had produced political dissension at home, pitting Francophile, Anglophile, and Neutralist factions against one another for supremacy within the nation. They could have described their catastrophic losses in battle, both abroad against the Hurons and at home defending themselves against the incursions of French-backed Indians. Most important, they could have related their tentative solution to the military and political problems they encountered in 1701: signing treaties in Montreal and Albany in which they pledged to remain neutral vis-à-vis the French and the English in all future conflicts. The main benefit to this arrangement, as they must have argued, was the freedom it gave them to maintain their lucrative trade with the English.[96]

Not only could the Iroquois have persuaded the Creeks to chart a neutral course, but Valero, the viceroy of Mexico, may have had some influence to the same effect. According to Spanish chronicler Barcia, the viceroy had urged the Creeks not to harm the English and the French lest they disobey the direct order of the king. Although Creek leaders proved wary of accepting his advice on those grounds alone, Valero's advice became common knowledge after the return of the Mexico City delegation. Because later generations of Creek leaders preserved the viceroy's words as part of their oral tradition, Valero must be considered an important influence on public opinion throughout the whole of Creek country.[97]

Drawing upon their own experiences with the Europeans and heeding the advice of others, the Indian leaders assembled in Coweta that fateful day fashioned a diplomatic policy that colonial officials and subsequent historians called neutrality, and that shall be referred to in this discussion as the Coweta Resolution. Among the first to hear about this new resolution was José Primo de Ribera, who was still resting in Sabacola. According to Primo de Ribera, on March 23 an unidentified principal Indian arrived to greet him with the news that the meeting had drawn to a close. The result, the Indian man informed him, was "to live in friendship with us [the Spanish in St. Augustine and Apalachee], Pensacola, Mobile, and the said English, if by some accident one should commence war upon the other."[98]

Although Indians met to discuss important political affairs frequently throughout the eighteenth century, the *junta general* of 1718 was a meeting of a different magnitude. The conclusions reached therein—the

Coweta Resolution—gained greater currency with the passage of time and ultimately outlived its authors. Brims's descendants, some of whom achieved similar positions of prominence, frequently recited their kinsman's instructions "not to shed the blood of white men" when asked to participate in European conflicts. Brims, according to their memory, had instructed them not to do so because he hoped his descendants "would not see the day when one [European power] should dominate the others." When Europeans, most often the English, sought to enlist Creek support for their various military schemes, Creek leaders regularly refused, stating that they would "remain neuter" because they had no business "to interpose among the white men's quarrels."[99]

In the aftermath of the war, Carolina officials sometimes lamented their inability to exert political control over the Creeks. In particular they singled out Brims as the source of their frustrations, giving him the backhanded compliment that he was "as great a politician as any American Governor."[100] Justifiably so, for Brims had asserted firm control over the peace process and used his own kinsmen and a "daughter" as go-betweens to establish ties to the respective European powers, thereby curbing the factional disputes that threatened to divide his people. Though historians have likewise praised Brims for his Machiavellian cunning, evidence indicates that we have only begun to probe the depth of his and his people's political thought, not to mention the significance of the Coweta Resolution.

The present discussion indicates that over the course of time, Brims and his people became well informed about the intricacies of the transatlantic marketplace, producing knowledge that laid the foundation for their political policies. Brims's plan to pay Carolina slave traders "little by little . . . in other commodities," for instance, demonstrates that he understood the intricacies of debt refinancing and the need to skew their economy toward trade in furs rather than in Indian slaves. Moreover, Chipacasi and Chislacaliche's long sojourns in St. Augustine suggest that they were aware that Spain's system of financial support, the *situado*, was often unreliable. Their desire to build a fort in Apalachee to facilitate trade with Havana furthermore indicates an understanding of Spanish trade routes. The Creeks did not use the Yamasee War as an opportunity to end trade with Europeans permanently, but rather to tap into—or, in this case, recreate—friendlier trade networks.

If their knowledge of the transatlantic economy shaped their political thinking, however, the Creeks' ability to differentiate between the various European colonial systems demonstrates the true depth of their political understanding. European empires, as the Creeks learned by 1718, were not all alike. The English were clearly the most aggressive appropriators of land and potentially their most dangerous military foes. For these reasons the Creeks knew to prohibit English settlement on the south side of the Savannah River, yet allowed the French to build a post in the heart of their territory. The Creeks encouraged the Spanish to build a fort in Apalachee and at times appeared sympathetic to Spanish plans to send missionaries to the Chattahoochee. Such seemingly contradictory policies indicate that the Creeks first had to demonstrate to the English that they had other equally important European friends before they could safely allow English traders back into their towns.

While it stands to reason that the Creeks should have been well informed about matters close to home, their knowledge of affairs in Europe is doubly remarkable. Specifically, it is evident that the Peace of Utrecht signed in 1713 was looked upon in Creek country with suspicion. While England was at war with Spain, the Creeks had proven themselves useful in Carolina's wars against the Catholic powers. With that impetus removed, however, Carolina traders had no incentive to send them en masse against French or Spanish forts or against their Indian allies. Consequently, Carolina traders and government officials saw less reason to extend to the Creeks any favors, such as writing off accrued debts, which soon sent them running to the Catholic powers. Once contact with the Catholic powers had been established, however, Indian leaders such as Brims and Chipacasi saw the glaring inconsistencies of the Europeans' definition of peace that allowed them to use the Creeks to fight their imperial wars by proxy. The Creek solution was to avoid European entanglements altogether or, in other words, "live in friendship with [all Europeans] if by some accident one should commence war upon the other."

April 15, 1715, and March 23, 1718, are two dates that have received differential treatment in Southeastern and Creek history. Because of history's general fascination with warfare, not to mention its pervasive Anglocentrism, April 15, 1715, became forever etched in the memory of South Carolinians and historians of the Southern frontier as the tumultuous outbreak of the great Yamasee War. The Coweta Resolution of March 23, 1718, though less dramatic, remained alive in the memories of successive generations of Creeks and deserves equal attention as one of Southern history's decisive turning points. On that date the Creeks resolved upon a policy to turn European imperialism to their own advantage and slow Carolina's western expansion. If there is any truth to the dictum that warfare is politics carried out by military means, then the Yamasee War should be seen as the Creeks likely saw it: an exercise in international diplomacy.

CHAPTER FOUR

The Challenge of Triple-Nation Diplomacy

Several weeks after the Creek leaders agreed on a foreign policy to avoid European entanglements and harmonize the factional interests within the Creek nation—an agreement that came to be known as the Coweta Resolution—Brims headed south to explain this new resolution to his friends in Spanish Florida. Brims left in April 1718 with 150 other Creek men, and once there, met with José Primo de Ribera, who was supervising the construction of the Spanish fort at Tomole (formerly the site of an Apalachee mission town). It was probably no accident that in addition to the numerous assembled chiefs and warriors, Brims brought an uncounted number of women and children to the Spanish captain. As the Creeks knew, the presence of women at diplomatic talks usually helped dramatize peaceful intentions in a way that the more militaristic warriors could not. In bringing their children the Creeks demonstrated their trust in the Spanish to defend, protect, and perhaps indulge the most dependent and defenseless elements in Creek (or any) society. The encounter was not, then, simply a meeting between warriors and diplomats, but a family affair in which both sides might engage in a more casual exchange of words and gifts.

However much Brims might have desired to send a peaceful message, he could do little to prevent Primo de Ribera from drawing his own conclusions as to the true intent of the Coweta Resolution. Primo de Ribera, who had become apprised of the recent gathering in Coweta in late March, had lingered in Sabacola for a week pondering the accord's significance. Concluding that the resolution was little more than a diabolical scheme that violated the obedience that the Creeks owed to the Spanish king, Primo de Ribera left Sabacola in a huff on April 1 to return to his post in Apalachee.[1]

To put Primo de Ribera's skepticism at rest, Brims apologetically affirmed "the great love he had for us [the Spanish]," in spite of his proclamations of neutrality.[2] Brims, displaying a newly acquired assertiveness that was lacking in his earlier diplomatic undertakings, boasted to Primo de Ribera that his kinsman Chipacasi had recently met the French governor at Mobile and emphasized the latter's inclination to distribute presents liberally. The French governor, Brims added, recognized that his people were valuable and formidable allies whom they dared not cross lest Brims make war on the French "with all his people."[3] Patronizing, if not threatening, in tone, Brims's apology did little to endear him to Primo de Ribera; Brims also did not succeed in convincing Primo de Ribera of his great love of the Spanish. Sensing that the Creeks had come merely to solicit food and presents, Primo de Ribera concluded that Spanish attempts to draw the Creeks away from the English would come to naught, reflecting a growing realization within the Florida government that "little confidence can be placed on their [the Creeks'] friendship."[4]

While it might come as no surprise that the Coweta Resolution strained the Creeks' relationship with Spain, more than a few of Brims's putative Indian allies likewise reacted coolly to the agreement. Adrian, the Apalachee chief who had been living among Brims's people, immediately decided "to gather all his people and move them to the [Spanish] fort," evidently in protest. Likewise, a group of Yamasees living near Chislacaliche's people at the Chacato old fields immediately packed their belongings, loaded their corn in boats, and moved to a settlement near the new fort. These Yamasees, it appears, had recently engaged in a heated verbal exchange with the Uchises, a dispute likely rooted in the Coweta Resolution. "They will say no more hostile words," a Spanish messenger related, "for fear of upsetting the Uchises." The Yamasees, he added, vowed "to die together with the Spaniards," a clear indication that they wanted little to do with the Uchises' brand of triple-nation diplomacy.[5]

As these events foreshadowed, the plan of peaceful coexistence that was set forth in the Coweta Resolution, though appealing in the abstract, presented the resolution's chief architect with a variety of challenges that made it difficult to implement in the decade that followed. Later generations of Creeks, of course, waxed romantically about the wisdom of the venerable ancestors who crafted the peace policy, with Brims's descendants being most inclined to invoke the author's ancient wisdom. Later still, at least one modern historian has dubbed the aftermath of the Yamasee War "the great period of the Emperor Brims" in an attempt to show how Brims artfully applied the policy of neutrality and how he helped to further the development of the "Creek Confederacy."[6] Though Brims rightly deserves credit for his political acumen, a more realistic assessment of the period suggests that Brims's neutrality policy did not immediately gain wide acceptance in places such as Charles Town or St. Augustine. Nor did it immediately harmonize the competing factions within his own nation. Brims spent the twilight of his life struggling hard to make the Europeans accept his multilateral diplomacy and, perhaps even harder, to retain a measure of control over competing Creek factions.

The English were primarily responsible for making the Coweta Resolution difficult to implement, and peace came with certain burdensome conditions. They ordered the Creeks to revenge themselves upon the Yamasees, who continued to wage a guerrilla-style war on the Carolina frontier. At the same time, Carolina officials exerted pressure on the Creeks to accept a peace settlement with the Cherokees so as to facilitate the restoration of the lucrative deerskin trade. However desirable from Carolina's perspective, many Creeks steadfastly resisted implementing these demands. Killing the Yamasees and embracing the Cherokees demanded that the Creeks forego their own notions of kinship, justice, and revenge. As many Creeks had intermarried with the Yamasees and considered themselves to be one people, at least in a metaphoric sense, the obligation to kill the Yamasees would have required them to commit to a fratricidal war. Conversely, to cease hostilities against their Cherokee enemies demanded that they ignore the laws of blood vengeance. Though inclined to ignore them, the Creeks could not easily disregard English demands because the Carolina traders remained the principle link to the new economy developing in the Southeast and exerted disproportionate influence over economic affairs. The Creeks of necessity implemented their brand of triple-nation diplomacy in a way that gave it a distinct tilt toward the English.

Adding to the difficulty of the Coweta Resolution's implementation was the decentralized nature of Creek kinship politics. Brims, it should be recalled, had never demanded that the towns under his influence forge a unified foreign policy. Rather, the Coweta Resolution permitted and even encouraged individual chiefs and warriors to develop their own political networks with one, or perhaps several, of the European powers, as they saw fit. In theory it was sound policy. In practice, however, certain individuals, aided and abetted by European supporters, built influential political followings and thus undermined Brims's traditional influence over foreign affairs. The decade following the venerable Coweta Resolution did not usher in the great period of Emperor Brims but instead witnessed the gradual erosion of Brims's influence and the proliferation of Creek political factionalism. In the long run, though, the Coweta Resolution nevertheless bore fruit as it enabled the Creeks to gain a measure of autonomy that a previous generation had not enjoyed.

A Rival on the Chattahoochee

In the several years that followed the restoration of peace in 1718, Brims's position as the leading man of the Creek nation remained unchallenged due to the respect he commanded among his own people, not to mention the favor he found in Charles Town and St. Augustine. The leaders in Charles Town in particular went to considerable lengths to concentrate Creek authority under Brims by commissioning him the headman of the Creek Indians and naming Brims's kinsman Ouletta as his heir. To help Brims monopolize the diplomatic channels between Creek country and Charles Town, in July 1722 Francis Nicholson, Carolina's first royal governor, gave Ouletta two metal plates inscribed with the royal arms: one for Brims and the other for anyone he might appoint to carry his "talk." The plates, Nicholson explained, would "give credit" to the veracity of any words coming from the nation, thereby making Brims's voice the only legitimate one.[7]

It would be an exaggeration, of course, to suggest that Brims was simply the creature of the British commissions that made him headman. Carolina's official policy at the time was to grant commissions "only to such Head Men as shall be voluntarily chosen and recommended by the Indians themselves," making it likely that Brims's own people readily consented to his exalted status.[8] Commissions were, after all, little more than pieces of paper; at best they were imperfect devices for inserting English influence over Native political systems or policy.

Yet given the almost universal recognition of Carolina's economic, political, and military power, many aspiring Creek leaders eagerly sought the British commissions as a way of enhancing their authority. Aspiring chiefs and warriors, for example, may have used the commissions as a symbolic marker of their contact with the colonies. For centuries Southeastern chiefs had hoarded exotic items to symbolize their connection to the outside world and their mastery of a wide array of esoteric knowledge. Because English commissions were exotic in their own way—cryptically encoded in an alien Roman script—they fit nicely into a centuries-old pattern of symbolic display.[9]

On a more practical level, the commissions gave Creek headmen tangible powers such as the right to speak as legitimate voices in Charles Town and to appoint friends and family members to subordinate positions of authority. In this sense English commissions granted individuals certain privileges that were worth having. Legal privileges, as customs backed by the sanction of tradition, were nothing new to the Creeks, of course. Creek men filled a variety of heritable civil and military offices that remained the property of particular families. Like the more traditional offices, Creek leaders began treating the English commissions as heritable property by passing their British-appointed titles from one generation to the next.[10] In time the English commissions acquired a similar veneer of tradition.

In this way English commissions became an inextricable part of the Creek political fabric. Because government-appointed agents ultimately determined who received the commissions, Carolina was able to exert a measure of hegemonic control over Creek political leaders whose authority was to some extent dependent upon the good favor—in the form of gifts—they received in Charles Town. In this sense Native and colonial politics became closely intertwined to the point of blurring the distinction between the two. What made Carolina's system of control possible, of course, was the fluid, localized nature of Creek politics. Though the Carolinians tended to commission only those who had been voluntarily chosen by the Indians themselves, determining which Indians did the choosing at times could be open to interpretation. When particular chiefs proved to be unreliable allies to the English, more amenable souls were usually waiting in the wings.

One individual who seized this opportunity was a Cussita war captain named Cusabo. It is fitting that a headman from Cussita challenged Brims, since Cussita ranked among the most prominent Lower Creek towns and was an ancestral home to Coweta. Soon after the Yamasee War Cusabo received notice from Carolina that he would be one of two men assigned to negotiate trade prices in 1718, a service for which the Carolina government awarded him one hatchet.[11] Three years later Cusabo appeared again, this time to discuss certain proposals for trade reform and to join Brims as a chief negotiator, an indication, perhaps, of his rising influence among the Lower Creeks.[12]

As it happened, Cusabo's rising influence came at an opportune time, for both Carolina and Cusabo. For several years Carolina had showered favors upon Brims and his kinsman Ouletta but, in the opinion of some Carolina leaders, had received little in return. Brims had not, in their view, done enough to support Carolina's guerrilla war against the Yamasees living near St. Augustine. Nor had he been able or willing to control his own people, some of whom committed occasional hostilities on Carolina's southern frontier. Rumors even suggested that the Creeks, acting in concert with Spain and the Yamasees, were drawing up plans to attack Fort King George, which Carolina had recently established near the mouth of the Altamaha River. As the Carolinians saw it, then, it was time to seek influence elsewhere among the Creeks. Governor Nicholson appointed Theophilus Hastings as the new Creek agent and ordered him to "go from town to town" and persuade the Creeks to turn on the Yamasees.[13]

Hastings established his agency among the Creeks late that summer but found few volunteers to spill Yamasee blood. By January 1723 the Commons House resolved to wield the only authority it had over the Creeks—withholding of trade—by withdrawing all traders from the Chattahoochee and requiring that they do business only from the safer confines of Fort Moore on the Savannah River.[14] In June, Carolina authorities placed a complete trade embargo upon the Chattahoochee towns, bringing five years of uninterrupted barter to a halt.[15]

By imposing the embargo the Carolina council hoped to show the Lower Creeks that their failure to fight the Yamasees would have dire economic consequences. Whether or not the embargo had its intended effect is open to interpretation. Evidence indicates that a few enterprising traders continued to operate illegally from the forks of the Altamaha River.[16] Unquestionably, though, the trade embargo coincided with the formation of several pro-English factions who were willing to spill Yamasee blood in order to restore the trade.

As the trade embargo went into effect, Cusabo began to take advantage of his relationship with Hastings, who undoubtedly had made Cusabo's acquaintance several years before. Cusabo had discussed trade reform with Hastings and Brims two years earlier, and circumstantial evidence suggests that Cusabo also had ties to several traders operating illegally at the forks of the Altamaha River. Although we cannot entirely verify Cusabo's political connections or motives, Cusabo's close ties to Hastings and other traders clearly predisposed him to be in favor of the English trade regime. Cusabo, one trader reported, believed that "they must in a short time be our friends [to the Carolinians] or else they would all be cut off."[17]

Unwilling to be cut off from English trade, in March 1723, at Hastings's bidding, Cusabo led a war party against the Yamasees living five leagues from the Spanish garrison at San Marcos, killing one man and capturing one woman. Cusabo might have been more successful had not some of his own people arrived ahead of him to warn the Yamasees of the impending attack. Cusabo and his men found the Yamasee town largely unpopulated and most of its inhabitants safely ensconced within the walls of Fort San Marcos.[18]

Although Creek runners friendly to the Yamasees were able to mitigate Cusabo's effectiveness on that particular occasion, the Cussita warrior's exploits were enough to generate a great deal of animosity among the people living on the Chattahoochee. Writing from Cussita that spring, Hastings reported that "there is a great deal of confusion amongst them about what is to be done, especially by those that are the Yamasees and Spaniards friends." As the instigator of the confusion, Hastings candidly had to admit that "my life is privately in danger." Cusabo's daring, however, appears to have emboldened the people of Cussita. "The Cussitoes," Hastings wrote, "says that as their town people has struck the blow, they will stand to it, and hopes that your excellency will encourage them in it."[19] Hastings promptly delivered his message to Charles Town by way of two Cussita men, who the council summarily rewarded with presents of clothing, powder, shot, paint, and a small English flag—all earmarked for the town of Cussita—to prove that fidelity to the English had its advantages. Hastings, not incidentally, received a reward of one hundred pounds for Cusabo's exploits.[20]

By earmarking such a large cache of presents in the midst of an embargo, Carolina solidified its relationship with the town of Cussita and widened the breach between it and Coweta. Predictably, the Cowetas—Brims and Ouletta in particular—began to fear that Cussita was becoming too influential. Seeking to put the pretentious Cusabo in his place, Brims and Ouletta countered Cusabo's "good talks" by circulating "bad talks" designed to shed unfavorable light on the Carolina regime. On June 5, 1723, for example, Ouletta returned to Charles Town, and during his stay received the governor's talk as well as two commissions that Nicholson ordered him to deliver to two Tallapoosa headmen, Oulatchee of Tuckebatchee town and Etchachawee of Oakfuskee.[21] That Nicholson employed Ouletta to deliver the commissions to Oulatchee, a Tallapoosa, and to Etchachawee, an Abika, suggests that Coweta's leaders still retained their traditional right to name subordinate headmen in their vaguely defined nation. Nicholson's strategy suggests that he too continued to recognize and support Brims's and Ouletta's claims as the principal "mouths" of the Creek nation.

On his return home, though, Ouletta happened upon several Cussita headmen who were then on their way to meet Nicholson. Ouletta, jealously guarding his right to carry talks to Charles Town, tried to persuade the four Cussita men to return home, stating that the governor "did not give a streight talk" and that certain English captains "were for knocking them in the head." Ouletta's alarming remarks convinced one of the four men to return with him to Brims's "cowpen" near Coweta, where Brims had assembled his "beloved men" to deliver a stern speech against the English. Directing his remarks at Cusabo, the "emperor" warned his listeners that "there would soon be war with the English," and advised them "to build forts in the most proper places."[22]

Brims's harsh words failed to cause Cusabo and his warriors to change their plans to carry out attacks against the Yamasees. Later that summer Cusabo attacked a Yamasee delegation that had come to Coweta to talk peace, killing one man and taking another prisoner. As if to add salt to Coweta's wounds, the Cussita warriors began a war of words to counter Brims's bad talks, sarcastically telling important Coweta warriors that they were looked upon as old women in Charles Town and reminding them that only they, the Cussitas, were allowed to trade with the English.[23] That the episode did not spark a fratricidal war between the Cowetas and Cussitas is a testament to the Cowetas' self-restraint. Not only did the attack occur in Coweta, but it is likely that the Yamasees had friends and relatives in that town, thus obliging the Cowetas to avenge the dead Yamasee man. Why the Cowetas chose not to fight their neighbors is open to interpretation. It was better, perhaps, to forego their responsibility to exact revenge than to start a cycle of violence with their neighbors across the river. Had the Cowetas turned on the Cussitas, the Carolina traders would surely not have returned any time soon.

By eagerly commencing the war against the Yamasees, by midsummer Cusabo had effectively placed Brims, Ouletta, and other Coweta headmen on the defensive. Though Brims still retained the preeminent title of headman, it had become clear that Cusabo could pull strings in Charles Town. Brims's people, the Cowetas, were forced to endure a trade embargo that left them short of gunpowder, shot, and other necessities for months to come. Cusabo's people, in contrast, received special favors from the Carolinians and exploited this privileged connection to build a wider following. Cusabo, moreover, continued to use his new-found influence to recruit accomplices among the Tallapoosas and Abikas, thus spreading the factionalism that Brims's neutrality was designed to contain.

The Upper Creeks Turn on Coweta

Thanks in part to Cusabo's actions, Brims's political problems did not stay confined to Cussita. Cusabo had been making occasional trips to the west, during which he secured promises from the Tallapoosas to attack the Yamasees on behalf of Carolina.[24] Why the Tallapoosas and later the Abikas chose to attack the Yamasees—both of which seemed to be in compliance with the demands of the Carolina government— is difficult to explain with any certainty. Perhaps the Upper Creeks had fewer friends and relatives among the Yamasees and therefore had fewer reasons to protect them. Indeed, the element of revenge cannot be entirely discounted. Many Creeks appear to have blamed the Yamasees for beginning a war that exposed them to the wrath of the Carolinians and threw their lives into disarray. Also significant is Brims's apparent sway among some of the Upper Creek towns. Though they had deferred to his voice in the past, some Upper Creek leaders may have come to believe that for political and economic reasons it was time to assert themselves. By assisting the Carolinians, the Upper Creeks had earned distinction among the leaders in Charles Town and had kept trade goods flowing into their villages.

Cusabo's effort to recruit Tallapoosa warriors, however, did not escape the notice of Brims and Ouletta, who began countering their Cussita nemesis by sending a series of scathing bad talks of their own to the Tallapoosa and Abika towns. Their blunt message was that the English talk was "rotten at the root."[25] Among those to hear and reject their message was Oulatchee of Tuckebatchee, who remained skeptical of Brims's motives. Oulatchee believed that Brims's bad talks threatened to upset their growing relationship with Carolina, a relationship that both sides had worked hard to mend in recent years. Concluding that Brims had stifled the talk, Oulatchee and other Upper Creek headmen resolved to assist the Carolinians and began making plans to go against the Yamasees that fall.[26]

Because the Upper and Lower Creeks communicated frequently, news that Oulatchee had resolved to set out against the Yamasees spread quickly to Coweta. Brims, apprised of Oulatchee's resolve to shed Yamasee blood, responded by declaring Oulatchee and his warriors enemies and threatening "to kill him if he [Oulatchee] should kill the Yamasees." Although hesitant at first to leave their villages exposed to Cherokee attacks, not to mention reprisals from the Cowetas, two-hundred Tallapoosa warriors set out against the Yamasees that September only to find that the "Yufaulas" living nearby had apprised the Yamasees of their approach. As a result, the Tallapoosas found the Yamasee villages deserted and killed only one stray woman before returning home.[27]

The Tallapoosas' initial expedition against the Yamasees, though rather insignificant in terms of its bloodletting results, marks the beginning of a growing rift between the Lower Creeks and their Tallapoosa and Abika neighbors to the west, a rift that spread well beyond Oulatchee's sphere of influence. Another instigator of the Tallapoosa war effort was none other than Tickhonabe, the head warrior of Tallassee who six years earlier had traveled to Mexico City on Brims's behalf. Tickhonabe's insubordination proved to be especially troubling for Brims in light of Tickhonabe's and his people's close ties to Coweta.[28]

By leading the war against the Yamasees in the fall of 1723, Tickhonabe distanced himself and his people from the anti-English militancy of Brims and the Chattahoochee towns, scoring political points with Carolina in the process. Naturally the Carolina government looked favorably on Tickhonabe's actions, and in June 1724 the Commons House rewarded him with a handsome English military suit and a diverse assemblage of gifts. Brims and the Lower Creeks, in revenge, placed a bounty on Tickhonabe's head and repeated their threats to declare the Tallapoosas enemies. To some observers it appeared that the Cowetas and Tallapoosas shared little common political ground.[29]

The Beloved Men

Despite the growing fault lines that the Yamasee problem carved across Creek country, the nation at large remained united in its pervasive fear of the Cherokees, who had not ceased their attacks on the Creeks since the murders in Tugaloo in 1716. Added to that fear was a simmering mistrust of the English, whom the Creeks still accused of providing munitions and intelligence to the enemy. The Creeks thus naturally directed much of their animosity toward Carolina's Cherokee traders, who were responsible for supplying the enemy, usually at bargain prices. The simmering hatred for the Cherokee traders finally boiled over in November 1724 when a Creek war party said to consist of two hundred men attacked John Sharp's trading store near the Cherokee town of Tugaloo. The attackers, led by an Upper Creek warrior nicknamed "Gogell Eyes," fired their muskets on Sharp's house and, after stripping him naked and beating him, confiscated his entire stock of trade goods.[30]

The assault on Sharp, combined with fresh reports that the Spanish and French were seeking to unite the tribes in a war on Charles Town, prompted Carolina officials to launch a comprehensive diplomatic campaign between 1725 and 1728, appointing two men on three separate occasions to serve as Carolina's Creek agents—"beloved men," in Indian parlance. Their ambitious intent was to end the Cherokee-Creek war, stifle Spanish and French influence, and settle, once and for all, the Yamasee problem. In many ways Carolina's beloved men met with much success, first by bringing the Creek-Cherokee war to an apparent end, and second by eliminating the Yamasees as a military threat. In accomplishing these goals, however, the beloved men opened new wounds that further promoted Creek factionalism.

The diplomatic campaign officially began in June 1725 when Carolina officials commissioned Tobias Fitch as Carolina's Creek agent. Fitch's mission was to spend four months among the Creeks to obtain satisfaction for the attack on Sharp, to propose a peace settlement with the Cherokees, and to induce the Creeks to exterminate the Yamasees. While most historians have mined Fitch's 1725 agency journals to demonstrate the tenuous relationship that then existed between the Creeks and the English, the journal also betrays a notable rift between the Upper and Lower Creek towns. At Oakfuskee, for example, Fitch pleaded with the Abikas and Tallapoosas to pay for the goods stolen from Sharp's store and to end their war against the Cherokees. Fitch emphasized the need to avenge the assault on Sharp because it was rightly assumed that an

Upper Creek headman had instigated the attack. By scolding Gogell Eyes before his peers, Fitch extracted a confession from the repentant chief and received promises from Tallapoosa and Abika headmen to pay for the goods. Significantly, Fitch did not feel compelled to discuss the Yamasee problem, since most people—including Fitch—agreed that the upper peoples had done their fair share to bring the Yamasees to justice in recent months.[31]

Once in Coweta, in contrast, Fitch adjusted his line of argument to fit a decidedly different and more hostile political climate. The Yamasees, Fitch noted, had friends or relations among the Cowetas, which made them reluctant to make war on them and hostile to those who did. Fitch found, for example, that the Chattahoochee towns were particularly angry at Tickhonabe, the Tallassee warrior who fought against the Yamasees on behalf of the English the previous fall. Knowing that Brims had earlier threatened Tickhonabe's life, Fitch defended him publicly in the Coweta square and stated that "Tickhonabe has done very well in following our King's orders and if you want satisfaction its of our king that you must seek it." Fitch added that "I am ready to answer [for] everything my king has ordered Tickhonabe to do."[32]

Fitch's journals expose the rift between the Tallapoosas and Cowetas and illustrate the growing political rivalry between Coweta and Cussita. On one occasion, for example, a Spanish soldier on a diplomatic mission from St. Augustine brought an escaped Carolina slave to the Coweta town square. Fitch urged Brims to hand over the slave so that he could be returned to his original owner. Brims refused to do so at first, causing Fitch to bring one hundred Cussita warriors to Coweta to influence the recalcitrant chief. The warriors' show of force, giving further proof that the Cussitas were greater friends to the English king, enabled Fitch to wrest the slave away from Brims. Toward the conclusion of this uncomfortable episode Fitch scolded the Cowetas, stating that "the reason I brought these [Cussitas] is because our king has always had a better character of them than you." An angry Brims responded that "as to the Cussitas being your best friends, I know the reason of it, but I should be glad if you would show me one instance where the Cussitas has expressed their friendships in better terms than we have done."[33]

At the root of this general intertown rivalry was a heated contest for the English commissions that named particular individuals as headmen in the nation. Brims had held that office among the Lower Creeks beginning in 1722, and had named his younger kinsman Ouletta as his heir. By 1725, however, Brims and his family were in danger of losing their exalted position among the English. Not only had Cusabo and the Cussitas gained influence in Charles Town but several months before Fitch's arrival Ouletta died near St. Augustine while trying to capture some Yamasee prisoners. Brims found himself without an heir that was answerable to the English and was therefore forced to make concessions to keep the headman commission in the family.[34]

Though certainly mourning the loss of his kinsman, Brims used the opportunity of Fitch's arrival that July to lobby for a suitable replacement, urging Fitch to name Chipacasi in Ouletta's place. Chipacasi, Brims confessed, was a rather unusual choice since he "has not been your Friend a great while but rather a Friend to the French and Spaniards." Ouletta's murder had caused Chipacasi recently to change his mind about the Yamasees, leading Chipacasi to pledge his friendship (if only briefly) to the English. Brims, hoping to keep the English commission securely in the hands of Coweta's ruling clan, had little choice but to name Chipacasi to the position, admitting that "there is not [one] left of my family but Chipacasi who is fit to take upon him the charge that I have." Brims's people must have generally agreed to the decision, because Brims explained that "its the general opinion of the people that he should [receive the commission]."[35]

If general opinion among the peoples living on the Chattahoochee held that Chipacasi should succeed Brims as headman, things may have been seen in a different light in Charles Town, not to mention in Cussita. On August 24 the Grand Council aggravated the investiture question by granting both Chipacasi and Cusabo a commission, thereby giving the two an equal voice in Charles Town. Fitch probably received the two commissions from the hands of a runner in September, giving one of them to Cusabo sometime before the end of the month.[36]

Curiously, however, Fitch did not deliver the commission to Chipacasi at that time. Instead, Fitch pocketed the commission for several months, implying that he would give it to Chipacasi only if Chipacasi went out and waged war against the Yamasees. In late September Brims learned of Fitch's action and called Fitch before him to discuss the commission controversy. Brims began by recounting to Fitch a set speech that Chipacasi had left behind, indicating his intentions to go to war. Though Chipacasi may have been willing to kill a Yamasee in revenge of Cusabo, his talk betrays his principal motivation to please Fitch and to "show you that I am really your friend and not the Spaniards nor

French." Chipacasi hoped that by pleasing Fitch he might receive the commission, humbly asking Fitch to leave it with his "father" (Brims), while he was away.[37]

After delivering Chipacasi's statement Brims expressed his dismay over Fitch's apparent breach of tradition, a tradition that had granted Brims the exclusive right to name his own subordinates. "I do not know the meaning that your King has Left [off] his former customs," Brims began, "for there was never a head man made here but such as I would recommend to your king." Lamenting the loss of his exclusive power to appoint warriors to commissioned offices, Brims added that "now any young Fellow that goes down and tells a fine story, gets a commission and they come here and they are head men."[38]

It has been argued that Brims's words betray the emergence of generational conflict in Creek country.[39] True, perhaps, but evidence indicates instead that Brims may have directed his complaint at the Cussitas in general and at Cusabo in particular. Brims argued further, for instance, that the Cussitas had also proved themselves to be fickle allies and "would not one man go out" when he ordered them to accompany Chipacasi against the Yamasees. Fitch dismissed Brims's accusation as typical Indian behavior, stating that "[a]s for my King appointing improper men to be head men, I know not how you can blame him, for these very Cussitas when they are down with our King tell him they will go to war with our enemies and if they will talk straight there and throw the talk away when they come here I know not how my king can help that." "Most of you" Fitch added, "are of one mind this day and another the next."[40]

Though Brims and Chipacasi may have been sincere in their words, it is reasonable to suspect Chipacasi's so-called expedition to "kill and destroy all the Yamasees they meet" may have been staged in order to pry the commission from Fitch's hands. Brims was careful to lower Fitch's expectations so that Chipacasi might receive the commission even if he failed to bring back a scalp: "Whether they shall have any success I cannot tell," Brims cautioned, adding that the Squire *mico* of Ocmulgee had sent runners ahead to warn the Yamasees of the warriors' approach.[41] When the warriors returned to Coweta on December 2, Chipacasi lamented that they had met with poor success in their campaign against the Yamasees, making Brims's earlier prediction a self-fulfilling prophesy. Chipacasi urged Fitch not to worry, and promised that this was simply the beginning of a great war. "Next time," Chipacasi predicted, they would have better luck, adding that "there shall not one [Yamasee] stay on this land."[42]

To demonstrate further his allegiance to the English, Brims made sure to inform Fitch that some of his warriors had lost their lives, hoping that this would be taken as evidence they were willing to die for the English cause. Fitch took note of the Cowetas' loss of warriors but seemed a bit skeptical that they had fallen in battle. "Its a wonder to me," Fitch mused before the assembled crowd, "that they did not do you a greater deal more Damage." If the Cowetas really wanted to prove that they were making a good faith effort to rout the Yamasees, Fitch recommended punishing the Squire *mico* for tipping them off, adding that "among us [English] such a man would be tied to four mad horses and driven to pieces" for committing such an act of treason.[43] Most likely Brims did not want to punish the Squire *mico*, as the *mico*'s espionage activities meshed well with Brims's and Chipacasi's desire to feign an all-out war with the Yamasees.

Reluctantly, Fitch nevertheless parted with the commission on that day, making Chipacasi the official commander in chief of the nation under Brims's direction. Fitch explained that the commission required him "to take all orders that shall come from my king," and, if he proved true to the English, "all men in this nation is to pay the said Chipacasi due obedience." Chipacasi, grateful that he had won this test of wills, thanked Fitch "with a streight heart" and promised to put the commission "in execution."[44]

As further evidence that Chipacasi's forays against the Yamasees were staged to provide apparent proof of his fidelity, Spanish sources indicate that shortly after Fitch left the nation on December 2, Chipacasi returned to St. Augustine and offered peace with the Yamasees and the Spanish. On January 29, 1726, several weeks after Fitch's departure, Chipacasi and several principal *caciques* arrived in St. Augustine to give obedience to the Spanish king and to guarantee peace between themselves and the "Christian Indians of this jurisdiction." If there had in fact been a breach between Chipacasi the Yamasees, it could not have been a particularly serious one. Given the timing of Chipacasi's visit, it is likely that he did not spend the previous fall killing Yamasees but rather in making peace overtures to them.[45]

In fact, the zeal with which Chipacasi and Brims sought to make amends with the Spanish and Yamasees indicates that their political sentiments had become increasingly pro-Spanish after Fitch's visit. Clearly

Brims and many of the Lower Creeks had come to mistrust the English for setting Cussita and Upper Creek warriors against the Yamasees. In addition, the Spanish were prone to recognizing rather than challenging Brims and Chipacasi's authority. For this reason Chipacasi's head was filled with grand schemes for a more Hispanic Southeast, one over which he would exercise greater authority. He argued, for example, that if the province of Apalachee could be peopled with Spanish families, they would be able to procure other infidel nations in their service to "cast off the injuries of the English and French" and propagate the Holy Catholic faith.[46] Though not explicitly stated, Chipacasi may have been baptized during his stay, as implied by his stated zeal to promote Christianity and his attempt to have Brims join him in baptism.

After rendering obedience in St. Augustine, Chipacasi and his attendants went to Fort San Marcos near the Gulf Coast to better guarantee the peace agreement. Chipacasi probably remained there for several months awaiting his aging kinsman, who he hoped would "come back to the holy faith." Brims finally arrived in San Marcos sometime before May in the company of "his sons and many other chiefs and principal men of his province" to ratify the peace and render obedience to Spain in the names of all the towns he governed. He promised to defend the Florida Indians—no doubt the Yamasees—"from the war that different nations have made, fomented by the English of Carolina." Evidence indicates that Brims, too, may indeed have been baptized at that time.[47]

By April, Carolina officials had learned of Brims's and Chipacasi's activities, concluding that the Spanish and French were actively courting the Creeks with their evil designs to attack Fort King George and Charles Town itself. To assert Carolina's demands more forcefully, the Carolina government once again ordered Fitch to return to Creek country as its agent.[48] On August 1, 1726, Fitch arrived in Coweta only to find Brims recently returned from Florida with some molasses, pipes, and a few Spanish pieces of eight. To his delight, though, Fitch learned that three towns—Cussita, Yuchi Town, and Osuche (King Hott's Town)—refused to go to Florida to ratify the peace accord, an indication that the fissures then existing between Coweta and Cussita had spread. When a Yamasee peace delegation arrived during Fitch's tour, these same three towns refused to meet with them, even further indication that the "English party" on the Chattahoochee was growing.[49]

Brims's political dilemma was compounded by the recent death of Chipacasi, who stole a keg of rum and proceeded to drink himself to death. Suffering personal loss once again, Brims again found himself without an heir to the British commission. Having run out of younger members of his family to fill the void, Brims this time turned to his brother Chigelly, whom Brims appears to have recommended to Fitch that summer. Though Fitch was probably aware that Chigelly had once fought the English during the Yamasee War and had not yet stepped forward as an ardent English supporter, Fitch nevertheless accepted Chigelly's appointment. The commission, Fitch argued, would "prevent him from further mischief" by making him answerable to the English.[50] For his part, Brims must have considered Chigelly a natural to assume the position as heir apparent. Being brothers meant that they were clan relatives, thereby preserving the Coweta ruling clan's monopoly of the English headman commission.

As a commissioned headman, Chigelly gradually assumed a leading role in Anglo-Creek diplomacy, thus initiating a long career as a chief liaison between Carolina and the Creeks. Chigelly was thus the fittest choice to represent the Lower Creeks at a round of talks in Tuckebatchee, which Fitch had arranged to discuss the Cherokee peace. The Tuckebatchee talks, which eventually began on September 23, 1726, drew headmen from all three Creek provinces. The presence of Chigelly, who spoke for the lower towns, may indicate that the Tallapoosas and Lower Creeks were now on friendlier terms than in the previous year. To promote Creek unity Fitch wisely avoided the controversial Yamasee issue and instead worked to cement a Creek-Cherokee peace, which the war-weary Abikas and Tallapoosas were eager to implement. Chigelly, however, in recalling the Cherokee massacre of Creek headmen in Tugaloo a decade earlier, refused to give his assent on the grounds that the Cherokees had not sent a present to demonstrate their sincerity. Because gift-giving was an important part of diplomatic protocol in Indian country, Chigelly succeeded in convincing the rest of the headmen to reject the Cherokee peace offer at that time.[51]

The Cherokees and the Creeks did, however, agree to meet South Carolina Council president Arthur Middleton in Charles Town to negotiate a peace agreement. In late January 1727 the Cherokee Long Warrior of Tunissee, Chigelly of Coweta, and the Abika headman Hobohatchey arrived in the colonial capital to discuss the peace proposals that Carolina's beloved man—Fitch—had proposed and that Chigelly had rejected weeks earlier. Throughout the proceedings the Tallapoosas and Abikas demonstrated that they were weary of losing loved ones at the hands of the Cherokees and wanted to sue for peace. So, too, did the Long Warrior of Tunissee, who feared that a festering war would have adverse effects on commerce.

In contrast, Chigelly's people, the Cowetas, still had not forgiven the Cherokees for the massacre at Tugaloo, indicating that Coweta had suffered most from the Cherokees' decade-old deadly trick. The Upper Creeks, though, had recently borne the brunt of Cherokee attacks. Thus the Abikas and Tallapoosas eagerly sought to convince Chigelly to accept the peace, which they viewed as an old grudge that needed to be buried rather than a fresh insult that called for vengeance. By pressuring the Cowetas to accept peace the Upper Creeks could then hunt in the woods without fear.

Thus, by isolating Chigelly politically, President Middleton, the Long Warrior of Tunnissee, and Hobohatchey appear to have humbled the stubborn Coweta warrior. The Long Warrior repeatedly berated Chigelly and his people, calling them rogues who seldom fulfilled their promises to the white people. With both former enemies and allies pressuring him to accept the peace, Chigelly capitulated and presented to the Long Warrior a white eagle's wing to signify his sincerity. Because he remained unconvinced that Chigelly's people had purged themselves of their rogue-like behavior, the Long Warrior at first was hesitant to receive Chigelly's gift but then consented to show President Middleton his gratitude for organizing the meeting. After exchanging the white wing, Chigelly, Middleton, and the Long Warrior each drank a toast to signify the peace, thus apparently ending an eleven-year feud.[52]

Although the January meetings brought an official close to the Creek and Cherokee war, the real peace negotiations transpired behind the scenes. During the official proceedings in the council chamber, the Long Warrior implied that the negotiations would continue when he remarked that "I shall talk further [about peace] to you when we meet and eat together in the woods."[53] No written record, of course, documents the further talks that took place. Nevertheless, the content of the discussion can be gleaned from extant sources, which indicate that the Cherokees demanded that the Lower Creeks bring Yamasee prisoners to Cherokee towns as a show of good faith.[54] Were they to resist, the Cherokees claimed, the peace then would be officially "spoilt," thus negating the peace accord agreed to in the council chamber.

Despite the Long Warrior's threats, the tentative conclusion of the war between the Creeks and Cherokees did nothing to induce Chigelly's people to bring in the Yamasees. In the ensuing months both the Cherokees and the Carolinians began to believe that the Lower Creeks truly were the rogues they feared. As the summer of 1727 approached, gangs of Indians continued to skulk on the Carolina border and all of Fitch's efforts "to make a strong party against the Yamasees" among the Lower Creeks did nothing to bring them underfoot.

The most shocking event, however, occurred in the summer of 1727 when a trader named Matthew Smallwood and four of his employees were found murdered at his plundered store situated at the fork of the Altamaha River. Trails leading away from the scene led toward the Lower Creeks and Chislacaliche's town, thus indicating that the "rogues" were up to their old tricks. On August 3, just one day after receiving word of the murders, the Carolina council put an immediate halt to the Lower Creek trade. Over the next few weeks Carolina officials made plans to commence a full-scale war against the Yamasees, the Lower Creeks, and Chislacaliche's people.[55]

With plans for an extensive ground and naval campaign in place, the council opted to direct its military efforts at the Yamasees and send another beloved man to the Creeks, the more formidable foe. Smartly, the council appointed Charlesworth Glover, a trader with much experience among the Creeks, to undertake the dangerous mission. Departing from Charles Town in October, Glover arrived in Oakfuskee on December 23 and remained in Creek country until May 1728.

Like Fitch before him, Glover found the Upper Creeks "hearty in our interest," indicating that public opinion on the Coosa and Tallapoosa Rivers favored fighting the Yamasees. To be sure, both Glover and important headmen were aware that the Lower Creeks had drawn some Upper Creeks into the scheme to murder and rob Smallwood, but most Upper Creek leaders sought to distance themselves from the violence perpetrated by the Lower Creeks. Since they had each concluded a separate peace with the Cherokees, they were free to send their warriors south against the Yamasees without fear. War captains from Okchay, for example, promised to send warriors as soon as their men returned from their winter hunts. Likewise, Glover secured the services of the "Tuckesee King" to lead a party of thirty men against the Yamasees. At Abika the enthusiasm for war was not as strong, but only because most of the town's warriors were unwilling to travel such a great distance during the winter hunting season. In general, however, Upper Creek headmen appeared willing to send warriors, an impressive show of allegiance given that "the sickness" had recently killed five hundred people among the Tallapoosas.[56]

Glover found the Lower Creeks, in contrast, to be in a greater state of political turmoil, a situation exacerbated by a more effective trade embargo. As Glover noted, the Lower Creeks were lacking gunpowder and were poor because they lacked trade goods. Lacking gunpowder, the Lower Creeks felt vulnerable to attack from all quarters, not knowing "who shall be the first" to take advantage of their weakened military state.[57] The embargo and the poverty it caused was having a divisive effect on the Lower Creeks, some of whom favored an attack on the Yamasees to appease Glover and others who remained in favor of Spain and the Yamasees. Two towns in particular stood out as pro-Spanish partisans: Apalachicola and Coweta. As Glover noted, the two "had declared for the Spaniards." "The rest," he added, "declared for us," indicating that Brims, by turning increasingly toward the Spanish for support, was out of touch with many of his people.[58]

Brims may have been so unpopular, in fact, that his own people felt compelled to circumvent his authority and appoint someone else to negotiate with Glover. Upon hearing of Glover's arrival in the area inhabited by the Upper Creeks, a number of little towns on the Chattahoochee River appointed the Long Warrior of Coweta and one Tom Slohi to plead with Glover to restore trade. It is likely that the little towns selected those two as their representatives because they each carried an English commission and neither was burdened, as Chigelly and Brims were, by what the English considered a belligerent record of lies and deceit.[59] It was hoped Glover would believe their professions of peace.

On January 15 the two Lower Creek warriors arrived to speak with Glover. The Long Warrior apologized for Smallwood's murder, blaming it not upon the headmen but on the mad and wild youths who could not control their animosity for the English. In an attempt to show that they meant to punish the perpetrators of the deed, the Long Warrior explained to Fitch that they had killed one of the men responsible for Smallwood's murder but could not deliver the scalp because it somehow had been given to the Tallapoosas. Glover was not satisfied with this minimal show of obedience, and insisted that the Lower Creeks bring in ten Yamasees and Chislacaliche himself to atone for Smallwood's murder. Only by doing so, he argued, "may you see rum and all other English goods in as great plenty among you as they have been in the past."[60]

After residing for a month among the Upper Creeks, stirring the warriors to action, Glover still feared that the Lower Creeks would not make peace with Carolina. Two Cussita men arrived on February 12 to inform Glover that the Cowetas and the Apalachicolas were actively working against the English interest and hindering their people "from doing what they promised." In the following weeks Glover learned that two Apalachicola warriors named Chocate and Madumee had assembled sixty supporters, marched to St. Augustine, and offered their services. Reports also indicated that the French and Spanish had accepted their offer of assistance and were assembling an army near Fort San Marcos.[61]

The month of March 1728 proved to be a pivotal one for the English and for the inhabitants of every village on the Chattahoochee. The Lower Creeks received visits by Glover and several delegations of French and Spanish ambassadors, each seeking to recruit warriors for their various schemes. Courted on all sides, some Lower Creeks were clearly picking their favorites. Brims, as Glover noted, was decidedly in favor of the Spanish and made no apparent effort to assist the English. Nor did Brims deign to speak with Glover when he appeared in Coweta on March 13, prompting Glover to conclude that Brims "has all the power and his heart is for the Spanish."

Brims did not, though, have all the power on the Chattahoochee. While Brims may have had considerable sway over a cadre of Coweta and Apalachicola warriors, he could do little to contain the pro-English sentiment that had grown within towns like Cussita or Yuchi, or among King Hott's Osuches. Glover reported, for example, that Licka, or "Liquor" (of the Yuchis) had sent five warriors to the Apalachee old fields to fight stray Yamasees. Though the war party spent much of its time "killing beef," they succeeded in killing a Spaniard and a Yamasee and brought their scalps to Cussita to display triumphantly before Glover.[62]

The most convincing evidence that King Hott's Town, Cussita, and the Yuchis were acting in the English interest occurred on March 21, when an English trader named Daniel Roche and King Hott heard the conspicuous sound of a gun echoing from the town of Apalachicola. Roche and King Hott at first believed the gunshot signified the return of Capt. John Musgrove's party. Musgrove, having a discernible influence among the Lower Creeks, had earlier been deputized to raise his own faction, and appears to have successfully recruited at least one war party. Brims, we might guess, did not approve of Musgrove's action, thus exposing the limits of kinship the two men felt by way of Coosaponakeesa and Musgrove's son. To Roche's shock, however, the gunshot signified the arrival of a Frenchman, the Frenchman's linguist, and several Spanish soldiers in the Eufala Town located south of the major towns on the Chattahoochee.

Two hours after first hearing the gunshot, two headmen arrived from Apalachicola and reported the arrival of the Spanish and French party, alerting Hott and Roche to the fact that three large canoes of pro-Spanish partisans had departed toward the south from Apalachicola. The two headmen, whom Roche assumed had come from Apalachicola, were clearly partial to the English. One of the men, referred to only as "the Dog King," told Hott that "he would immediately go after his neighbors." At that point Hott and the Dog King, accompanied by ten other warriors, grabbed their guns and went away in haste to challenge their pro-Spanish neighbors.

Two days later a runner from the town of Cussita arrived at King Hott's Town to report that they had located the Spaniards and intended to "tie or hyde them." This turned out not to be necessary because Roche soon learned the Euphalas and Apalachicolas had turned on the Spanish. Madumee, the Apalachicola warrior who had recently offered his services to the Spanish, had seized the Spanish captain and his linguist and had taken them back to Euphala, where they remained prisoners under the care of Tubbasigo, the *mico* of Apalachicola.

While it should not be surprising that individuals from Cussita or King Hott would assist the English, the fact that the Euphalas and Apalachicolas seized the Spanish captain suggests that something happened that March to turn public opinion on the Chattahoochee in favor of the English and against the Spanish. Why, after "declaring for the Spaniards" and defending the Yamasees, did these groups suddenly turn on the Spanish captain and his men? Glover may have had some influence, since the Lower Creeks knew that they would have to comply with at least some of his demands before he would restore trade. Moreover, Glover had spread rumors that the Spanish had placed a bounty on Chigelly's head, which may have prejudiced him against the Spanish.[63]

Though Glover's not-so-subtle persuasion might have convinced enough Creek leaders that the Spaniards were their true enemies, other evidence indicates that the Eufalas and Apalachicolas seized the Spanish in order to punish them for being poor trade partners and military allies. Juan Jacinto, a Spanish soldier who was seized on the day in question, remembered years later in an interview that he had asked his captors why they treated their Spanish "friends" in such a deceitful way. They responded, Jacinto recalled, "that the Spaniards never have complied with their offer to populate Apalachee, and to bring there what they should need."[64] Evidently, Jacinto's captors recalled promises made in 1718 to repopulate Apalachee and establish a trading store at the rebuilt Apalachee fort, which the Spanish had abandoned in 1723.

Because of Spain's inability to trade, the Indians believed that the Spanish "had deceived them in their hopes" and that "it was not so with the English," for when they "promised to do something they put it in execution." Jacinto did not specify the promises that the English were praised for executing, but one can venture to guess that it had something to do with trade. Evidence shows that the Creeks respected Carolina's ability to provide them with the trade goods that had become a necessary part of everyday life. The fact that the Creeks were suffering the effects of a trade embargo at the time of Jacinto's imprisonment likely made him a scapegoat for their suffering.[65]

The Creeks respected more than Britain's economic might; they believed the English were formidable foes capable of executing a military campaign when circumstances demanded it. They had proved it on numerous occasions: as allies against the Apalachees during Queen Anne's War and, more recently, in the Yamasee War when Carolina militias proved themselves capable of stifling Indian resistance in the backcountry.

For years the Carolinians had been threatening to annihilate the Yamasees and they successfully accomplished this task too, when Col. John Palmer, a veteran of the Yamasee War and Commons House member, led two companies of soldiers and Indian auxiliaries over land from Charles Town to St. Augustine. At dawn on March 9 they attacked the Yamasee stronghold of Nombre de Dios, killing thirty and capturing or wounding fifteen more. After circling St. Augustine for two more days, Palmer's forces laid waste to Nombre de Dios, burning the chapel as well as the Indian town. The event marked the end of the Yamasees as a military threat and demonstrated to the Creeks that the English were brazen enough to search out and kill their enemies, even under the shadows of the Castillo de San Marcos. The Lower Creeks apparently knew about Palmer's success at the time of the seizure, for on March 27 they brought news of the event to Glover, who was then residing in Oakfuskee among the Upper Creeks.[66]

On April 14, in Okchay, Glover received official notice of Palmer's victory, confirming what the Creeks had told him weeks before. Shrewdly, Glover made his way back to Coweta and called Brims and Chigelly before him to boast that "Palmer hath cut off a town of the Yamasees and burnt Augustine town, [and] killed & took near 50 Indians," including a warrior from Coweta "which Colonel Palmer let go again." By the time they received this bit of news, Brims and Chigelly had apparently resigned themselves to Carolina hegemony in the region. Brims, for example, expressed astonishment that the English had not killed the captured Coweta warrior, calling him "he who bred all the mischief." Confident that the Creeks had "stopped the path to Augustine," on April 15 Glover ordered the trader Miles Mackintosh to set up shop among the "Euchechees" of the Lower Creeks, thus ending the on-again, off-again embargo that had been in place for over five years.[67] By ending the embargo Glover was able to act on his conviction that trade rather than warfare was the surest way to govern the Creeks.

In the weeks that followed the restoration of trade, Glover found the Lower Creeks to be a somewhat more compliant people: "These people," Glover reported from Coweta, "are more of them going out [against the Yamasees] to try what they can get." Glover was happy to add that almost every town had sent out at least one war party. Only the Cowetas, Glover noted, "are not yet gone," which made him suspect that they "may have an opportunity to make peace with the Spaniards again." According to Glover, Brims still harbored pro-Spanish sympathies and it would be necessary to win him over before Carolina's influence in the region would be complete.[68]

Noteworthy in Glover's final remarks is the degree to which Brims, the celebrated emperor of the Creeks, had become a politically isolated figure in the decade following the Coweta Resolution of March 1718. In those days Brims had spoken as the voice of a people dedicated to taming the Carolina trade regime through a policy of neutrality. By betrothing his kinswoman Coosaponakeesa to the young John Musgrove and by deputizing his kinsman Ouletta to conduct diplomacy in Charles Town, Brims had taken the lead in welcoming the English back to the Chattahoochee region. But as the Carolinians stepped up their demands to root out the Yamasees and threatened Brims's traditional right to name subordinate chiefs, Brims increasingly looked to the Spanish to protect his own interests but isolated himself politically in the process. In the end a majority of the Lower Creeks may have welcomed or at least resigned themselves to the presence of the English and their demands. Brims, in contrast, sacrificed some of his own political influence to maintain a political ideal that reserved a less influential role for the English.

A Free People

On April 26, 1731, the Consejo des Indias reported to the Spanish king that the English of Carolina had returned to the "province of the Emperor of Coweta, he who was formerly in our devotion," and now held sway over his people. English traders, the report continued, had ensconced themselves among the people, learned their language, married their women, and corresponded with that province's various chiefs. The report accused the English traders of belittling the Spanish nation, "saying to the Indians that they are all liars and poor people that have no valor, and at the same time prejudic[ing] them against our Holy and True religion." The Indians, the report concluded, "easily believe all their lies."[69]

At first glance the Consejo's report might indicate that very little had changed since 1715. Like many Spanish accounts written by an earlier generation, the report lamented the loss of an Indian province centered in Coweta and bemoaned the grip that English commerce had asserted over the Coweta people. Moreover, the Indians had still not embraced Catholicism, shunning it and instead succumbing to the lure of English trade. Probing the recent history of the region, however, we find that the resurrection of the English trade regime in Creek country, though impressive, was nonetheless incomplete. The fact that the English had to tell so many lies to sway the Creeks in the first place suggests that something rather remarkable had taken place since appearance of the Coweta Resolution.

One piece of evidence indicating that something had changed after 1718 was the spread of political factionalism in the 1720s. Rather than a sign of political infirmity, the presence of competing factions in Creek country was a sign of its political health.[70] The spread of factionalism was, in fact, a product of the Creeks' kinship-based political system, which remained fluid, localized, and lacking in the punitive mechanisms or institutions necessary to ensure obedience to a single course of political action. In short, a kinship system like the one found among the Creeks made the Coweta Resolution possible and enabled individual leaders to cultivate alliances with whomever they saw fit. By encouraging a multilateral policy the Creeks could in theory entertain the advances of three imperial suitors rather than just one, theoretically taming the worst impulses of each.

This is not to say, however, that Creek leaders predicted or desired the kinds of disputes that emerged between individuals such as Tickhonabe and Brims, between towns like Coweta and Cussita, or between different riverine populations such as the Lower Creeks and Tallapoosas. At times various Creek leaders appear to have been frustrated by their lack of control over their own people and their inability to define foreign policy. Brims, for example, had no way of stopping attacks against the Yamasees and could therefore not mitigate English influence in the region. Conversely, some headmen who favored attacking the Yamasees often had a difficult time convincing their warriors to abandon their winter hunts, thereby jeopardizing their friendship with English officials. The Abika headman Hobohatchey, for example, on one occasion admitted to Charlesworth Glover that his efforts to stir his warriors to battle with kind words had been to no avail: "I have given the people a good talk till I am weary," Hobohatchey said, adding that "now I will give them a bad talk and see what that will do."[71]

So long as war leaders as great as Hobohatchey could do little more than issue good or bad talks to their people, Europeans found it difficult to mold Indian behavior. For this reason the Spanish and especially the English exerted pressure upon the Indians to model their political institutions after their own. It is clear, for example, that the Spanish wished to create a quasi-feudal Creek state in which leaders such as Brims would play a prominent role. They sought to make Brims a king as early as 1717 by bequeathing to him a silver baton signifying his rule as generalissimo.[72] Moreover, Spanish officials sought to create an incipient noble class by offering headmen landed estates in Apalachee.

The English, by way of contrast, were less concerned about molding the Creeks into a feudal state. Nevertheless, the Carolina government did its best to centralize authority by using British military commissions. Though this system was designed to advance explicitly English goals, the system served Creek purposes as well. Brims in particular appears to have uttered no protests when he or his kinsmen received headman commissions from Carolina or metal plates that in theory permitted them to monopolize talks with Charles Town.

Brims eventually found good reason to view the commissions with ambivalence, however, as the acceptance of a British military commission made the recipient answerable to officials in Carolina. These same officials made vexing demands to kill Yamasees and embrace Cherokees that Brims and his people found troubling. Most important, the commission system afforded British officials the opportunity to manipulate the Creek political system when they commissioned men who were not or were unqualified to be headmen. Brims, who staunchly defended his right to name headmen within the nation, clearly viewed the commissions held by Cusabo and others as a direct affront to his own political authority, if not an assault on the sovereignty of his nation.

Centralizing pressures also came by way of persuasion. Carolina's beloved men, for instance, applied consistent pressure upon the Creeks to speak with one voice. On one occasion Charlesworth Glover explicitly warned them to do so, stating to the stubborn Chigelly that "you are on the broad path to destruction by fighting against one another," and adding that "your towns can never stand unless you are of one mind and one tongue and one people."[73] Glover may have been right in predicting that the Creeks were on the broad path to destruction if a civil war had erupted in Creek country during those years. But, despite occasional death threats, civil war never came. One aspect mitigating this potential was a culturally determined disposition against internal violence.

In Creek country, as in many other areas of the world where kinship political systems persist, responsibility for enacting punishments rests in the hands of clans rather than in a single absolute authority. When a murder occurs, for example, the victim's family reserves the right to avenge the death of its kinsman. This method of justice has the potential to spiral into a fratricidal war of cyclical revenge, but the Creeks lived in what might be called a provincial or small-town world that was intimately bound by ties of kinship and in which persons had much face-to-face contact with their peers. This intimacy, coupled with the threat of retribution or even witchcraft, discouraged punishments and politically motivated murders.[74] For these reasons Brims found no one willing to take Tickhonabe's or Cusabo's head for killing a few Yamasees, nor would any pro-English partisan dare to challenge Brims militarily.

This inability—or unwillingness—to punish is what the English found particularly difficult to overcome. For this reason, Carolina's beloved men made efforts to persuade the Creeks to change their ways. Tobias Fitch, for example, chastened Brims for allowing the Squire *mico* of Ocmulgee to warn the Yamasees of the Coweta warriors' approach, thereby spoiling one of their punitive raids. Fitch argued that traitors in his country would be torn limb from limb by wild horses, hoping that Brims would take note and do the same.[75] Likewise, when the Long Warrior of Coweta explained to Charlesworth Glover his inability to keep his people "within my sight," Glover urged him to take tough measures: "If you will punish one or two of your rogues when you find them as we do," Glover scolded, "it would make all the rest good and afraid."[76]

The difficulties that the beloved men faced in trying to bend the Creeks to Carolina's will demonstrates that though imperial authorities in London, Madrid, or Paris could talk about Indians as their pawns, persons in Coweta or Tuckebatchee most often could not. The Spanish Consejo des Indias, as noted previously, liked to believe that in 1715, 161 towns had become vassals of the Spanish king and sought to force them to cut off all ties with the English. Likewise, in later years British officials gleefully seized upon the fact that the Spanish sometimes referred to the Creeks as "our [Carolina's] Indians," which, they presumed, was a concession to Britain's territorial claims.[77]

The real triumph of the Creeks' brand of triple-nation diplomacy was that it forced the three European empires to recognize Creek sovereignty for the purposes of expediency. As sovereign, the Creeks earned the right to make alliances with whomever they chose. Consider the following example. When a French diplomat, a laced-coat-wearing dandy described as the "King of France's son," met Charlesworth Glover in Coweta in March of 1728, the Coweta chiefs made it known to Glover that they wished to hear the Frenchman's talk in private. Consequently, Glover spent that evening in Cussita in deference to their demand for privacy. The following day Glover returned to Coweta and was obliged to listen to a staged talk, demonstrating that the Frenchman posed no serious threat to Carolina's interests. Annoyed that a lone overdressed Frenchman could command such respect in Coweta, Glover responded to the Frenchman by saying, "Sir, these people are a Free People," and conceded that "I suppose you are as welcome here as I."[78] Brims's power, then, lay not in his ability to command his own people but in his ability to force the English beloved men like Glover to come to the same important realization.

CHAPTER FIVE

Oglethorpe's Friends—
and Enemies

Through the ages the city of London has seen its share of foreigners come and go, but rarely has it been treated to the spectacle that took place between July and October 1734. That year a small delegation of Creek Indians traversed the "great water" and became the first of their people ever to set foot on English soil. The Creek dignitaries had come by invitation of James Edward Oglethorpe, the leader of the new colony named Georgia in honor of the British king, George II. At the head of the Creek delegation was an elderly man named Tomochichi who had befriended Oglethorpe a year earlier and had granted Oglethorpe permission to plant his new colony on the Savannah River.

Oglethorpe recognized that Georgia's survival required the favor and protection of the Creek Indians, whose proximity to the Catholic powers made them a valuable ally and a potentially dangerous foe. Tomochichi, the leader of a nearby group of Creeks known as the Yamacraws, was the critical intermediary between the Creeks and the Georgians. Thus when Tomochichi's party arrived in London that July, British officials went to extraordinary lengths to impress upon them the grandeur and benevolence of the British state. On August 1, Tomochichi and his followers were privileged enough to meet with King George and Queen Caroline, who dutifully listened as Tomochichi pledged his friendship.

As the London press had it, Tomochichi's visit with the royal couple was a festive affair marked by numerous symbolic acts that renewed the ancient peace between the English monarchy and the Creek Indians. *Gentleman's Magazine*, a popular London periodical, portrayed Tomochichi as the king of an entire "Creek nation" and loyal to King

George.[1] Not everyone in London at the time, however, was naive enough to accept the shallow glossing of a men's magazine as the truth. It just so happened that Joseph Ramos Escudero, who was in London on a secret mission for the Spanish governor of Florida, had come to spy on Tomochichi and his followers.

Disguised as a Dutch diplomat, Escudero, a Franciscan friar, infiltrated the British court and gained access to the Creek visitors. Escudero soon became suspicious, though, when he noticed the absence of several influential Creek men, especially Yahoulakee, whom Escudero believed was the "emperor" of Coweta. A somewhat confused Escudero therefore surmised that Tomochichi's party was nothing but an assemblage of minor chiefs and that Tomochichi was a mere pretender to Yahoulakee's position. To verify his suspicions, Escudero at one point turned to a Creek man sitting beside him in court and asked sarcastically, "When will I see the Emperor of Coweta?" The Creek man, hesitant to reveal the emperor's absence, replied defensively, "I don't know, [but] he is here."[2]

For several weeks Escudero lingered like a phantom in the shadows, needling the Creek diplomats for further information about Yahoulakee and the visiting chiefs. Eventually Escudero directed his questions to the Creek interpreter, John Musgrove, who was forced to admit that the new emperor of Coweta was not in London but pleaded that "he had been begged to come, but . . . was afraid of the sea."[3] Musgrove, in order to gloss over this inconvenient matter, responded by styling Tomochichi as the "second man" in the nation to whom the present chief of Coweta and others might defer in times of war or other serious matters. The Creeks added their own spin, stating that the English had crowned Yahoulakee supreme king eight or nine years prior, and had given him a crown, a scepter, and a suit of "popish vestments" believed to have been worn by the British king. These attempts, Escudero was informed, were not received with general applause because Yahoulakee was a "cruel and barbarous" leader and because the Indians in general did not recognize such absolute authority.[4]

As Father Escudero's penetrating remarks suggest, the shifting state of political authority in the Creek nation was inextricably tied to the imperial struggles taking place between Britain and Spain. One beneficiary in this struggle was "King" Tomochichi. An outcast from the town of Apalachicola, Tomochichi gained remarkable political influence in the

1730s by way of his relationship to the new Georgia Colony and its leader, James Oglethorpe. Tomochichi's pilgrimage to London, therefore, should not be seen as an isolated or accidental event, but rather the cornerstone of a prolonged effort to enhance his status in the Creek nation. To this day one can view Tomochichi's conspicuously placed memorial in Wright Square in downtown Savannah. Local legend even has it that Tomochichi still speaks from the grave to anyone bold enough to run around his memorial three times in rapid succession. A fruitless exercise, perhaps, but the legend serves as a lingering reminder of the degree to which Tomochichi had become an indelible fixture in the new colony.[5]

While it is understandable that Georgians of Oglethorpe's generation might have found it in their own interest to enhance the prestige of a friendly Indian chief, historians have simplified an important chapter in Creek and British history by falling prey to the same impulse. By adhering too closely to the paper trail left by Oglethorpe and the Georgia trustees, historians have effectively placed Tomochichi and his small band of Yamacraws at the center of Georgia-Indian relations, leading at least one historian to portray the Creeks as "Oglethorpe's friends."[6]

Father Escudero's correspondence suggests, to the contrary, that the establishment of Georgia in 1733 catalyzed not only an imperial contest between Britain and Spain for the "debatable land" between the Savannah and St. John's River but also a struggle for power among the Creeks themselves over the definition, if not the destiny, of their "nation." Oglethorpe, to be sure, found a good number of friends among the Creeks. But he made no small number of Creek enemies, some of whom exploited the Spanish and French alliance to challenge the Georgia-Creek alliance that Tomochichi and Oglethorpe worked so hard to build and maintain.

Georgia and the Making of the Yamacraws

Since the days of Henry Woodward a half century before, English interlopers had eyed the territory south of the Savannah River as a potential site for colonization for reasons both economic (for the proliferation of its rice plantations) and strategic (as a defensive buffer against Spanish Florida). Early attempts to colonize and fortify what eventually became Georgia foundered, though, and serious plans to colonize the Southern frontier did not resume until the early 1730s. At that time a group of religiously inspired reformers sought to establish a new colony to ameliorate the desperate condition of the London poor, burdened as they were by a draconian legal code that committed common debtors to London jails. These reform-minded individuals, led by James Edward Oglethorpe, petitioned the Crown "for obtaining a grant of lands on the south-west of Carolina for settling the poor persons of London." The Crown, sensing that a new southern colony in North America would be of great strategic value to the empire, consented to Oglethorpe's plan and Georgia Colony was born.[7]

Though Oglethorpe and his associates in London were inclined to view the territory south of the Savannah River as a vacant land waiting to be settled, the Georgians were not the first to plant a colony in the vicinity of Savannah. Once the region's indigenous peoples, the Guales and the Escamacus, had been largely eradicated by the 1680s, the Savannah River and its environs attracted a variety of Indian colonizers seeking to tap into the burgeoning trade with Carolina to the north. Among the first to settle in the area were the Yamasees, who settled just to the north of the Savannah in 1685. A generation later, members of the Creek town of Apalachicola took up residence on the north side of the Savannah River some sixty miles upstream from the coast. Although the Apalachicolas and Yamasees eventually abandoned that territory in the wake of the Pocotalico Massacre in 1715, the southern margins of the Carolina colony continued to attract stray bands of Creeks and other Indians who hunted there and traded with the local white inhabitants. One area of particular importance was the young John Musgrove's lands in nearby Colleton County, upon which were settled some of Musgrove's Creek relatives. Most conspicuous among those relatives was Coosaponakeesa, known in the colonies as Mary Musgrove, who came to play an important if somewhat infamous role in Georgia-Indian affairs. The final and most influential Indian group to settle near the mouth of the Savannah River was Tomochichi's displaced band of Creeks known as the Yamacraws, who had come to the region roughly one year before Oglethorpe.

The origin of Tomochichi's Yamacraw community and the reasons for their exodus are somewhat obscure, though it is evident that they came to the Savannah River under circumstances not of their own choosing. Tomochichi himself rarely discussed the reasons for his banishment, but the Earl of Egmont, a leading trustee of the Georgia Colony, once recalled that Tomochichi had been accused of "cutting down a Popish Chappel, which the French were endeavoring to erect, with design to convert it to a fort."[8] Circumstantial evidence appears to support Egmont's claim. In

March 1729 the French commander of Fort Toulouse sent a lone priest to "the [Cowetas] . . . to see if they would be willing to have missionaries." Brims of Coweta personally ventured twice to Mobile between October 1729 and November 1730, a clear indication that the Cowetas and the French were then working to solidify their alliance.[9] Coweta, we may presume, led in the effort to banish the Yamacraws.

As for the composition of the Yamacraw group, evidence suggests kinship played an important role in determining its membership, because it appears that Tomochichi and many of his followers were clan relatives from several Creek towns. Colonial officials, for instance, described the Yamacraws as derived from several towns but members of the same "tribe," (a term sometimes used to denote kinship).[10] In addition to Tomochichi's Apalachicolas, the Yamacraws appear to have drawn members from the pro-English point towns, particularly Osuche, the town of origin of three brothers closely affiliated with Tomochichi.[11] Reports that the early migrants consisted of an assemblage of Creeks and Yamasees suggests further that Tomochichi's people may have had close ties to the Yamasees, who themselves may have had ethnic links to Osuche.[12]

But why choose to settle precisely at Yamacraw Bluff? Tomochichi was no doubt familiar with the territory in question, as he had probably lived among the Apalachicolas on the Savannah River between 1708 and 1715. For this reason, perhaps, Tomochichi described his wanderings as a "search for the tombs of my ancestors." In addition, Tomochichi likely had acquaintances, if not a few relations, living nearby in the Carolina settlements on John Musgrove's land.[13] The Musgroves—John and his wife Mary—were, if not directly related to Tomochichi, at the least sharers of a common Creek ancestry and served as important go-betweens between the Yamacraws and the Georgians. Years later Mary recalled that she had been instrumental in facilitating the peaceful working relationship between the Yamacraws and Oglethorpe's colony by using "her influence and interest with the said Indians" to gain for Oglethorpe "a peaceable and quiet Possession in that Country in behalf of His Majesty."[14] The Yamacraws appear to have returned the favor by inviting John and Mary to settle near Yamacraw Bluff in order to establish a trade outpost, an offer the Musgroves accepted. Tomochichi was drawn to the coast, then, because he had a past history there and because he probably had a Creek network of support with important contacts in the colonies.

Once situated in their new homes, the Yamacraws, derived from several towns, were initially required to reinvent themselves as a people and to craft a new political identity. The first task would have been to establish a new town, for eighteenth-century Creeks regarded the town (*talwa*) as central to an individual's social and political identity and the mark of a people governed by law (as opposed to those who lived beyond the pale of civilization, as the Creeks understood it). Living as exiles would have likewise required the Yamacraws to establish new hierarchies of political and military offices that would have recently been thrown into disarray.

At the head of the town political hierarchy, of course, was the town *mico*. Though Tomochichi assumed that role soon after the establishment of the new town at Yamacraw, he was not known as a town *mico* before his exile. Nor should it be assumed that Tomochichi was the leader of the exiled people when they first arrived on Carolina's southern frontier. Sources indicate instead that a man named Bocatchee may have been the head of the immigrant Creeks when they first arrived in 1732.[15] Tomochichi should therefore be regarded not as a geographically displaced traditional town *mico* but as a recently appointed one who may have found it necessary to go to extraordinary lengths to cultivate his political gravitas.

Thus in 1733, when the first Georgia colonists arrived, Tomochichi's need to solidify his position and James Oglethorpe's desire to secure an Indian ally brought the two men together on common political ground. Tomochichi remained Georgia's staunchest Creek ally (until his death in 1739) and in the process resurrected himself as the *mico* of a new Creek town—Yamacraw. Oglethorpe, by using Tomochichi as his chief intermediary with the Lower Creeks in the nation proper, built a small but influential pro-English coalition around Tomochichi, thus buying a measure of security for the exposed infant colony.

Tomochichi met Oglethorpe for the first time on February 1, 1733, when he, his wife, and several subordinate chiefs greeted Oglethorpe and company on Yamacraw Bluff. Peter Gordon, an associate of Oglethorpe's and witness to the proceedings, summarized this first encounter as the Indians' attempt "to pay their obedience to Mr. Oglethorpe." To individuals unfamiliar with Indian diplomacy this description might have appeared apt. Upon closer inspection, though, it seems that Tomochichi's overtures of obedience were designed to draw Oglethorpe into the Yamacraws' own kinship orbit, thereby cultivating the ties of reciprocity that obliged the Georgians to protect and defend the upstart Yamacraw community.

In form the Yamacraws' performance before Oglethorpe is reminiscent of the ritual that the Creeks had staged before the Spanish in April of 1717. As the Creeks had done on that previous occasion, the ceremony began with a reciprocal exchange of gunfire. Soon after, the Yamacraws commenced their march toward Oglethorpe's tent, preceded by a leading (and in this case lone) warrior who had adorned his head with white feathers, a sign of peace. While shaking rattles the warrior sang and danced, thereby preparing the way for Tomochichi, his chief attendants, and the rest of the people, all of whom marched toward Oglethorpe in a formation according to their respective ranks.

Conspicuous among Tomochichi's attendants was Senaukey, his wife, who could often be found at her husband's side whenever the Yamacraws and Georgians held rituals of peace and even joined her husband on his pioneering voyage to London. Though Senaukey typically played a silent role in most proceedings, her very presence at the first talks suggests that the Yamacraws, like many Indian groups in eastern North America, at certain times used women to demonstrate in a more conspicuous fashion their peaceful intentions.

Once ensconced with Oglethorpe in Oglethorpe's tent, Tomochichi delivered his first formal speech, the contents of which emphasized peace and Oglethorpe's obligations as protector of the Yamacraw community. As was common among the Creeks, Tomochichi began first by presenting Oglethorpe with a gift: a buffalo robe painted with the head and feathers of an eagle. That Tomochichi used the imagery of the eagle to decorate his buffalo robe is of special significance, for the Creeks regarded the eagle as the king of all birds, the ruler of the upper World, and a symbol of peace. As Tomochichi explained, "the eagle signified speed and the buffalo strength. That the English were as swift as the bird, and as strong as the beast; since, like the first, they flew from the utmost parts of the earth over the vast seas, and, like the second, nothing could withstand them." Having portrayed the English in such a flattering light, Tomochichi reminded Oglethorpe that this strength also entailed certain obligations, proclaiming that "the feathers of the eagle were soft, and signified love; the buffalo's skin warm, and signified protection." "Therefore," added Tomochichi, he "hoped that we would love and protect their little families."[16]

In the weeks that followed, Tomochichi, the Yamacraws, and Oglethorpe continued to exchange ritual gestures commonly used by Indians to cultivate fictitious kinship ties. Yamacraw hunters immediately set to work to provide the English with venison, and though Oglethorpe was know to pay "a very moderate rate" for their services, the Yamacraws would have understood this exchange of food as a way to fulfill their obligations to their new friends. Likewise, when the Yamacraws later met with Oglethorpe to conduct yet another peace ritual, the Yamacraws presented him with a supply of deerskins as a sign of their allegiance. A quick study in the art of Indian diplomacy, Oglethorpe responded in kind with a gift of cloth, thus fulfilling his own obligation to meet gift with gift.

While the Yamacraws appear to have utilized these initial rounds of diplomacy to cultivate reciprocal kinship ties with the English, it is evident that Tomochichi himself self-consciously began to identify closely with the English in an effort to shore up his political authority. To establish his historic connection to the English, Tomochichi made it known early on that he had long been their friend, stating that "he was not a stranger to the English, for that his father and grandfather had been very well known to them."[17] In the same breath Tomochichi humbly deferred to Oglethorpe in matters of war, as if to grant the English commander de facto powers normally reserved for Indian chiefs, stating that he "would not take revenge without Mr. Oglethorpe's consent and approbation."[18] Tomochichi and his followers even volunteered to assist Oglethorpe in ridding the fledgling colony of several Irish Catholic spies working for the Spanish, a further sign of Tomochichi's loyalty to English causes.[19]

Tomochichi may have even assumed a superficial English identity. On one occasion a young Creek man committed suicide in the vicinity of Charles Town by placing the barrel of a loaded gun in his mouth and pulling the trigger with his big toe. The young man's relatives, assuming wrongly that an Englishman had murdered him, threatened to wage a private war on the English colonies. Tomochichi personally averted disaster by seeking out the man's relatives and, upon finding them, exposed his bare breast and stated, "if you kill anybody, kill me, for I am an Englishman."[20]

If Tomochichi was in some ways willing to declare that his body was English, his actions and words also hint that his soul may have assumed a similar configuration. In the weeks following their first meeting, James Oglethorpe portrayed Tomochichi as a man with a keen interest in the English God. Just days after landing at Yamacraw Bluff, for example,

Oglethorpe joyfully reported to the trustees back in London that the Yamacraw chief and his second man "desire to be instructed in the Christian religion."[21] One month later Oglethorpe continued to boast that Tomochichi "comes constantly to church and is desirous to be instructed in the Christian religion."[22] Tomochichi's zeal for things Christian did not wane with the passage of time and we therefore cannot attribute this zeal simply as an initial attempt to ingratiate himself to Oglethorpe. Three years later Tomochichi would have the privilege of meeting the founder of the Methodist sect, John Wesley, whom he asked to "speak the great word to me and my nation."[23]

Moreover, as the *mico* of the Yamacraws, Tomochichi's duties would have included the education of an heir in the traditions of his people. Curiously, Tomochichi's plan for educating his nephew and heir, Tooanaway, demanded a large dose of Anglicization, including indoctrination in the Christian religion and instruction in the English language. To achieve this cultural transformation Tomochichi appears to have given Tooanaway to Oglethorpe for instruction, a common way in which Indian peoples helped to solidify kinship bonds. The project to educate Tooanaway in English ways appears to have worked, for in just a few short months the *South Carolina Gazette* proudly proclaimed Tooanaway an "apt Genius" who had "made a good Progress in the English language, having not only learnt to read the letters, but figures also."[24] Within a year Tooanaway gained enough facility in English to begin reading and reciting portions of the English Bible.[25]

Though Tomochichi may have effectively used his alliance with Oglethorpe to enhance his standing among his own people, he necessarily had to give something in return, thereby opening the door for Oglethorpe to make some of his own demands. On March 12 Oglethorpe scored what was perhaps his greatest coup by concluding a peace with Tomochichi, and securing from him a promise to "[give] up their right to all this part of the country." Oglethorpe, however, did not exactly define what he meant by "all this part of the country."[26]

Tomochichi's initial offer of land, though, did not conclude matters between the Creeks and the Georgians. Initially Oglethorpe and other British officials heralded Tomochichi as "the Mico, or chief of the only nation of Indians living near it [Georgia]." As they well knew, in truth the Yamacraws were only a "little Indian nation" comprised of banished Lower Creeks and lacking in authority to make such a transaction.[27] To secure Creek permission to settle the lands that Tomochichi had offered them, Georgia officials necessarily had to acquire the approbation of the towns in the nation proper. Moreover, Tomochichi's grant directly violated previous agreements made between the Creeks and South Carolina in 1717 and 1732, which placed a moratorium on English settlement south of the Savannah River.

In order to secure their claim to the lands Tomochichi offered and to mollify Creek fears of English encroachment, Oglethorpe invited a large delegation of Creek chiefs to Savannah to negotiate a peace settlement on behalf of the nation. Though often hesitant to make such a long journey, particularly in the midst of planting season, the Creek chiefs responded promptly to Oglethorpe's call, a sure indication that the establishment of yet another English colony—with Tomochichi's assent, no less—had created a good bit of alarm back in Creek country.

One piece of evidence indicating that Tomochichi's actions had alarmed the Lower Creeks was the relative size of the Lower Creek delegation that arrived in Savannah on May 18. According to the official records of that visit, the delegation numbered no less than fifty-two people from eight Chattahoochee towns, including Yahoulakee, the recently appointed *mico* of Coweta, and three other *micos*. Rarely if ever had Charles Town received such a large and high-ranking Creek delegation, which demonstrates that the Creeks used the opportunity of the May meeting to make a diplomatic show of force.

The first to speak at the May conference was a tall, elderly man from the tribe of the Oconees named Oueekachumpa, a self-described relative of Tomochichi who thanked Oglethorpe for the kindness the Englishman had shown to the banished chief.[28] Oueekachumpa emphasized Tomochichi's wisdom, courage, and past deeds as a great warrior, stating that it was for those reasons "that the banished men chose him king." Oueekachumpa's spoke not to flatter Tomochichi, who had absented himself, but to force others to recognize Tomochichi as the *mico* of a new town.

Tomochichi and the Yamacraws later joined the discussion, facing their countrymen for the first time, perhaps, since their exile. Although Tomochichi styled himself a king in the presence of Englishmen, he assumed a much more humble posture when confronted by his own people—a sure indication that the other Creek chiefs may have hardly recognized him as a *mico* much less an important one in the nation. Standing before Oglethorpe, Tomochichi bowed very low and, in an almost pitiful show of self-deprecation, stated "I was a banished man. I came here poor, and helpless, to look for the Tombs of my Ancestors."

After finishing his speech Tomochichi sat down next to Oglethorpe, prompting Yahoulakee, the *mico* of Coweta, to rise and issue his own talk. "I rejoice," he began, "that I have lived to see this day, and to see our friends that have long been gone from amongst us. . . . Our nation was once strong, and had ten towns," he added, "but we are now weak, and have but eight towns." Directing his speech at Oglethorpe, Yahoulakee continued by stating, "you [Oglethorpe] have comforted the banished, and have gathered them that were scattered like little birds before the eagle. We desire therefore to be reconciled to our brethren, who are here amongst you."[29]

Superficially, Yahoulakee appears to have sought merely to reconcile the differences between his and Tomochichi's people. Perhaps the pernicious threat of fratricidal war, combined with the ravaging effects of the recent smallpox epidemic, had put the Lower Creek chiefs in a conciliatory mood. A closer reading of his speech, however, indicates that Yahoulakee was also trying to exert a measure of control over Tomochichi and any further migration to the Yamacraw tract. Yahoulakee concluded by stating "we give leave [permission] to Tomochichi, Stimoioche, and Illispelle, to call the kindred that love them out of each of the Creek towns, that they may come together to make one town." He urged Tomochichi to "recall the Yamasees, that they may be buried in peace among their ancestors . . . and that they may see their graves before they die."[30]

By explicitly granting permission to Tomochichi and the Yamacraws to form their town, Yahoulakee was effectively claiming authority over the new settlement. His plea to "call the kindred that love them out of each of the Creek towns" suggests that they were tacitly trying to purge themselves of other members of Tomochichi's tribe or that they expected these kindred to migrate in the near future, a process that either way he wished to control. Moreover, the fact that Yahoulakee encouraged them to form only one town illustrates that he feared chaos might ensue if other renegades established yet more towns in the vicinity of Savannah.

Thus it appears that by connecting themselves to a potentially powerful new English colony, the once banished Yamacraws effectively rehabilitated themselves in the eyes of their countrymen. The new Yamacraw settlement gained distinction as a legitimate Creek *talwa*, and

Tomochichi likewise garnered recognition as the legitimate Yamacraw *mico*. Such was the true benefit of the 1733 meetings as far as Tomochichi and the Yamacraws were concerned. Regarding the new English settlement, however, much work was yet to be done, as the lands upon which it was to be settled could only be granted by the Creek nation proper and the Creeks first had to determine precisely what was theirs to give.

The Invention of the Creek Empire

The three following days of talks between the Lower Creeks and the Georgia colonists concluded with the ratification of seven Articles of Peace and Commerce. In some respects the 1733 articles mimicked earlier treaties between the Creeks and South Carolinians, most of which were primarily concerned with the issues of commerce, peace, and dispute resolution.[31] The 1733 treaty differed in its reflection of the desire of Georgia and British officials to secure title to the "debatable" Georgia territory. Article three, for example, introduced the "chain of friendship" metaphor that British officials consciously exploited to claim Indian territory. The metaphor had first been used in the South three years earlier in the Cherokee Treaty of 1730, as well as the Creek Treaty of 1732, and was an attempt on the part of the British to link the southern Indian nations to the Iroquois whom they considered subjects of the British crown.[32]

Linked to the chain of friendship metaphor found in article three was article four, which later proved to be a source of contention between the English and the Creeks. In article four the Creek chiefs appear to have granted the Georgia trustees and their successors and assigns the right to "make use of and possess all those Lands which our [the Creek] Nation hath not occasion to use."[33] The problem inherent to article four was its ambiguity, which left "the lands which our Nation hath not occasion to use" as vague and undefined.

At first glance it may appear that the Creeks had conceded much to Georgia and to the British Empire. By granting Oglethorpe the lands that they had no occasion to use, however, the Lower Creeks committed an imperial act of their own by defining what specifically constituted their territory. While most historians have portrayed the struggle for the debatable Georgia territory as a two-way contest between the British and Spanish empires, the 1733 treaty proceedings illustrate that the contest involved not two but three competing nations. Though it is justifiable to assume that the South's indigenous peoples should naturally have a prior claim to Georgia territory, an argument can be made that the Lower Creeks' claims were also in some sense debatable.

According to records of the treaty proceedings, the Lower Creeks at that time claimed all the lands "from the Savannah River, as far as St. Augustine, and up to the Flint River, which falls into the bay of Mexico," including "all the islands in between said rivers. The Creeks also appear to have considered the territory from the "Bay of Apalachee" to "the Mountains" to be their own, a swath of land that necessarily encompassed the Apalachee old fields.[34]

The Lower Creeks proudly boasted that this expanse of territory, roughly approximating and even exceeding the current boundaries of the state of Georgia, was theirs by ancient right. A critical examination of recent history to 1733, however, indicates that the definition of ancient was in the eye of the beholder. For example, Spanish documents from the mission period suggest that prior to 1680 the peoples of the Chattahoochee River may have had little or no contact with the original inhabitants of the Georgia coast—the Escamacus, the Guales, and the Mocamas. Thus it is likely that very few persons from the Chattahoochee River even saw the Georgia coast before that date.[35] Moreover, recall that north Florida remained largely in the hands of missionized Indian groups such as the Timucuans and Apalachees until the first decade of the eighteenth century. How, then, could the Lower Creeks claim to have an ancient right to territories far beyond the middle course of the Chattahoochee River? Because the Lower Creeks were a diverse people who harbored remnants of nations that once lived in the Georgia interior, such as the Ocheses and Ocutis, it is reasonable to suggest that certain elements within the Creek nation remembered their historic link to this territory and believed it was their right to defend it.[36]

Although one can speculate that some Creeks with ancestral links to the Georgia interior continued to regard that territory as their own, more substantial evidence for the Creek belief that Georgia was rightfully theirs can be found in their imaginative use of human bones. Whereas literate peoples such as the British and Spanish used the power of the written word to stake their claims to disputed territory, to commodify it, and to colonize it, the Creeks, like other nonliterate peoples throughout the world, believed that the ritual deposition of ancestral remains established perpetual spiritual links to the land. One recent study indicates, for example, that the when the Choctaws established new towns they transported bundles of ancestral bones and buried them in a ritual manner to establish a settlement charter to the new territory. By burying ancestral bones in this way, Choctaw communities were able to mitigate the upheaval caused by relocation, using the ancestors' remains to link past and future generations to the new territory.[37]

Evidence that the Creeks also used ancestral bones to establish settlement charters comes from the mouth of Tomochichi, who described his exodus to Yamacraw Bluff as a search for the tombs of his ancestors. Tomochichi was referring, of course, to the bones of Apalachicola peoples who had lived and died on the Savannah River during the first decade of the eighteenth century and, according to tradition, still rested there. Tomochichi and the Yamacraws had used this metaphor on earlier occasions, arguing that the bones of a long-dead chief king lay under a high mount of earth located approximately one-half mile from Savannah, conveniently near their current home on Pipemaker's Bluff.[38]

While it is unlikely that a chief king of Apalachicola was ever buried at that precise location, Tomochichi's and the Yamacraws' claim that such a tomb did exist demonstrates the spiritual dimension of the Indians' sense of place; ancestral bones served to link past with present and future generations. The supposed presence of the bones can also be read in light of Tomochichi's territorial and political goals, as the bones' convenient location would have given Tomochichi (a descendant) the right to serve as *mico* and claim the territory in question.[39] It is difficult to determine the extent to which the Creeks still living on the Chattahoochee felt similar spiritual bonds to the Georgia territory that they or their ancestors had occupied between 1691 and 1715. But the indisputable presence of historic Creek burial sites at Ocmulgee and other locations in central Georgia suggest that, if pressured to do so, other Creek towns could have made a similar historic claim to the Ochese Creek territory.[40]

Not only did the Creeks use the presence of the bones of their ancestors to assert their territorial rights, they also used the bones of their enemies to signify their recent conquests on the Georgia coast and in north Florida. Historically speaking, the Creeks could argue with some justification that their assaults upon the Florida mission provinces prior to the Yamasee War entitled them to the now-vacant lands. In subsequent negotiations with Oglethorpe the Creeks argued that they could prove their right to the conquered territory by showing "the heaps of Bones of their enemies slain by them in defense of the said lands."[41] Whereas the bones of ancestors established a charter of settlement, the bones of enemies established a charter of conquest that the Creeks used as one part of their ideological claim to the debated territory.

The Lower Creeks had good reason to make such territorial claims, because they stood to gain in two important ways: first, by granting to the English only the territory they "hath not occasion to use" the Creeks secured, at least in theory, the right to limit the spread of English settlements; and second, this territory was economically valuable in view of the fact that the Georgia woods and plains harbored extensive herds of white-tailed deer (the number of which likely had been artificially inflated due to the recent lack of human occupation). The protection of these herds was essential to the Creeks' nascent market-driven hunting economy, which at the time was on its way to a full recovery after the shocks of the Yamasee War and subsequent trade embargoes.[42]

Creek warriors often carried out their conquests armed not only with British muskets, powder, and steel, but with the British war commissions that empowered them in the use of those arms. There lies the rub. British officials, seeking to undermine Creek claims to their territory, made this fact a cornerstone of their historic defense of Georgia territory. Six years later, in another treaty, Oglethorpe included a clause hinting that the Creeks understood they had "gone to war by commissions from the Governors appointed by the said Kings and Queens of England and that the Spaniards nor no other nation have a right to any of the said lands."[43] Thus, these conquered lands belonged not to the Lower Creeks but to the kings and queens of Britain under whose banner the Lower Creeks fought. In this way war commissions became an important hegemonic tool for British imperialists, who used them to empower ambitious war chiefs and to establish a paper trail claiming the territories they conquered.

A few short weeks after the treaty was signed, Oglethorpe proudly boasted to the trustees in London, "[W]e have concluded a peace with the Lower Creeks, who were the most dangerous enemies to South Carolina and formerly friends to the French and Spaniards."[44] Oglethorpe may have been right to boast of this peace, but his use of the past tense to describe the Creeks' alliance with the French and Spaniards exposes a myopic view of Creek politics. In the years to come Oglethorpe found not only friends among the Lower Creeks but also a good number of enemies, an indication of the contested nature of leadership and foreign policy among the Creek nation.

A Contested Alliance

The 1733 Articles of Peace and Commerce signaled the beginning of James Edward Oglethorpe's and the Georgia government's prolonged attempt to draw the Creeks (through Tomochichi) into a mutually convenient alliance. But it would be a mistake to view Anglo-Creek diplomacy within the confines of a political vacuum since many in the nation did not share Tomochichi's political goals and looked upon Georgia's apparent territorial and military aspirations with suspicion. As a result, the creation of the Georgia colony did not simply catalyze a group of "Oglethorpe's friends" but led to the appearance of other Creek factions dedicated to the preservation of the Spanish and French alliances.

It is ironic, perhaps, that on June 26, 1734, just days after Tomochichi's party arrived in London, twenty-three Creek chiefs and warriors approached the gates of Fort San Marcos in Apalachee to pledge their friendship to Alvaro Lopez de Toledo, the garrison commander. Leading the Creek delegation was Chocate, a warrior from Coweta whom Lieutenant Lopez took to be "the first in authority." Accompanying him was Quilate of Apalachicola, Ysques, a *cacique* from the town of Achito [Hitchiti], and Opugilele, who was described as a *cacique* of Cussita.[45] The chiefs, in an apologetic and friendly tone, argued that they had come to San Marcos "to obtain news of the manner by which the Governor treated the natives." Fortunately for Lopez, several Indian runners from St. Augustine had recently arrived at the fort and attested to the familiarity and affability of the new governor, Francisco de Moral Sanchez. Ysques and Quilate, encouraged by their reception, informed Lopez that they would soon call a meeting of all the nations to discuss reinvigorating the Spanish alliance. If successful, they planned to pay Governor Moral Sanchez a complimentary visit in October to demonstrate their sincerity.[46]

News of the anticipated Creek visit to St. Augustine, however, may not have been the most important occurrence at San Marcos that day. That distinction belongs to the fortuitous arrival of Don Juan Ignacio de los Reyes, one of the aforementioned runners from St. Augustine. Ignacio, a virtually unknown figure in the annals of Creek and Southern history, was commonly known to be an Uchise Indian by birth. Ignacio, reputed to be near thirty-five years of age, was a resident of Pocotalaca, an Indian village located near St. Augustine that harbored the last remnants of the Yamasee tribe. As a courier for the presidio Ignacio had developed a reputation as a man of honor who delivered messages with punctuality. A literate Christian with an apparent facility in the Castilian tongue, Ignacio was quite familiar with the ways of the Spanish, which made him a valuable go-between.[47]

Although pro-Spanish factions had emerged among the Creeks on previous occasions, the June meeting at San Marcos catalyzed the formation of a faction dedicated specifically to thwarting Oglethorpe's plans to subjugate the Lower Creeks. Chocate, the faction's leader, was a subordinate chief of Coweta who harbored a longstanding grudge against the English. Back in the winter months of 1728 he had offered to help the Spanish oust South Carolina Indian agent Charlesworth Glover from the Lower Creek towns. Chocate, moreover, was noticeably absent from the talks held in Savannah the previous May, indicating that his hatred of the English had not waned.

Quilate, whom Lopez judged as second in command, was the head warrior of the town of Apalachicola. He first appears in the historical record in May 1733 as a representative of his town at the grand conference with Oglethorpe in Savannah. Oglethorpe's hospitality, apparently, had done little to comfort Quilate's fears of the building of yet another English settlement, prompting him to join Chocate's mission to San Marcos. From that day forth Quilate would play a prominent role in counter-English espionage, forming critical links to Ignacio and other Indian informants living near St. Augustine.

One suspects, then, that it was this newly formed communication network that first tipped off Governor Moral Sanchez to Oglethorpe's plan to bring Tomochichi to London. Hence, we find Joseph Ramos Escudero in the British capital later that fall, tormenting the Indians with his incisive questions about Tomochichi's authority to act on behalf of the Creek nation. Escudero's correspondence suggests, moreover, that this Creek cabal may have informed Escudero or perhaps Governor Moral Sanchez that Yahoulakee of Coweta should have been considered the true emperor of the Lower Creeks rather than Tomochichi, the pretender.

If Oglethorpe's initial congenial overtures to the Creeks were enough to cultivate mistrust, his increasingly aggressive brand of Indian diplomacy gave further incentive to the Creeks to hold fast to their alliances with the Catholic powers. Beginning in 1734, Oglethorpe not only brought Tomochichi to London but he appointed an acrimonious Scot named Patrick Mackey as Georgia's first Indian agent. In the year following his initial appointment Mackey pressed for Creek permission to build a fort in their territory, which most Creeks considered an affront to their political autonomy. Mackey repeatedly used the authority of his office to monopolize the Creek trade for the colony of Georgia, resorting to strong-arm tactics to oust Carolina traders and seize their merchandise. Circumstantial evidence suggests that Mackey, acting on vague orders from Oglethorpe, tried to draw the Creeks into a war against the Spanish, an enterprise that many Creeks read as a thinly veiled attempt to use them as warriors-by-proxy in Britain's quest for empire.

Thus when Mackey arrived in Creek country in December 1734, he succeeded only in souring the relationship between Georgia and the Creeks. In Coweta on March 10, Mackey ordered all the Lower Creek traders to return to their trading houses, forbidding them "to stir from their habitations" and effectively placing an embargo on the Lower Creek trade. The following month Mackey began confiscating trade goods and expelling traders at the Upper Creek town of Oakfuskee, subsequently granting a trade monopoly to a company of eleven men, many of whom were believed to have formed a partnership with the feisty agent. Later that summer Mackey expelled two Lower Creek traders and in September three of his deputies began seizing more trade goods and expelling the traders to whom the goods belonged.[48]

Most important, perhaps, was Mackey's heavy handed approach that threatened to disrupt the intricate web of social relationships that had developed between the Carolina traders and their Creek hosts. Like earlier generations of Indian traders, the Carolina traders had gained access to the Creeks by immersing themselves in the local communities and learning the protocols of kinship that lubricated commercial transactions. The more socially adept traders likely had married into prominent Creek families or had entered into a privileged relationship with a local chief, who sometimes acted as the trader's guardian or landlord, and thus ensured the protection of the trader's person and property. To have their traders replaced necessarily required the Creeks to educate a new group of men in local etiquette and added yet another burden to the hardships caused by the dwindling supply of trade goods. To counteract Mackey's handiwork, Creek leaders from both the upper and lower nations lobbied to restore the trade to the status quo as it existed before Mackey's arrival. On July 6, 1736, Charles Town officials listened as Obeyhatchey, the king of the Abikas, who spoke on behalf of a small delegation who wished to see their old traders back in their respective towns.[49] Officials in Savannah simultaneously assented to the request of a Lower Creek chief named Emalageechee to have George

Coussins, a trader whom Mackey had expelled the previous year, sent back to his town.[50]

Regardless of how greatly Mackey's efforts to monopolize the Indian trade for Georgia had offended the Creeks, his naked ambition to secure Creek military assistance against Spain and France drove certain Creek chiefs, many of whom were predisposed to favor the Spanish, to seek succor in Florida. Once again problems stemmed from Mackey's first confrontational encounter in Coweta on March 10, 1735. According to a deposition taken several months after the event, Mackey interpreted Oglethorpe's vague instructions to "presume that there is a war with France or Spain" literally rather than conditionally, and began to pressure the chiefs to declare "whether they were willing and would go to war with him?"[51] To placate Mackey the Creek chiefs assented to his request, replying in unison that "they would stand by him with their lives."[52] Mackey must have believe that he had gained some influence, because a few weeks later he stated that, "the chief men of the Indians behave with greater civility and seem to respect us . . . more within these [past] twenty days than they did before."[53]

Still, even the boastful Mackey at his most optimistic moments could not have failed to notice undercurrents of hostility among the Lower Creeks. "It is incredible," he wrote, "how much they are overawed by that silly place in possession of the French called Fort Toulouse and by Saint Marks [San Marcos]." Such awe, Mackey deduced in a moment of Machiavellian epiphany, indicated that "the Indians are governed more by the principles of fear [than] as love." This awe of the French and Spanish led Mackey to find them to be "a sullen, morose people of few words, very ambiguous in answering questions, mighty deceitful and covetous."[54]

Covetous enough of their own autonomy, that is, to go to the Spanish for assistance. On April 5, just weeks after Mackey began his campaign to enlist the Creeks as military auxiliaries, an unnamed chief from the Lower Creeks came to Fort San Marcos requesting a Catholic baptism. The garrison commander seized the opportunity to obtain intelligence about British activity and questioned him as to why his people had not yet rendered obedience to Spain. The man responded that "they were all loyal vassals of his majesty, but they were waiting for an English captain with five-hundred men." The reason his people remained in their towns, he argued, was "to discover his [Mackey's] motives and to oppose him."[55] Although Mackey made some effort to pose as an agent of goodwill, many Creeks understood his motives as patently imperialistic and threatening to their interests. Though this particular chief probably inflated the number of Mackey's force from a modest dozen to an inconceivable five-hundred men in a conscious effort to gain Spanish assistance, the fact that he did so also underscores the Creeks' intuitive understanding and pervasive fear of British imperialism.

Mackey probably refrained from publicly revealing Britain's imperial goals to the Creeks. British officials commonly kept such discussions to themselves. To the Georgia trustees, for example, he claimed that "if I was to demand all their [Creek] territories, they have not a countenance to deny me, tho I believe anything they yield is against their inclinations. Its my opinion that five hundred men with what Indians could be raised in this Nation (if Britain were engaged in a war with France and Spain) would put Britain in possession of all of Florida, and to the Mississippi River."[56]

The Creeks shrewdly recognized Mackey's requests for military assistance, "if" Britain should become engaged in a war with the Catholic powers, as a thinly veiled plan for conquest. Many Creeks came to this understanding during Mackey's tour of duty, as if privy to his private correspondence with British officials. The messenger at San Marcos, for example, warned the Spanish commandant that "they understood that the English wished to populate the province of the Talapuses and Uchises and to continue in Apalachee," echoing almost precisely some of Mackey's words to the Georgia trustees.[57]

Creek chiefs partial to the Spanish continued to keep Governor Moral Sanchez and his subordinates apprised of Mackey's activities. Their accounts differ considerably from English accounts of the same events and indicate that Mackey may have acted more militantly than his superiors knew. On May 20, 1735, Moral Sanchez listened as Yahoulakee, appointed by his people to make the journey to St. Augustine, divulged that twelve Englishmen had come to their provinces bearing flags, war commissions, and munitions. Yahoulakee explained that the Englishmen had called a general meeting in the town of Coweta and offered a supply of guns, powder, and bullets to any town that agreed to "raise the English flag against the Spaniards." The Englishman, Yahoulakee added, promised to distribute these and other gifts to each person in the compliant towns. Only two towns accepted Mackey's offer: Osuche and [Chehaw]. "None of the others" accepted the gifts, Yahoulakee protested, because they knew "the bad intentions of the English."[58]

Mackey had met with Chislacaliche, the Spanish partisan, in an attempt to win him to the English cause. English and Spanish accounts show that Mackey had urged the chief to abandon his current town at the forks of the Chattahoochee and Flint Rivers and relocate among the Lower Creeks, an offer the chief refused unconditionally. Mackey reported that Chislacaliche rejected the offer because he feared Spanish encroachment and because his present location afforded him the opportunity to spy on the Spaniards in behalf of the British.[59]

Yahoulakee's account of the same meeting, in contrast, indicates that Chislacaliche did not intend to spy for the British but rather for the Spaniards. What Mackey failed to reveal was that Chislacaliche had become enraged at Mackey's pretentious demands and that he and Yahoulakee had left Apalachicola in a huff. Together the two men returned to the forks, and Yahoulakee proceeded from there to St. Augustine. Chislacaliche was privy to Yahoulakee's secret mission and thus complicit in his anti-British espionage. Later dispatches also suggest that Chislacaliche was an important link in the intelligence network that kept the commanders of Fort San Marcos in Apalachee well apprised of English activities.[60]

Though Spanish accounts demonstrate that Patrick Mackey's militancy generated a degree of mistrust of the British among Creek leaders, they may have exaggerated the degree to which the Lower Creeks considered him to be unconditionally bad. Mackey could be useful at times, for his influence in Savannah enabled them to counter Tomochichi's attempts to capitalize politically from his London voyage. Tomochichi's party had arrived in London the previous summer and remained abroad much of that fall; the group did not return until late December 1734, first stopping in Charles Town and then proceeding to Savannah in the following weeks.[61]

Although Oglethorpe had intended to parade the Yamacraw delegation through London to drum up support in England for his Georgia schemes and to impress Tomochichi with the grandeur and benevolence of the British people, it was Tomochichi who gained the most politically by choosing to venture to England. On a metaphysical level the act of traveling to such a hitherto unknown are of the world—across the "great water," no less—likely conferred spiritual power upon Tomochichi. Southeastern Indian chiefs had long claimed power on the basis of their mastery of the outside world, which the Indians considered to be both dangerous and powerful. Conquering the barriers of geographical distance therefore required the traveler to manipulate spiritual powers to protect him or herself. Tomochichi's successful return home to Georgia, then, was likely seen by the Creeks as evidence of his mastery of geographical distance and as evidence of the good favor he found with the spirits that protected him on his journey.[62] On a practical level Tomochichi earned respect as a seasoned traveler able to provide a firsthand account of the English people in their element. Tomochichi successfully negotiated the terms of a trade agreement with the Georgia trustees and secured for his people a gift from them that came in the form of a large cache of trade goods.

Though certainly a favorable development, the gifts had a divisive effect on the Creeks and caused their leaders to squabble when it came time to distribute them. At first Tomochichi sought to monopolize the distribution process by sending his personal messenger Senteche into the nation to invite his own "private friends" to Savannah for their reward.[63] Mackey became apprised of Tomochichi's scheme and forbade Senteche from carrying out Tomochichi's orders on the grounds that "the presents should be bestowed on the most deserving and of the most Interest and Power among them here," rather than "lavished away" by Tomochichi.[64]

Heeding Mackey's advice, Thomas Causton, the Georgia official responsible for distributing the trustees' gift, convinced Tomochichi to compile an official list of Creek chiefs deemed worthy to receive the gifts. Like many documents born of a political compromise, Tomochichi's list contained a number of omissions and inclusions that betray the political factionalism then present in Creek country. The most conspicuous divide existed between Tomochichi's friends and the Spanish partisans. Tomochichi was quick to earmark gifts for persons of little political importance who appear to have been related to him or to other Yamacraws. Tallapholechee from the Osuche town, for example, was a man of little note who happened to be the brother of a recently deceased Yamacraw war captain and thus probably a member of Tomochichi's own clan. Other interesting inclusions are Himolatche (or Malatchi) of Coweta, a man of no more than twenty-five years who just happened to be a kinsman of the late emperor Brims. That Malatchi made the list is curious, for Mackey considered him at the time to be little more than "a drunken fellow . . . and entirely in the French interest."[65] Tomochichi perhaps saw in Malatchi a means by which to gain more influence in Coweta, a town that likely had played a role in ousting Tomochichi's people several years before.[66] Tellingly, Tomochichi was careful to omit Yahoulakee and Chocate of Coweta, who had recently reinvigorated the Lower Creeks' contacts with Spanish Florida. Quilate, a leader in that enterprise, somehow made the list, perhaps due to Tomochichi's ignorance or to his desire distribute gifts to as many headmen from Apalachicola, his town of origin, as he could.

The political battles over the gifts finally came to a head in June 1735 when the Upper and Lower Creeks descended upon Savannah for the distribution ceremony. Predictably, the event did not go according to Tomochichi's plans. Tomochichi, it was learned, had intended for half the presents to go to the Lower Creeks and half to go to the upper nation. Georgia officials, however, diverted a disproportionate share to the Upper Creeks, most likely as a reward for granting Mackey permission to build a small—and, as it turned out, inconsequential—fort at Oakfuskee the previous April. Thomas Causton later reported that the Georgians had frustrated Tomochichi's self-serving plans. "Tomochichi," Causton wrote, "was again uneasy believing Mr. Mackay had again disappointed his intentions. . . . Indeed," Causton added, "I found that though Tomochichi had invited some of the upper Nation he did not intend to have so many of them [here]."[67]

Tomochichi's problems did not end with the Upper Creeks. Chigelly of Coweta challenged in a more direct way Tomochichi's presumed authority to distribute presents as he saw fit. Sensing that the time was right to inform the Georgians of the "real" vectors of power within the Creek nation, Chigelly seized the opportunity to stake his own claim as the Creeks' preeminent voice and to assert Coweta's historic role as the Creek nation's head town. Chigelly traced the Creeks' history, delivering a speech lasting two days that Thomas Causton recorded in English on a buffalo robe using black and red ink. Though the original has not survived, Chigelly's account is now known to scholars as the Cussita Migration Legend.[68]

Briefly, the Cussita Migration Legend explains the origins of the Cussita peoples' sacred ritual practices and relates their migration from a mystical point of origin in the west to the Chattahoochee River. Because of its rich ethnographic detail, the Cussita Migration Legend has long attracted the attention of anthropologists, historians, and archaeologists alike. In the process of becoming an object of scholarly fetish, though, it now exists as an ossified cultural artifact far removed from the historical and political context in which it was composed.[69] By inserting it back into that context we find that the Cussita Migration Legend was not a Creek "Book of Genesis" but a ritualized performance intended to demonstrate Cussita's—and, by association, Coweta's—supremacy over other Creek towns and especially over the person of Tomochichi.

The migration legend itself was first brought to the attention of the British in Savannah on June 11, 1735, when Chigelly and Antiche, a Coweta warrior, proceeded to explain how the Cussitas came into being by emerging from a hole in the ground somewhere in the west. After discussing the origins of their sacred war tomahawk and busk medicines, the speakers related how they migrated eastward and established their preeminence over the Chickasaws, Alabamas, and Abikas. A brief discussion of the metaphorical significance of the eagle segued into a discussion of the Cussitas' more recent migration from Coosa River to the Chattahoochee, where they first met the people of Apalachicola.

After resolving a brief dispute, the Apalachicola and Cussita peoples decided to "be all one." "Ever since," Chigelly continued, "they have lived together and shall always live together, and bear it in remembrance." Chigelly made it known that the alliance was not between two equals, infusing his historical narrative with political rhetoric favorable to him and the Cowetas. The Cussitas and Cowetas, he asserted, were one people that were "[recognized] to be the head towns of the upper [and] lower Creeks." Chigelly demanded recognition as the leader of the Creek nation, arguing that "I am from the eldest town and was chosen to rule after the death of the Emperor [Brims]."[70]

The question that arises is, Why did Chigelly choose to deliver such a politically motivated speech on that particular occasion? Given Tomochichi's cozy alliance with Oglethorpe, it is evident that Chigelly sought to counter the Apalachicola man's rising influence. Chigelly did not fail to note, for example, that Tomochichi came from Apalachicola which, unlike Coweta, was not one of the two specified head town. Chigelly took the time to explain that they looked upon Tomochichi as the father of the Yamacraws, revealing Chigelly's belief that Tomochichi's right to rule depended upon the consent of the rest of the Lower Creek nation. Furthermore, it was well known that Georgia officials wished to distribute the trustees' presents to the most influential and friendly chiefs, which perhaps may explain why Chigelly promised to serve the British king and why he declared his own town to be the eldest and his own mouth to be the strongest, presumably among the whole nation.[71]

A second question that arises is the degree to which Chigelly's migration legend accurately represented the historical canon of the Creek nation. According to many anthropologists and linguists, Chigelly's method of storytelling was a common way for nonliterate peoples to communicate historical knowledge. Historical accounts similarly produced can vary over time and according to the context in which they are told. As such, oral traditions can be manipulated easily to reflect the views of the individual telling the tale, the audience, or the current political climate.[72] Not everyone who heard Chigelly's speech, then, was likely to agree upon its accuracy. There may have been as many migration legends as there were storytellers. Just days after the event, for example, Thomas Causton related that the "Hetchitaws and [A]palachicolas" promised him a further account of the migration legend, an indication that Chigelly's was somehow inaccurate. The new account, Causton added, "they say will be an improvement on this," suggesting that Coweta's status as the eldest town or Chigelly's role as the strongest mouth were points of contention on the Chattahoochee and beyond.[73]

Jenkins's Ear, or, The Apparent Proof of Fidelity

While the Cussita Migration Legend reveals certain fissures among the Creeks, an analysis of the behavior of Creek leaders in the years that followed its delivery indicates more directly how the Creek nation itself was a far cry from united, at least as their unity pertained to foreign diplomacy. Evidence suggests, on the one hand, that a core group of Oglethorpe's friends—consisting primarily of the Yamacraws, the Lower Creek point towns, and various individuals with kinship ties to the Yamacraws—had coalesced around Tomochichi. On the other hand, a distinctly pro-Spanish group among the Lower Creeks appears to have formed around individuals such as Yahoulakee and Chocate of Coweta and especially Quilate of Apalachicola. Though these two factions undoubtedly held influence within the nation, we should not assume that every Creek individual was eager to identify too closely with either group. Rather, it appears that the majority of Creek leaders sought to steer a middle course as the War of Jenkins's Ear loomed on the horizon.

The War of Jenkins's Ear (1739–1743) remains one of colonial America's most enigmatic wars due to its odd nickname, opaque origins, and inconclusive results. The conflict's name emanates from an incident that occurred in 1738, when hawkish members of the British Parliament recruited a one-eared smuggler named Robert Jenkins to argue before the House of Commons that Spanish atrocities on the high seas merited British retribution. Jenkins testified that seven years before, while he was attempting to trade in the Caribbean, Spanish sailors had seized his ship, imprisoned him, and severed one of his ears, the dried remains of which Jenkins proudly removed from a handkerchief and displayed before the astonished MP's. Hawkish members of parliament exploited the event in the London press, successfully steering British public opinion in favor of war. In response to the Britons' new-found martial spirit, Prime Minister Robert Walpole abandoned his policy of peaceful coexistence and reluctantly declared war on Spain in October 1739.[74]

Although the war owes its name to the dramatic events in Parliament, its true origins can be traced obliquely to the unresolved territorial disputes between Spain and Britain dating to 1670 and to more recent disagreements over Britain's right to trade in the Spanish Caribbean. Though principally a naval war, regiments from South Carolina and Georgia, together with their Indian allies, engaged Spanish forces on land on three notable occasions, resulting in a virtual stalemate as the year 1743 drew to a close. Peace, however, did not come officially until the Treaty of Aix-la-Chapelle, signed in 1748, ended the widespread series of conflicts in Europe known as the War of Austrian Succession. Although it successfully ended the war in Europe, the Treaty of Aix-la-Chapelle failed to address adequately the territorial disputes in the New World between Britain, Spain, and France that remained fundamentally unresolved until the Treaty of Paris in 1763.[75]

Despite its inconclusive results, historians working in the traditions of British imperial and U.S. colonial history have generally declared the War of Jenkins's Ear a modest success, citing the young Georgia colony's very survival as evidence for Britain's growing strength on the Southern frontier. Some historians credit Georgia's success to James Oglethorpe's aggressive Indian policy which, they argue, succeeded in bringing the Creeks "fairly well under the sway of Georgia" at the outbreak of war.[76]

Historians working within these historiographical traditions are correct to point out (in hindsight) that the stalemate enabled Britain to solidify its position vis-à-vis Spain on the southern frontier. But most have neglected to ponder Creek perspectives on the war and to explain why the Creeks responded to Britain's and Spain's call to arms in a variety of ways. Some Creek warriors, to be sure, fought valiantly for Oglethorpe and willingly sacrificed their precious lives for Britain's cause. But most warriors in the nation remained rather aloof in the conflict. Those who chose to fight for Britain actively refrained from carrying the war to its ultimate conclusion, much as an earlier generation of Creek warriors had done in the waning years of Queen Anne's War. The Creeks, then, were not "generally under the sway of Georgia" but content merely to show their apparent proof of fidelity to the British and yet not get drawn too closely into the larger imperial squabbles.

This is not to say, however, that Creeks never fought against the Spanish or their Indian allies, for evidence indicates that some Creeks carried on a guerrilla war against the Florida presidios for the better part of a decade. Oglethorpe, nevertheless, should not be credited with bringing the Creeks under his sway. The Creeks had their own reasons for fighting such a war and at times were able to conflate their and Oglethorpe's goals to make it appear that they were fighting on behalf of British imperialism.

Blood revenge, for instance, undoubtedly motivated some to risk their lives in the shadows of the Spanish presidios. Such was the case for Licka, the *mico* of Osuche who, at the behest of Patrick Mackey, set out toward St. Augustine in late March 1735, where he killed one Spanish soldier and returned the scalp to Savannah that summer to receive an undisclosed present from the Georgia trustees.[77] Though at first glance Licka appears to have been working in Mackey's employ, evidence suggests that his principal aim was to avenge the death of a brother killed by the Spanish sometime before then and from "whose skull," in Licka's words, "they drink at Augustine."[78]

Even Georgia's most dependable allies, the Yamacraws, appear to have waged war not because of Oglethorpe's influence but for blood revenge or perhaps because of the lure of plunder. For example, in 1736 Oglethorpe began building a series of forts on the Georgia coast that were put in place both to defend the Savannah settlement and to stake Georgia's claim to disputed territory. To assist in this enterprise Oglethorpe enlisted the Yamacraws to help feed his soldiers and scout the territory. As Oglethorpe was not yet willing to encourage his Indian allies to attack the Spanish, he conveniently struck a deal with Governor Moral Sanchez in 1736 whereby they agreed not to go to war and not to set their Indian allies against each other. In doing so both men hoped to shift the burden of imperial affairs upon the shoulders of diplomats in London and Madrid.[79]

Oglethorpe, though pleased to hear Tomochichi and Tooanaway

pledge that their people would live and die by the English, remained apprehensive when he learned of a rumor that Tomochichi's Creek allies "designed to fall on the Spanish." Seeking to avert a premature war against Spain, he urged Tomochichi to bring no more than two hundred men, a number he deemed "sufficient for any service we can have for them."[80]

Oglethorpe's apprehensions proved to be well-founded, for in the years that followed Tomochichi's Yamacraws and other Creek warriors independently waged a guerrilla war against the Spanish presidios. On April 4, 1736, for instance, a body of Uchises and Tallapoosas ("the wild Indians," in Oglethorpe's words) launched an attack of their own against Fort Pupo, a small Spanish garrison on the St. Johns River located sixteen miles from St. Augustine, killing one Spanish soldier in the process.[81] Such small-scale attacks continued during the following years in spite of Oglethorpe's and Moral Sanchez's attempts to establish peace. The attacks did not abate even as Britain and Spain remained officially at peace until the fall of 1739.[82]

Beneath the veil of Creek complicity in fulfilling Britain's overall imperial aims, however, we find more than a murmur of discontent within Creek country being sounded principally by Quilate and other Spanish sympathizers who made themselves useful to the Florida regime. Some Lower Creeks accomplished this service by continuing to provide Spanish officials with intelligence, an enterprise that ran counter to the wishes of Oglethorpe's friends living at Yamacraw and beyond. In September 1735, for instance, English traders reported the presence of three Spanish diplomats among the Lower Creeks. They had come to the Creek towns to invite the chiefs to fulfill earlier promises to meet Governor Moral Sanchez in St. Augustine.[83] Though unable to meet the governor at the time, pro-Spanish Creeks continued to keep the governor apprised of British activity. On October 12 a runner sent by Yahoulakee arrived in St. Augustine to inform the governor that three Englishmen, subalterns to Patrick Mackey, had returned to Apalachicola carrying war flags. Their intent, the runner added, was to enlist Creek warriors in a "propose[d] war" aimed at "reducing" St. Augustine and San Marcos.[84]

Pro-Spanish Creeks continued to provide intelligence to the garrison at Fort San Marcos, which remained the Lower Creeks' principal link to the Florida regime. On April 25, 1736, Moral Sanchez reported that his lieutenant at San Marcos had recently received word that three hundred Englishmen had arrived to build a fort among the "Talapuces." Rumor ominously indicated that the British planned to build another two forts on the Chattahoochee during the upcoming summer. The Creek Indians, the governor was informed, hoped to challenge Britain's ambitions but "could not oppose them without help" from Spain.[85]

While the establishment of Georgia itself was enough to force Spanish officials to come to Florida's defense, Creek pleas for help played a significant role in determining Spain's specific course of action. By intentionally inflating the number of British soldiers stationed in their territory and by portraying Patrick Mackey's meager attempts to fortify Creek country as an unprecedented intrusion of British soldiers, the Indians forced the Spanish to invest a substantial amount of time, energy, and money into cultivating their alliance. As a result, the Creeks secured a new (though unreliable) source of the European goods upon which they now depended. The Creeks effectively used the threat of their military might to buy a lucrative peace with the Catholic powers.

Evidence of the effectiveness of this Creek strategy comes from the pens of the governors of Spanish Florida and French Louisiana themselves. In the opening months of 1736, Moral Sanchez began entreating Governor Bienville of Louisiana to help Spain pacify the "Kouitas" with gifts, noting that the English habit of providing opulent gifts had prejudiced them against the Catholic powers.[86] Bienville, unwilling to see Spain's possessions fall to the British, readily complied, and hosted a large gathering of Creek chiefs at Fort Toulouse in January 1737. The French commander stationed at Fort Toulouse used the opportunity to disburse a large present of powder and shot to each chief, with Governor Moral Sanchez agreeing to pay for the Lower Creeks' portion of the gift. By sharing expenses the two Catholic powers compensated for their local poverty, and both Spanish and French officials believed that the presents mitigated Kaouita aggression.[87]

The threat of Creek hostility also appears to have resonated loudly in Cuba. Well aware of English attempts to buy the Creeks' loyalty, Cuban governor Juan de Güemes y Horcasitas embarked upon his own plan to fight fire with fire by buying a like measure of Creek loyalty for Spain.[88] On January 18, 1738, Güemes y Horcasitas dispatched from Havana Capt. Juan Marquez del Toro on a ship bound for San Marcos de Apalache. On board was a large cache of presents ranging from red jackets garnished in silver and gold to more mundane items such as combs, knives, and hatchets. Because Toro aimed not only to give the Creeks useful gifts but also to regale them in a ceremonial manner, he included in his inventory a sizable quantity of food such as maize, beans, and rice, as well as the social lubricants of choice in Creek country— tobacco and brandy.[89]

Catering to Creek vices, however, was not Güemes y Horcasitas's principal goal. Rather, the Cuban governor sought primarily to coax the Creeks into rendering the obligatory obedience to Spain. For this reason Toro carried with him a set of instructions ordering him to dispense with the gifts in a politically expedient manner. The governor specifically instructed Toro to bestow gifts upon important chiefs only, particularly those who took the time to see him in person. Most important, Toro's instructions included a list of seven points that contained a demand to render unilateral obedience to Spain and "not allow any English or other foreigners in their towns."[90]

Encumbered by these imperious instructions, Toro arrived at San Marcos on February 18. Three days later Juan Ignacio, Florida's most useful Uchise Indian ally, reported to Toro and set out from San Marcos on February 22 carrying Toro's invitation to the various towns in the Creek nation. It should be noted that Juan Ignacio's arrival was not simply a fortuitous stroke of luck but a calculated ploy on the part of Florida and Cuban officials to tap into the network of communication established several years before. Governor Güemes y Horcasitas, not incidentally, had met Juan Ignacio previously in Cuba and believed him to be a "skillful man of trust"; he specifically instructed Toro to use Ignacio as a messenger upon his arrival in Apalachee.[91]

Predictably, the first to heed Toro's invitation to San Marcos were well-known Spanish partisans with ties to Juan Ignacio, including Chocate of Coweta, Chislacaliche, and Quilate of Apalachicola, whom the delegates recognized as the "head of all present" at the gathering. In the coming weeks Juan Ignacio successfully convinced more than 140 Creeks to venture to Fort San Marcos to receive gifts and hear Toro speak, culminating in a grand conference held on April 14, the largest of any Spanish-Creek meeting in the 1730s.

In many ways the April 14, 1738, meeting between Toro and the Creeks was reminiscent of many such meetings that had occurred in the wake of the Yamasee War and reflected the aspirations of a bygone era. Toro read the contents of his superior's instructions, directing Quilate to plead with his people to shun the English and repopulate Apalachee. Quilate, though eager enough to ally with Spain, was unwilling to commit wholeheartedly to Toro's requests. Quilate had a few demands of his own, indicating that his own desire for the alliance was conditional. He implored Toro, for example, to build and garrison a Spanish fort at San Luis de Apalachee complete with a store furnished with all the necessary trade goods. Quilate, disappointed by Spain's failure to fulfill similar promises in years past, gave the Spanish one year to fulfill this demand, stating that their failure to do so would only prove that English insinuations of Spanish poverty were well founded.[92]

Fortunately for Oglethorpe, Britain retained a substantial number of friends in the Creek nation, many of whom appear to have been dismayed by the sudden rise of pro-Spanish sympathies among their people. This hawkish pro-English faction appears to have been composed of Tomochichi's own townspeople living in the generally pro-English towns of Osuche and Chehaw, as well as residents of less partisan towns such as Ocmulgee and Apalachicola, Tomochichi's town of origin.[93]

In October 1738 an impressive delegation of 86 Creek chiefs and warriors journeyed to Savannah to invite Oglethorpe to a grand meeting of their own, to be held the following summer in Coweta just in time for the annual Busk festival. The Creek chiefs, led by the *micos* of the Chehaws, Ocmulgees, Osuches, and Apalachicolas, begged Oglethorpe to come on the pretense that his failure to do so would steer their countrymen into the bosom of Spain. They further enticed Oglethorpe with the promise that upon his arrival, "the nation would march one-thousand warriors wherever he should command them."[94] Though Oglethorpe was somewhat hesitant to make the long voyage to the Chattahoochee, Tomochichi encouraged him to accept the invitation, arguing that his presence might convince the Creeks to shun the Spanish and "entirely settle them in an unanimous resolution to adhere to his [Britannic] majesty."[95]

Most important, perhaps, Creek promises to field a large army for good King George induced Oglethorpe to let his imagination run wild with unrealistic expectations of Indian military assistance. Initially the Creeks hinted to Oglethorpe that they could field up to one thousand warriors, but reports indicating that other Indian nations would send delegates to Coweta led him to think that he might be able to recruit seventy-five hundred Indian warriors for the British cause. Thus, with inflated expectations of Indian military assistance, Oglethorpe commenced his journey from Fort Frederica in July 1739, arriving on August 9 at Coweta, where Chigelly greeted him with the customary displays of friendship.[96]

Oglethorpe's momentous visit to Coweta culminated in the ratification of a second Anglo-Creek treaty two days later. The treaty recapitulated many of the points expressed in Georgia's 1733 treaty with the Lower Creeks. The Creeks asserted their prior territorial claims and reaffirmed Georgia's original land grant on the sea coast. Though similar to the agreements reached six years earlier in Savannah, the 1739 treaty lowered the price of trade goods in the Creek nation, perhaps by as much as one-third. Oglethorpe's intention, of course, was to lure the Creeks with this discount and recruit more warriors to the British cause.[97] Ultimately, however, Oglethorpe was sorely mistaken to think that the majority of the Creeks could be bribed into helping Britain raise the Union Jack over St. Augustine.

Nevertheless, Oglethorpe returned to Savannah in late September, brimming with optimism for Creek assistance in the (as of yet undeclared) war effort. "In conversation," William Stephens wrote, "he [Oglethorpe] was pleased most agreeably to inform us, how unquestionably he had the Friendship of the lower and upper Creek Indians secured to us." As a consequence of this self-confidence, Oglethorpe spent more than a month "waiting for his Indians" as he assembled a main army of Scottish highlanders.[98] Oglethorpe grew tired of waiting, however, and returned to Fort Frederica in early November. When Spanish interlopers killed two unarmed Georgians on Amelia Island, Oglethorpe decided that war was at hand and soon thereafter set out with his army toward Florida.[99]

In the three or so years that followed, the British and Spanish fought four major battles before the so-called War of Jenkins's Ear ground to a stalemate and caused Oglethorpe to be recalled to England (permanently, as it turned out) to defend his apparent ineptitude. The first such battle occurred in late December 1739, when the Georgians briefly captured Forts Picolata and Pupo on the Florida frontier, only to abandon them weeks later when their position appeared indefensible. The following spring Oglethorpe launched an extended siege of St. Augustine, which eventually foundered when Spanish sloops evaded a British blockade. Spain retaliated in the summer of 1742 by invading St. Simon's Island, only to be repulsed by the Georgians and their Indian allies during a series of skirmishes known as the legendary Battle of Bloody Marsh. Oglethorpe staged a final siege of St. Augustine in the spring of 1743, but once again failed to raise the Union Jack over St. Augustine.

Though it is clear that Oglethorpe successfully recruited Indian allies at every stage of the war, the extent to which the Creeks actually fought is questionable. Both Spanish and English sources attest to the fact that the number of Creek warriors who actually fought for Oglethorpe fell far short of the 1,500 promised to him in Coweta in August 1739.[100] In the initial foray against Fort Picolata on December 29, for example, Governor Manuel de Montiano reported that the attack party consisted of approximately 150 Englishmen but only 30 Indians. Forty-six Uchise warriors, he added, had attacked the Indian town of Ayamon, indicating that the total number of active Indian troops may not have exceeded 80 warriors.[101]

Montiano's correspondence during the siege of St. Augustine that summer tells a similar tale. Though Montiano believed that British forces had numerous Indian allies scouring across Florida territory, evidence indicates that relatively few Creek warriors actually fought. Spies revealed that Oglethorpe's army during the summer siege was comprised of approximately 130 Indian warriors, an estimate far shy of the most boastful British accounts, which claimed that 500 Indians had assisted them in the siege. In addition, another 35 Indians may have participated in the attack on Fort Mose and, in the wake of the fort's capture, stayed there as a part of the garrison.[102] One Spanish soldier who took part in the Battle of Bloody Marsh estimated that Oglethorpe had no more than 100 Indian allies, only 50 of whom appear to have played an active role in the skirmishes.[103]

Numbers, however, tell only part of the story. A second strain of evidence indicating that the Creeks may have been lukewarm to the Georgia cause can be found in the composition of the war parties that actually fought. The British, it appears, drew a substantial portion of their auxiliaries not from the Creek nation proper but from among the small dependent Indian nations established near the English settlements. Both the Yuchis, who lived near Fort Palachicola on the Savannah River, and the eastern Chickasaws, who had recently taken up residence near Augusta, appear to have constituted the bulk of his Indian army.[104] The Indians who helped—and failed—to guard Fort Mose, for example, were described by Montiano as a party of "Yuches and Uchises, with a white man for a chief."[105] Another telling piece of evidence comes from the pen of Oglethorpe himself, who reported that 20 to 30 Yuchis lost their lives during the siege of St. Augustine, an indication that many of the most active warriors had come from that nation. Evidence also indicates that many of the Indians who fought at Bloody Marsh were Chickasaws and Tomohetans, a migrant people that had resided from time to time among both the Creeks and the Cherokees. [106]

Britain's staunchest Creek allies came not from the nation proper but were drawn from among the Yamacraws and lesser-known coastal Indian settlements. The pro-English Creeks were led by Tomochichi's heir Tooanaway and the Cowkeeper, a so-called island chief who lived on the Georgia coast. Tooanaway, for instance, first volunteered to lead 200 Creek warriors in the fall of 1739 and eventually suffered a fatal wound in the Battle of Bloody Marsh in 1742. His presence and ultimate sacrifice suggests that many of the Creeks who fought were Yamacraws. The Cowkeeper, a Lower Creek chief who lived on one of Georgia's barrier islands, reported to duty in the midst of the siege on St. Augustine with 45 warriors, indicating that he too had cultivated a pro-English following. [107] The Creeks, as one scholar of Spanish Florida has noted, may have made useful raiders and scouts, "but they were not decisive in turning the balance of power overwhelmingly to the English" and were therefore not "the key to victory" in the War of Jenkins's Ear. [108] The question that remains is, why not?

Understanding why the Creeks appear hesitant to help Oglethorpe raise the Union Jack over St. Augustine demands that we consider the War of Jenkins's Ear as the Creeks might have seen it. Undoubtedly, a number of Creeks held grievances against the Spanish and their mission Indians and proved willing to engage in small-scale raids for scalps and plunder. To escalate this activity into an imperial war would not only have required the Creeks to sustain great numbers of casualties but also demanded that they abandon the wisdom articulated in the Coweta Resolution, which held that Creek security was best guaranteed by maintaining peaceful relationships with all three European powers.

Some prominent Creek leaders, such as Quilate of Apalachicola, appear even to have assisted Spain in its defense so as to preserve the contested political environment. In August 1739, just as Oglethorpe had assembled in Coweta all chiefs of the nation, Quilate sent a runner into St. Augustine in an apparent attempt to warn the Spanish of the upcoming invasion. Quilate's runner explained that a slave rebellion had recently broken out in South Carolina and that the British intended to build a fort somewhere on the Southern frontier. [109] Of more immediate concern were the two large bodies of Indians that had gone out, one set to attack St. Augustine and the other San Marcos de Apalachee. Quilate, according to this same report, claimed to be "investigating everything, particularly where they intended to build the fort."[110]

Spain's most valuable ally in the course of the war proved to be none other than Juan Ignacio, who slipped in and out of Oglethorpe's camps during his two attacks on St. Augustine and provided Governor Montiano with much valuable intelligence. For example, Ignacio was responsible for first reporting the initial attack on Fort Picolata on December 29, 1739, and he was the first to inform the governor of the fall of Fort Pupo in January. Juan Ignacio also put himself at risk by spying on Oglethorpe's army and providing Montiano with accounts of British movements and troop strength.[111]

Moreover, the Creeks who came to Florida to assist Oglethorpe regarded his sieges merely as opportunities to acquire scalps, slaves, or a bit of plunder from the Spanish presidios. In the wake of the first attacks on Forts Picolata and Pupo in January 1740, Governor Montiano observed that the Uchise warriors spent most of their time in search of Indian slaves, the primary source of which were to be found on the Florida coast south of St. Augustine. Other shreds of evidence suggest that the Creeks spent much time pursuing the horses and cattle that roamed northern Florida. Furthermore, during the siege of St. Augustine, Thomas Jones reported that his party of Creeks were loath to participate in the siege and did little more than scout the territory. In the course of his military duty, Jones had warned his superiors that his warriors would not abide by Oglethorpe's war plans, stating that "they would soon be tired with that way of Proceeding, for that they loved to go and do their business at once and return home again." Predictably, Jones's warriors departed after a mere three weeks of service.[112]

One of the most intriguing pieces of evidence indicating that the Creeks may have been feigning war rather than fighting it comes from the pen of Edward Kimber. Kimber, an Englishman who participated in the aborted March 1743 siege of St. Augustine, later composed a romanticized narrative of the event, giving a somewhat contradictory account of Oglethorpe's Indian allies' martial prowess. Kimber was at first impressed by the religious solemnity with which the Indians pursued warfare. On one occasion he noted that Britain's Indian allies often absented themselves to a remote part of the forest to perform "physick" rituals, undoubtedly a reference to war purification rituals common among Southern Indians. Kimber likewise appeared impressed when it was reported that the Indians had set numerous fires in the vicinity of St. Augustine that "had spread near a mile, destroying all before it." The fires, Kimber presumed, had been set by the Indians to intimidate the Spanish.[113]

Britain's Indian allies, Kimber revealed in contrast, at the same time exhibited tepid passion for combat. Kimber noted not only their tendency toward drunkenness but also the ease with which Spain's Indian allies repulsed them. Kimber explained how on March 28 a war party had set out against St. Augustine but had "advanced no farther than the Grove, where they were repuls'd by the Yamasees, who, it seems, were out and one of them wounded." "They appeared," Kimber added, "prodigiously jaded and fatigued" as a result of this brief engagement.[114]

Though we might attribute this kind of behavior to the Indian method of warfare, a more plausible explanation is that the Creeks purposefully chose to fight this way. By doing so they could avoid costly casualties and at the same time receive presents and a cut in trade prices from the English for "services rendered." Oglethorpe himself appears to have believed that such was the case, complaining to his superiors that his Indian allies would not fight unless he continually distributed presents, food, and alcohol.[115]

Oglethorpe, it appears, was correct in his assessment. After the war, Spanish officials learned from a Christian Yamasee Indian named Francisco Luis that much of the Creek war effort, particularly the aborted 1743 siege of St. Augustine, had been staged. Luis, who served as an interpreter at St. Augustine, had several close acquaintances in the Creek nation who divulged to him the Creeks' true war aims. Though not necessarily fond of either the Spanish or the English, Luis explained that the Creeks went to war in order to milk the English of their gifts. During the recent siege of St. Augustine, he argued, most of the Creeks who participated did so only to steal horses; for this reason they resisted British attempts to subordinate them under British commanders. Furthermore, the bonfires Kimber described were little more than a lie designed "to prove [to the English] that they had taken some action against the Spanish." Their goal, he concluded, was not necessarily to do the Spanish harm but merely to give the English an apparent proof of their fidelity.[116]

The Creeks' lukewarm effort in the War of Jenkins's Ear stands in stark contrast to the confident pronouncements of loyalty that Tomochichi made to King George scarcely a decade before. While ambitious British officials, not to mention a few conspicuously complicit Indians, strove at times to create a loyal Creek Nation, the Creeks' fluid, kin-based political system virtually guaranteed that James Oglethorpe would find among the Creeks as many enemies as he did friends. Moreover, Tomochichi and Oglethorpe tended to draw their allies specifically from the Lower Creek point towns, a pattern that indicates that the Lower Creek confederation, like the "Creek Nation" itself, was still a work in progress.

By enhancing Tomochichi's authority and by pressing the Creeks to cede land, British imperialists forced the Creeks to look inward and ponder the state of their own nation. In effect, the establishment of Georgia in 1733 prompted the Creeks to assume ultimate authority over most of the territory claimed by the state of Georgia, and thereby define "the nation" in reference to its recent conquests. Likewise, Tomochichi's rise in influence prompted chiefs such as Chigelly to assume authority as the principal mouths of the entire Upper and Lower Creek nation. These events, while important in their own right, set important precedents for a future generation of Creek leaders caught between the peril of subjugation and the opportunities for personal aggrandizement that British imperialism offered. One figure who would soon find himself caught in this dilemma of leadership was a young man from Coweta named Malatchi, a kinsman of Brims, who sought to navigate these new political waters and to further define the Creeks as a nation in the process.

CHAPTER SIX

The Twin

Ominous news awaited Coweta's leaders as the year 1746 drew to a close. With Chief Tomochichi dead a full seven years, the Yamacraws found themselves on the defensive as the "white people" of Georgia began extracting "a great deal of timber" from the Yamacraw reserve at Pipemaker's Creek. Tomochichi's widow, Queen Senaukey, issued a formal protest with the Georgia magistrates, who rebuffed her complaints about the logging by saying that the Indians who crossed the "Great Water" years before—Tomochichi and Senaukey included—had given away their lands to the English. When she demanded a sizeable gift of rum as payment for the illegally appropriated timber, Senaukey was rebuffed again, causing her to look to Chigelly of Coweta, then in Augusta on other business, for help. Chigelly, hesitant to recklessly enter into the dispute, decided to return home to Coweta to "[enquire] of my people" about the affair.

The news was no better in Coweta. Chigelly, eager to ascertain the true extent of the Lower Creeks' land grant to the Georgia colony, employed their trader, George Galphin, to interpret an old copy of the 1739 treaty that Chigelly had signed in the presence of James Oglethorpe. Galphin, one of the more fluent interpreters of the Muskogee language, dutifully reported to Chigelly that by virtue of the 1739 treaty the Creeks had in fact given away substantial tracts of land along the Savannah River.[1] Chigelly was much vexed "to think that the white people should give us Papers and tell us they were all for the good of us Our wives and children when at the same time they were to take away our lands."

Chigelly, of course, knew they had been duped because "we could not read" the treaty.

Entering into the fray was Chigelly's younger kinsman, Malatchi, who was on hand to hear Galphin disclose the contents of the treaty. In the months that followed Malatchi became increasingly embroiled in the land controversy. A year later Malatchi made the arduous trek to Fort Frederica to make his views of the matter known to the recently installed commander of His Majesty's forces, Alexander Heron. Introducing himself as the "*opiya mico* Emperor of the upper and lower Creek Nation," Malatchi informed Heron of his noble bloodline by stating that "my Father was Emperor of the Creek nation," a status rooted in the claim that his "father" was "the first man that received white people on these lands."[2]

Malatchi proceeded to give Heron a history lesson that chronicled the triumphs and tragedies of the Anglo-Creek alliance, relating several events that occurred either prior to his own birth or during his early boyhood. Recalling the Yamasee War, Malatchi remembered that the Creeks and English had "lived together as Brothers for some time" until the traders "began to use us very ill and wanted to enslave us." This, he argued, had occasioned a war until the governor of Carolina sent his beloved man, Col. John Musgrove, to make peace by having both sides ritually bury their war implements.

Malatchi was particularly adept at recounting the past treaties his people had concluded with the English, paying particular attention to the details concerning land. Malatchi reminded Heron that the original peace treaty forbade white people from settling or allowing their animals to roam on any land "to the Southward of the river Savannah" (which was "the boundary between the white people and us"). He acknowledged that his people had amended the terms of the original agreement by allowing Oglethorpe to settle "upon the river Savannah as far as the tide flowed and along the Sea Coast, excepting the three Islands, Sapalo [Sapelo], St. Catherine's, and Ossabaw, which we reserved for ourselves."

All agreements sat well with the Georgia colonists, Malatchi thought, until Oglethorpe "gave us a paper, which he said was for the Good of us all . . . but did not let us know the Contents of it." The signing of that paper, he argued, marked the beginning of the controversy over land, and Malatchi wanted to see this land restored to its rightful owners, the Indians. Before departing Malatchi issued a stern warning to King George II: "I am now Emperor of the Creek Nation, that I have 2,000 fighting Men under my Command, as well as the Care of their wives and Children. . . . [I] think myself obliged to speak every thing for their Good, and that I shall wait for his [the King's] answer thereto, and make all my people easy in the mean time."[3]

Few eighteenth-century Creek leaders drew more attention to them-selves than did Malatchi of Coweta in boldly issuing this stern warning to the king. Highly esteemed among his own people, Malatchi's physi-cal presence and abilities as warrior and statesman likewise impressed colonial officials. Georgia magistrate William Stephens described him as a very engaging person, just shy of six feet tall, of a "clean" make, and "perfectly well shaped from Head to Foot, as he appears when naked to his skin." When he donned European garb Malatchi duly im-pressed the often-haughty Europeans as their equal. As Stephens put it, "when he puts on a Coat and Hat, his Behaviour is such, that one would rather imagine from his Complaisance, he had been bred in some European Court, than among Barbarians." Possessed of a courtly polite-ness, Malatchi's presence nevertheless tended to mystify: "At the same time," Stephens added, "though the Features of his Face were inviting, and shew Tokens of Good-Nature; yet there is something in his Aspect which demands Awe."[4]

However awesome he may have appeared to his contemporaries, Malatchi has yet to receive the same attention from modern scholars, who have devoted more effort to the study of preceding Creek leaders, such as Brims or others who followed Malatchi generations later, such as Alexander McGillavray. Among the first to focus attention on Malatchi was John Swanton, who acknowledged Malatchi as the Creek emperor but casually dismissed him as a mere "headman, probably a [Cussita] In-dian," and overlooked his relationship to the previous Coweta emperor, Brims. Later generations of scholars, in contrast, have fixated almost exclusively on Malatchi's place in the Coweta chain of emperors and offered various explanations as to his biological relationship to Brims. David Corkran, taking at face value the English documents (which typi-cally depict Malatchi as Brims's son), believed that Malatchi was Brims's biological son and speculated that Coweta's rulers consciously founded a patrilineal dynasty by absorbing the offices of *mico* and head warrior into one. More ethnographically informed revisions of Creek political history, however, posit that Malatchi was more likely Brims's biological nephew, an interpretation more consistent with the rules of matrilineal succession.[5]

Most existing analyses of Malatchi's political career devote attention to what others of his time believed Malatchi was and, in the process, neglect to explore fully what exactly he did or how he might have regarded himself. As a result, Malatchi's life as an important epoch in Creek political development has largely gone unnoticed. Referred to variously as the "twin," the "prince," the emperor," the "son of Brims," and the "real chief" of the Creek Indians, Malatchi's precise status within the nation sometimes confused colonial officials and often confounded his Creek contemporaries. By looking at Malatchi's manipulation of traditional political channels, though, we find a man who consciously worked to gain regional influence. Born in the influential town of Coweta into an influential clan that earlier had staked claims to political prestige, Malatchi was well-positioned to exert political influence throughout much of the Creek nation. Though he was no emperor or prince in the European sense of the term, and was keenly aware of the limits of his political influence, Malatchi nevertheless appears to have asserted and defended the concept of his national leadership, thereby building upon earlier precedents set by his kinsmen Brims and, to a somewhat lesser extent, Chigelly. Fitting it was, then, that Malatchi was "obliged" to emerge in 1747 as the leading Creek opponent of Georgia expansion into Creek lands.

By virtue of his clan and town connections, Malatchi was probably the most intellectually prepared person to fill the role of leader, since the defense of Creek lands required a thorough knowledge of Creek and colonial history and tradition as well as an ability to innovate when needed. Though it is true that many other affairs occupied his time, Malatchi's defense of Creek lands may be viewed as his most important contribution in crafting a new definition of the Creek nation as a territory with precise (and presumably defensible) boundaries. And, as the defense of Creek lands required him to invoke old Anglo-Creek treaties and occasionally use the power of the written word, Malatchi helped to establish the "Creek Nation" as a legal term. Indeed, Malatchi may or may not have fully understood the significance of his innovation. The abstract, legal concept of a Creek Nation, moreover, may have had little meaning to the clans scattered among the various towns on the Chattahoochee, Tallapoosa, and Coosa Rivers. But as land struggles became more commonplace later on, the concept of the territorially circumscribed and legally defined Creek Nation assumed an increasing level of concreteness. Malatchi, it might be argued, was the first to give a definite shape to the idea of a Creek Nation.

The Twin

Though his early life is clouded somewhat in obscurity, we know with some certainty that Malatchi was born the second of two male twins and was referred to frequently as such, even late in his life. Malatchi's status as a twin must therefore be considered fundamental to his identity. The Creeks and most Southeastern Indians believed that twins possessed special spiritual powers associated with divination and prophecy, particularly second-born twins, who were often credited with protecting and guiding the older twin on the journey from womb to world.[6]

Malatchi's life as a twin would have been exceptional even as he drew his first breaths, for the Creeks treated twins differently than they did other infants. Instead of allowing the infant to suckle soon after birth, Malatchi's mother might have refrained from nursing him for up to four days, instead feeding the infant corn gruel mixed with several kinds of pulverized roots and tubers. These foods, in lieu of mother's milk, were thought necessary for nourishing a twin's prophetic gifts. Furthermore, the infant Malatchi probably remained isolated in his mother's house for four months rather than the customary four days. Like special foods, this prolonged period of isolation was thought to enhance a twin's powers to prophesy which, with proper training, might someday make him a doctor (elicktca) or medicine man (hilis haya).[7]

Despite, or perhaps because he was a twin thought to possess spiritual gifts, Malatchi's people were likely to have viewed him with ambivalence. Spiritual power was an attribute that all Creeks valued, and those who could demonstrate their mastery of it generally earned the respect of their peers. But all Indians recognized that such powers could be used both for good and for evil, which made spiritual persons simultaneously respected and feared within their communities. Much of this ambivalence derived from the Creek belief that twins regularly spoke with the "little people," a race of spirits who inhabited treetops, hollow logs, and caverns. Because the Creeks believed that the little people caused sickness and insanity, twins like Malatchi would have been feared because of their association with the spirits.[8]

In addition to being a twin, evidence indicates that Malatchi's life began in about the year 1710.[9] The timing of his birth should be considered fundamental to Malatchi's identity since the world he knew growing up was decidedly different from the world inhabited by his predecessors. Like many Lower Creek men of his age, Malatchi was probably born at Ochese Creek, Coweta's temporary home between 1691 and 1716. If so, he was part of an entire generation that could claim Ochese Creek as the land of their birth, which may help to explain why Malatchi was particularly hostile to white encroachment on that territory.

By virtue of the timing of his birth, Malatchi came into the world more than twenty-five years after British traders had established steady commercial relations with the Creeks and may have regarded European technology as familiar, if not traditional. For example, he would have considered it natural to skin a deer using a metal knife, and may have preferred wearing British woolens to dressed deerskin. Having no firsthand memory of life without European goods, Malatchi would have been loath to give them up, thus making him and his generation dependent upon English traders to satisfy their material wants.[10] Nor did Malatchi have any firsthand memory of life as it was lived before the intrusion of Europeans, whose presence had, by the turn of the eighteenth century, become commonplace for most Creeks. Malatchi would have grown up knowing the benefits and the dangers of the European presence. Among the most disturbing events in the young twin's life was the Yamasee War, which acquainted him with the harmful effects of the British trade regime. Malatchi's earliest memories, therefore, may have been rooted in fear as his people struggled to avoid becoming slaves to the Carolinians.

The Yamasee War may have had the corollary effect of instilling in Malatchi a life-long hatred of the Cherokees, due in part to the assassination of sixteen Creeks and Yamasees at Tugaloo in 1716. Some of the victims of this assassination were undoubtedly related to Brims, Chigelly, and other members of the Coweta elite, making it likely that the five- to six-year-old Malatchi was intimately acquainted with the rituals of mourning during those troubled times.[11] As an adult Malatchi fought frequently against the Cherokees, perhaps invoking the memory of lost relatives as added inspiration.

The Yamasee War also probably caused Malatchi's boyhood to be defined by material deprivation and want. When the Yamasees initiated their attacks on English traders on Good Friday of 1715, they put an abrupt end to the trade in skins and slaves that had enabled the Creeks to acquire English trade goods, rendering the Creeks poor by 1717. Likewise, we may imagine the young boy struggling to keep up with his family as they trekked from their homes on Ochese Creek west to the Chattahoochee River, where in the spring of 1716 they reestablished their old towns permanently after a twenty-five-year exile. Malatchi, by then of a more competent age, probably assisted with the difficult work that accompanied such a move: collecting and carrying personal belongings, felling trees, building new houses, and planting enough corn to avoid starvation when winter came.

Not incidental to Malatchi's life was his place of birth, Coweta, which had recently ascended to political prominence, aided in part by the town's alliance with the Carolina trade regime. But it was not enough simply to be born in Coweta. For Malatchi to rise to prominence he must have been born into the right family, one with a historic claim to the Coweta chieftaincy and an apparent regional influence. Politically speaking, then, Malatchi's relationship to Emperor Brims appears to have been most important and to this day continues to be a subject of dispute. British colonial officials typically regarded him as the son of Brims, believing that by rising to power among the Creeks, Malatchi was rightly following in his father's footsteps.

This view, however, should not be taken at face value, because the patriarchal norms of European culture often blinded British officials to the matrilineal kinship systems typically operating among Indian groups in eastern North America. We may never know the precise biological relationship between Brims and Malatchi, but in the Creek matrilineal system the office of *mico* typically passed from uncle to nephew so as to keep the office within the same matrilineal clan. A Creek chief customarily established a close relationship with a favored nephew, who lived with the chief to undergo a period of instruction in the art of governance and in the traditions of his tribe. As Thomas Nairne put it, "the Chief and [beloved men's] sons never enjoy their fathers place and dignity." Instead, the honor of chief went to their sisters sons, who were "taken into their Cabins when young, [to] hear their consultations," guaranteeing that the selected successors "are instructed in their customs [so] that when it comes their Turne they may know how to rule The Town."[12] Thus, any adopted nephew taken into the chief's household could easily appear as a son to Europeans predisposed to assume that authority flowed through patrilineage. Malatchi, we may therefore surmise, was a member of the Coweta ruling clan and more than likely not Brims's biological son but a nephew according to European kinship conventions.[13]

Whatever their precise biological relationship, Brims undoubtedly played a singularly important role in educating Malatchi in governance, an education that began rather early in the boy's life. Malatchi's introductory lesson in foreign diplomacy, for example, began in the midst of the Yamasee War when his kinsman allowed him to meet the Spanish governor in St. Augustine in September 1715. On that particular occasion Malatchi would have watched as Brims submitted to the Spanish Crown, probably in exchange for a handsome suit of vestments and the Spanish military title of "generalissimo." In time Malatchi undoubtedly learned that the Spanish were capable of supplying clothes, candy, and rum, but could not give the Indian chiefs the items they wanted most at that time: cloth, gunpowder, and bullets.[14]

Brims continued to instruct Malatchi as he grew from a boy to a young man, bequeathing to him the knowledge that an earlier generation had gained only through hard-won experience. Malatchi's own recollections indicate that Brims devoted much time instructing him in the concept and goals of neutrality as articulated in the Coweta Resolution. As an adult Malatchi occasionally recalled his "father's" words of warning to not "spill the white man's blood" in an Indian town. Most important, Brims warned the young man of the impending slavery his people might suffer in the event that one European empire was able to dominate the others.[15]

Another individual who played an important role in Malatchi's life was Brims's brother Chigelly. Cognizant of his impending mortality, the aging Brims late in life appointed Chigelly as Malatchi's guardian. At the same time, Brims appointed the soon-to-be Coweta *mico*, Yahoulakee, as the guardian to Malatchi's twin brother Essabo. As Malatchi's guardian, Chigelly was duty bound to continue the young man's political education in the event of Brims's death, which occurred in 1732 or 1733. Chigelly continued to operate in this capacity past Malatchi's thirtieth year of age and can be credited as being the first to introduce Malatchi to Georgia officials. Throughout his life Chigelly worked as a trusted aide to Malatchi and together the two often conferred on important political matters.

Malatchi's privileged birth in turn left him in a favorable position to exploit preexisting connections to the European powers and to stake a claim to leadership over the entire Creek Nation. Coweta's ruling clan had been "the first" to accept British traders into their town and, on at least two occasions, had married their women off to important British traders such as Henry Woodward and John Musgrove. The British continued to recognize these important connections throughout the early part of the eighteenth century, first by commissioning Brims as the singular Creek headman and second by appointing Brims's younger kinsmen—Ouletta, Chipacasi, and Chigelly—as his heirs. Spanish connections also ran deep. The Spanish, recall, had dubbed Brims "generalissimo" and later recognized Chipacasi as Brims's second in command or campmaster general.

Most important, by virtue of his connection to Coosaponakeesa, Malatchi had more direct access to the British colonies than most Creeks. Coosaponakeesa, betrothed in the peace settlement following the Yamasee War, wed the young John Musgrove in 1725 and lived in Colleton County, South Carolina, until 1732 when the Yamacraws invited the couple to move to Georgia to open a trade outpost. From that point on Coosaponakeesa, with the assistance of her three husbands (in succession, John Musgrove, Jacob Matthews, and Rev. Thomas Bosomworth), served James Oglethorpe as translator, diplomat, and trader, making her the most important go-between for Georgia Colony and the Creek Indians. Significantly, though, Coosaponakeesa and Malatchi likely shared a common ancestry. Both were born at Coweta on Ochese Creek, and Coosaponakeesa's mother was the sister to Brims and Chigelly. Malatchi, whom Coosaponakeesa described as a near relation, most likely was born into the same matrilineal clan. Malatchi, then, had more than a friend living in Georgia; she was a "sister" to whom he grew increasingly close as he emerged as Coweta's leader in the 1740s.[16]

As it happened, then, Malatchi was fortunate in birth in more ways than one. As a twin born with prophetic gifts, his people would have been prepared to look to him for guidance about future events. That he happened to be born in Coweta, arguably the most ancient or head town among the Creeks, was certainly no political handicap. As Brims's favored kinsman he would have found ample opportunity for political instruction and advancement, and was therefore probably among the more culturally conscious and cosmopolitan Creek leaders of his generation. The facts of his birth combined with precedents set during previous generations paved the way for a life not merely as a medicine man but one deeply enmeshed in political affairs. It would take quite some time, however, for Malatchi to grow into this role.

Opiya Mico

According to the anthropologist Fred Gearing in his classic study of Cherokee politics, *Priests and Warriors*, a "good" Indian man was someone who, over the course of his life, was able to master important skills in self-control.[17] The Creeks, like all Southeastern Indians, believed that age conferred wisdom and allowed a person to temper his youthful passions to become deliberative, thoughtful, and a ritually pure individual. Indian leaders, particularly chiefs and head warriors, were expected to exhibit more self-control than most of their countrymen as a prerequisite of office. Malatchi's transition to adulthood can therefore be characterized as a quest for self-mastery, a long and at times difficult process that became evident at about age thirty when Malatchi threatened to "take the government out of Old Chigelly's hands." The process of self-mastery likely culminated in his thirty-sixth year when he finally shed his youthful reputation as a "drunken fellow" to assume a position as Coweta's head warrior (*opiya mico*).

Though leadership required mastery of self, the establishment of regional influence also demanded a certain kind of mastery of others. For a town leader to become a regional "big man" he first had to develop political connections to outsiders, both Indian and European and, if possible, to monopolize such connections so as to gain leverage back home. Aspiring regional leaders also faced the demands of providing gifts and services that indebted others to him so as to oblige some form of repayment when needed. Generously bestowing gifts most often served as the best means of establishing such social relationships. Malatchi's rise in influence therefore can also be attributed to the wide web of influence he self-consciously spun during his growth to adulthood.

Malatchi first briefly surfaces in the historical record in August 1732 when South Carolina officials singled him out as the leader of a small Lower Creek and Tallapoosa party that had plundered and murdered two traders on the Flint River.[18] Carolina traders later exonerated Malatchi of the murders, but in the eyes of both the English and the Creeks he remained unfit for conducting public business.[19] Though this reputation may have been a function of his tender age, evidence that his twin brother Essabo had already begun to play a prominent role in the community suggests otherwise. When a Lower Creek delegation first gathered in Savannah to welcome Oglethorpe in May of 1733, for example, Essabo is identified as one of Coweta's two representatives (and known then as the town warrior and later as the "young prince").[20]

Malatchi, on the other hand, did not attend the 1733 proceedings and Georgia's first Indian agent considered him a "worthless drunken fellow and entirely in the French interest."[21]

Malatchi's life may have taken an unexpected turn, however, in March 1735 when Essabo died at Silver Bluff on the Savannah River. Essabo's death caused problems for James Oglethorpe, who had recently appointed Essabo as the young prince in an effort to establish a predictable and malleable chain of authority among the Lower Creeks. Essabo's death left open the position of young prince and paved the way for Malatchi to assume his brother's position of prominence.

Malatchi, however, was young and inexperienced. At only twenty-six he was a political neophyte by Creek standards. The Creeks believed that young persons were unfit to conduct public business because of inexperience and a perceived inability to control their own passions and rage. Such qualities may have enabled young men to become effective warriors but it did not make them fit to become chiefs or war leaders, whose duties required that they be deliberate in all their undertakings and able to exercise a cool head when passions reigned.

Responsibility for educating Malatchi in his leadership role and in the intricacies of Anglo-Creek affairs undoubtedly fell upon the shoulders of Chigelly, Malatchi's guardian. Chigelly first introduced his young nephew to James Oglethorpe at Fort Frederica in the summer of 1736. There, at Chigelly's side, Malatchi look on silently as Chigelly and several other Lower Creek chiefs performed diplomatic rituals intended to renew their friendship with the British. To guarantee that Georgia officials recognized Malatchi as an important person, Chigelly first asserted his own authority in the nation by promising to "keep the people in order whilst he live." Then, pointing to Malatchi sitting at his side, Chigelly explained that "the man that sits by him would govern after him."[22]

Several days after this first exchange, Oglethorpe met with the Creek chiefs for a second time and acknowledged Chigelly's high rank by removing his coat and giving it to Chigelly as a gift. Everyone would have recognized the red officer's jacket as a symbol of chiefly authority and an exotic good to which few Creek leaders had access. As such, Oglethorpe's coat legitimized Chigelly's right to rule and represented Malatchi's right to succeed him, prompting Oglethorpe to remark that "that young man after you [may wear it]."[23] Once recognized as Chigelly's heir, Malatchi began to transform himself from an undependable drunken fellow into Coweta's most successful and influential warrior. Like most young men, he began his public career by playing an inauspicious and silent role. During the 1736 meetings that officially made him the heir to the Creek government, Malatchi uttered not a single word, instead deferring to the voice of Chigelly and the other older chiefs. Gradually, however, Malatchi began to acquire his own voice in the following three years. The first evidence of his political coming of age appears in August 1739 during the negotiations in Coweta that resulted in Oglethorpe's second Creek treaty. Although Chigelly headed the Coweta delegation, Malatchi received notice in the treaty minutes as one of three Coweta chiefs who agreed to the treaty on behalf of their town.

Having shown signs of political influence, Malatchi may have begun to chafe under the tutelage of his guardian, Chigelly. To emerge from under Chigelly's shadow, however, Malatchi must have found it necessary to garner support within the British colonies so as to extend his web of political connections beyond the confines of Coweta. Evidence for Malatchi's growing independence surfaced first in the spring of 1740 when Oglethorpe began recruiting Creek warriors to conduct a massive siege of St. Augustine. Chigelly, who feared that Creek participation in the war against the Spanish would make them vulnerable to Choctaw attacks, was unwilling to "meddle with" or "interpose" among the "white man's quarrels," preferring instead to refrain from military action and to seek French support for his nonintervention policy.[24]

Meanwhile, as Chigelly courted the French, Malatchi held his own meeting with General Oglethorpe at Fort Frederica. Shrewdly, Malatchi dismissed Creek support for the Catholic powers as the work of French and Spanish emissaries[25]: "The main body of people" Malatchi said, supported Oglethorpe and the British and he was "at the head" of the pro-English majority. Malatchi even threatened to use violence against his mentor, stating that if Chigelly opposed him he would "cut off his head." When later arriving in Savannah, Malatchi divulged his political aspirations to magistrate William Stephens, arguing that he had proven himself as a warrior. Stephens was impressed enough to convince himself that Malatchi had become the most highly esteemed man in the nation. Malatchi, as Stephens related, later argued that "he never intended to take the government out of Old Chigelly's hands, but let him die possessed of it, had he ruled for the good of his country; but now if he shows no longer regard to the pleasing of his people, it is time to put an end to his power; and he thinks himself of Age sufficient to take his own right, being near thirty. And his ability, as well as his good will to the English, is not to be questioned." Malatchi's protestations caused Stephens to surmise that Malatchi was now "the greatest man of that or most other nations." To symbolically demonstrate the young Indian's status, Stephens gave Malatchi a scarlet officer's coat as if to signify that Malatchi's influence had finally equaled that of his guardian, Chigelly.[26]

Having secured recognition as a leading "red coat wearer" in Georgia, three years later Malatchi set his sights on South Carolina, casting his web influence even further. On June 22, 1743, Malatchi traveled to Charles Town to speak with South Carolina's lieutenant governor, William Bull. No record of their conversation exists, but it is clear that Malatchi made a strong impression on Bull, who was the first to refer to Malatchi as the chief of the Lower Creek Indians. The following day Malatchi delivered another talk to Bull, after which he received an unspecified present. Malatchi, already familiar to Georgia officials, could now count on South Carolina officials to recognize him as a person of importance.[27]

Though colonial officials may have recognized Malatchi as a leading man by 1743, his own people did not do so officially until the busk ceremony in the summer of 1746. Busk, the Creeks' most important communal ceremony, was infused with many rituals that in the course of eight days of fasting and celebration dramatized the rebirth of the people. While many busk rituals were intended to ensure that the community would endure in perpetuity, other rituals signified the rebirth of particular individuals whose personal achievements entitled them to a higher rank within the community's political hierarchy.

Like most Southeastern Indians, Creeks signified personal merit and achievement by occasionally bestowing or acquiring new titles in a ceremony performed during the annual busk. The acquisition of such titles, or busk names, entitled the bearers to certain privileges such as the right to take an important seat at council meetings, the right to lead war parties, or the right to speak with colonial governors in an official capacity. The acquisition of such titles was particularly important for up-and-coming warriors, who naturally were eager to reap the political and social benefits of their new status. A good title could even help a young man find an attractive spouse, which might explain why they often failed to sleep the night before the naming ritual.[28]

For Malatchi, the busk of 1746 was probably filled with just this sort of anticipation, because on that occasion the people of Coweta renamed him *opiya mico*, a distinguished war title reserved for the head warrior of a particular town.[29] That Malatchi appears to have served in Coweta both as a civil authority (*mico*) and as head warrior (*opiya mico*) was not inconsistent with Creek practices, since it was common for Creek men to assume war titles and civil offices at different times in their lives.[30] Malatchi's status as a warrior likely only enhanced his political influence in Coweta and beyond, and it must have reminded others that he had mastered all the skills needed in peace and in war. Though we do not know specifically which martial exploits earned him this distinction, it is likely that Malatchi played an important role in the ongoing conflict with the Cherokees, with whom the Creeks had recently begun fighting—again. Malatchi also appears to have taken part in at least one of the military engagements that occurred between Georgia and the Spanish several years earlier.[31] Perhaps he met with success there, too. Malatchi's demonstrable connections to the British colonies likewise may have enhanced his reputation as a man of distinction.

Malatchi, like most *opiya mico*s, was not Coweta's only head warrior, but rather was a particular kind of war leader possessing both religious and military responsibilities.[32] According to British trader James Adair, the *opiya mico* was a war priest who enforced the purification rituals that kept the spirits appeased and ensured victory in battle. For instance, the *opiya mico* saw to it that his warriors fasted in the appropriate manner while away at war, allowing them only to eat parched corn that the *opiya mico* distributed from his own hand. Likewise, the *opiya mico* kept his warriors ritually pure by prohibiting sexual contact with women while they were engaged in warfare.[33]

Although maintenance of ritual purity was one of the *opiya mico's* principal functions, his role in warfare went even deeper. Translated literally, *opiya mico* means "far off king." Specifically, the word *opiya* denotes the ability to work magic from afar and also can be defined as "seeker."[34] Thus the *opiya mico* was not simply a warrior, but a wizard whose ability to work magic on an enemy from afar would have enabled his warriors to succeed where others might fail. Given the literal meaning of the title, it is likely that the *opiya mico* was responsible for interpreting dreams and other portentous signs that predicted victory or defeat in battle. Malatchi's people (and Malatchi himself) may have believed that he was fit for that role because he was born a twin and had an innate wizard's ability to read signs.[35]

Finally, because the *opiya micos* were responsible for regulating the behavior of their warriors, they gained notoriety for their extraordinary ability to control their own impulses and themselves became the most ritually pure of the warrior class, a good Indian. In this light, his acquisition of the title *opiya mico* in the summer of 1746 suggests that Malatchi, a thirty-six-year-old man, had finally shed his reputation as a drunken fellow and had matured into a person who was fit to rule in Coweta and perhaps beyond.[36]

Being recognized as an *opiya mico* in Coweta, however, did not guarantee Malatchi the kind of regional sway exercised by his elder kinsman Brims a generation earlier. Malatchi tacitly understood that the cultivation of a political following demanded tangible proofs of his largess. One way a chief could give such proof, of course, was to secure presents for his warriors. Circumstantial evidence indicating that Malatchi pursued this strategy can be seen in the speech he delivered to Alexander Heron at Fort Frederica in 1747. At issue were the military services Malatchi and his followers rendered on behalf of Georgia during the War of Jenkins's Ear. James Oglethorpe, recalled to London to explain his military failures, promised to speak to King George on the Creeks' behalf so as to procure "a ship with presents for us." Meantime, Oglethorpe pleaded with the Creeks to continue providing assistance against the Spanish.

As the Creeks apparently joined the Georgians simply to acquire presents in the first place, the arrival of the gift-bearing ship would have been important to Creek military leaders, including Malatchi, who faced the burdensome task of recruiting warriors. To Malatchi's chagrin, the Creeks later "came down as usual to go to war" but found that "the Great Ship was not come with presents." Malatchi argued that lack of presents aboard ship "made us think that he [Oglethorpe] had made peace with the Spaniards and did not want our assistance." Malatchi, demonstrably aware of the political costs of Oglethorpe's broken promise, described his young men as being cross that they could not go to war to get presents. Malatchi's concern did not appear to abate anytime in the following four years, being apprised that "some of my people went to Augusta to ask for powder and Ball as usual." Captain Kent, the commander at Augusta, responded that if they wanted any gunpowder "we should have it out of the mouth of his great guns [cannons]."[37]

Procuring gifts of ammunition, however, was only one of the methods Malatchi employed to enhance his political standing. British war commissions also figured prominently in Malatchi's plans to shore up his political base. By procuring war commissions for others, Malatchi could help to create headmen answerable not only to the British but also to him. In November 1746, for example, in response to an invitation by South Carolina governor James Glen, Malatchi journeyed to Charles Town with a retinue of thirty-nine men and one boy representing various towns in both the Upper and Lower Creek nations. To gain an immediate audience with the governor, three of Malatchi's accomplices presented old military commissions dating to the previous decade. At the time Malatchi appears to have pressed the governor to prepare a commission for him and for Enachtanatchee of Okchay, better known to the English as "the Gun Merchant." Having secured his own commission, Malatchi pressed Glen further by stating that of the many men present, "none had commissions but those who at [present] produced them." Glen summarily asked Malatchi if there were any headmen "to whom it would be proper to give commissions." Malatchi named four men, all of whom received commissions at that time.[38]

Malatchi's procurement of British commissions for people of his nation did not occur randomly or without purpose. Malatchi, who put the issue before Glen in the first place, assumed personal responsibility for naming the individuals worthy of commissions. Thus, all privileges the commissions conferred were owed directly to Malatchi's influence. The identity of the four men receiving commissions suggests that Malatchi strategically distributed them so as to extend his influence beyond Coweta. One individual receiving a commission at Malatchi's request was Thpahatchee, or the War King of the Cussitas. Tellingly, the other three men—Uchlepayhagio of Pucantallahassee, Kelesenecha of Hillabee, and Enanawgy of Oakfuskee—hailed from Abika towns. The question that arises, then, is why Malatchi chose to name these particular men to receive commissions. Perhaps Malatchi's choice reflects kinship connections, because it is plausible to suggest that Malatchi may have had clan relations in the Abika towns. Equally possible as a motivating factor was the fact that the Abika towns were relatively far removed from Coweta and historically less subject to Coweta's influence.[39] In this light, British war commissions served as political tools not only for the colonial governors but for aspiring young leaders like Malatchi, who in this instance used them to secure loyalty from Creek towns that may have not have deferred as readily to the wishes of Coweta and its leaders.

The Prince

Having earned distinction as a leader both at home and abroad, Malatchi soon found himself in the unenviable position of defending Creek lands against the intrusion of Georgia settlers and the pretended authority of the British Crown. As his people were the first to open the path to Charles Town and had traditionally held disproportionate sway over English diplomacy, perhaps Malatchi felt personally obliged to step into such a role. Malatchi's attempt to define and place himself at the head of the Creek Nation, though, proved to be an awkward, contested enterprise. At issue was the method for determining who, precisely, had the authority to conduct land transactions on behalf of the imagined Creek Nation. Most Creeks, who continued to view their territory as communal property, believed that land cessions required the consent of the nation as a whole.[40] Malatchi, though cognizant of his people's communal territorial beliefs, nevertheless attempted to secure that power for himself, albeit for the good (as he saw it) of his people. In the process Malatchi earned a new title—"prince"—that reflected his involvement in the deepening crisis between the Creeks and the Georgians.

Because Malatchi eventually became deeply immersed in the defense of his people's lands, no study of his political career would be complete without first placing it in the context of colonial Georgia's most serious and prolonged land dispute, the Bosomworth Affair. The Bosomworth Affair was a nearly twenty-year fight between the colony of Georgia and two of its infamous residents, Mary (Coosaponakeesa) and Thomas Bosomworth, over a tract of land on the Savannah River and three coastal islands, Sapelo, St. Catherine's, and Ossabaw. The affair may have originated in 1737 when Tomochichi ceded to Jacob and Mary Matthews (later Bosomworth) "two or three hundred acres" of Indian land on the south side of the Savannah River.[41] Mary, who had served Georgia Colony as diplomat and interpreter to the Creek Indians—indebting herself in the process—believed that the Georgia trustees owed it to her to affirm her land claims as a reward for her service.

Taking the initiative to secure title to her land, Mary petitioned the Georgia trustees in 1741 to recognize the legality of Tomochichi's grant. As Mary and her Creek relatives saw it, the specified lands belonged to the Creek Indians and had not at any time been ceded to Georgia. Because Tomochichi and Mary were both Creeks, Tomochichi had full right to give the land to her, making it an Indian-to-Indian transaction over which Georgia officials had no say. However, because Mary had

long lived in the English settlements, had received a Christian education, and had wed an Englishman—an ordained Anglican minister at
that—Georgia officials viewed Mary as a subject of King George. British
officials, moreover, forbade private individuals from purchasing or acquiring Indian lands directly from the Indians because they believed
that such transactions caused instability and directly infringed upon
the royal prerogative.[42] Though they appreciated Mary's service as interpreter, the Georgia trustees could hardly afford to allow Mary's claim
to stand and, predictably, the trustees denied Mary's petition.[43]

In the wake of the 1741 petition, Mary and her new husband, Thomas
Bosomworth, waged a legal war with Georgia officials to confirm their
right to the disputed lands. Finally, in 1759, after eighteen years of haggling with Georgia and British imperial officials, Mary struck a deal by
which she relinquished most of her land claims in exchange for title to
lands on St. Catherine's Island and a lump sum of cash.[44]

In defending her land claims, Mary found a willing ally in her kinsman Malatchi who, as a chief and fellow clan member, may have felt
obligated to come to her defense. The specific lands in question may
not have been vitally important to the Creeks in the nation proper, as
Chigelly and Malatchi remarked when they initially declared that had
Mary given the lands away herself: "we should not think much of it."[45]
Yet Malatchi knew deception when he saw it and understood that Georgia's claim to the specified lands set a dangerous, if abstract, precedent.
If Georgia could deny Indian land claims on this one occasion, what
was to stop them from grabbing more land from the Creek Nation on
another?

Like most legal disputes, the Bosomworth Affair was not fought with
guns and steel, but with paper. Mary, with a life's worth of experience in
business affairs, and Malatchi, well informed of the provisions of past
Anglo-Creek treaties, both recognized the power of the written word as
a tool of conquest. For instance, when Mary first begged the assistance
of her kinsmen in Coweta in December 1746, she employed Malatchi to
deliver a sharp message to George Galphin in which she denounced
James Oglethorpe. Declaring Oglethorpe a rogue, Mary argued that
Oglethorpe had given away Indian lands to the king to defray criticism
of his failed military ventures. In recognition of the philanthropic designs of the Georgia trustees, Mary predicted that "when the war [with
Spain and France] was over, the King [of Britain] intends to send over
all his poor people and settle all their land." The danger, she added,

lay in the practice of deceiving Indians with their papers; she warned the Creeks to be "on their guard with the traders" who "were always writing down against the Indians."[46]

Malatchi, who delivered the above message to Galphin, no doubt understood its contents and perhaps even helped to compose it, having previously expressed his vexation upon hearing the ominous provisions of the 1739 treaty. A year later, when Malatchi confronted Alexander Heron on the same issue, he continued to fixate on the problem of the paper that Oglethorpe had deceptively influenced them to sign. The problem began, Malatchi insisted, when he "immediately went with a Paper General Oglethorpe gave us when in the nation." Galphin, he added, "told us the Contents of that Paper was that we had given away all our lands to the King." This information, Malatchi admitted, "made us very uneasy, to think that he should impose upon us so, and give us a Paper to take away our Lands and not let us know anything of it."[47]

If Mary and Malatchi recognized the power of paper as a tool of conquest, however, both understood that the written word could also be employed in self-defense. To create a paper trail favorable to themselves, Mary and Thomas, in conjunction with Malatchi, began devising a series of documents that made it appear that the Creeks acknowledged Mary and Malatchi's preeminent right to conduct land transactions. Empowered as such, Mary and Malatchi simultaneously produced a series of deeds that confirmed Mary's rights to the disputed lands. To impress skeptical British officials, Mary and Thomas wrote these documents using a language they could understand, depicting Mary as the Creek Nation's "natural princess" and Malatchi as its "natural prince." Of necessity, the Bosomworths likewise depicted the Creeks as a politically centralized, territorially bounded nation familiar to Europeans. The Creek Nation as a legal entity was born.

The creation of this imaginative paper trail began in December 1747 when Mary and Malatchi met with Alexander Heron at Fort Frederica. Heron, recently installed as commander of that garrison, appears to have lent a friendly ear to the two as they fashioned themselves into the prince and princess of the Creek Nation. As Heron confided to a superior, Mary had been instrumental as interpreter and diplomat, adding that "since the Emperor Malatchi's arrival here I am more than ever convinced that she is looked upon by the whole Creek nation, as their Natural Princess. . . . Any Injury done to her," he added, "will be equally resented as if done to the whole nation."[48]

At Frederica, Mary and Malatchi, with the assistance of Heron, drafted a windy declaration identifying "Malatchi, *opiya mico*" as the natural prince of the Creek Nation. By naming him prince, the document accorded to Malatchi, using the legalistic verbiage of the day, "full power and authority . . . to transact all affairs relating to our nation as firmly and fully to all intents and purposes as we or the whole nation might or could do if present."[49]

Though it might appear that the entire Creek Nation deferred to Malatchi's rule, it is important to remember that only sixteen Lower Creeks signed the declaration in question, throwing into question the document's use of the term "we or the whole nation." Not only were the signatures of Tallapoosa or Abika chiefs missing, but many of the persons who did sign it were warriors, most likely young devotees of Malatchi. Among the noteworthy omissions was Chigelly, who might have contested the claim that Malatchi had the full power and authority to transact the nation's affairs. Also missing were prominent individuals such as Chocate of Coweta and Quilate and Tubbasigo of Apalachicola, both of whom Spanish officials still considered influential Uchise chiefs.[50]

Untroubled by such inconvenient facts, on January 4, 1748, Malatchi signed a deed that gave to the Bosomworths the islands of Ossabaw, Sapelo, and St. Catherine's.[51] As a reward, the Bosomworths gave Malatchi ten pieces of strouds, twelve pieces of duffel cloth, two hundred pounds of powder, two hundred pounds of bullets, twenty guns, twelve pistols, and one hundred pounds of vermilion (which Southern Indians used to make red war paint). By any measure it was a significant gift, and Malatchi could have in turn distributed parts of it to male and female supporters alike, thereby shoring up his own standing as a prince who could deliver the goods. In addition to handsomely outfitting Malatchi for war, the Bosomworths gave him thirty head of breeding cattle that they had raised on their (illegal) plantation on St. Catherine's Island.[52]

Because it was illegal for private individuals to purchase or trade for Indian lands, Georgia officials promptly charged Mary with treason. To fight these charges, Mary and Thomas traveled to Coweta that July, at busk, to invite Malatchi to Savannah to plead with Georgia authorities on their behalf. In return, Mary promised to send her brother-in-law Abraham to London to speak to colonial authorities about the Creeks' concerns for their land. Believing that the older Bosomworth's influence might be beneficial, and entertaining rumors that Mary might be hanged, Malatchi and at least eleven other Lower Creeks promptly accompanied the Bosomworths to Georgia, arriving in Savannah in early August 1749.[53]

The talks that ensued between the Georgia authorities, the Creeks, and the Bosomworths were unpleasant, to say the least, and resulted in a drunken romp through Savannah that led to the arrest of Abraham Bosomworth and Mary herself. Malatchi, meanwhile, found himself humiliated before Georgia officials as he listened to repeated assaults on the Bosomworths' character and his own. At one point William Stephens, a rabid foe of the Bosomworths, even went so far as to deny Mary and Malatchi's kinship ties, arguing that "she is not of your family, being a Daughter of a Woman of the Tuckebatchee Town (of no note or family) by a White Man." To defray the animosity swirling within the Savannah courthouse, Malatchi deferred to the Georgia assistants, denied the validity of the deed he had written to Mary Bosomworth, and later summoned Georgia officials to drink with him in a local tavern. Stephens, however, remained skeptical, stating that Malatchi's waffling "gives too much reason to doubt the sincerity and continuance of his professed friendship."[54]

While Stephens was wrong to accuse Malatchi of malfeasance, Stephens was right not to trust Malatchi entirely, as he consistently refused to play the role of English pawn. In 1746, with a state of war then existing between Britain and France, Gov. James Glen of South Carolina implored Malatchi and several other chiefs to allow the British to build a fort in their nation to counteract the influence of the French fort. Malatchi summarily denied the request and likewise refused to take up Glen's subsequent offer "to cutt off the Alabama fort."[55] After rebuking Glen's requests, Malatchi had proceeded directly to Fort Toulouse to inform its commander of Glen's various schemes, effectively killing Glen's plans to establish British hegemony in the region. Though Malatchi's own experiences as an ambassador may have prompted him to challenge British ambitions, Malatchi's tutelage under Brims had conditioned him to respond as he did. Explaining his behavior a year later, Malatchi argued that all the bad talks then circulating "put me in mind of the words of my Father." Echoing the spirit if not the substance of the Coweta Resolution of 1718, Malatchi remembered the warning he had received from Brims that "the English were come from the East, to settle upon our lands, the Spaniards towards the South, and the French towards the West." Brims's wish, Malatchi added, "was that you may not see the day when they will be for taking your Lands from you, and making Slaves of your Wives and Children."[56]

The acrimonious confrontation in Savannah in 1749 appears only to have strengthened Malatchi's resolve to abide by the wishes of his "father" and to assure that the day of European encroachment would not occur so long as he drew breath. Behind the scenes in Savannah, for instance, Malatchi convinced ten of his followers to put their marks to yet another Bosomworth "Recognition," which this time conferred upon Mary her rights as the official princess of the Creek Nation.[57]

The August meetings had so infuriated Malatchi, in fact, that he traveled to Mobile the following spring to receive presents from the commanding French officer. To return the favor, Malatchi invited the French to pay him a visit in Coweta, prompting three French officers to make a rare visit to the Lower Creek towns in mid-July. Because the chiefs conducted all talks with the French in their private homes, however, British traders failed to learn the nature of their business. Rumors did suggest that the French wished to purchase some land to build a fort. To the relief of British officials throughout the empire, the French fort never materialized. But Malatchi issued a symbolic protest against British aggression by replacing the British flag that flew in the Coweta square with the French *Fleur de Lys*.[58]

The French ambassadors were still in Coweta when Abraham Bosomworth arrived on July 29, 1750, bearing more documents for the Creeks to sign on behalf of Abraham's brother and sister-in-law. Abraham may have found it difficult to convince anyone to support them, but he obtained Malatchi's consent by promising to send Mary to England to speak to the king on behalf of the Creeks. Persuaded that the Bosomworths would faithfully represent their interests in London, Malatchi promptly lowered the French flag and signed three more documents that on paper reaffirmed her status as the princess of the Creek Nation and confirmed their deeds to the disputed lands.[59]

On paper, then, it appeared that Malatchi and Mary had established a chain of evidence that favorably positioned them as prince and princess of the Creek Nation. The problem with this strategy, however, was that the tradition of English literalism was not their own and left Mary, and especially Malatchi, vulnerable to challenge on the same legal grounds. In fact, though Malatchi clearly supported Mary's land claim, evidence indicates that he may have had little real knowledge of the various documents the Bosomworths pressured him to sign. In Savannah, for instance, Stephens informed Malatchi that by signing those documents he had consented to Mary's claim as the "Empress and Queen of the Creek Nation." Malatchi answered "with some warmth" that he did not understand how he could be "ranked with an Old Woman," arguing instead that he was chief. Some days later Malatchi presented a copy of his paper to Georgia officials, saying that he "looked upon it as nothing."[60]

The use of written evidence, moreover, rendered Malatchi vulnerable to new threats, as British officials then had opportunity to employ similar methods in defense of their own agendas. Take, for example, Malatchi's leadership of the entire Creek Nation. Georgia officials, particularly those hostile to Mary and Malatchi, knew that though Malatchi was influential, he did not have the full support of the Lower Creeks much less the Creek Nation.[61] This fact underscores the contested nature of Malatchi's leadership and illustrates that the constituent parts of the Lower Creek confederation did not always recognize the preeminence of Coweta or its chiefs.

Leading the resistance to Malatchi were the headmen from Osuche, a town that had demonstrated its defiance of the Coweta chiefs on many previous occasions. In September 1749, just weeks after the infamous Savannah incident, twenty Osuche men came to Savannah to speak with President Stephens and his assistants. The Osuches explained that the whole uneasiness that had recently occurred in Savannah "proceeded from Mary and Malatchi." Reluctant to accept Malatchi's aggrandized status as prince, the men further complained that Malatchi "had no superior right to them or any other chiefs in the nation to give away their lands." The Osuches even offered to "destroy all the cattle that the Bosomworths had put on their islands," a telling reminder that many Creeks harbored deep suspicions of Malatchi's and Mary's motives.[62]

Thus the following summer, as Malatchi began courting the French, Georgia officials called a party of Lower Creeks to Savannah to establish a more pliable chain of command in the nation. Consequently, Georgia officials offered a commission to Wehoffkee of Oconee, appointing him "to command the whole nation" and accept "all talks concerning the English."[63] Fortunately for Malatchi, Wehoffkee refused the offer. Yet Wehoffkee's refusal did little to stop subsequent attempts to find more pliable leaders, as the Georgians later commissioned an Upper Creek man named Tunape as the Tallapoosa emperor. Tunape, who later emigrated to the Apalachee old fields, appears never to have gained much recognition, either at home or abroad, as emperor. It nevertheless was clear that the Georgians wanted to "introduce some discontent among the two [Tallapoosa and Coweta] nations," thereby making it easier to subjugate the Creek Nation as a whole.[64]

Moreover, many leaders among the Upper Creeks, most of whom rarely made use of the coastal islands or the "Indian tract," had little to gain in the Bosomworth dispute. For reasons of expediency, then, Upper Creek leaders were more than willing to deed the lands away with little or no fuss. Shrewdly hoping to exploit this schism within the Creek Nation, Georgia officials embarked upon a policy to have Upper Creek leaders "resign the [Bosomworths'] deeds to the three islands."[65] To accomplish this end, the Georgia government appointed Patrick Graham as Indian agent and ordered Graham to produce a new deed in repudiation of the deeds granting the disputed lands to the Bosomworths.

Graham arrived in the Upper Creek town of Okchay on May 28, 1750, receiving a warm welcome from Enostonakee, the Gun Merchant of Okchay, who Graham styled as the "head king of all the upper Creeks." When confronted with the Bosomworth Affair, Enostanakee affirmed— curiously in tortured legalistic prose—that "we are willing and fully satisfied that . . . the English should possess and occupy all the lands on the Savannah River commonly known by the name of Indian lands, as also the three islands called Sapola [Sapelo], St. Catherine's, and Ossabaw." In return, the Gun Merchant's people were to receive "a valuable parcel of cloth, guns, ammunition, hatchets, beads, paint, and other goods and manufactures."[66] Knowing that these lands were of little concern to the Upper Creeks, Graham's offer was one the Gun Merchant could not refuse. To cement the deal, Enostanakee abruptly agreed to sign "any necessary paper," resulting in a deed of repudiation that placed the questioned lands in the hands of the British Crown.

By using the written word—"any necessary paper"—to exploit schisms within the Creek Nation, British officials rendered Malatchi little more than the paper prince of a fictitious legal entity, the Creek Nation. Malatchi, who signed every document the Bosomworths presented to him, was not entirely innocent of playing the same game of aggrandizement, asserting unprecedented authority to conduct land transactions on behalf of an entire nation. Nevertheless, Malatchi's claims to political influence beyond Coweta had some merit. The unlettered Malatchi may not have been—or may never have claimed to be—a prince, but he knew how to be a chief. As chief of the Cowetas, Malatchi could exercise influence through more traditional political channels in order to accomplish other political goals, even goals concerning more serious matters of life and death.

The Executioner

As important as the Bosomworth Affair may have been, Creek foreign relations involved far more than the sometimes tense relationship with Georgia. While Malatchi and Mary were busy haggling with Georgia officials over the disputed lands, the Creeks remained at war with the Cherokees, whom they had been fighting intermittently since 1743. Despite Gov. James Glen's repeated attempts to end the conflict, fighting flared up on several occasions—in 1749 and particularly in the springs of 1751 and 1752—that resulted in the destruction of all but three Lower Cherokee towns. Glen invited the Cherokees to Charles Town again in early 1752 to lay the groundwork for a truce. Desperate to put an end to the fighting, one hundred Cherokees descended upon Charles Town in March 1752 to gain audience with the governor.[67]

Unexpectedly, however, several parties of Upper and Lower Creeks soon appeared in Charles Town and took up lodging at a house that had been set aside for Indian guests. A dozen Cherokee men from the town of Estatoe, returning to Charles Town to have their guns mended after a hunting excursion, found that the Creeks had taken up temporary residence where they themselves had been staying. Thinking that the Cherokees had come to attack them, the Creeks took up their arms in a threatening manner, painted themselves, and raised the infamous war hoop. Bloodshed appeared imminent, Governor Glen recalled, until "some of our people" from the colony prevented them from "doing any mischief." Urging the impassioned Creeks to restrain themselves, the South Carolinians offered the reminder that, while in Charles Town, the Cherokees were under their protection and they would look upon the killing of any Cherokees "the same as if they killed white men."[68]

Tempers subsided and the next day the Creek and Cherokee parties made peace, and later danced, smoked tobacco, and exchanged blankets. The ritual gestures made the two parties appear so sincere that Governor Glen was compelled to believe that "it should not only be Peace betwixt these two parties" but a general peace that the two nations might later confirm more generally. The Estatoe men set off for home a day later; a large body of Lower Creeks met them on the path, offering to travel and hunt together as friends. After traveling a little way, the Cherokee men decided to rest, laying aside their guns in a thicket and thinking all was safe. The Creeks fired on the unsuspecting Cherokee party, killing four on the spot and seizing another as prisoner.

Word of the massacre soon began to trickle into Charles Town. Rumors, which later proved to be true, suggested that the perpetrators were the twenty-six Lower Creeks who had recently arrived in Charles Town. English traders traveling the same path reported that the Creeks mutilated and scalped the murdered men and, in a display of exultation, repeatedly cried out "Cowetas, Cowetas."[69] Believing that the Coweta party bore sole responsibility for the murders, Governor Glen initially had little reason to suspect the Upper Creek party still in Charles Town of any wrongdoing. Glen became suspicious of them, however, when eleven Upper Creeks skipped town that evening without waiting to have their guns repaired, collect the presents allotted to them, or even say good-bye.[70]

As the Carolinians had taken the Cherokees under their protection, Governor Glen regarded the murders as a direct affront to the colony. Moreover, Glen understood that Carolina-Cherokee relations rested upon reciprocity, making it necessary for the Cherokees to obtain satisfaction for the murders. To do otherwise would have breached the kinship etiquette upon which the Anglo-Cherokee alliance rested. Aware of the significance of the murderous act, Governor Glen immediately resolved to get the Cherokee prisoner returned home and have the Lower Creeks—who at the time were the principal suspects—punish those responsible.

Colonial governors, though, were well aware that Indians hesitated to punish their own, particularly for killing their ancient enemies. Glen knew that any agent he sent into the Creek Nation had to be well respected and uncommonly influential. Thomas Bosomworth's rather infamous reputation was no secret in South Carolina, but on July 2, 1752, Governor Glen nevertheless appointed him as the colony's agent. Glen instructed Bosomworth to have the Lower Creeks punish (by way of death) the murderers and urge the Creeks and Cherokees to come to peaceful terms. Most important, Glen understood that Bosomworth's success depended upon the influence of his wife Mary, "who is said by her Relation with some of the Head Men to have an Interest in the Creek Nation." Glen clearly expected Bosomworth to exploit his wife's interest, instructing him to preface his speeches with the reminder of the "near relation you stand in to them."[71]

Glen was shrewd to exploit the considerable influence of the Bosomworths and skillful enough to recognize Malatchi and Chigelly of Coweta as the two persons most likely to obtain satisfaction for the Cherokee murders. Glen instructed Bosomworth that once in Coweta, he should immediately "repair to the house of Malatchi" rather than conduct business in the town square. "At the same time," he continued, "you are to send for Chigelly, and in the presence of these two head men only, you are to produce and read your Commission" and therefore keep the affair a private rather than public matter.[72] One day later the Bosomworths set out for Coweta, arriving on July 24 after a three-week journey.

Malatchi, meanwhile, had spent that summer fighting against his archenemies, the Cherokees, on behalf of a slain friend, only to return to Coweta to find the Bosomworths awaiting him. Three days later Bosomworth explained the bad news, imploring Malatchi and Chigelly to "give the satisfaction demanded" by "punishing with death some of the most considerable offenders."[73] At first the two men responded to Glen's demands with silence, and Bosomworth noted that "an air of deep concern was visible in their countenances." Chigelly spoke first, stating with disgust that "never in his life had [he] heard of such a demand for such a crime." Chigelly knew that the murder of a white man might merit such drastic punishments but, he noted, "to kill their own people for killing their enemies [the Cherokees] was what he could not understand."[74]

Wary of making a rash decision on the matter, Chigelly and Malatchi consulted together for four days in solitude, then finally called an assembly of headmen on August 10 to bring the matter to everyone's attention.[75] After conferring with other Lower Creek leaders and the Bosomworths, Malatchi recommended a compromise plan whereby only the leader of the murdering party would be executed. Conveniently for Malatchi—a bit too conveniently, perhaps—the individual singled out as the leader was not a Lower Creek man at all, but an Upper Creek man known as Acorn Whistler.

Ironically, perhaps, Acorn Whistler was the "white king" of the Tallapoosa town of Little Oakfuskee, a more recently established community that appears to have branched off from the town of Oakfuskee proper. Acorn Whistler's contemporaries regarded him as a noted warrior; he commanded seven towns among the Tallapoosas. In his own towns, however, Acorn Whistler was not particularly well-liked in all quarters. Beginning in 1745, for example, Acorn Whistler developed an annoying habit of showing up unexpectedly at Charles Town, begging for presents and causing South Carolina officials to incur unwanted expenses.[76] Nor can it be said that he was universally liked by the Creeks. In the summer of 1749, as Upper Creek leaders worked to secure peace with the Cherokees, Acorn Whistler and his party set out to attack the Cherokees, brazenly ignoring the Wolf of Muccalassee's plea to stop. Acorn Whistler's militancy jeopardized a tenuous truce between Okchay and the Cherokee town of Tellico that their respective leaders had worked hard to secure.[77]

More recently, Acorn Whistler happened to be the leader of one of the Upper Creek parties that had come to Charles Town the previous March and was in the company of James Glen when rumors of the Cherokee murders first came in. Glen questioned Acorn Whistler about the murders at the time but released him after the Indian denied any knowledge of the affair. Creek investigations, however, revealed that Acorn Whistler had met with the twenty-six Lower Creeks on his way to Charles Town, inviting them to join him there. Finding the Cherokees in town, Acorn Whistler convinced the Lower Creeks to feign peace with the Cherokees and kill them later at a time they least expected it. Malatchi, who met up with Acorn Whistler on his return home, confirmed Acorn Whistler's malfeasance. As Malatchi reported, Acorn Whistler continued to circulate bad talks, stating that "the Governor had taken away all the Indians' Arms, and wanted to kill them," causing Acorn Whistler to "flee for his life like a slave." Acorn Whistler, Malatchi continued, "used all the arguments in his power to induce him [Malatchi] to kill all the Englishmen in the Nation directly." When Malatchi refused, Acorn Whistler threatened to "kill some white man himself" for which the entire nation would be obliged to make war.[78]

Malatchi, who played a more subtle political game with the British, likely viewed Acorn Whistler as a threat to rather than a patriot of the Creek Nation, and recognized the poisonous results that his bad talks had caused. So poisonous, in fact, that Malatchi would have rather sacrificed Acorn Whistler than kill the traders and commence a war against the English colonies. Urging Acorn Whistler not to kill any of the white men, Malatchi warned him that "if he did he should die for it."[79] Thus, even before the Bosomworths' arrival in Coweta, Malatchi had already formed a bad opinion of Acorn Whistler and no doubt would have welcomed an excuse to get rid of him.

Planning an execution was one thing; carrying out such a deed was another. It was an especially difficult task for tribal people like the Creeks, whose primary allegiance was to the clan rather than to an ambiguous national entity. The tradition of blood vengeance required that Acorn Whistler's relatives mete out punishment against the appointed executioners. Malatchi knew, moreover, that the execution of Acorn Whistler posed particular challenges since he was considered a great man who had "so many relations in both the upper and lower Creek Nation" that might insist upon exacting revenge against his executioners.

Malatchi understood that the execution had to be accomplished by manipulating established kinship connections. The solution was to have Acorn Whistler's own relations carry out the killing. At Malatchi's behest, the Lower Creeks hastily recruited Acorn Whistler's young nephew to do the dirty deed, fabricating the lie that the young man's uncle "was Mad and wanted to kill him," reputedly because they were competing for the affections of the same woman. By arranging the execution in such a way, Malatchi and others hoped that others would view Acorn Whistler's death as a private act of vengeance rather than a public execution committed in the name of the nation.[80]

A week later, on August 18, one of Acorn Whistler's relatives returned to Coweta and informed Bosomworth that "the business was done." Not only had the young nephew killed Acorn Whistler, but some of the young man's own relatives had put the nephew to death, too, after he had carried out his act. The nephew had been put to death, Bosomworth later learned, in order to keep him from revealing why he had been recruited to kill Acorn Whistler in the first place.[81]

Although it may be true that dead men tell no tales, it proved impossible to keep secret the real reason for Acorn Whistler's execution. The victim's relations were demanding an explanation for his death, stirring rumors in Coweta that they might commit mischief against the traders or the Lower Creeks unless they could be pacified.[82] Malatchi, together with the Bosomworths, wisely decided that it would be prudent to confer with the Upper Creeks "to endeavor to convince all his relations there of the justice and necessity of his suffering [and] to remove all obstacles to a good understanding betwixt the English and their nation."[83]

As with the orchestration of the execution, Malatchi likewise understood that pacifying Acorn Whistler's Upper Creek relations required the deft manipulation of the clan system. Malatchi handpicked a delegation of Acorn Whistler's Lower Creek relations to accompany them to the Upper towns. Isspuffnee of Coweta, for instance, was a near relation of Acorn Whistler, as was the Cussita *mico*. Several other relations of the Acorn Whistler also joined this group. Chigelly, working in close consultation with Malatchi, advised the party not to apologize for the execution but to "boldly declare" that Acorn Whistler had "broken the Chain of Friendship" with the English and that only his "Blood" would "make all streight again."[84] Malatchi's party then set out a day later, headed for Upper Creek country and arriving in Tuckebatchee on September 2.

More likely than not, the Lower Creek delegation's decision to proceed to Tuckebatchee was not accidental. As the Bosomworths, Malatchi, and Chigelly recognized, their mission stood more chance of success if they could enlist the support of their own Upper Creek relations for hospitality, political support, and protection in the event that Acorn Whistler's relations called for vengeance. Bosomworth's instructions from Governor Glen, however, directed him to conduct business farther north, in Oakfuskee, requiring that he depart somewhat from his orders. As Thomas Bosomworth put it, the Lower Creeks chose to conduct business in Tuckebatchee because Acorn Whistler's death was "a very ticklish point." "In case of the worst," he added, "it would be necessary to have some Friends to stand by us." The leading men of Tuckebatchee, Bosomworth knew, were Mary's "own relations and secured in our interest." We may therefore infer that Malatchi and Chigelly, Mary's clan-kin, shared this relationship, which helps to explain why the two men steadfastly refused to go no further than Tuckebatchee. "Nothing could be done at the Oakfuskees," Bosomworth concluded, "which could not as well or more effectually be done here."[85]

After a nearly three-week interlude, interrupted only by the occasional talk given on the Bosomworths' behalf, a general meeting of all the traders and headmen of the Upper Creek nation commenced. Bosomworth read his commission to the assembled chiefs, explaining that the heinousness of the crimes committed near Charles Town demanded satisfaction by way of Acorn Whistler's spilt blood. Acorn Whistler's execution, Bosomworth added, "was not for killing the Cherokees as their enemies, but for staining the white beloved Town [Charles Town] with the Blood of our Friends," who, he added, "were under our immediate protection." Bosomworth's message, of course, would not have been lost upon the assembled chiefs, who knew that the rules of blood vengeance demanded that friends obtain satisfaction for those under their protection.[86]

Though present in Tuckebatchee at the time, neither Malatchi nor Chigelly uttered a single word during the general meeting, wisely deferring to Acorn Whistler's relations, all of whom could weigh in with more legitimacy on that particular issue. In succession the Ottassee king and Oakfuskee captain both spoke in defense of Acorn Whistler's execution. As the Ottassee king put it, "the execution [was] done by his own relation" so that "all past injuries might be forgiven and forgot." Sacrificing Acorn Whistler, he believed, was "for the good of our own nation." Isspuffnee of Coweta went even further in justifying the execution of the executioner, Acorn Whistler's young nephew. Lamenting the fact that one innocent man had to suffer with the guilty, Isspuffnee nevertheless recognized that the nephew's death prevented Acorn Whistler's relations from turning against the English "in their fury" and engaging "the whole Nation in a war." Surprisingly, perhaps, no protests were uttered in Acorn Whistler's defense.[87] It appears, then, that the man who had nearly caused a war between the Creeks and "our Best friends" would not be entirely missed.

Having brought the Acorn Whistler affair to a conclusion, Malatchi and the Bosomworths soon returned to Coweta to discuss plans for a proposed visit to Charles Town that spring. Days after returning, however, ominous news arrived that a man from the emigrant Chickasaw community of Breed Camp on the Coosa River had fired on and killed a trader named William Mackrachun. Bosomworth understood that Acorn Whistler's recent execution might foment jealousy if the Carolina government were to forego demanding satisfaction from the Chickasaws (for killing one of their own traders, no less). Bosomworth could not, of course, see this through without the help of Malatchi, who he recruited to accompany him to the Upper Creeks.

To have the Chickasaw man put to death, Malatchi and Bosomworth employed a strategy similar to the one they had taken with respect to Acorn Whistler: relying upon Malatchi's personal sway and the network of his and Mary's relations living in the upper towns. As before, Malatchi and Bosomworth set out for Tuckebatchee, arriving on October 12. There, Bosomworth communicated the nature of their mission, explaining that Mackrachun's death demanded that the Chickasaws execute his killer. Malatchi recommended to Bosomworth that "it might not be amiss" to call a general meeting of all the headmen to legitimize and to enhance the diplomatic effectiveness of the execution.[88]

Two weeks later the headmen assembled yet again to discuss Bosomworth's demands, this time in the Abika town of Abiccouchee, where the Gun Merchant of Okchay, arguably the most influential Abika chief, seems to have played host. Also arriving in town was the "king" of the Chickasaws and a handful of his relatives, who came into the council house conspicuously well-armed. Listening to Bosomworth's demands for satisfaction, the Chickasaw king responded that the murderer was his own flesh and blood, in effect stating that Bosomworth would have to kill him before he would hand over his relative. After this insult, Bosomworth issued a final warning that the Chickasaws had until "the sun was at its height tomorrow" to give a final answer.[89]

Into this fray stepped Malatchi, who assumed the floor to make "a long and excellent speech, showing the reasonableness and necessity of their granting the demand." Malatchi thus appears to have played the critical role in bringing the Upper Creeks to see Mackrachun's murder through Bosomworth's eyes. That Malatchi chose to assert himself among the Abikas suggests that he enjoyed a certain amount of influence there not unlike the influence he held among the Tallapoosas. So influential, in fact, that the leading Abika chief, the Gun Merchant of Okchay, sided enthusiastically with Malatchi, delivering a speech that equally favored Bosomworth. The next morning both Malatchi and the Gun Merchant held a private consultation with Bosomworth, offering to "compell them [Chickasaws] by force of arms" to comply with Bosomworth's demands.[90]

Conveniently for Malatchi and the Gun Merchant, force proved unnecessary when the appointed hour came for the Chickasaws' final decision. As it happened, the murderer's uncle stepped forward and offered to sacrifice himself on the grounds that "the man that has committed the mischief is my own flesh and blood." If his nephew was afraid to die to keep the peace, "he would sacrifice his own life for him." Orders were then given to have the man shot, but before they could do so the Chickasaw man obtained a knife and plunged it into his gullet and died almost immediately from his self-inflicted wound.[91]

Once the ritual (self-)execution was over, the Creeks and Chickasaws met again with Bosomworth the following day to bring closure to the bad episode. While ostensibly an affair between the Chickasaws and the British, Malatchi realized that he had played a significant role in bringing about the Chickasaw man's death and therefore bore some responsibility for placating the dead man's grieving relations. Addressing the Chickasaws, Malatchi stated that he had "come a long way" to advise them as "an elder brother." Malatchi's choice to position himself as such was no accident, as the Creeks regarded the Chickasaw immigrants as subordinate younger brothers. Malatchi pleaded that the Chickasaws were "settled by permission" in the Creeks' country. As the murder of the trader had occurred in Creek country, "satisfaction would be required at their Hands."[92]

Retrospectively, the successful orchestration of not one but two executions in the fall of 1752 indicates that Malatchi held far greater sway than any other man at that time in the Creek nation. No Creek leader, of course, had enough personal sway to single-handedly order the execution of the nation's rotten members, as the clan system's rules of blood vengeance tended to limit the unilateral use of force. But influential men could manipulate those same kinship connections to achieve the same end. It was no accident, then, that this burdensome task fell principally upon Malatchi and Chigelly. As Bosomworth related, "it was entirely through their means that this satisfaction was obtained. . . . Not a man in the nation," he added, "durst attempt or go about such an affair but themselves."[93]

The Real Chief

Given Thomas Bosomworth's close connections to Malatchi and Chigelly, it is tempting to attribute his depiction of their political largess to Bosomworth's self-interest. Of course we should dismiss outright any notion that Malatchi was the Creeks' emperor. But Malatchi's own actions and words reveal a man who consciously regarded himself as the leading voice of his nation, not simply when it came time to carry out politically expedient executions but as it pertained to matters of peace and war as well. Malatchi's leadership role cannot be dismissed as a function of his own active imagination because many influential Creeks deferred to his voice and looked upon him at home and abroad as the real chief of the Creek Nation.

Evidence that Malatchi perceived himself as uniquely influential can be seen in how he jealously guarded the British commission that named him commander of the entire Creek Nation. Malatchi was not the first Coweta leader to assert this privilege, of course, as Brims had complained of South Carolina officials' attempts to bypass his influence in naming headmen a generation earlier. Malatchi, we can presume, was well aware of the precedent set by Brims, given the instructional relationship the two men shared. Fitting it was, then, that in the aftermath of the nearly disastrous Acorn Whistler affair, Malatchi found cause to complain to Governor Glen that their young people had become increasingly ungovernable, committing "mad actions which they ought not to do." Echoing the protest that Emperor Brims had made years before, Malatchi blamed the white people for the youthful insubordination that had become commonplace as of late, accusing them of aggrandizing individuals "who had no right to command," by "making Captains and great men by Commissions granted them." Particularly alarming was Georgia's effort to commission Wehoffkee, the Long Warrior of the Oconees, "to command the whole Nation." Bitterly recalling an episode that had occurred a full two years earlier, Malatchi expressed his relief that Wehoffkee had wisely refused the commission on the grounds that "he, Malatchi, was the King of the whole Nation."[94]

Indeed. Wehoffkee appears not to have been alone in considering Malatchi the supreme voice of the nation, particularly as it applied to the proposed truce with the Cherokees. During the latter stages of the general meeting of Upper Creek chiefs at Tuckebatchee in September 1752, for instance, Thomas Bosomworth reminded his audience of the earlier promises to commit to peace, inviting them to see Governor Glen "either at Augusta or Charles Town in order to make a new Chain of Friendship." The Upper Creeks appeared willing to declare their friendship with the English, but many demurred when pressed to declare their intentions toward the Cherokees. Speaking on behalf of the Upper Creeks, the captain of Pucantallahassee declared the peace talk to be "very agreeable" to them, but hesitated to commit to it until they had consulted Coweta on the grounds that "the Cowetas was the Great Town of both the Nations and Malatchi the Great King and Son of the Emperor of both nations." Only when they heard "his resolution on the matter," he added, would they give a "final answer." "Whatever Malatchi agreed to," the Pucantallahassee captain concluded, "the whole upper Creek nation would ratify and confirm."[95]

Closer to home, the Lower Creeks likewise deferred to Malatchi's wisdom when Bosomworth floated a similar peace proposal, just weeks later, in the Coweta square. On October 4, Chigelly called for a general council of Lower Creek headmen to consider Bosomworth's invitation to meet with Governor Glen that spring. In council Chigelly and the headmen had failed to form a consensus; they "did not know what answer to give in Regard to the Satisfaction demanded." Unsure of themselves, the council unanimously "left the Management of the affair entierly to Malatchi." Whatever he decided to do, Bosomworth was informed, "they all promised to ratify and confirm."[96]

Thus empowered, Malatchi did not hesitate to act decisively, agreeing to settle a series of minor incidents as prerequisites to the establishment of peace with the Cherokees. Citing his authority to speak for the Upper and Lower Creek nations, Malatchi then agreed to "comply with every thing the governor desired." Hunting season was soon to begin, however, and Malatchi knew that he had to act quickly to prevent mischief in the woods. Hoping to prevent any accidental breach of the peace, Malatchi agreed to issue immediate orders forbidding "any of their Nation from going to war in the Enemies' country." Likewise, Malatchi accepted Governor Glen's offer to meet with him at any time and place the governor should appoint.[97]

That winter, traders and Indians living in both the Upper and Lower Creek nations confirmed that the warriors had stayed home and that several parties had already exchanged tokens of peace with the Cherokees.[98] Encouraged by these favorable signs, in February 1753 Glen invited the headmen of the Creek Nation to meet him in Charles Town at their earliest convenience.[99] That May at least ninety-three Creek headmen descended upon Charles Town, making it the largest gathering of Indians that city had seen for quite some time. For a full week Glen, the South Carolina Council, and the Creek headmen held several talks, during which they discussed a series of pertinent issues such as the Cherokee peace and the need to lower the price of trade goods.

Malatchi, appointed by the Upper and Lower Creeks to speak on the nation's behalf, predictably emerged at that meeting as the principal mouth of the nation. Having already demonstrated his influence back home in bringing about the execution of Acorn Whistler, Malatchi used the Charles Town meetings as a forum to lay forth his own agenda: specifically, to resurrect the Bosomworth Affair and urge his countrymen to repudiate the infamous Graham Deed that had rescinded the Bosomworths' claims to the disputed lands in Georgia. To gain Governor Glen's favor, Malatchi exploited the influence his people had given him and, in a series of subtle verbal moves, convinced Glen and the assembled Creek headmen to recognize him as the "real chief" of the Creek Nation.

However adept politically, Malatchi did not have to work too hard to gain Glen's ear, as Glen had singled out Malatchi as a man of influence by way of his association to the previous "emperor, Brims. "I see the son of our good friend, the worthy Old Brims," Glen began, as if to acknowledge the longstanding friendship between the Creeks and the British. But Malatchi, Glen argued, deserved recognition for his own merits, stating that although he respected him as the "son" of South Carolina's old friend, "he is still to be valued upon his own account as he is an honest, brave man, and a good friend to the English."[100]

In the council chamber Glen began the proceedings by summarizing recent events, such as the Acorn Whistler incident, and by urging the Creeks to strive for peace with the Cherokees and the Iroquois. The first Creek to respond was Malatchi, who recounted his people's ancient friendship with the English and presented Glen with a handsome present of deerskins, an attempt to reestablish "an old custome before my time," as Glen put it. By presenting a gift in this manner, Malatchi was clearly trying to use traditional gift-giving in a way that created mutual ties of reciprocal obligations consistent with older Creek customs of practicing politics.[101]

When talks resumed the following day, Malatchi again spoke first. Referring to the recent peace proposals, Malatchi expressed his skepticism that the Creeks, the Iroquois, and the Cherokees could ever conclude an effectual peace. Abruptly Malatchi then switched the subject by airing his displeasure over the Colony of Georgia's treatment of his "sister," Mary Bosomworth. According to his understanding of the first treaty with Oglethorpe, the Creeks had granted the Georgians permission to settle one town, but they had "ever since encroached upon us ever from that time of their first settlement." Malatchi went on to complain that Doctor Graham had recently come into the nation and obtained a grant for Creek land. "But here are some of the head men to deny it," he added, stating that the lands belonged to Mrs. Bosomworth by virtue of the fact that "she is an Indian, intitled to all the rights and privileges of an Indian and was entitled to the Lands she possessed."[102]

After praising Malatchi as "the head and mouth of your nation," Glen invited other Creek chiefs to state their opinions on the land controversy. The *fanne mico* or Red Coat king of Oakfuskee, one of the supporters of the Graham Deed, declined to speak, citing his advanced age. In his place the Wolf king and head warrior of Oakfuskee both affirmed that they, like Malatchi, hoped that the Cherokee peace would be "effectuall," but insisted that there was not one but two great men in the nation who "agree to peace or order war." Malatchi, of course, was one of these great men. The other, they implied, was the absent Gun Merchant, who had also worked hard recently to keep his warriors at home.[103]

The Oakfuskee head warrior's insinuation that two great men lived among the Creeks thus set the stage for a verbal confrontation, which finally occurred when talks resumed on Sunday, June 2. After a discussion of the Cherokee problem, Malatchi recounted his version of the Bosomworth Affair, complaining that the "pretend[ed]" Graham Deed should be considered null and void. Malatchi explained that he had asked all the headmen present if they ever signed such an agreement that granted the disputed lands to Georgia, and challenged anyone in the room who did so to stand up and be counted. "Now I desire," he exclaimed, "that the head men here present who are said to have signed that Grant may declare before your Excellency whether ever they assented to any Grant or not?"[104]

At first Malatchi's challenge to the supporters of the Graham Deed drew no response. Malatchi finally drew his foes into the conversation by refusing to renegotiate trade prices, thereby muting a request for lower trade prices that several Upper Creek representatives had made the previous day. Malatchi's refusal to address the Upper Creeks' trade interests quickly drew the scorn of the Head Warrior of the Oakfuskees and the Oakfuskee captain, who bitterly argued that Creek trade prices should be lowered to match the Cherokees' more favorable terms of trade. Then, citing his ill luck, the Oakfuskee captain returned the commission that Glen had issued to him several years before and stormed out of the room. Other Creek warriors, presumably those hailing from Upper Creek towns, soon followed in the Oakfuskee captain's wake, leaving behind the presents that Glen had given them as a sign of protest.[105]

Though the Upper Creeks' abrupt departure momentarily threatened to undermine the Creek-Carolina talks, the din of silence that ensued presented both Malatchi and Governor Glen with a rare opportunity to further their own converging political interests, which required the Creeks to recognize Malatchi's pretended national authority. In a timely fashion Malatchi broke the din of silence first by apologizing for his compatriots' behavior: "Some of our People who call themselves Head Men and Warriors," Malatchi mused, "are unacquainted with the Nature of Public business and the true interest of their own Nation." "They ought to be considered as children," he said, "[for] they in a very rude and abrupt manner broke in upon my discourse without any Power or Commission from me or the Nation. My talk," he continued, "is the only true talk and shall be ratified and confirmed. Everything else is to be considered as wind."[106]

By positioning himself as the true voice of the Creek Nation and dismissing others as children, Malatchi convinced Governor Glen, at least for the moment, that he was the best suited to conduct public business. The Creeks in attendance would have recognized such wording as a slight as well, for they viewed children as unequipped emotionally and experientially to assume leadership roles. Malatchi's verbal sleight of hand initially produced material rewards, for Glen gave Malatchi control of the Upper Creeks' unclaimed presents so that he could distribute them "to those that you shall think most worthy of them." When tempers subsided and talks finally resumed two days later, Governor Glen urged the Creeks to unify their government under Malatchi's leadership, noting that his "extreamly good" behavior in Charles Town was "becoming [of] a king."[107]

Glen was painfully aware, of course, that the Creeks lacked a notion of absolute authority and knew from firsthand experience that their nation lacked a real king. Urging innovation, Glen pressed the Creeks in attendance to invent such a position to honor Malatchi. Singling out Malatchi, Glen argued that "had he not been born a King, he deserves to have been made one, the Head King of the Nation, and happy is that Nation that has such as a Head." In an effort to convince the Creeks that Malatchi was fit for such a role in a language they could understand, he emphasized Malatchi's mastery of the dual facets of leadership: war and peace. "By his Prudence," Glen implored, "he is capable of conducting their affairs in times of Peace, and by his Valor he is able to defend them from their Enemies in Times of War, and to lead them to certain Victory."[108] In this way Glen, seasoned by several years of "occular inspection" of Southeastern Indian cultures, sought to conflate the dual leadership roles common among the Creeks. As Glen would have it, Malatchi was wise enough to be a chief brave enough to be a warrior.

If anyone in the nation could challenge this assertion it was Gun Merchant of Okchay, the *mico* of the leading Abika war town and commissioned by South Carolina on the very same day as Malatchi. As many of the Upper Creek warriors who stormed out of the proceedings looked to the Gun Merchant for leadership, Glen and Malatchi knew that the Creeks would have to be reconciled before any single chief would be recognized by the nation at large. Glen urged the Creeks to "consult among yourselves and concert what you have to say, and agree upon a proper Person to be your Mouth and empower him to speak and treat fully upon that affair." Though Glen conceded that the Gun Merchant was a great man who could be "commissioned for the upper Towns," Malatchi was Glen's first choice as the proper person to speak for the whole nation.[109]

Glen and Malatchi's political maneuverings appear to have momentarily humbled the Oakfuskee head warrior and captain into submission. When the talks concluded that day, an unnamed Indian chief from the Upper Creeks apologized for their rash behavior, stating that their hostile talk was "an inadvertent word" that he compared to "a sudden gust of wind which is spent and gone." Hoping that his slip of the tongue would soon be forgotten, the Upper Creeks conceded defeat and suggested that, although the Upper towns looked upon the Gun Merchant as their headman, Malatchi "should speak for us all."[110] In the end the Oakfuskee captain, who led the exodus from the council chamber two days before, apologized for his misdeeds and took back his commission, stating that he would "continue a true friend of the English until the Day of My Death."[111]

In the wake of the May and June meetings, Governor Glen confidently predicted that the British Empire had found an influential and enduring friend in Malatchi. In an attempt to distance himself from earlier comments that suggested that Malatchi was no more than the headman of the Cowetas, Glen tried in earnest to convince the Board of Trade that he was "the greatest leader they [the Creeks] ever had." "His speeches," Glen boasted," were delivered with the Dignity of a King, and with the Greatest distinctness." This ability, he further argued, showed that Malatchi was "a man of admirable sense, and that his whole behavior during his stay has charmed everybody." "There are other considerable men in that Nation," Glen concluded, "but he [Malatchi] is really the chief and is chiefly to be noted by us."[112]

Malatchi's performance in the South Carolina Council chamber in 1753 proved to be the pinnacle of his important career in European diplomacy. For a while it appeared that he had established firm control over the Lower Creek warriors, enabling him to bring about the peace with the Cherokees that Governor Glen had entreated him to make. Upon his return to Coweta in June, Malatchi forbade them from taking up arms for three moons in order to determine the veracity of

Cherokee promises to halt their attacks. When the said three moons had expired, the Cherokees agreed to send a northern Indian slave to the towns of Coweta and Oakfuskee so that they could be burned to avenge the Creeks that the northern Indians had slain in previous years.[113]

Malatchi's ability to secure Governor Glen's support in Charles Town appears to have humbled the Gun Merchant into repudiating the Graham Deed. When William Little, a Georgia official, spoke with the Gun Merchant in December 1755, the Gun Merchant admitted that he had dispensed with the lands because they were "of no value to them [the Upper Creeks]." In recognition of Malatchi's earlier attempts to give the lands to the Bosomworths, however, the Gun Merchant conceded that Coweta was "the head and most ancient" town: "To pretend to countermand or invalidate any grants of lands made by [the Cowetas] to their friends would be acting like children." Consequently, the Gun Merchant repudiated the Graham Deed, stating that Mary Bosomworth should be allowed to keep the land "for the rest of her life."[114] The Creeks eventually ceded this land to Britain in less than three years, and the compromise that concluded the Bosomworth Affair was settled four years later in London, independent of Creek wishes or influence, a sign of worse things to come.

The Legacy

Within a year of the Charles Town meetings Malatchi began to show signs of an illness that kept him confined to Coweta for much of the rest of his life. As Malatchi's health declined, so too did his political influence, illustrating the old dictum that personal attributes figure prominently in the world of politics. Political institutions, historical precedent, or an individual's pedigree might be important, but no surer sign of an individual's political efficacy can be found than his or her physical prowess.

That Malatchi's physical decline paralleled his sagging political fortunes is evidenced by the peculiar dispersal of political influence in Coweta that occurred in the mid 1750s. In Coweta, for instance, Chigelly, aged and lacking the use of one arm, appears to have regained some of the influence he had lost during the previous decade. Antonio Micono, a Spanish emissary who visited the Lower Creeks at that time, described Chigelly as their reigning emperor and reserved for Malatchi a somewhat subordinate role as a "kinsman who governs" due to Chigelly's advanced age.[115]

This decentralization of political influence is most apparent, though, in the younger generation of leaders that later replaced Malatchi and Chigelly. Whereas in an earlier era the two men tended to dominate Coweta politics, after Malatchi's death political influence appears to have been conferred upon a cadre of men, none of whom emerged as singularly dominant. Among the more important leaders was Malatchi's brother Sempeyoffee, who emerged as Coweta *mico* by 1758. Though influential, Sempeyoffee never monopolized diplomatic talks in the way his predecessors had, instead relying heavily on a small group of men to whom Indian superintendent Edmund Atkin referred as "four vile brothers" who "owned" the Coweta Town square. Arguably the most important of these four young men was the eldest, Scotchaby (Escuchape to the Spanish), who Sempeyoffee singled out as the next in line to become emperor of the Lower Creeks in 1763.[116] Atkin concurred in believing Scotchaby was the most important of the four brothers, describing him as the "Chief Warrior . . . who overrules all when on the Spot."[117]

Scotchaby, however, never seems to have been recognized at home or abroad as the one voice of his people. Another figure of importance was Togulky, who many regarded as Malatchi's "son" but who might best be thought of as his nephew. When he was a young man both British and French officials bestowed upon him the honor of emperor, though his inexperience and apparent lack of leadership ability never allowed him to convincingly defend that position. Coweta leaders thus presented a confusing picture of the man's position in his own town. Malatchi's guardian, Sempeyoffee, for instance, referred to Togulky as "the Head of our Nation" in Savannah in 1759, entirely ignoring Scotchaby's claim to a similar title.[118]

In addition to the lack of a discernible emperor, in the wake of Malatchi's death the dispersal of political influence in Coweta is observed more generally in the number of different men who served as ambassadors, speakers, and signers of treaties. Ufylegy, the second man of Coweta, was Scotchaby's younger "vile" brother. Also important were "Half-Breed Abraham" and Assttuttee (variously known as the White King or Red King of Coweta).

These other Coweta leaders appear to have had the opportunity to grow—prematurely, in some cases—into their political roles because, in his final years, Malatchi concerned himself less with politics and more with his illness, seeking an explanation for his premature afflictions. To find the source of his suffering Malatchi called upon the prophetic gifts with which he had been born. By exercising this innate ability he might have been able to expose the witches who were working their evil magic upon him. Initially Malatchi pointed his finger at English sorcerers, who he believed had used on him a "slow poison" (a euphemism for witchcraft).[119]

Despite being born with the gift of divination, Malatchi failed to develop this skill during his adult life, due in part to the fact that the exigencies of war and diplomacy had lured him into a political rather than a priestly life. Lacking the skills to root out his own afflictions, Malatchi sought the advice of various Indian doctors who charged him handsome fees for their diagnoses. Malatchi resorted to their cures so often, in fact, that he was forced to part with many of his own personal possessions in return for services rendered. Responding to Governor Glen's invitation to visit him in Charles Town in the fall of 1754, Malatchi explained that he was very ill and could not visit, adding "nor have I any thing left me but my body" and that he had "been obliged to give all I had to the Doctors."[120]

For a brief while it appeared that Malatchi might recover from his afflictions, as Malatchi himself predicted. The following February, the trader Lachlan McGillavray reported that Malatchi was "upon the recovery"; by March he was well enough to resume his travels, entertaining offers from the French and Spanish to visit their respective outposts. That summer Malatchi made a brief excursion to Fort Toulouse, causing British officials to look upon him, once again, as a foe.[121]

Malatchi's exertions that summer, however, appear to have caused his mysterious illness to reappear as autumn approached. In November the trader David Douglas reported that Malatchi "is very bad," an apparent reference to his declining health. Douglas invited Malatchi to attend a meeting at Fort Moore, scheduled to take place the coming April, in order to discuss a proposed alteration in trade prices. Malatchi died before the scheduled meeting could take place, succumbing, at last, to his lingering illness while hunting in the woods in early January 1756.[122]

In some respects, then, Malatchi of Coweta's life as a public figure was important because his career marked the end of a particular era in Creek history. Though later Coweta leaders might have toyed with the concept of emperor, none exhibited the political skills nor exercised the regional influence as Malatchi or his elder kinsmen Chigelly and Brims had. Moreover, Malatchi's death seems to have occurred simultaneously with Coweta's demise as a center of influence among the Creeks. Studies of subsequent periods of Creek history indicate that political power in the wake of Malatchi's death later shifted to the more numerous Upper Creeks. Coweta's influence on the Chattahoochee River also steadily declined, as British officials increasingly found influence among the Lower Creek point towns located farther south, particularly the town of Chehaw.[123]

If not entirely successful in perpetuating Coweta's legacy as the most influential town in the nation, Malatchi seems to have succeeded in perpetuating the legacy of the Coweta Resolution devised by his elder kinsman Brims. For Malatchi the Coweta Resolution was not simply a rhetorical device but rather a political habit that steered him toward the French and Spanish when compelled by British Indian policy to do so. But Malatchi's version of the Coweta Resolution departed somewhat from the strict neutrality it recommended. Malatchi, born long after the presence of English traders had become commonplace, recognized that the Anglo-Creek alliance was more important than alliances with the Spanish or the French. "With his last breath," it was reported, Malatchi urged his people "to hold the English fast, as their truest friends, and most capable to serve them."[124]

Malatchi's willingness to place more importance on the English alliance suggests, moreover, that his own career signified the beginning of a new era in Creek politics. As it was his misfortune to be Coweta's leader at the time of the first significant Anglo-Creek land dispute—the Bosomworth Affair—Malatchi of necessity became the first leader to defend Creek claims to the debatable Georgia territory. Defending the Creek Nation on the basis of its land claims thus made Malatchi the first to define his society more precisely as a territory, which many anthropologists recognize as a marked shift away from the more vague territorialism seen in tribal societies.[125] Willing to position himself as the defending prince of this territory-based nation, Malatchi might also be thought of as the first leader possessing a national scope. Malatchi's mortality did not put a stop to these political trends, as the issues of territory, national leadership, and triple-nation diplomacy came to the fore again in the impending era of the French and Indian War.

CHAPTER SEVEN

The Invention of the Creek Nation

"In the Name of the Most Holy and Undivided Trinity, Father, Son, and Holy Ghost. So be it." These pious words began one of the most important peace treaties in the history of the modern world, the Treaty of Paris, ratified on February 10, 1763, in the name of "His Brittanick Majesty, the Most Christian King [of France] and the king of Spain." A lengthy and complex document, the Treaty of Paris officially brought to an end the epic struggle for empire known in America as the French and Indian War (1754–1763), which had relied on and drawn in the participation of Indians throughout eastern North America. Not incidental to Indian political concerns, the treaty distributed contested colonial possessions in the "four parts of the world" to the several European nations involved in the conflict. In peace as in war, the big winner was Britain, which gained legal control over recently conquered French territories and their inhabitants. The most important of these territories—Canada—had been in British hands since the fall of Quebec in 1759. Britain's gains were no less impressive in the southeastern quarter of North America which, although an unconquered territory, came under British dominion by virtue of the treaty.[1]

Thus, by a single stroke of a pen the European powers brought their longstanding imperial contest to a (as it was then perceived) permanent end. Historians have long recognized the French and Indian War and the "peace" that came after it as an important watershed event in the history of North America. Unencumbered by imperial rivalry, the British Parliament and Crown began to look inward and devote attention to the enduring goal of bringing the colonies into proper subordination. As even most schoolchildren are aware, Parliament's attempts to impose new taxes and demands on the colonists provoked the colonists first to resist, then to rebel against the aggressive regime that threatened to enslave them. The Treaty of Paris did not cause the American Revolution per se, but it did play no small role in creating the political conditions that made the revolution, and the subsequent territorial expansion of the United States, possible.[2]

The treaty also had revolutionary implications for the Indian peoples in North America, who recognized that their own independence was best maintained within a climate of imperial rivalry and not one of British encirclement and hegemony. Consequently, the abrupt departure of the most Christian king's troops from their North American posts caused a nostalgic longing among some Indians for the return of their French "father." Fear of British encirclement also caused Indians to look for spiritual solutions to their predicament, as an indigenous, pan-Indian, millenarian movement inspired by the Delaware prophet Neolin spread throughout the continent. Political conditions thus set the stage for Ottawa chief Pontiac's revolt against British efforts to evict them from their recently acquired territory in the Great Lakes region. For nearly three years Pontiac and his allies attacked forts that had recently belonged to the French, notably the encampments at Detroit, Niagara, and Michillimacinac. Though ultimately unsuccessful, Pontiac and Indians who came after him continued to pine for the return of their indulgent French "father" as Anglo-American settlers began spilling beyond the Appalachian Mountains.[3]

The outcome of the French and Indian War had revolutionary implications for the Creeks as well. They understood that a British victory might render precarious their own political independence and expressed dismay and outright hostility when informed of ominous provisions of the Treaty of Paris. Yet even during a nine-year war of much bloodshed, the Creeks had generally fought on a diplomatic rather than a military front to achieve two basic goals: to remain neutral at a time when many other Indian nations were choosing sides, and to defend Creek territory from the unwanted intrusion of backcountry settlers (who began filtering into Creek hunting grounds at an unprecedented rate) and British imperial officials (who strove to appropriate lands by treaty). In light of the diplomatic methods Creeks employed to achieve these ends, the Great War for Empire as experienced in Creek country might best be thought of as a "cold war" not entirely unlike the imperial conflicts that preceded it.

If not entirely a war in the military sense of the term, the era of the French and Indian War nevertheless witnessed the convergence of historical trends that required the Creeks to apply more concretely the concept of the Creek Nation in the execution of their political goals. With a hot imperial war raging around them, the avoidance of warfare demanded rigorous and widespread application of the precepts of neutrality, which in turn consolidated the nation more directly under the banner of the Coweta Resolution. Neutrality in essence became more than a diplomatic policy; it was a political, if not ethnic, marker sanctioned by tradition that distinguished the Creek Nation from its neighbors.

Likewise, as the Creeks had long feared, a British victory posed an imminent threat to Creek territorial claims, which increasingly were subject to challenge during the era of the war. On two separate occasions during the conflict, British officials convinced reluctant Creeks to sign away territory in Georgia that the Indians had once called their own, a harbinger for the land cessions that ultimately led to their removal to Indian Territory in the 1830s. To execute these cessions both the British officials and the Creeks relied upon the legal construct of a "Creek Nation" to endow the transaction with legitimacy. Initially a vaguely defined product of cross-cultural diplomacy, the use of the concept of the Creek Nation for the purpose of defending, defining, or ceding land permitted the Creeks to invent themselves as a "society as a territory" rather than as a tribal society that just happened to exhibit territorial tendencies. In this way the Creek Nation assumed a concreteness it had not hitherto possessed. And, if ill-formed in an institutional sense, the threat of war and Creek territorial aspirations may rightly be attributed to the invention of the Creek Nation.

The Indigenous Origins of the Creek Nation

For a legal Creek Nation construct to have been invented in the first place, and for it to have been accepted to some extent by the people to whom the concept applied, we should expect to find a degree of social convergence among the towns and clans that comprised it. Without such a foundation of social connection, Creek nationhood itself was unlikely to take root and grow into a more mature form, just as it did in the latter part of the eighteenth century. Of course it is difficult, if not impossible, to pinpoint the precise moment at which this social convergence took place. But if we accept Charles Hudson's assertion that the Mississippian chiefdoms were intensely provincial in nature, and if we bear in mind the demographic catastrophes and social dislocations of the century following the first Spanish *entradas*, we must assume that the convergence of coalesced peoples like the Creeks came later rather than sooner.[4] Though one can see signs of this social convergence occurring in the late seventeenth century, more demonstrable proof can be found in the mid-eighteenth century on the eve of the French and Indian War. Pressures exerted by the colonial powers likely promoted this bonding process, and Creek social convergence might therefore be understood as a function of frontier conflict. The Creeks, though, would have understood this social convergence in terms of their own notions of kinship and social organization. The Creek Nation had in effect become an extended family, and here one finds the roots of what might best be called the "indigenous origins" of Creek nationhood.

That the Creek Nation appeared to be growing somehow was not lost upon the eighteenth-century observers who knew them best. In 1775, just as the rebellion in the American colonies took a violent turn, a James Adair published his famous historical account of the Southeastern Indians. Adair, who had considerable firsthand knowledge of the events and personalities described here, was therefore well-prepared to offer an opinion on the formation of the Creek or Muskogee Nation. Noting that many other Indian groups were "visibly and fast declining," Adair observed that the Muskogee Nation, in contrast, was growing. He attributed this growth in part to an "artful policy" that enabled the Muskogees to replenish their numbers by "inviting decayed tribes to incorporate with them. . . . I am assured," he added, "[that] they have increased double in the space of thirty years."[5]

Yet, as evidence of Indian social convergence comes to us largely through the paper trails left by Europeans, we should approach the study of Creek nationhood with a healthy dose of skepticism. The three European colonial powers often had dissimilar goals and approaches to Indian affairs, and it should come as no surprise that dissimilar portraits of Creek social and political configurations emerge. Part of the problem stems from the fact that the term "Creek" was a British invention, a catch-all label that simplified not only the clan system but also the ethnic and political diversity found among Creek peoples. This tendency to homogenize might have proved to be a benign practice had the Creeks and the British Empire not begun competing for the same territory after the founding of Georgia in 1733. Beginning with South Carolina governor Robert Johnston's attempt in 1732 to subordinate the Creek Nation under its perceived chain of friendship, the term Creek Nation became not simply a term of convenience but a legal entity that British officials endowed with powers attributable to modern nation-states: to make treaties, cede land, and enter into military alliances.[6] Imperial considerations, then, explain why the use of the terms "Creeks" and "Creek Nation" became widespread, most especially among the colonial governors, Indian agents, and metropolitan officials seated in London.[7]

Such was not generally the case among the Catholic powers, whose colonial officers never adopted the word Creek nor any other homogenizing term to refer to this same group of Indian peoples. In fact, if we were to write Creek history using only the paper trails left by the Spanish and the French, we might very well conclude that no single nation or confederacy ever existed. Typically the Spanish used the term "province" to refer to an agglomeration of no more than a dozen towns loosely allied to larger towns such as Apalachicola or Coweta; sometimes Spanish officials used the term to refer to all such towns occupying a single river system. For instance, when Bishop Calderon first conduct a survey of the interior in the 1670s, he described the Creek peoples as inhabitants of two distinct provinces, Apalachicola (the Chattahoochee towns) and Tavasa (the Coosa and Tallapoosa towns). After the Yamasee War, when Spanish officials restored contact with the *enemigos*, they generally referred to the so-called Lower Creeks as the Uchises or, on occasion, the Uchises and Cavetas. Typically, the Spanish regarded the inhabitants of the Coosa and Tallapoosa Rivers as a different political entity that they called "Apiscas" and "Talapuces." Occasionally Spanish officials even believed that the Uchises and Tallapoosas were declared enemies of each other. Spanish officials did note, however, that the Apisca and Tallapoosa towns were particularly close, and sometimes referred to them as confederates or allies.[8]

Likewise, the French also portrayed the Creek Nation as a decentralized, multi-ethnic polity that defied easy description. French officials typically refrained from using a homogeneous term and instead referred to the Creek peoples in the plural: Alabamas, Abikas, Tallapoosas, or Kawitas, albeit with some variations. Occasionally French officials did try to invent a single homogenizing term, but their efforts to do so appear strained and suggest that the Creeks' political system did not merit such simplification. Among the most awkward labels were "the party of the Alabamas," the "nations of this region," "those comprised under the name Alabamas," "the nations of the region of the Alabamas," or, tellingly, "the Indians under the name and territory of the region of the Alabamas."[9]

Also complicating the picture is the fact that the social and political convergence of the Creek peoples was brought about in part by a process of exclusion, as certain elements of the Creek Nation withdrew—voluntarily, for the most part—to fulfill specific political goals. Fission as much as fusion, therefore, distinguished the Creek Nation at midcentury. Henry Ellis, the second royal governor of the Colony of Georgia, noted this complication on one occasion when he discussed the regulation of trade with his counterpart in South Carolina, William Lyttleton. In recent years, Ellis complained, many unlicensed traders living on the southern outskirts of the colony had bartered with Indians who were nominally judged to be Creek. Not only was the current trade regulation act too loose to be effectual, Ellis noted, but also it "may easily be avoided from the difficulty of proving who are or are not of that nation."[10]

The difficulty that Ellis encountered in determining which towns were a part of that nation was a reflection of the Creek tendency toward mobility during the eighteenth century.[11] Although for centuries the Southeast's native inhabitants had tended to drift geographically, this process accelerated during colonial times. Among the Creeks it was particularly true, once the decimating wars against the Florida missions opened the previously occupied lands for Creek settlement.

The lure of trade drew a great number of Creeks from their towns, which had the tendency to make them—and their young warriors, in particular—increasingly ungovernable. Documentary evidence attests to the fact that, over time, more and more Creeks could be found on the paths traveling to Augusta, Charles Town, Savannah, or Fort Frederica, sometimes to trade illicitly with the locals and sometimes to solicit gifts from colonial officials.[12] Occasionally the more able-bodied men "rambled" through the woods for a year or more at a time, particularly during the war years when the opportunity for intrigue proved most tempting.[13] Many Indians and whites crossed paths at Augusta, which one colonial official described as "the seat of all disorderly doings."[14]

Not only did individual mobility pose a threat to frontier stability, it also had revolutionary consequences for the Creeks' own social and political order, particularly because Creek traditions were uniquely adapted for small, face-to-face communities bound tightly by real and imaginary bonds of kinship. In such communities the old men typically exercised the most authority and ultimately made decisions relating to peace and war. Though they rarely used force against their own people, the power of shame within these small communities was strong. Social pressures enabled Creek leaders to retain a measure of control over their people, often by evoking the memory of long-dead ancestors whose judgment they regarded as infallible. By midcentury, however, Creek youths were becoming increasingly ungovernable and prone to causing mischief when away from their elders' watchful eyes. As the increase in frontier violence in the latter half of the century attests, the presence of hot-tempered young Creek men in woods that were quickly filling with Anglo-American traders, farmers, and their livestock proved to be a volatile and deadly mix.

This generational rift was not the only revolutionary implication for Creek mobility. As both British and Spanish officials occasionally testified, the lure of trade and the availability of vacant lands were beginning to draw a few enterprising Creek leaders away from their towns of origin. By midcentury a few of them appear to have left permanently, thereby initiating a gradual process of fission (referred to here as "Seminolization").[15]

It has long been known that the Seminoles of Florida were not indigenous to the region, but rather were migrants who had originally constituted a part of the Creek nation. Nevertheless, it has not been possible until recently to date precisely the beginnings of this migration.[16] Seminolization, or, as the Creeks themselves might have termed it, the outward migration of Creek communities that "pay obedience to no-one," in one sense began shortly after the Yamasee War of 1715 when Chislacaliche, a pro-Spanish chief, reoccupied the Sabacola old fields at the confluence of the Flint and Chattahoochee Rivers. Chislacaliche's town, and another like it established near Fort San Marcos by his nephew in the 1750s, were fiercely "Hispanophile" and at least superficially Catholic, and their leaders were conspicuously absent from most Lower Creek gatherings.[17]

Chislacaliche was not alone, however, among Creek chiefs who established independent communities in the two decades following the Yamasee War. In the 1720s, for instance, the town of Eufala, originally located in the Upper Creeks, split into two. One faction, which earned a reputation for lawlessness, migrated south and established a town on the Chattahoochee roughly midway between the forks and the southern extremity of the Lower Creek towns. In a similar vein, Tomochichi's "tribe," which founded the settlement at Yamacraw in 1732, might also be labeled Seminole due to the fact that many other Creeks in the nation proper considered them renegades who lived beyond the pale of legitimate Creek authority.[18]

Though early migrations did not immediately revolutionize the Creek political system, they nonetheless paved the way for other migrations in the 1740s and produced the first true Seminole communities. The first such villages—family encampments, really—arose in the Alachua region of north-central Florida in territory that at one time harbored several Timucuan settlements and a large Spanish cattle ranch. Leading the way into this region was the wayward chief of the Oconees who was most commonly known by his nickname, the Cowkeeper. The Cowkeeper's band appears first to have settled on one of Georgia's sea islands only to migrate to the long-abandoned Alachua region during the War of Jenkins's Ear so as to prey upon the Spanish presidio and its relatively defenseless Indian population.[19] By the mid-1750s the Cowkeeper had distanced himself from his countrymen almost completely, asserting in 1757 that he had "not been in the nation these four years" and therefore not claiming to speak on its behalf.[20]

A revealing element in the story of Creek Seminolization was the tendency of a few headmen to establish their own settlements in colonial territory. One such noteworthy individual, a Cussita headman nicknamed Captain Elick, was an influential "doctor" who claimed English ancestry and proved to be one of Britain's closest allies during the French and Indian War. Though his origins, like the Cowkeeper's, are obscure, we know that by midcentury Elick inhabited a plantation called Sancta Sevilla located near the Georgia coast on the south side of the Altamaha River.[21]

While it is true that many wayward Creeks such as the Cowkeeper and Elick allied themselves to the Georgians, not everyone who founded new communities did so for the same reason. Some midcentury Spanish documents attest to the fact that many Creek Indians began spending much of their time abroad, roaming the Apalachee old fields in order to communicate more regularly with Spanish officials, hunt deer, or round up stray cattle.[22]

Hints that the Apalachee region would become fertile ground for permanent Creek colonization can be found as early as 1747, when Spanish officials in Pensacola claimed that they were receiving unprecedented numbers of Creek visitors to the presidio. Likewise, in November 1749 an anonymous individual reported that at least five Kaveta Indians had come to St. Augustine to receive instruction in the Catholic faith. Visits from these Indians increased so fast that Manuel de Montiano, during his last year as governor, complained that the six thousand pesos annually earmarked for the Indian fund was now insufficient due to the influx of persons from the "provinces of Kaveta."[23] His successor, Melchor de Navarrette, boasted in May 1751 that in the previous year he had received visits from exactly 714 Indians from "Kaveta, Ocone, Apalachicola, Yufala, Kasista, and Nadele," and had made a like plea to the viceroy for more money.[24]

This unprecedented influx of Creek people into Florida territory appears to have set the stage for more permanent migrations to the panhandle, which in fact occurred in the ensuing years. By 1753 migrant Creeks had established two towns in the abandoned Apalachee territory, one named Escambe after the old Apalachee town upon which it arose, and the other, Puntarrasa. Both towns appear to have had close ties to the Spanish colonial administration in Pensacola, which viewed the new communities as dependencies of the Spanish Crown. At Escambe, for example, Spanish soldiers erected a small fort—a "pen"—that housed a half-dozen or so infantrymen. Escambe's Indian leaders, who often adopted Spanish names, appear to have spoken Spanish fluently, acquired literacy skills, and professed the Catholic faith.[25]

During the war years Creek leaders in the nation proper became suspicious of these two Indian towns because of their close relationship to the Spanish, who were suspected of entering into a secret alliance with the English so as to encircle Creek country from the east and the south. Among those who became wary of Escambe and Puntarrasa was Acmucaiche, the Tuckebatchee *mico*, who believed that the two migrant communities were acting in favor of European rather than Indian interests. To reassert Creek authority in the region, in the spring of 1759 Acmucaiche sent his "son" (perhaps a nephew) into Apalachee to establish a new village that he named Talagache. Although nominally under Spanish authority, in February of 1760 Creek warriors used Talagache as a rendezvous point to launch a punitive campaign against the Spanish possessions. Those attacks resulted in the destruction of both Escambe and Puntarrasa, forcing the inhabitants to flee to Pensacola and ultimately to migrate to Cuba. Shortly after those attacks, Acmucaiche's people abandoned Talagache and returned home to Tuckebatchee, perhaps because their work there had been done.[26]

At first inspection, then, the Creek Nation appears inchoate, subject to fission, perhaps even a figment of the collective British imagination. Ethnographic evidence, however, suggests a remarkable degree of social interaction and convergence among the Creek peoples, connections that made it possible for them to identify with an extended if somewhat imaginary community that transcended town and clan. Since the Creeks generally understood all human relationships in kinship terms, it is plausible to suggest that a foundation of kinship ties based upon recognizable blood relationships was a necessary prerequisite for the formation of a national consciousness.

Because the Creeks rarely if ever revealed to Europeans the intricacies of their own kinship systems, evidence supporting Creek clan affiliation is severely lacking. Nevertheless, enough evidence exists to suggest that the increasingly mobile eighteenth-century Creeks, particularly members of elite families, did in fact forge region-wide kinship ties. The ruling clan of Coweta was no exception. The best evidence of this comes by way of Mary Bosomworth, who left a vague paper trail indicating the extent of her—and, by association, Malatchi's and Chigelly's—kinship ties within the Creek Nation. In the summer of 1750, for instance, Mary made plans to attend busk in Tuckebatchee, where a few unnamed relatives resided. Likewise, when Mary ventured into Creek country in the summer and fall of 1752 to repair the breach caused by the infamous Acorn Whistler episode, Mary used her influence among her relations in Tuckebatchee to calm the Upper Creeks. Mary also revealed that her kinship ties extended to other Lower Creek towns. Thus, in August 1752 we find Mary chastising her Lower Creek relations, urging them to reveal the instigator of the recent murders of the Cherokees. When imploring her relations to confess, Mary addressed herself to a man named Hiacpellichi, whom she described as "a relation of her own." Hiacpellichi, heeding Mary's advice, then singled out Acorn Whistler as the cause of all the mischief. Hiacpellichi, though, appears not to have been one of her more famous Coweta relations, but instead was described as "a young fellow of the [Osuches]," indicating that Mary, Chigelly, and Malatchi claimed kindred from that town.[27]

Ironically, perhaps, the individual for whom we have the most evidence for an extensive network of kin is the infamous Acorn Whistler of

Little Oakfuskee, whom Malatchi described as "a great man [who] had so many relations both in the upper and lower Creek Nation." Among Acorn Whistler's Lower Creek relations was an unnamed nephew— the man assigned the unenviable task of killing his infamous uncle— who resided in either Coweta or Cussita. Likewise, Thlackpallacke, who first reported Acorn Whistler's death, was known as a relation of Acorn Whistler and probably lived in either Coweta or Hitchiti town. Isspuffnee, the Coweta beloved man who later assisted Malatchi in pacifying Acorn Whistler's grieving Upper Creek relatives, regarded himself as a near relation to Acorn Whistler. Circumstantial evidence also suggests that the chief of Cussita counted himself among Acorn Whistler's kin. Among the Upper Creeks, both the Atasi king and the captain of Oakfuskee regarded themselves as Acorn Whistler's relatives.[28] Malatchi was right, then, to note that Acorn Whistler's extensive kinship ties made his execution a difficult task, as both Upper and Lower Creeks from no less than four towns claimed him as one of their own.

Another means by which we may trace the more intimate connections of kinship shared between and among Creek communities is by examining the annual busk ritual. Busk was the most important ritual in the Creek calendar and its ceremonies were conducted in part to renew the reciprocal relationships between people who—at least ceremonially— shared the same fire. It is therefore plausible to suggest that by tracking the participants of any given busk we may gain at least a vague understanding of which towns or clans did or did not consider themselves related. A busk attended by a wide variety of towns, for example, may be taken as evidence for widespread social and kinship relations; a busk attended by fewer towns may be evidence of a more parochial community.

Existing records reveal very little pertaining to busk during this early phase of Creek history, as the Creeks generally guarded their most sacred rituals and traditions from the prying eyes of Europeans. Still, extant evidence suggests that by midcentury, the Cowetas and Cussitas, in particular, conducted busk rituals that were regional in scope. Take, for instance, the busk of 1750 held in Cussita. That year Abraham Bosomworth just happened to be present and was able to coax Malatchi and others to sign three deeds to the disputed lands claimed by his sister-in-law, Mary Bosomworth. Abraham was wise to present himself at that particular season, as busk tended to draw in people who might otherwise have been engaged in war forays, hunting, or various other pursuits. Wisely, just two days after the completion of the busk rituals

Bosomworth had Malatchi call a general council to urge the other leaders to consider signing Bosomworth's documents. Given the timing of events, it is likely that each of the deed signers had also been in Cussita two days before at busk. Therefore, the composition of the party signing the deeds may reflect those in attendance at the recent busk in Cussita.

An examination of the group that signed Bosomworth's deeds in fact indicates that the Cowetas and the Cussitas shared a ceremonial relationship with their neighbors that extended through most of the Lower Creek province. Though originally immigrant communities, this pattern of relationship suggests that by the middle of the eighteenth century the Cowetas and Cussitas shared their "fire" with communities that may have been indigenous to the Chattahoochee River. Not surprisingly, the Cussita warrior king placed his mark on the deed immediately after Malatchi, no doubt in recognition of the close ties shared by the towns of Coweta and Cussita. More important as it applies to Coweta's regional connections, though, were the marks of Jockcagey the king of Hitchiti town, and Ahomathley, the king of Apalachicola, both of whom may have been descended from people who were indigenous to the Chattahoochee. Also signing the deeds and likely in attendance at that busk were Elachegegey, the king of the Chehaws, and Tintlapuyey, "king of the Ossuhees," both Creek towns that may have derived from the Georgia interior. As further evidence that the Cowetas shared historical connections to at least some Upper Creek communities, one finds on the Bosomworth deeds the mark of JuClechumbey, the king of the Tuckebatchees who likely lingered on the Chattahoochee after fulfilling his busk obligations.[29]

As the rules of reciprocity governed Creek kin and social relationships, we should likewise expect to find the Cowetas obliged to take part in the busk rituals held in other Creek towns. In the summer of 1752, apparently after completing busk rituals in their own town, Malatchi and Chigelly ventured south to Hitchiti to engage in busk.[30] Their presence suggest that the two men shared an unspecified kinship relationship with some of the Hitchitis or, as the leading men of their town, the two were obliged to represent their town at the ceremony. Either way the reciprocal attendance at busk in these two towns—one group likely descended from people indigenous to the area and the other group descended from an immigrant community—suggests that for ceremonial purposes, the Hitchitis and Cowetas reckoned themselves people of the same fire.

Although much has been said here and written elsewhere about the relative independence of the Creek towns, the evidence concerning busk stands as a reminder that the Creeks tended to regard themselves and their towns as part of a larger whole. Evidence of regional or multi-community leadership roles is suggestive of the same trend. Coweta's leaders, for instance, clearly exercised influence among both the Upper and Lower Creeks. But the evidence is not just limited to Coweta. Other Creek leaders also claimed authority to speak for more than one town, indicating that political leadership, like ceremonial life, tended to integrate rather than divide Creek communities.

Take, for example, the case of Tupajatqui, a leading man from the town of Chiaja (Chehaw) who in 1738 was named the single head of the three Lower Creek towns of Ocmulgee, Osuche, and Chehaw. Both Spanish and English documents verify that in the 1730s these towns regularly acted in concert, usually on behalf of the English. Because of their close political connection, British authorities tended to identify the three towns as a single unit—the so-called point towns—for much of the remainder of the colonial period.[31] Likewise, in 1758 the pro-English chief Wolf of Mucculassee claimed that his authority extended well beyond his hometown to "four or five other little towns" that recognized his exalted status as a *micho thlacco* ("big king"). Wewoka, Canhatke, Euphale, and Little Oakfuskee all appear to have deferred to Wolf of Mucculassee's "mouth." The same may have been true of Fushatchee, whose principal war leader may have been a near relation. Despite his exalted status, the Wolf never claimed to be one of the nation's leading men, but nevertheless insisted "no man's mouth is heard in his towns but his own."[32] The infamous Acorn Whistler also claimed to speak for seven towns, further indication of the tendency toward multi-community political leadership within Creek country.[33]

If these miniature inter-Creek confederacies are suggestive of political and social convergence between towns, what, then, of the larger divisions within the nation? Prior to the first European invasions the Creeks' ancestors' recognized the existence of much larger imagined communities typically referred to as chiefdoms. Although much scholarly debate has covered the efficacy of the term and the degree to which such polities persisted into the historic period, it is clear that multi-community polities within a single river system would have seemed natural to the Creeks and other southern Indians. For this reason Creek leaders, when referring to themselves collectively, tended to use a different indigenous term for the three principal clusters of towns on the three river systems. The Chattahoochee Lower Creeks, for instance, appear to have referred to themselves collectively as the Cowetas or the Uchises, possibly in recognition of Coweta's influence or the Lower Creeks' ties to Ochese Creek. On the upper reaches of the Coosa and Tallapoosa Rivers, the people preferred the term Abikas. Farther south, toward the confluence of the Coosa and Tallapoosa Rivers, Tallapoosas was the term of choice. Though many persons—European and Indian alike—reverted to the more simplistic modifiers of lower and upper to distinguish the different regional divisions in Creek country, it is clear that the Creeks imagined themselves as a nation comprised of three rather than two riverine divisions.

The existence of three riverine divisions within the nation, though, ought not to be thought of simply as a barrier to a national identity. It should be stressed that the inhabitants of both the Chattahoochee and the Tallapoosa-Coosa river systems had forged links among themselves. The core of this linkage appears to have been the towns of Coweta and Tuckebatchee, which considered themselves friend towns by the middle of the eighteenth century.[34] The towns' friendship may be attributed to Coweta's apparent residence on the Tallapoosa River long ago. Some of the Tuckebatchees, moreover, appear to have immigrated in 1690 to the Chattahoochee River near Coweta, thus making it more likely for inhabitants of the two towns to intermarry and forge political and military alliances. One should also note that throughout much of the eighteenth century a trading path connected Coweta and Tuckebatchee, thus facilitating communication and the maintenance of such familial and political ties.

Consistent with this evolution of blood, ceremonial, and political ties within the nation was the Creeks' gradual embrace at midcentury of what may be called a Muskogee identity. In part the Muskogee identity may be understood as a linguistic marker, since the Muskogee tongue was the most commonly spoken language along the three river systems. Several other related languages, however, were commonly spoken as well, such as Alabama, Hitchiti, Koasati, and the unrelated tongues spoken by the Yuchis and Savannah immigrants. The Muskogee moniker, therefore, did not apply to all who lived in Creek country although Muskogee became known as the mother tongue, no doubt because of its widespread use in Creek country.[35] The pressure to speak it could be considerable, and some immigrant groups that spoke foreign tongues appear to have adopted it. One group of immigrants, the Tomohetans, who spoke a dialect similar to Southern Cherokee, adopted Muskogee as their own language as the younger generation of Tomohetans—born and bred among the Creeks—began using the language of their adoptive people. The Cherokee Long Warrior of Tunnessee, speaking before Carolina Council president Arthur Middleton in January 1727, summarized the linguistic assimilation of the Tomohetans in this way: "In those times they [Tomohetans] talked the language of the Lower part of the Cherokee Country up to and after they were separated." The young people, he noted, "picked up a different language from the Sea Part Indians [a Cherokee euphemism for the Creeks] which is what they talk now."[36] This process may have continued as the century progressed; the British-American traveler William Bartram noted that even the Natchez immigrants living among the Upper Creeks spoke Muskogee.[37]

National identities—linguistically based or otherwise—tend not to germinate in isolation but are forged in relation to others. Consequently, it is quite common for ethnic groups to adopt foreign terms by which to refer to themselves. In this way the Ojibwe-Anishinaabeg peoples of the upper Great Lakes region became known as the "Chippewas" and the Lakota and Dakota peoples of the Great Plains became widely known by the Chippewa-derived term "Sioux."

Indeed, this appears to have been the case with the term Muskogee, which likely was derived from a Shawnee term for "swamp" or "wet ground" and was adopted rather late in Creek history. As John Swanton noted, most Creeks of the early twentieth century had little clue as to the word's meaning and used it "for want of a native term to cover all the Muskogee tribes."[38] Even more important, though, the Creeks do not seem to have used this term with much frequency prior to the 1750s when it first begins to appear sporadically in colonial documents. We may therefore assume that the term Muskogee came into vogue roughly at midcentury when the Creek peoples felt compelled to adopt a catchall term to distinguish themselves from others.[39]

In sum, by the middle of the eighteenth century the Creek peoples had developed a regional network of clans and towns that shared common rituals and perhaps even a common name. It might therefore be asserted that the social foundations for nationhood had already been sown as the Great War for Empire loomed. But we should be careful not to assume the inevitability of this process, as the Seminolization of the Creek Nation suggests that ethnic and political fissioning occurred simultaneously. Nor should it be assumed that the social convergence seen among the Creeks translated neatly into a form of political consolidation. Political and ethnic identities, though correlative, may emerge at different times in response to different kinds of pressures.[40] Creek nationhood, therefore, must be explained historically, not simply as a function of social and cultural convergence but as a function of politics. Hence the importance of Creek neutrality in the new and dangerous era of imperial warfare.

It Is the Sense of the Nation to Remain Neuter

Experienced as they were in the world of international politics, the Creeks of the early to mid-eighteenth century rightly deserved the label that historian Verner Crane bequeathed to them long ago: "custodians of the wilderness balance of power in the South."[41] Well situated between the colonial outposts of three European empires, the Creeks had managed in impressive fashion to maintain commercial and diplomatic relations with all three. Their unique position, moreover, enabled them to play important intermediary roles between the respective colonies and other Indian nations and facilitated, for example, French diplomacy in Cherokee country and English trading with the remote Choctaws.

Thus the French and Indian War placed the Creeks, the "custodians of the balance of power in the South," in the middle of myriad tugs-of-war for their allegiance. The French and the Cherokees tugged from one direction, repeatedly attempting to drag the Creek Nation into a war against English settlements in South Carolina. At the same time British emissaries tugged from the other, pressuring the Creeks to build a fort in their nation and later lending military support against French posts in Alabama. Given the decentralized nature of political authority in the nation, it was perhaps inevitable that some Creeks chose to fight on one side or the other. By and large, however, most Creeks opted out of the conflict altogether, content to avoid bloodshed and adhere to the precarious status quo of neutrality.

Neutrality, moreover, by that time had become much more than a wise policy that the Creeks resurrected from time to time to avoid the serious consequences of imperial intrigue. Rather, Creek neutrality—and Brims's famous Coweta Resolution in particular—had become deeply woven into Creek oral traditions. Attributed to the venerable wisdom of their ancestors, the policy of neutrality assumed an air of religious significance as it, like many other Creek customs, was endowed with the sanctity of tradition. More than a quaint oral tradition, neutrality served conspicuously as a mark of Creek cultural identity, distinguishing the neutralist Creeks from surrounding nations who were more willing to choose sides and shed the white blood that most Creeks thought best not to spill.

Traditionally, the French and Indian War has been depicted as an epic struggle between two empires and their respective Indian allies. As most of the fighting occurred in Ohio country, upper New York, and Canada, the war's northern theater has tended to draw the most attention from historians, writers, and filmmakers alike.[42] British officials, however, did in fact draw up plans to attack French possessions in the South beginning in 1758. The British "southern strategy," as it might be termed, called for coordinated land and naval attacks on the French posts at Mobile and Fort Toulouse.[43] Creek villages, of course, guarded the approach to Fort Toulouse, which thus forced British officials to court Creek assistance.

British military leaders, however, were well aware of the Creek tradition of neutrality and the fact that success would depend as much upon diplomacy as the exercise of military might. The entire chain of the British military command structure made diplomacy with the Creek Nation a high priority. William Pitt, the prime minister, ordered Governor Lyttleton of South Carolina to "engage, if possible, any of the Indian nations to join therein" in the planned attack. Lyttleton, knowing that the Creeks were the effective gatekeepers to Fort Toulouse, warned British navy commander Adm. Edward Boscawen that Creek political sentiments posed a serious challenge to their war strategy. Although the Creeks were "not ill disposed to us," Lyttleton warned Boscawen, the land campaign might be difficult because "it is a fix'd principle with them to observe a strict neutrality between us and the French." Lyttleton also made sure to warn Maj. Gen. Jeffrey Amherst, the new commander of British forces in North America, that they might encounter some opposition from the Creeks who, he added, "are desirous to keep the French in their nation, and maintain the [French] Fort."[44]

To counter the Creeks' "fixed principle," British officials called upon Edmund Atkin to enlist Creek warriors or, at the very least, to obtain tacit Creek support for the attack on Fort Toulouse. Atkin, a former member of the South Carolina Council and self-proclaimed Indian expert, had been appointed two years earlier as the Crown's superintendent of Southern Indian Affairs. His duties had kept him occupied on Virginia's northern frontier, and Atkin had yet to set foot in Creek country. But he knew the Creeks well enough to know that their longstanding tradition of neutrality would make the task of razing Fort Toulouse a difficult one.

In a report on Indian affairs that Atkin penned prior to receiving his commission, Atkin singled out the Creeks as the "most refined and Political Indians" with their tradition of neutrality depicted as something of a distinctive cultural trait. "The Policy of the Creeks," Atkin wrote, "leads them to live in Peace with all their Neighbours" and made them want to "preserve a good Understanding with all the white people, English, French, and Spaniards." This message, he went on, "is frequently inculcated by some of the Chiefs in their harangues." Most tellingly, Atkin was even apprised (accurately, it seems) of the long history of this Creek tradition. The principle of neutrality, Atkin reminded his readers, "was enforced by the dying charge of the Old Emperor Brim to his Son Malatchi . . . never to suffer the Blood of any white men to be spilt on his Ground." "The conduct of the Creeks conformable to those Principles," Atkin concluded, "hath rendered them of superior weight among the Southern Nations, as holding the ballance between their European Neighbours, and esteemed or feared by the rest of the red People."[45]

Though knowledgeable of Creek political principles, Atkin nevertheless found it difficult to articulate Britain's war aims in a way that was acceptable to the Creeks and caused him to deny outright the Southern strategy he was charged with implementing. During his stay among the Upper Creeks, Atkin repeatedly denied Creek accusations that he sought to make war on the French forts and instead insisted that his only goal was to maintain Britain's historic friendship with the Creeks: "My business," Atkin once explained to an assembly in Tuckebatchee, "is to see whether you are his [King George's] friends or not, and to inquire how the traders behave towards you in their dealings."[46]

The Creeks, moreover, saw the truth through Atkin's charade. Evidence that they understood the real motive of his mission comes to us from Spain's Indian spy, Andres Escudero, who first alerted Spanish officials of Atkin's doings in July of 1759. According to Escudero, Atkin had come to Tuckebatchee that summer with a flag bearing the image of an Indian arm (the Creeks) and an English arm (King George) clenched in a bond of friendship. Escudero revealed that Atkin made the Indians swear their allegiance by kissing a book that was thought to be the Bible.[47] Escudero reported that Atkin "wanted the Indians on his side to seize New Orleans and Mobile," echoing precisely the details of the secret British military strategy. Not only did Escudero learn the targets of the British military, but also their strategy for executing the attack. Escudero explained, for instance, that a fleet of ships was in the north waiting to do the same on the Gulf Coast, an unmistakable reference to Boscawen's fleet in Nova Scotia.[48]

That even a spy working for the governor of Pensacola could discern Atkin's real motive explains why the Upper Creeks were reluctant to meet with Atkin that July, forcing him to wait in the woods for three weeks before receiving him in Tuckebatchee. It also explains why Atkin was obliged to deny repeatedly that his government had plans to attack the French possessions. Given that the Creeks knew his real motive, it is little wonder that Atkin concluded at the end of his mission that any attack on the French forts would be futile: "At present," he wrote, "such an expedition this year, or even perhaps the knowledge of such an intention, would I verily believe have cost the lives of all the King's subjects in this Nation. . . . The reduction of that fort," he added, "must be gone another way about."[49]

As it turned out, the reduction of the fort was never to occur. Though Atkin scored notable diplomatic victories—concluding treaties of peace and commerce with the Alabamas and the Choctaws—his mission to the Creeks in 1759 failed to lay the necessary groundwork for the planned conquest of Alabama. The Creeks, in fact, appeared to view Atkin as a noxious presence due to his numerous threats to withdraw traders from the Creek towns of Okchay and Cussita. His threats eventually prompted one mad Cussita man to twice strike Atkin on the head with a tomahawk as Atkin was giving a speech in the Tuckebatchee town square, causing a wound that nearly made Atkin a martyr for Britain.

Perhaps more irritating to Atkin than the wound he suffered in Tuckebatchee was the Creek tradition of neutrality, which proved to be the greatest obstacle to Britain's war plans. In Coweta, for instance, he tried to install a puppet headman who he deemed sufficiently in the "British interest," only to find that their leading headmen held commissions from all three European powers. Atkin's first choice to lead the puppet government was the lieutenant of Coweta, Scotchaby, who was known to be sympathetic to the British and carried a British commission. The lieutenant, however, had not yet returned home from the hunt, so Atkin sought to name another influential man in his place. The second choice, Ufylegey, known as the lieutenant's brother, quickly fell out of Atkin's favor when Ufylegey showed him a French commission that empowered him to make war on "all the enemies of the French nation." Atkin then received the Spanish commission made out to "Malatchi's brother" (Sempeyoffee), which named the Creeks as Spanish subjects. Another man, presumably Atkin's fourth choice to lead the puppet government, delivered up a similar Spanish commission, which prompted Atkin to postpone his attempt to mold Coweta's government to suit Britain's needs. In frustration, Atkin concluded that "a fine precedent this [is] for the other Commissions in being."[50]

In Coweta we can see one town's attempt to practice triple-nation diplomacy by allowing its individual members the leeway to cultivate alliances with whichever European power they saw fit. On other occasions Atkin found individuals who tried to play the game of triple-nation diplomacy single-handedly. One such person was Acmucaiche, the Tuckebatchee *mico*, whom Atkin first met on July 24. Atkin took special care to sway the chief in Britain's favor because Acmucaiche was rumored to be a French sympathizer and had recently raised the French Fleur de Lys in the Tuckebatchee town square.[51] Furthermore, Acmucaiche had recently rendered obedience to the Spanish crown by signing a peace treaty with the governor of Pensacola. Unbeknownst to Atkin, Acmucaiche had established a Tuckebatchee colony in Spanish territory, naming his "son" Anatichi as its titular chief.[52]

When Atkin called upon Acmucaiche to explain his duplicitous behavior, Acmucaiche argued that he was only doing what past generations had done in accordance with the Coweta Resolution: "I have formerly heard our old people say that we should take fast hold of the hand of all white people, & push none away. That is what I stand to—upon the news of your coming." The French flag flying in his town square, he argued further, did not necessarily preclude him from maintaining his alliance with Britain.

Acmucaiche then revealed that he simultaneously held both French and Spanish commissions. The French commission, he argued, came to him recently from the commander of the French fort. Evidence indicates Acmucaiche received his Spanish commission from the commander of Pensacola in April 1758. To assure Atkin that this practice of holding dual commissions was not unique, Acmucaiche later admitted "there are many down along the River who have both English & French commissions. . . . Yet they mean no harm by it. I believe that they love the English very well."[53]

Though Atkin disagreed, the Creeks did not interpret the practice of holding multiple commissions as duplicitous. Acmucaiche therefore spoke sincerely when he argued that the Creeks, even those who held French commissions, "love the English very well." Although the Creeks considered it practical to maintain alliances with all three European powers, the Creeks' love for the English indicates that the British alliance was always more important for several reasons, not the least of which was Britain's important role as the Creeks' principal trading partner. Atkin, of course, recognized that Britain's decades-old commercial relationship was his strongest selling point. He shrewdly played the "trade card" to convince Acmucaiche to give up the French colors and replace them with the British standard. Atkin realized that trade with the British had acquired the sanctity of tradition and was felt strongest in Tuckebatchee, Acmucaiche's own town. Old Bracket, the elderly *ispocoga mico* (an order of chiefs involved in the ritual preparation of busk medicines) of that town, served as a living reminder of the ancient friendship and, as everyone knew, had been one of the first Upper Creek leaders to restore the peace with the English after the Yamasee War. The Tuckebatchees, particularly Old Bracket and his relatives, had long worn this achievement as a badge of honor. Using Old Bracket's ancient act of friendship as an example to be emulated, Atkin reminded Acmucaiche that his townsmen had served as the caretakers of the Anglo-Creek alliance ever since. Acmucaiche, responding to Atkin's logic, hastily returned the French flag to Atkin and raised the British flag over Tuckebatchee.[54]

Atkin employed a similar rhetorical strategy when he returned to Tuckebatchee several months later. Having suffered a tomahawk wound while delivering an acrimonious speech the previous day, on September 29 Atkin shifted his rhetoric in a way that acknowledged the wisdom of the Creek neutrality policy in an attempt to win over a hostile crowd. The Creek audience had just grown silent after Atkin berated the French yet again for being poor trade partners and for pressuring the Creeks to act as mercenaries. Wisely, Atkin then began to applaud Creek political cunning, evoking the memory of the wise ancestors who authored the Coweta Resolution: "Among your ancestors there were many very wise & good men." Evoking the memory of Brims, Atkin continued by admitting that he knew "what was the advice of the wisest of them . . . to hold fast all three, English, French, & Spanish." "Take care and never quarrel with any of them" were Brims's words, causing the silent crowd unanimously "[to signify] their approbation with a visible change in their countenance." Atkin conceded that their policy "was the only way for you to thrive," adding that the "wise men . . . gave very good advice to you."

Knowing that some Creeks were then hatching plans to assist the French, Atkin used the Creeks' own logic to turn them against war: "I say to you as your own forefathers did, Live quiet in your own land & mind your hunting." This policy of inaction, Atkin reminded them, was necessary so that "your children and the white people's children may grow up together like brothers." Even facing this tough crowd, Atkin's speech caused the assembled Creeks again to signify their approbation as if Brims himself were speaking to them.[55] Brims was not, of course, in attendance, but Atkin's assumption of his voice at that time brought Brims back to life and the crowd's response suggest that Brims's words— the Coweta Resolution—had not been forgotten.

Edmund Atkin's 1759 mission to the Creeks, though, is but half the story of Creek neutrality in the French and Indian War. Creeks hostile to the British regime began hatching plans to enlist the French and the Cherokees in a war against the English. Leading this effort was the venerable Yahatustunagee of Okchay, better known to the British as the Mortar, whom Edmund Atkin described as "the man possessed of the most wisdom" who had "no man equal to him in the nation." Having acquired chief command over the head warriors, even his brother-in-law the Gun Merchant could do little to influence him.[56] However influential, the Mortar also found Creek neutrality too much to overcome and, like Atkin, failed to achieve his goal of ridding Creek country of the English menace.

The Mortar's plan—or conspiracy, as it has been characterized—was an unintended consequence of the Cherokee-Creek peace concluded in the year 1753. Mortar's town, Okchay, played a significant role in the peace negotiations. Okchay was one of two towns that had agreed to exchange tokens of peace with the Cherokees back in 1753 to end their decade-long war. Following some initial gestures, Creeks and Cherokees began meeting with each other regularly in order to renew their initial peace agreements. Many such meetings took place during busk rituals in which the Creeks and the Cherokees used an ancient adoption custom to form permanent alliances between ritually adopted *micos* who were responsible for maintaining friendly relations between allied towns. The Mortar, who had many friends in that nation, may have been ritually adopted by the Cherokee town of Chota. As a result, some of the Upper

Creeks and Overhill Cherokees became close, thus building a foundation for a military alliance.[57]

Having established kinship connections with the Creeks, Cherokee emissaries then took the opportunity to establish contact with the French fort at the Alabamas, facilitated, it appears, by like-minded Creeks.[58] Recognizing that Cherokee support was essential to protecting French interests in the region, French emissaries began making covert visits to Cherokee country as well. The individual most responsible for maintaining this covert alliance was one Louis Lantagnac, a French spy who posed as a deserter and obtained a license to trade in Carolina. Using his trade license as a cover, Lantagnac began distributing gifts to the Cherokees ostensibly from Governor Kerlerec of Louisiana. By 1756 Lantagnac had successfully cultivated a pro-French faction among the Overhill Cherokees.[59]

Why the Mortar attracted a small but zealous following among the Creeks and Cherokees during the war is not difficult to discern. The Cherokees, for their part, had allowed the British to build three forts in their country that quickly became the object of Cherokee resentment. Likewise, the Cherokees joined the British on no less than two military ventures into Ohio country, losing notable warriors in the process and coming to blows with white settlers in the Virginia backcountry. For the Creeks' part, the war years witnessed the unwanted intrusion of white settlers into Creek hunting grounds, particularly at Briar Creek in Georgia. Eventually some small bands of Upper Creeks and white settlers came to blows in September 1756, resulting in the deaths of at least three Upper Creek men. Adding to Creek disillusionment was South Carolina Indian Agent Daniel Pepper, sent into Creek country just a few months later to mend the wounds caused by the Briar Creek murders. Most grating on Creek nerves, however, was Pepper's effort to coax the Upper Creeks to permit the British to construct a fort, which even Pepper conceded was looked upon by the Creeks as a synonym for slavery.[60]

Following the initial meetings between Creeks, Cherokees, and the French, the Mortar worked behind the scenes for three years to plan and execute his bold plan of conquest. By May 1759 the Mortar's followers had hastily constructed Etoahatchee, a small camp on the Coosa River where it joins with a smaller tributary, the Coosawattee Creek. Intelligence indicated that the camp was to serve as the rendezvous point for

Creek and Cherokee warriors and French soldiers (who were to assist the Indians in their long-anticipated attack on Fort Loudoun). From there the war was to spread to the backcountry settlements and result in the evacuation of the British from Creek and Cherokee territory. Though little evidence indicated that French troops had entered the region, rumors held that French officers from Fort Toulouse had been making regular visits to the camp, presumably to encourage the Indians to go to war on France's behalf. One young lad named Maximillian Moore reported more tangible and ominous signs of the French, including finding a cache of "sails, oars, etc.," which indicated that French boats "had come there."[61]

The Mortar's plans for an Indian-French conquest appears to have assumed a continental dimension, as French-allied Canadian Iroquois—the Nottawagas—sent an ominous-looking wampum belt to the Southern Indians in the summer of 1759. The belt, as described by a Creek informant, depicted three headless Englishmen garnished with red paint, an unmistakable sign of the Nottawagas' hostile intentions. Its arrival in Cherokee country in the spring of 1759 coincided fortuitously with the establishment of Etoahatchee. Evidence indicates that the Mortar learned of the belt and had approved of its message long before it arrived in Coweta later that summer. By the summer of 1759, then, the Mortar seemed to have all the necessary elements in place to lead a widespread Indian revolt: promises of French military assistance; a camp to use as a base of attack; and an alliance with both the Cherokees and the Iroquois. If the intelligence gathered by British officials was any indication, the Indians planned to attack "at the first fall of the leaf" (autumn) of 1759.[62]

The Mortar's plans failed to come to fruition, however, because most Creeks did not share his political views or military goals. Nor was the Mortar a typical Indian of his day. He might even be described as "too Indian." Atkin noted, for instance, that the Mortar was little known to most British traders, which suggests that he, unlike many of his countrymen, rarely bartered directly with them. Because of the Indian's anti-European attitude, Atkin also characterized the Mortar as "the compleatest Red man in principle," adding that it was his personal policy to "[scorn] a commission from any European power." The Mortar even seems to have held in disdain Indians who did not share his nativist views. Atkin's Creek allies informed him, for example, that the Mortar was known to liken an Indian wearing a hat to a mushroom, as if to say that Indians who assumed the trappings of the Europeans were little better than fungi.[63] Unlike the Mortar, most Creeks refused to take sides and decided to "stand neuter" as the British pacified the Cherokees, the result of two military campaigns conducted in 1760 and 1761.[64]

Before the outbreak of the war in January 1760, the nation was deeply divided over whether or not to choose sides in the impending conflict. As the Wolf of Mucculassee put it, "this Nation . . . was then divided against itself, into several parties; not only the Miscogas (Creeks) themselves, but likewise the Alabamas."[65] As a consequence of these divisions within the Creek Nation, the Cherokees and pro-French Creeks found it difficult to coordinate their war plans. Militants from both nations called for war, but the two sides agreed on this point only so long as the plans remained abstract. When the time came to put words into action, the Creeks and Cherokees had a difficult time determining who would strike first. Some evidence suggests that the Cherokees were designated to strike the first blow, which was to be followed by a general Creek uprising against the traders. Others sources indicate, on the other hand, that the Creeks were supposed to begin the war by murdering the traders, after which the Cherokees would begin their attacks on the British forts and settlements.[66]

When war eventually came to Cherokee country, both the British and the Cherokees recognized that the Creeks' response might ultimately determine the war's outcome. British officials, the Mortar, and the Mortar's Cherokee allies all appealed to the Creeks to fight on their respective sides. Pessimistically, though, all suitors expected the Creeks to declare their allegiance only after it became easier to determine the outcome of the war. One trader summarized this perception of Creek intentions: "If the Cherokees should get the better of us, we may expect the Creeks to join them, otherwise, not."[67]

Given the diversity of political opinions held in Creek country at that juncture, it is not surprising that only a minority of Creeks chose to fight on behalf of one cause or the other. The Mortar, who continued to facilitate communication between the Cherokees, Creeks, and French, appears to have attracted a small following of Upper and Lower Creeks who fought actively on the Cherokees' behalf on the South Carolina frontier and assisted in the Cherokees' siege of Fort Loudoun.[68] On the other side, the Cowkeeper's Alachua bands escalated their attacks on Spanish St. Augustine to forestall the development of a Franco-Spanish alliance. Conspicuously, leaders of the Lower Creek point towns fought actively on Britain's behalf, occasionally bringing in a Cherokee scalp for a reward. Though not active militarily, the Coweta *mico*, Sempey-offee, appears to have led a pro-British faction that worked behind the scenes to allay the anti-British attitudes held by some of his townsmen, particularly Malatchi's "son" Togulky, a French partisan.[69]

That most Creeks chose not to fight can be attributed to the influence of exerted by numerous Creek leaders, who understood the wisdom of the Coweta Resolution and the dire consequences that would inevitably follow if English blood was shed in their towns. These leaders' understanding of the benefits of peace can best be seen in their actions during the abortive uprising that occurred among the Upper Creeks in late May 1760. The uprising, directed at the English traders, was rumored to have been premeditated by the Mortar, who had called upon the Creeks to slay their own traders and then join the Cherokees in their attacks on the settlements. The murder of English traders began in the Upper Creek town of Suglepoga when the son of the headman of that town and other associates killed the traders there. From Suglepoga the combatants proceeded to Oakfuskee, killing the unsuspecting traders there. At Oakfuskee, in an attempt to drum up more support, the combatants began spreading false rumors that the Lower Creeks had begun killing their own traders. From Oakfuskee the war party moved to the towns of Caiolegee and Fushatchee. In all, the Creek belligerents killed eleven traders and forced most others to flee for their lives.[70]

To anyone able to recall the events that began the Yamasee War of 1715, the violent acts committed against the English traders in the spring of 1760 likely had a familiar ring. As with the Yamasee War, Creek men began killing the traders in their midst with plans of then turning their attention to the English settlements. But the trader murders of 1760 did not degenerate into a repeat occurrence of the Yamasee War because this time many Creeks helped bring the uprising quickly to an end. For example, as with previous wars between the Indians and the English, Creek women appear to have apprised some of the traders of the plot and assisted in their escape. Among the fortunate was a packhorse man named Robert French who, after being warned by the niece of the Oakfuskee captain of the murderous plot, had managed to escape.

Most important, many of the leading Upper Creek men responded quickly to put an end to the spree of violence, demonstrating that it was their traditional duty to avoid bloodshed in the towns and reflecting their general belief that the English alliance was worth preserving. Among the staunchest defenders of the English traders was the Wolf, the *mico* of Mucculassee. Several traders, upon hearing of the advancing war party, fled immediately to Mucculassee, gaining the protection of the Wolf. In an attempt to defend the traders from the anticipated advance of the belligerents, the Wolf ordered his warriors to paint themselves for battle as if to send a clear signal to the belligerents that no traders were to be murdered in his town.[71]

The Wolf did not act alone, of course, in defending the English traders. The Gun Merchant of Okchay, acting contrary to the wishes of his infamous brother-in-law, the Mortar, gave some of the fleeing traders a safe haven in his town. Also singled out for ending the murder spree was Devall's Landlord (chief of Pucantallahassee), the war captain of Oakfuskee, and several Tallassee headmen. The Tallassee *mico*'s son, in fact, appears to have been so distraught by the murders that he promised to bring 117 of his own warriors to Savannah to fight for the English. The Lower Creeks, upon hearing of the murder spree, hastily escorted their traders to the safer confines of Savannah.[72]

The Creek leaders who sheltered the traders later pleaded ignorance of the murderous plot and soundly denounced the murders as the actions of a few brash young men, noting that the headmen had not condoned such actions. Devall's Landlord dismissed the unhappy episode as the actions of "mad young men." The Wolf of Mucculassee made a similar excuse, arguing that some of the young people had been listening to the bad talks circulating between Cherokee country and the French fort. Creek leaders, in fact, appear to have been so intent upon demonstrating their disapproval that they called several general meetings in the weeks that followed, disavowing the belligerent actions of a few in the council squares of Mucculassee, Tallassee, and the Lower Creek towns.[73]

British officials, once apprised of the murders, demanded that the Creeks obtain satisfaction by killing or capturing the perpetrators, many of whom appear to have fled to Cherokee territory for protection. Though some Creek leaders promised to apprehend the murderers, few took the initiative to do so. Nevertheless, the Upper Creeks sought to restore the peaceful balance between themselves and the British in their own way. In the weeks that followed the Creeks began the grisly task of collecting the bones of the dead traders. Once collected and stripped of the remaining flesh, the bones were then wrapped in a dressed deerskin that had been bleached white, the color of peace and harmony. Preparing the bones in this way, the Creeks were said to have performed the necessary rituals "to wipe away remembrance of the bad." The bones were then buried at an undisclosed location in Creek country.[74]

That the Creeks would give the murdered English traders a distinctively Creek burial not only signifies the Creeks' desire to "forget [past] grievances" but also demonstrates a continued perception of their alliances with Europeans was an extension of their own kinship relations. The burial preparations closely mirror a common Southeastern Indian burial custom performed specifically for individuals who died far from home. The Creeks, like most Southeastern Indians, believed that the spirit of a person who had died under such circumstances could only enter the realm of the spirits only after such a ritual burial of his or her bones had occurred. According to James Adair, one of the few Europeans to witness an Indian burial, the handling of the bones was a dangerous enterprise because the performance of such funeral duties caused the living to become "unclean." Such dangerous work was therefore typically reserved for the relations of the deceased who themselves had to undergo a series of purification rituals to be restored to a clean state.[75] In a nutshell, a Creek burial should properly be regarded as a collective mourning ritual that appeased not only the spirit of the deceased but also his or her clan-kin. By according the traders' remains the same degree of respect given to their own kin, the Creeks had effectively treated the dead traders as their own.

Repeatedly throughout the conflict the Creeks defended their military inaction and defense of the English traders on the grounds of neutrality. On March 22, 1760, the *South Carolina Gazette* reported that Scotchaby, the young lieutenant of the Cowetas whom British officials had once feared, had recently spoken with officials at Augusta and stated that "it was the sense of his nation to remain neuter."[76] On April 7 a group of Upper Creek leaders assembled at Mucculassee and declared their displeasure with the Cherokees' practice of parading white scalps through their nation. "Some of the Indians," the newspaper reported, "threatened to knock them on the head, saying that they would not allow the French to receive either scalps or provisions."[77] Later that summer Devall's Landlord even indicated that the Upper and Lower Creeks had recently held a general meeting, during the course of which they decided to "hold fast" to the English and remain decidedly neutral in the war.[78]

That the Creek peoples refused by and large to join the Cherokee war effort testifies to the fact that British imperialism had a differential impact on the "Red peoples" in eastern North America. As many

Creeks themselves realized, the Cherokee revolt was rooted principally in the unwanted effects of their intimacy with the British. The Creeks, in contrast, had managed to thwart British attempts to build a fort in their territory or to enlist them in either the foreigners' southern or northern military campaigns. Thus when the option of war presented itself to the Creeks, the Creeks' relationship to the British remained primarily commercial and continued a two-generation-long series of hard-fought efforts to maintain independence, This was accomplished, in part by adhering to the advice of the ancestors to remain neutral in accordance with the ancient wisdom of the Coweta Resolution.

Though the dynamics of the situation may be obvious from our historical perspective, all contemporaneous evidence indicates that the Creeks were aware of their privileged though precarious historical predicament. Sempeyoffee stated his people's case most succinctly. When questioned about the likelihood of Creek participation in the expected war in September of 1759, Sempeyoffee admitted that the Cherokees had recently come to them bearing grievances against the British including, but not limited to, "their grievances of losing a great number of their best men in Virginia and the daily Incroachments of the white people." Sempeyoffee emphatically declared, however, that their arguments carried little weight with him and that he would remain a friend to the English.[79] Sempeyoffee added that the Cherokees would have attacked long ago had they not feared Creek "resintments," which made the Cherokees "be slow in their measures and so long hesitate about taking full satisfaction for the many Injurys they have received from the English." The Creeks, he added, generally blamed the Cherokees for their misfortunes but he insisted that the error was theirs "in giving unbounded libertys to the whites in regard to lands and forts and all for the sake of a low trade. That their too great intimacy and familiarity with the white people was the origin and cause of the present disturbance and quarrel between them."[80] For this reason, Sempeyoffee concluded, he would not "engage in the behalf of his countrymen the Creeks to take any part in the present quarrel between the Cherokees and English."[81]

That the Creeks were proud of their tradition of neutrality was not lost upon the Cherokees, who regarded the policy as the distinguishing characteristic of the Creek Nation. A decade earlier, when the Cherokees were at war with the Creeks, the Cherokee chief Skiagusta of Keowee explained to South Carolina governor James Glen the reasons that the Creeks could not be brought to heel: "We suppose it will be a hard matter for you to make a peace between the Creeks and us," attributing Creek recalcitrance to their favorable position vis-à-vis the other European powers. "They [the Creeks] have the French and Spaniards to apply to in case you won't supply them," the chief added, implying that the Cherokees, by way of contrast, were not so favorably blessed with allies.[82]

The Lands of Our Ancestors

The behavior of certain factions during the era of the French and Indian War makes it tempting to differentiate between Creeks who were neutral, pro-British, or pro-French. In fact, Creek pronouncements of their desire to hold fast to the British during their darkest hours superficially makes it appear that Creek neutrality itself served Britain's war aims. This simplistic formula, however, should be eschewed in favor of an interpretation recognizing Creek rather than European goals. The Creeks behaved as they did not simply to assure a favorable outcome in the French and Indian War but to achieve the commonly held goal of maintaining their territorial and political sovereignty. While the need to defend land was not new, the era of the French and Indian War marked a turning point; disputes over Creek lands gradually replaced imperial intrigue as the most important element of Creek foreign affairs.

As the British Empire developed into the most territorially acquisitive of the three, the Creeks wisely singled out the British colonies as being the most dangerous to their own interests. Three generations of Creeks had watched as South Carolina's slavery-based plantation system spread south into the Georgia low country and west into the Carolina and Georgia backcountry. Not lost upon the Creeks was the exponential growth of the British colonies, which far exceeded the anemic growth of the Catholic colonies in Florida and Louisiana. Also ominous was the construction of three British forts in Cherokee country, which the Creeks equated with military occupation and slavery, and causing them to forbid the erection of similar posts in their own country. Nor could the Creeks forget the as-of-yet unresolved Bosomworth land dispute through which the Crown repeatedly asserted its right to Indian land.

No doubt many Creeks themselves viewed their relationship to the British colonies with ambivalence; the British traders had served three generations of Creeks yet ironically the British posed the greatest threat to Creek territorial integrity. The territorial acquisitiveness of the British colonies may in fact be uniquely important to the story of the development of Creek nationhood. As anthropologist Morton Fried argues, regionally integrated tribes do not emerge in isolation but are *"ad hoc* responses to ephemeral situations of competition"* and may well be "the product of processes stimulated by the appearance of relatively highly organized societies amidst other societies which are organized more simply."[83] Anthropologist Marshall Sahlins concurs, arguing that external pressures cause the integration of small-scale societies into more regionally complex ones.[84] The Creek Nation, then, likely did not come into being on its own, regardless of how profound its indigenous origins. British territorialism, it appears, served as the most influential external pressure on the Creeks to invoke the innovative concept of the territorial Creek Nation to protect the land that the Creeks called their own.

That the Creeks interpreted the emerging conflict of the French and Indian War as a struggle to protect their territory can be seen in the early stages of the conflict, when most of the fighting remained confined to the north. In December 1754 more than one hundred Creek ambassadors descended upon (French) Mobile to hear the governor of Louisiana's pleas for peace with the Choctaws and seeking assistance in the expected military campaigns. Employing rhetorical flourishes intended to alarm his Creek audience and spur them to action, the governor reminded his listeners of Britain's territorial ambitions: the British "were coming upon them, and . . . were preparing to cutt them off entirely." The ultimate British goal, the governor warned, was to "take possession of their [Creek] lands."[85] Throughout the war years French officials continued to warn the Creeks of Britain's true aims, reminding them repeatedly of the impending slavery that might ensue after a British victory.

Sensitive as they were to British encroachment, the Creeks did not have to look far to find confirmation of their worst fears. Beginning in 1755, settlers from Virginia and the Carolinas began spilling into Creek hunting grounds at Briar Creek, a southern tributary of the Savannah River, and into Creek hunting territory on the Ogechee River. As many on both sides predicted, violence erupted in the first week of September 1756 when seven Tallapoosas stole horses and some other property from two of the Briar Creek settlers. The settlers gave immediate chase to the Tallapoosa party and, after tracking them for fifty miles, a melee ensued that left three of the Tallapoosas dead.[86]

The Ogechee Incident, as it became known, strained the Anglo-Creek relationship at a time when neither side could afford a breach with their ancient friends. Georgia officials immediately dispatched an agent to calm the fears of the Lower Creeks, who accepted the Georgia governor's apologetic rhetoric at face value on the grounds that the Upper Creek affair was not their concern.[87] Upper Creek consternation, however, proved more difficult to assuage, causing the South Carolina government to dispatch Daniel Pepper into Creek country to bury the "little affair" by distributing presents to the headmen and relatives of the deceased. Pepper scored some diplomatic victories while in Creek country, as the gifts persuaded the Lower and Upper Creeks to affirm their longstanding alliance with the British and bury the Ogechee Incident. Pepper erred, however, by lingering in Creek country to drum up support for building an English fort that South Carolina officials wanted to see erected somewhere in Tallapoosa country. Pepper's efforts predictably divided the Creeks, most of whom opposed the fort on principle alone. Pepper, though diligent, seems only to have assisted the Mortar in recruiting disillusioned Creeks and Cherokees to entertain ideas of the emerging French conspiracy against the British plantations.[88]

With the Anglo-Creek alliance temporarily on solid footing, Georgia officials saw fit to bring the Bosomworth Affair, a thorn in the side of both the English and the Creeks that had festered for more than a decade, to a permanent resolution. Important to this climate of reconciliation was the February 1757 arrival of Henry Ellis, appointed to succeed John Reynolds as royal governor of Georgia. Ellis recognized that in the climate of imperial warfare, the Georgia colony could ill afford to give the Creek Indians any cause for grievance. Ellis's strategy, therefore, was to disengage the Creeks from the land dispute and reconcile it internally. "It is of importance that the Indians should be disengaged," Ellis wrote, adding that "the dispute should rest between the King, and his natural born subjects" Thomas and Mary Bosomworth.[89] The disengagement process effectively began in May 1757 when Ellis received a fifteen-hundred-pound consignment of royal presents earmarked for the Creeks. That August, Ellis dispatched Joseph Wright to invite Lower and Upper Creek leaders to meet with him in Savannah. On October 29 more than 150 Creeks from at least twenty-one towns descended upon Savannah for the most well-attended and elaborate reception the colony had ever witnessed.

For four days Ellis entertained the Creek Indians at his private home, where he delivered a speech of reconciliation from King George and reminded his Creek guests that the presents were "a token of his paternal regard." The Creeks, themselves desirous to restore the British alliance to its proper equilibrium, conceded that their friendship had brought great rewards to the Creek peoples. Speaking for the entire delegation, Stumpee (Sempeyoffee) of Coweta made it known that he viewed the gathering as an "opportunity towards confirming and renewing our antient Friendship with our Brothers the English." "Our fathers," Stumpee reminded his countrymen, "were poor, but you [the English] have made us rich." Holding fast to the English, he added, was "the surest means to continue secure in their present happiness."

Sempeyoffee's speeches and the subsequent actions taken by the Creeks in Savannah attest to the Creeks' willingness to put an end to the Bosomworth Affair, even if that meant abandoning the Bosomworths in the process. Referencing the long-disputed lands, Sempeyoffee explained "these we left in the Hands of an Old Woman (meaning Mrs. Bosomworth) to keep for Us." Mary, he argued, had not been innocent in the affair, arguing that she "by pretending to have bought [the lands] and that they belonged to her, occasioned great animosities between us and the white people." Sempeyoffee then rescinded all previous Creek claims to the lands, stating that "we now declare that we did not Sell them to her." "We desire," he concluded, "that your Honour [Ellis] will take them under your care in trust to put an end to future disputes concerning them."[90]

Since the emergence of the Bosomworth Affair and the attempts on the part of Mary and Malatchi to assume unilateral authority as prince and princess to do as they pleased with the lands, most Creeks had maintained that land cessions required the consent of the entire nation. Mary and Malatchi, however, appear only to have obtained the consent of a small faction of the Creek Nation, whom they pressured to sign the various deeds and recognitions that had established the paper trail upon which the Bosomworths staked their claim. The same could be said, of course, of Georgia's efforts to establish a paper trail favorable to the Crown's cause. The infamous Graham Deed, for example, was made without the consultation of the Lower Creeks and featured the signatures of only the Upper Creeks, led by the Gun Merchant of Okchay. Though stated as the official policy of the Creek Nation, the Creeks had never managed to forge a consensus that was truly national in scope and would have legitimized the Creek position on the disputed lands.

Steps toward achieving a national consensus emerged, though, in Savannah later that year. On November 3, twenty-four Creek leaders representing twenty-one towns made put their mark on a treaty that officially placed the disputed lands in Governor Ellis's hands. Most important was article four, in which the Creeks denied that they ever "did sell or alienate the same [lands] to the said Coosaponakeesa alias Mary Bosomworth, or to any private person whomsoever." Though not every Creek town nor every important headman appears to have been present, delegates from most of the important Upper and Lower Creek towns touched pen to the treaty. Sempeyoffee signed for the Cowetas. The Wolf accepted the treaty's terms on behalf of Mucculassee. Lower Creek towns such as Cussita, Oconee, Chehaw, and Sabacola were represented. Oakfuskee, Tallassee, and Tuckebatchee each had at least one individual give consent. The nation, at long last, had spoken on the Bosomworth Affair.[91]

Following the ratification of Ellis's 1757 treaty in Savannah, Georgia officials imposed yet again upon the Creeks to sign away the disputed lands. Fulfilling that mission was agent Joseph Wright, who ventured into Creek country the next spring bearing an official cession that required Creek signatures. On April 22, in the friendly confines of Mucculassee, Wright obtained the signatures of twenty Upper Creek headmen representing all of the important towns. The Wolf of Mucculassee led the signers, followed by venerable persons such as the *ispocoga mico* of Tuckebatchee (Old Bracket), the Okchay captain, and the captain of Tallassee. Less than two weeks later Wright descended upon the Lower Creeks, obtaining in the Apalachicola square the signatures of fifteen headmen. Sempeyoffee signed once again for Coweta, as did the leaders of Apalachicola who were absent from Savannah the previous fall. In addition the Cussita king consented, as did the leaders of the Oconees, Hitchitis, and Uchesees.[92]

Thus the land cession of 1757 enshrined the convergence of two related though not necessarily identical ideas of the Creek Nation. The first, which we might call the aboriginal Creek nation, encompassed the Creek people and the kinship relationships that bound them together into clans and towns. Based upon more concrete and observable relationships of clan and town affiliations, the aboriginal Creek nation existed largely independent of European influence. The second Creek Nation, on the other hand, was a legal entity empowered to cede or protect the land claimed by the nation as a whole. An imaginary construct—the legal configuration of "Creek Nation"—emerged only intermittently, most obviously when Creeks and Europeans met to discuss land transactions. The term's invention, therefore, ought to be regarded as a product of frontier diplomacy, since the legal construct in part owed its origins to the Europeans who helped define it.

Most important among the European powers were the British, who played the greatest role in causing the Creeks to invent and invoke the name Creek Nation. The process did not begin in 1757, of course, because the British had pressured the Creek peoples on numerous occasions in the past—using the threat of a trade embargo or a war, or the lure of British military commissions—to unite in common cause against the Yamasees, the Spanish, and the French, albeit often with less than the anticipated success. More than anything, the defense of their land from the territorially inspired British stimulated among the Creeks a need to define themselves as a territory and thus led to the invention of the Creek Nation as a territorially circumscribed legal entity. It is no accident that the Creeks preserve in their oral tradition the memory of past Anglo-Creek treaties, particularly provisions that touched specifically upon land.[93]

Evidence for the singular importance of British influence on Creek territorialism is brought most directly to light when the Anglo-Creek relationship is compared to the Creeks' relationship to the Catholic powers and to other Indian nations. The French fort, for example, seems not to have caused any existential crisis among the Creeks since they maintained that they had only lent to the French the territory upon which the fort was built.[94] The land was not purchased, and the French did not ask for any further significant cessions. Nor did the Creeks have much to fear by way of the Spanish, whose rumored attempts to purchase land in the Apalachee old fields never materialized. Likewise, the Creeks' indigenous neighbors—such as the Cherokees and the Choctaws, both of which were "enemies" for much of the eighteenth century—did not cause the Creeks to define their northern and western borders with the same precision they had used with the British to the east. The following example stands as evidence for this imprecise reckoning of Creek borders. In July 1759, when Edmund Atkin ventured into Tuckebatchee, he floated the idea of a Choctaw-Creek peace. In an attempt to delineate the territorial claims of the two nations, Atkin asked the headmen in Tuckebatchee which river represented the dividing line between the Creek and Choctaw nations. Apparently the question had never been put to them this way before; the Creeks responded that "there was no such thing" as a border between their two nations.[95]

Though the Creeks appear to have readily acquiesced to the British on the point of the disputed Bosomworth lands, it is clear that they saw the ominous implications of a British victory in the Great War for Empire. Up to that point the Creeks had managed to use their alliances with the weaker Catholic powers to restrain British territorialism. But the French and Indian War seems to have impressed the Creeks as a climactic moment in the region's imperial history. As evidence of Britain's ultimate military victory mounted, the Creeks bristled at the idea of a new imperial order featuring only one rather than three European powers. When Atkin boasted of "our [British] great success in Canada, the taking of Port Mahon, destroying many French men of War & the prospect of the King's stopping up the Rivers of Mississippi & Mobile," he at once realized that, contrary to their hopes that such news would sway the Creeks to fight for Britain, the Creeks looked upon British successes with alarm. Atkin warned his superiors to "beware of saying to them, fall on & help us."[96]

"It is just the reverse," Atkin later wrote. "They receive the least intimation thereof with profound silence & an apparent want of satisfaction, or joy at it, for which reason I have been very backward in telling them that kind of news."[97] Atkin explained that the Creeks behaved this way for their own good reasons: "The meaning of it is this. They have an opinion, that sooner or later they shall lose their freedom & become subject to one of the European Powers. And they would keep that day as far off as possible. Wherefore the greater our Success is, the more they are inclined in their hearts to assist & prop up the tottering French; not so much out of compassion or real love to them, as out of a true regard to themselves & their independency."[98]

Fearing the loss of their independence, Creek leaders were curious to know of the war's outcome in other quarters of the continent and looked on in anticipation of the details of the final peace settlement. Jean-Bernard Bossu, a French traveler who visited Fort Toulouse in the spring of 1759, noted that the Creeks were an inquisitive people when it came to matters of self-interest, adding, "they also ask about the war in Canada and inquire about their father, the King." In the spring of 1761, Togulky, the young kinsman of Malatchi, traveled first to Mobile then to New Orleans to pay the governor a visit, the timing and duration of which suggests that he wished to learn more about the war and France's precarious grip on its continental possessions. Reports from South Carolina indicated that the Creeks had even sent emissaries to Canada just to confirm that reports of the British conquests were true.[99]

As it became increasingly apparent that France and Spain were likely to lose the war, the Creeks lent their ears to a series of rumors that the British troops stood ready to strike out against them. Though unfounded, the prevalence of such rumors indicates that the Creeks feared that Britain's impending conquest did not bode well for them. On May 15, 1762, the *South Carolina Gazette* reported that the Creeks had been persuaded that "a very large body of British troops were collecting in order to take Mobile, with a view, from thence, to attempt the extirpation of the Creeks." The following week that same newspaper stated that Ephraim Alexander, an English trader who lived on the southern boundary of Georgia, was spreading rumors among the Creeks that the English intended to destroy the Indians once they had defeated the European powers.[100]

Sensing that the political conditions under which they had maintained a degree of independence were about to change for the worse, a good number of Creeks made last-ditch efforts to renew their peace agreements with the Catholic powers, as if to spare themselves an expected fate. In the spring of 1762, for instance, the Cowkeeper's "gang," which for years had waged a small-scale war of attrition against the *presidio* at St. Augustine, ceased its attacks after becoming apprised of the impending transfer of power. Months later, representatives of the three Lower Creek point towns, which had a history of animosity toward the Spanish, began making regular visits to Pensacola presumably to trade and cultivate a new-found alliance.[101] Likewise, in February 1763 at the precise time when diplomats were putting the finishing touches to the Treaty of Paris, a Creek delegation, led by an unnamed emperor of Coweta, the emperor's nephew, Scotchaby, and "other principals from the Talapuze nation," confirmed peace with the newly installed Spanish governor Melchior de Feliú.[102] The Creeks never fully abandoned the French, whose military assistance they continued to court even on the very eve of their departure from Fort Toulouse.[103]

When the Creeks did learn of the important articles of the Treaty of Paris, they reacted in a manner befitting a people who equated their own independence with the maintenance of imperial rivalry. On June 4 the *Gazette* reported an ominous-sounding reaction: "They doe not seem to relish the news; that they declare they will not suffer them to depart; and insist, that in case the French and Spaniards should be taken from them, we have no right to possess the lands that were never given to us; and they will oppose all our attempts in that way." The newspaper's account is telling, for it suggests that the Creeks considered the Catholic possessions as their own and implies their reluctance to have the Spanish and French "be taken from them."

This reluctance to see the Catholic posts be taken from them prompted many Creeks to descend upon Mobile, Pensacola, and St. Augustine when British troops began arriving there in the fall of 1763. Although they appear to have committed few if any direct acts of violence against the British, evidence indicates that the Creeks made their presence known by occasionally waving their tomahawks in a bellicose manner and by conferring with the newly installed garrison commanders about the limits of Britain's new possessions. Predictably, Creek efforts to fix these boundaries were little more than an attempt to make sure that British settlement would not spread too far, which had not been much of an issue when Spain and France controlled those lands.[104]

While the Treaty of Paris may have established a Christian, universal, and perpetual peace between the European powers in North America, British officials in the colonies knew that there was much diplomatic work left to be done in Indian country. To bring the Southern Indians officially under British jurisdiction, the newly appointed superintendent of Indian affairs, John Stuart, called for a great congress to be held at Charles Town between representatives of the five Southern Indian nations—Cherokees, Creeks, Choctaws, Chickasaws, and Catawbas—and the governors of Georgia, South Carolina, North Carolina, and Virginia.[105] Once informed that the Creeks refused to travel so far, however, Stuart instead summoned the parties to Augusta, Georgia, which became the site of the great Augusta Congress held the first week of November 1763.

At the Augusta Congress the Creeks earned their reputation as the least friendly Indians in the entire Southeast. Some of their animosity was directed toward other Indians, who they believed had capitulated too easily to the British. In September, for example, reports indicated that relations between the Creeks and Cherokees were deteriorating due in part to the Cherokees' refusal to join them in a proposed war against the British and the murder of two Cherokees by Upper Creeks. Moreover, one of the two Choctaw delegates arriving at Augusta in October reported that two of his people had been murdered while traveling through Creek territory, forcing most of his delegation to return home. Likewise, the Chickasaw delegates complained of the Creeks' "extremely insolent" behavior while making their way through Creek territory.[106]

Much of this animosity became manifest, however, when British officials and Creek representatives met face-to-face at Augusta during the first week of November. One of the striking features of the official journal of those proceedings, published in 1764, was the degree to which the Creeks' behavior differed from that of the other Indians. Particularly noteworthy was the tendency of Cherokee, Chickasaw, Choctaw, and Catawba delegates to offer conciliatory speeches full of praise for the great King George. Also, representatives of each of those Indian nations gave strings of beads to the southern governors and Stuart as a sign of their loyalty and affection. Not so for the Creeks who, in a series of preliminary talks held on November 7 and 8, generally refrained from speaking in such a conciliatory manner and failed to exchange beads or any other tokens of peace.[107]

The fact that the Creeks behaved in a less-than-friendly manner toward the British officials invites the inevitable question: why? Again, the official journal of the Augusta proceedings, combined with other pieces of evidence, suggests that the new political order described in the Treaty of Paris had a disproportionate effect on the Creeks. Their concern, it seems, revolved around a single issue: land.

Many Creeks perceived that the Augusta Congress, as it concerned them, was little more than a thinly veiled attempt to divest them of territory they had claimed since the beginning of the century. In September, just weeks before the proposed congress was scheduled to take place, Lower Creek headmen issued a talk to John Stuart in which they expressed their fear that "the governor of Charles Town intends to buy our lands from us, as far as Ogeechie, and as high up as Broad-River." The Creek headmen also informed him of a similar rumor indicating that "the governor of Savannah intends to buy from us, [our land] as far as the fork of Altamaha." Likewise, the governor of North Carolina was reported to have his eyes set upon Creek land "as far as the Okonies." Stuart and the governors assured the Creeks these were merely rumors spread by "ignorant people, who do not know the great king's intention," but his protests did little to assuage alarm among the Creeks.[108]

The Creeks tacitly understood more about the king's intentions than Stuart or the colonial governors let on. That fall the Crown issued an official royal proclamation by which an arbitrary line was to be drawn separating the British colonial settlements from Indian territories. Though in some ways the proclamation made conciliatory gestures to Indian territorial sovereignty, its text carried ominous words that applied to the Creeks: "We have also annexed . . . to our province of Georgia all the lands lying between the rivers [Altamaha] and St. Mary's." In effect, the proclamation would have stripped thousands of miles of territory from the Creeks had it been implemented according to the text.[109]

At Augusta, Stuart and the other southern governors listened as Telletcher, the chief of Ocmulgee, articulated in no uncertain terms the Creeks' desire to defend their ancient territories. Recognizing the futility of keeping the whites confined to the north side of the Savannah River, Telletcher conceded the disputed lands between the Savannah and Ogechee Rivers but, in an attempt to confine the white people to the territory north of the Ogechee, Telletcher insisted that the lands between the Altamaha and St. John's Rivers should remain in Creek hands. Telletcher also argued that "no settlement should be made by the white people at Pensacola, but within the ebbing and flowing of the tide," a familiar refrain that an earlier generation of Creeks had used in their failed attempt to keep Georgia confined to the coast.[110]

British officials, happy to acquire territory without shedding blood, eagerly accepted Telletcher's proposals and incorporated them into article four of the Treaty of Augusta, signed on November 9, 1763. Therein the Creeks officially ceded the territory between the Ogechee and Savannah Rivers and, in return, were guaranteed the right to posses their remaining lands in Georgia. As a further show of His Brittanick Majesty's beneficence, British officials agreed not to seek punishment for those who had committed hostilities during the recent war, which in effect granted amnesty to the Mortar and his fellow conspirators.[111]

The list of signers of the Augusta treaty, not incidentally, ought not to be regarded as entirely representative of the Creek Nation. Many of the signers had demonstrated on previous occasions a tendency toward accommodation with the British. Leading the list of treaty signers was Elick, whom colonial officials recognized as the chief of Cussita. Elick's identity, however, was much more complicated than of most Creek chiefs. Elick described himself as a mixed-blood, boasting at Augusta that "half of his body is English, and half Indian, and therefore he holds both by the hands." Elick not only claimed English parentage, he owned a Sancta Sevilla, a plantation on the south side of the Altamaha River and close to the southern margins of Georgia Colony. During the era of the French and Indian War, Elick had served British officials loyally as a spy and scout. Elick's unique personal history thus made him a valuable go-between for both the British and Creek nations. Nevertheless, Elick's attempt to speak as the mouth of the entire Upper and Lower Creek Nation was likely an act of self-aggrandizement.[112]

Furthermore, most of the other Creek leaders who participated in the Augusta proceedings came from towns that historically had shown a predilection to support the British. Their political opinions, then, may not have been representative of political opinions of the nation at large. A majority of the treaty signers came from the so-called point towns of Ocmulgee, Chehaw, and Oconee, all of which had sided with the British on many occasions after the 1720s. Telletcher, the chief of Ocmulgee, for example, did not sign the treaty but his speeches directly led to the cession of the disputed territory north of the Ogechee River. Evidence for point town complicity can also be found in the Treaty of Augusta itself, for one of its signers was the *mico* of Chehaw town. Another signer was the Wolf of Mucculassee, who had been a loyal friend of the British throughout the duration of the Great War for Empire. Coweta's lone signer was Sempeyoffee, the Coweta *mico* who courted British support in his ongoing struggle to defray the pro-French tendencies exhibited by some of his own kinsmen.[113]

The era encompassing the French and Indian War, brought to a conclusion by both the Treaty of Paris and the Augusta Congress, should be viewed as a distinct turning point in the history of the Creek Nation. For two generations the Creeks had managed to use the venerable Coweta Resolution as a device for preserving and maintaining a competitive imperial environment. Not only had this strategy of neutrality allowed the Creeks to hold the balance of power among Indian nations in the Southeast but its application and preservation in oral tradition endowed the strategy with the sanctity of tradition. No other Indian nation in the South at that time had developed nor could develop such a policy, making the Coweta Resolution something of a defining Creek cultural trait. The Treaty of Paris, though, brought the wise policy of following the tradition of the Creeks' ancestors to an unceremonious end. "The day of British encirclement," which the Creeks had worked so hard to avoid, had indeed come.

Out with the old, in with the new. Anglo-Creek land disputes gradually came to replace imperial intrigue as the centerpiece of Creek foreign policy. In this decidedly new political climate the Creek Nation found life and became a legal entity that bridged the kinship-based, acephalous political systems of the Creeks and the state-centered politics of the British Empire. Neither wholly Indian nor wholly European, the Creek Nation was the work of many minds and an outgrowth of the Southern frontier environment that assumed a corporeal form whenever and wherever the Creeks met with the British to discuss territorial rights, yet disappeared, phantom-like, when those talks ended. Inextricably tied to the defense of their ancient lands, the invention of the Creek Nation forced the Creek peoples to define themselves more abstractly as a territory rather than as a people united in kinship. Anthropologists regard this evolution an important if not inevitable step from tribalism toward nationhood. But the Creek Nation had a more complicated historical life, as the precise institutional mechanisms for its governance had yet to be worked out. Political authority in Creek country remained diffuse and, as events finally revealed, could be manipulated by outsiders; the emerging nation could be and was divested of the very land that was said to define it. Though this process was already at work at Augusta in the fall of 1763, succeeding generations of Creeks would produce their own "captain" Elicks who made similar awkward compromises that gradually eroded the Creek Nation's territorial foundation.

Epilogue:
The Legacy of the Imperial Era

The ink had scarcely dried on the treaty signed at Augusta when a Chickasaw headman approached British officials to offer a sour note of pessimism: "Nothing done here will be confirmed by the absent [Creek] leaders, in comparison of whom the present chiefs are inconsiderable."[1] The Chickasaw man had good reason to make such a prediction, because in fact many Creek leaders did not attend the Augusta meetings. The Upper Creeks, in particular, were underrepresented, possibly because the Lower Creeks sought to dominate the talks. As the Wolf of Muccalassee explained it several months later, many Upper Creek chiefs were angered because "the lower Creeks would not let us speak a Word."[2] As a consequence, many Upper Creek headmen chose to absent themselves from the gathering. The Gun Merchant of Okchay declined on the grounds that he was unable to find a reliable person to mind his livestock in his absence. Also missing was the Mortar, who believed that the British might punish or kill him for leading the French conspiracy. Moreover, influential men from the friendly towns of Tuckebatchee and Oakfuskee failed to attend, as did several important Cowetas, most conspicuously Scotchaby.[3]

One reason why many "considerable" Creeks may have been hesitant to confirm the peace made with the British at Augusta rests in the Paris Peace Treaty's ominous mandate. Just as Brims and earlier generations of Creek leaders had feared, the day of British encirclement had finally come, requiring the Creeks to adjust, yet again, to new political circumstances. Superficially at least, the Creeks seem to have made the adjustment admirably well. In John Stuart the Creeks found a reliable go-between who faithfully articulated their concerns to British imperial officials, causing the Creeks to look to him as an elder brother.[4] British encirclement, while undesirable on the one hand, presented opportunities as well. The Tallapoosas, recognizing that they might be supplied with British trade goods more efficiently from another venue, lobbied the British to reroute the trading path through Mobile or Pensacola. Moreover, Anglo-Creek diplomacy became more standardized. Not only could the Creeks conduct diplomacy with a single Crown appointee—John Stuart—but both sides appear to have adopted Iroquois diplomatic protocol to bridge the cultural gap between the Creeks and the British.[5]

Still, old habits proved hard to break and later generations of Creeks sought to replicate the conditions of imperial rivalry whenever the opportunity presented itself. This tendency indicates not only that tribal peoples tended to fare better wherever imperial rivalry thrived, but it testifies to the durability of the political instincts forged in the years prior to 1763. The Creeks and Spaniards, for instance, maintained regular if infrequent contact with each other for several years after the transfer of power was completed in 1764. James Adair recorded one notable occurrence in 1767, when a Cuban vessel coasting off the coast of Florida dropped anchor to entertain a party of Creeks that happened to be there. Rumor, as Adair related, hinted that the Spanish sought to purchase the Apalachee old fields. William Bartram, the famous American naturalist who traveled through Creek territory in the 1770s, noted that Spanish fishing ships coasting along the Florida panhandle commonly stopped to trade with eager Creeks waiting on shore. Ambitious Creek individuals also ventured to Havana on occasion, in order to visit the Cuban governor and, if they were lucky, to return home with a cache of Spanish gifts.[6]

The Creeks also found many opportunities to replicate the conditions of imperial rivalry after the American Revolution. As a product of the Treaty of Paris of 1783, which ended the war in the colonies, Florida was returned to Spain in recognition of that nation's support for the American war effort. Once the new Spanish regime was restored to power, the influential Creek leader Alexander McGillavray sought to establish diplomatic and economic ties with St. Augustine to counter the territorial aggressiveness and economic influence of the Americans. Spanish officials, eager to solidify their own claim to Florida territory, readily complied with McGillavray and granted a trade monopoly to a group of British loyalists. That group of loyalists, who founded the firm Panton, Leslie, and Company, traded regularly with the Creeks until the Spanish permanently ceded Florida Territory to the Americans in 1819. Some estimates suggest that a majority of Creek deerskins found their way to Panton, Leslie, and Company's Pensacola store during that time.[7] Brisk trade with Pensacola not only provided the Creeks with another outlet for their skins and produce but it enabled them to acquire the firearms and munitions that allowed them to resist American intrusions until the time of the Red Stick War of 1813–1814.

The Red Stick War was a civil war between assimilationist Creeks who wished to benefit from the new American order and nativists who, inspired by a series of prophets, sought to resist the Americans and adhere to traditional economic and cultural practices.[8] The U.S. Government, which viewed the Red Sticks as a threat to western expansion, quickly sent Andrew Jackson, future president, into Creek country to put down the revolt. Once the rebellious Creeks had capitulated, the treaty of Fort Jackson, signed in 1814, divested the Creeks of much of their Georgia territories and paved the way for later territorial concessions and, ultimately, Removal.

As with earlier conflicts between Anglo-Americans and the Creeks, the U.S. Government believed that the Creeks' intimacy with the Spanish and British traders in Florida had played no small role in the rebellion. Article three of the Treaty of Fort Jackson demanded that the Creeks "abandon all communication, and cease to hold any intercourse with any British or Spanish post, garrison, or town," an obvious attempt to mitigate the Creek habit of obtaining military supplies from Panton, Leslie, and Company traders.[9] Perhaps the most telling legacy of imperial rivalry occurred later that year, when one of the leaders of the rebellion, the prophet Hilis Haya, avoided capture and caught a ship to London, where he pleaded with British officials to furnish the Creeks with trade goods. Hilis Haya's attempt to enlist British assistance may have been a desperate move, but it was no aberration; rather, it was consistent Creek political practice rooted in the Yamasee War a century earlier.[10] We may imagine that Brims, the venerable architect of the Coweta Resolution of 1718, would have made a similar desperate move had he been born a century later.

Another obvious explanation for the Chickasaw man's prediction that the Creeks would not confirm the business of the Augusta Congress of 1763 was that the Creek Nation was underrepresented at the talks.

Many considerable men had exempted themselves in protest, making the treaty that came out of those talks the work of but a fraction of the nation's leaders. Moreover, the treaty left the southern boundaries of the Creek Nation undefined with respect to the new colonies of East and West Florida, which had recently passed to British hands by virtue of the Treaty of Paris.

The confirmation of the Augusta Treaty of 1763 therefore required John Stuart to call for subsequent congresses to finish the business. In 1765 the Upper and Lower Creeks met Stuart at Pensacola to establish the boundary of West Florida. In November of that year a large delegation of Lower Creeks and Seminoles met with Stuart again at Fort Picolata to confirm the boundary of East Florida. The Lower Creek boundary was drawn again in 1768, and finalizing the Upper Creek boundary with West Florida required the Upper Creeks to convene yet again at Pensacola in 1771. In all, confirming the respective boundaries between the Creek Nation and the British colonies required an additional five congresses held in the subsequent decade, proof positive that the Chickasaw man was right to be skeptical of the outcome of the proceedings held at Augusta in 1763.[11]

Consistent with the precedents set during the French and Indian War, the cession of Creek lands in the postwar era catalyzed an the apparent need to centralize and institutionalize the leadership of the Creek Nation so as to avoid spurious actions taken on its behalf. Toward that end, the Upper and Lower Creeks exhibited a tendency for unity, as the many Creek towns appear to have been well represented at various congresses held during the 1760s and 1770s. Though no single national leader appears to have emerged at the time, a handful of men came to dominate Creek politics. Tallechea of the Oconees and Captain Elick spoke consistently in behalf of the Lower Creeks. Rising to prominence at the same time among the Upper Creeks was Emistisiguo and the Mortar (now a peace chief of Little Tallassee), who tended to speak in the behalf of the Coosa and Tallapoosa towns.[12]

Adding to this demand for political innovation was the traffic in rum and the increase in violence between whites and Creeks on the southern frontier. Likewise, the American Revolution nearly divided the nation as the Americans and the British both courted Creek assistance throughout the conflict. Avoiding these troubles required not only national unity but a willingness to exercise power to stay the violence when necessary. Alexander McGillavray, born of a Creek woman and the Scottish trader

Lachlan McGillavray, emerged in the wake of the American Revolution as the Creeks' most influential leader. Known as the Great Beloved Man by the Creeks, educated by whites, and well apprised of the workings of the larger world around him, McGillavray was well positioned to defend Creek land from, as he termed it, the "ambitious and encroaching Americans."[13] Uniquely among his Creek countrymen, McGillavray recognized that the protection of Creek lands demanded Creek unity. Knowing full well the United States's tendency to practice divide and conquer politics, McGillavray saw pan-Indian tribal unity as a solution to the Indians' territorial dilemmas.[14]

Historians often credit McGillavray as having founded the first Creek National Council, which eventually encompassed all of the towns in the Creek Nation. Born and bred in the Upper Creek town of Octiapofa (Little Tallassee), however, McGillavray spoke primarily for the Upper Creek towns since the nation had yet to form a truly national assembly. According to anthropologist John Swanton, the Creeks held only irregular councils in the eighteenth century and remained deeply divided even before Removal. The different sections of the nation, he concluded, tended to counsel apart from one another.[15] Subsequent researchers have found a similar lack of evidence of a Creek National Council. Kathryn Braund, for one, argues that there was no such body, dismissing the National Council as a "proper noun and little more" and McGillavray as but the most influential Upper Creek leader.[16]

Yet the pressure exerted by the new American nation upon the Creeks lends credence to John Swanton's assertion that "in the last quarter of the eighteenth century conditions were ripe for the evolution of a still more closely knit state."[17] Spurring the Creeks along this path was Benjamin Hawkins, appointed by George Washington in 1796 as the U.S. Government's first agent to the Southern Indian nations. As the official U.S. Indian policy at that time was to "civilize" the tribes remaining in the eastern United States, Hawkins's mission was to introduce the Creeks to the arts of cotton cultivation, cloth spinning, animal husbandry, and Christianity, all elements of civilization as understood by the Americans.

As a part of his "civilizing" strategy, Hawkins introduced important political innovations that were to give the Creeks the appearance of national unity and erode their clan- and town-based political system. For example, Hawkins made the Creek National Council more of representative body by creating legislative districts with appointed delegates. Hawkins encouraged the formation of an executive council and later named Tuckebatchee and Coweta the nation's two capitals. A police agency, the "law menders," meted out punishments to persons who broke Creek laws and gave the nation a monopoly of the use of force which once had been exercised by the various clans only.[18]

While the Creek government forged under Hawkins's direction may have assumed the configuration of a nation-state, the transformation was but superficial.[19] Southeastern Indian cultural traditions proved durable and Creek politics were no exception to the rule. In fact, political factionalism within the Creek Nation during the Removal crisis bears a striking resemblance to the schisms that emerged nearly a century earlier under Malatchi. The issue then, as it became in the 1820s, was Coweta's authority to control the cession of Creek lands, which most agreed required the consent of the entire nation. To facilitate Removal, U.S. officials, according to Swanton, "strove to make as much of the primacy of Coweta as possible" by singling out Coweta leader William McIntosh as the nation's mouthpiece. McIntosh, who favored removal, met with resistance from the Upper Creeks when the U.S. officials met to discuss land cessions at Indian Springs in 1825. McIntosh, knowing that "no part of the land can be sold . . . without the consent of the nation," nevertheless signed a secretly prepared treaty extinguishing Creek claims to their ancient lands in Georgia.[20] The Creek National Council wasted no time passing a death sentence on McIntosh and a handful of his followers, which was carried out promptly in the name of the Creek Nation.

Following their eventual Removal to Indian Territory, peace and unity often evaded the Creeks. The U.S. Civil War tore the nation asunder, as did the subsequent allotment of Creek lands preceding the emergence of Oklahoma statehood.[21] Even into the twentieth century Coweta's status as the head town of the Creek Nation remained a subject of dispute. Writing in 1928, Swanton found the Creeks divided on the issue: "Today upper Creeks will generally tell you that Tuckabatchee stands first." The Lower Creeks, he added, "will assign the place of honor to Coweta," indicating that even in Swanton's day the Creek Nation remained something of a work in progress.[22]

In the end, the South's imperial era set important precedents for the internal and external politics of the Creek Nation. During an era fraught with imperial rivalry, the Creeks forged a lasting foreign policy—neutrality—that conditioned Creek leaders of subsequent generations to seek succor wherever they could find it. A political habit of mind that many Creeks shared, the doctrine of neutrality set the Creek Nation apart from its Indian neighbors, who looked to them as an example when it became necessary to defend their own independence. A nation led by the influential head town of Tall Coweta, the terms of the debate over Creek nationhood were set during the imperial era. And, even if a contested idea, the Creek Nation owes its existence in no small part to Brims, Malatchi, and others who first forged the ideology of Creek nationhood. That we speak of the Muskogee (Creek) Nation today is a lasting reminder of the invention of the Creek nation that first occurred during the South's imperial era.

Notes

Introduction

1. *South Carolina Gazette*, May 15, 1762.

2. The Mortar and the Gun Merchant to James Wright, May 8, 1763, in Juricek, *Early American Indian Documents: Georgia Treaties, 1733–1763* (hereafter GT), 352.

3. Provincial Council of Georgia, July 14, 1763, which included the Lower Creek talk of May 15, 1763, Juricek, GT, 356.

4. *South Carolina Gazette*, September 18, 1762.

5. On the triple-nation transfer in the South, see Gold, *Borderland Empires in Transition*. For a discussion on political discontinuity in North America, see Adelman and Aron, "Borderlands to Borders." See also "Forum Responses" by Evan Haefeli, Christopher Ebert Schmidt-Nowara, John R. Wunder, and Pekka Hamalainen, and Stephen Aron and Jeremy Adelman, AHR 104.4 (October 1999): 1221–1239.

6. *South Carolina Gazette*, June 4, 1763.

7. Timothy, *Augusta Congress Journal*, 6,7; *South Carolina Gazette*, June 4, 1763; *South Carolina Gazette*, September 24, 1763; *South Carolina Gazette*, October 22, 1763.

8. *South Carolina Gazette*, November 19, 1763.

9. *South Carolina Gazette*, October 22, 1763.

10. For the treaty provisions, see Timothy, *Augusta Congress Journal*, 38–41.

11. Timothy, *Augusta Congress Journal*, 42.

12. Increasingly, historians are coming to terms with the continental significance of the peace treaty of 1763 as a turning point in Native American history. See Richter, *Facing East*, 191–223.

13. Crane, *Southern Frontier*, 255; Corkran, *Creek Frontier*, x.

14. Braund, *Deerskins and Duffels*, 22; Green, *Politics of Indian Removal*, 22.

15. Axtell, *The European and the Indian*, 5.

16. Some examples: G. C. Anderson, *Kinsmen of Another Kind*; Price, *The Oglala People*; Kugel, *To Be the Main Leaders of Our People*; Richter, *Ordeal of the Longhouse*; Dennis, *Cultivating a Landscape of Peace*; Dowd, *War under Heaven*; and Piker, *"'White and Clean' and Contested."*

17. A majority of scholars argue for the early formation of the "Creek Con-

federacy," while a growing minority insist that Creek unification occurred at a later date. For the "early" interpretation, see Crane, *Southern Frontier*, 185; Swanton, *Early History*; Debo, *Road to Disappearance*; Corkran, *Creek Frontier*, 48–60; Braund, *Deerskins and Duffels*, 6; Durschlag, "First Creek Resistance," 5, 7–8; Rayson, " 'Great Matter to Tell,' " 307; M. T. Smith, *Aboriginal Culture Change*, 129–142; and Harris, *Here the Creeks Sat Down*, 1–30. For contrary opinions see Knight, "Formation of the Creeks," 373–392; Hann, "Seventeenth-Century Forebears," 66–80; and the written exchange between Richard Sattler and John T. Juricek conducted in the pages of *Ethnohistory* 40 (spring 1993): 407–409.

18. Adair, *American Indians*, 277; Bartram, *Travels*, 383–392.

19. See Swanton, *Early History*, 9–31; Swanton, "Social Organization," 31.

20. Crane, "Origin of the Name," 339–342.

21. Gatschet, *Migration Legend*, 1:168.

22. Braund, *Deerskins and Duffels*, 25, 139.

23. Green, *Politics of Indian Removal*, xi, 14.

24. Saunt, "New Order of Things," 1–11; Durschlag, "First Creek Resistance," 5, 7–8.

25. Fenton, *Great Law and Longhouse*, 72–73.

26. On factionalism, see Waselkov, "Historic Creek Responses," 123–131; Galloway, "Choctaw Factionalism." On Creek localism, see Opler, "Creek 'Town' and Problem of Creek Reorganization," 165–180; Opler, "Report on Creek Organization and Government," 30–75; Haas, "Creek Inter-Town Relations"; and Spoehr, "Brief Communication," 134.

27. On the issue of ethnogenesis and "boundary maintenance," see Galloway, *Choctaw Genesis*, 264–337; Barth, *Ethnic Groups and Boundaries*.

28. Hobsbawm and Ranger, *Invention of Tradition*; B. Anderson, *Imagined Communities*.

29. On the importance of land in the evolution of political societies, see Sahlins, *Tribesmen*, 6; Fried, *Evolution of Political Society*, 229; Engels, *Family, Private Property and the State*.

30. Fried, *Notion of Tribe*, chap. 13.

31. Vine Deloria Jr. once wrote that a "tribe means a group of people living pretty much in the same place who know who their relatives are" (*Skull Wars*, 229), thus underscoring the localistic, kinship-rooted concept as expressed by at least one prominent Indian writer. For a discussion of the meaning of "tribe" to Native Americans, see David H. Thomas, *Skull Wars*, 227–321. On the Latin derivation of the word "nation" see Simpson, *Cassell's Dictionary*, 387.

1. Tall Coweta

1. Martin and Mauldin, *Dictionary*, 226.

2. Swanton, "Social Organization," 54.

3. Swanton, "Social Organization," 54.

4. Swanton, "Social Organization," 58.

5. Swanton, "Social Organization," 58.

6. Swanton, "Social Organization," 54–55.

7. Swanton, "Social Organization," 68–69.

8. Swanton, "Social Organization," 307.

9. Young and Fowler, *Cahokia*, 274, 287–309; Pauketat, *Ascent of Chiefs*; Worth, *Timucuan Chiefdoms*, esp. vol. 1; Steoponaitis, "Contrasting Patterns," 193–228; Beck, "Burke Phase."

10. The literature on prehistoric Southeastern chiefdoms is voluminous. For an overview, see Hudson, *Knights of Spain*, 11–30, 215–217; Worth, *Timucuan Chiefdoms*, 1:1–18; DePratter, "Prehistoric and Historic Chiefdoms"; Widmer, "Structure of Southeastern Chiefdoms"; D. Anderson, *Savannah River Chiefdoms*; and Scarry, "Mississippian Societies," chap. 2.

11. For some good examples of the elite Mississippian material culture, see DePratter, "Prehistoric and Historic Chiefdoms," 179–203; Galloway, *Southeastern Ceremonial Complex*; and Pauketat, *Ascent of Chiefs*, 168.

12. Knight, "Symbolism of Mississippian Mounds"; Halley, "Platform Mound Construction."

13. Worth, *Timucuan Chiefdoms*, 1:12.

14. Hudson, *Knights of Spain*, 203–219; Worth, "Account by Rodrigo Rangel," 284–294; Worth, "Account by Luys Hernandez de Biedma," 252; Robertson, "Account by Gentleman from Elvas," 92–94.

15. Hudson, *Southeastern Indians*; Hudson, *Juan Pardo Expeditions*; Hudson, *Knights of Spain*; Hudson and Tesser, *Forgotten Centuries*; Depratter, "Prehistoric and Historic Chiefdoms"; M. T. Smith, *Aboriginal Culture Change*. For some more skeptical views of the "collapse" thesis, see Galloway, *Choctaw Genesis*; Muller, *Mississippian Political Economy*, esp. chap. 4; Kelton, "Southeastern Smallpox Epidemic"; Galloway, "Colonial Period Transformations," 230; Richter, *Facing East*, 33–36.

16. Worth, *Timucuan Chiefdoms*, vol. 1; Arnade, "Cattle Raising in Spanish Florida"; Hann, *Apalachee*; Hoffman, "Convento de San Francisco"; Waselkov, "Seventeenth-Century Trade"; M. T. Smith, *Aboriginal Culture Change*, esp. chap. 3.

17. Crosby, "Virgin Soil Epidemics"; Ramenofsky, *Vectors of Death*, 21; Dobyns, *Their Number Become Thinned*, 343; Worth, *Timucuan Chiefdoms* 2:1–26; M. T. Smith, *Coosa*, 96–117; Kowaleski and Hatch, "Settlement in Upper Oconee Watershed"; Worth, "Prelude to Abandonment," 40–45.

18. Crane, *Southern Frontier*, 6–21; Hahn, "Invention of Creek Nation," 62–70. On the Chiscas, see Worth, *Timucuan Chiefdoms*, 1:120, 122.

19. M. T. Smith, "Aboriginal Population Movements in the Postcontact Southeast," in Ethridge and Hudson, *Transformation of the Southeastern Indians*, 3–20.

20. M. T. Smith, *Coosa*, 50–117; Martin, "Rebalancing the World"; Keyes, "Myth and Social History in Early Southeast."

21. Knight, "Formation of the Creeks."

22. Martin, "Rebalancing the World."

23. Muller, *Mississippian Political Economy*, 40–41, 257–287; Haas, "Creek Inter-Town Relations."

24. Martin, "Rebalancing the World," 94.

25. See Swanton, "Social Organization," 64–71; Piker, "Fani-Micos of Oakfuskee"; Nairne, *Muskhogean Journals*, 40, 62–63.

26. Hudson, *Southeastern Indians*, 234–239; Swanton, "Social Organization," 286–306; Hultkrantz, *Conceptions of the Soul*, 51–114; Lankford, "Red and White"; and Chadhuri and Chadhuri, *Sacred Path*, 28–51.

27. Nairne, *Muskhogean Journals*, 63; Green, *Politics of Indian Removal*, 7–11; Swanton, "Social Organization," 156–166.

28. Swanton, "Social Organization," 157.

29. Hudson, *Southeastern Indians*, 234–239; Swanton, "Social Organization, " 286–306; Haas, "Creek Inter-Town Relations."

30. Hulkrantz, *Conceptions of the Soul*, 51–114; Tooker, "Clans and Moieties."

31. Nairne, *Muskhogean Journals*, 63–64.

32. Saunt, *New Order of Things*, 11–37.

33. Martin, "Rebalancing the World," 94–95.

34. Fairbanks, "Function of Black Drink."

35. Green, *Politics of Indian Removal*, 4–6; Swanton, "Social Organization," 170–174; Nairne, *Muskhogean Journals*, 33, 61. For a discussion of the gendered dimensions of the use of kinship language in diplomacy, see Shoemaker, "Alliance between Men."

36. Nairne, *Muskhogean Journals*, 62–63, 65; Stiggins, *History*, 28.

37. Hudson, *Knights of Spain*, 220–249.

38. Hudson, "Spanish-Coosa Alliance." On "Caxiti," see Fr. Domingo de la Anunciacion and Others to Luna, August 1, 1560, in Priestley, *Luna Papers*, 1:225; Anunciacion to Luna, in Priestley, *Luna Papers*, 1:223, 229–231, 237; Soldiers' Testimony, 1562, *Luna Papers*, 2:287, 291.

39. Migration Legend, Candler, Coleman, and Ready, *Colonial Records of the State of Georgia* (hereafter CRG), 20:381–387; Antonio Matheos to Gov. Juan Marquez Cabrera, May 19, 1686, Ross Papers, folder 88, no. 27.

40. Reasons for placing "Colossa" at the lower Talapoosa are twofold: first, the name of the town "Muccolassee" is suggestive of "Colossa"; and, as will be demonstrated below, the Cowetas appear to have had frequent contact with lower Talapoosa towns such as Tallassee, Atasi, and Tuckebatchee, suggesting a recent connection.

41. Worth, "The Lower Creeks."

42. Testimony of Nicolas Ramirez, December 10, 1688, in Residencia of Governor Juan Marquez Cabrera, Archivo General de las Indias, Escribanías de Camará (hereafter AGI-EC) 156C, Pieza 22–26, f. 108, P. K. Yonge Library, reel 27-M.

43. Worth, "Prelude to Abandonment"; Worth, *Struggle for Georgia Coast*, 18–30; Hann, "Seventeenth-Century Forebears," 66–80; Manuel Cendoya to the King, November 8, 1671, AGI-SD 839, and Antonio Somoza to the King, January 7, 1673, Archivo General de las Indias, Audiencia of Santo Domingo (hereafter AGI-SD) 848, in Stetson Collection, reel 13.

44. Woodward, "Westoe Voyage," 133; Bishop of Cuba Gabrial Diaz Calderon to the Queen, 1675, AGI-SD 151, Worth Collection, reel 3, no. 2.

45. Somoza to Fr. de Madrigal, January 7, 1673, AGI-SD 848, Stetson Collection, reel 13; Calderon to the Queen, 1675, AGI-SD 151, Worth Collection, reel 3, no. 2.

46. Gov. Alonso de Aranguiz y Cotes, Auto, October 23, 1659, AGI-SD 839, and Aranguiz y Cotes to the King, November 11, 1659, AGI-SD 839, in Worth Collection, reel 14, no. 14; Aranguiz y Cotes to the King, September 8, 1662, AGI-SD 225, Ross Papers, folder 53, no. 32; Worth, *Struggle for Georgia Coast*, 15–16.

47. Matheos to Cabrera, January 12, 1686, AGI-SD 839, Ross Papers, folder 88, no. 27, 217–218; Matheos to Cabrera, February 8, 1686, AGI-SD 839, Ross Papers, folder 88, no. 27, 233–234; Testimony of Nicolas Ramirez, December 10, 1688, AGI-EC 156C, P. K. Yonge Library, f. 108, Marquez Residencia.

48. Calderon to the Queen, 1675, AGI-SD 151, Worth Collection, reel 3, no. 2.

49. For a summary of the Stuart Restoration, see Smith, *Emergence of a Nation State*, 364–368. For some of the details of Carolina's exemptions from trade restrictions, see Carolina Charter, 1663, in Saunders, *Colonial Records*, 1:20–33.

50. Fr. Jacinto Barreda peticion, April 30, 1692, AGI-SD 227B, reel 7; Gov. José de

Zúñiga y la Cerda to the King, September 30, 1702, AGI-SD 858, Worth Collection, reel 5, no. 8.

51. Earl of Shaftesbury to Henry Woodward, May 23, 1674, Sainsbury, *Calendar of State Papers, Colonial Series* (hereafter CSP), 7:58.

52. Crane, *Southern Frontier*, 12–21; Barker, "Blood and Treasure," 189–201.

53. Cabrera to the Viceroy of New Spain, May 19, 1686, AGI-SD 839, Worth Collection, reel 6, no. 2, f. 555.

54. Woodward, "Westoe Voyage," 134.

55. Hita Salazar to the King, June 8, 1675, AGI-SD 839, Stetson Collection, reel 14.

56. Hita Salazar to the King, November 10, 1678, AGI-SD 839, Stetson Collection, reel 15.

57. Declaration of the Lords Proprietors, April 10, 1677, CO: 5/286, f. 120. See also Crane, *Southern Frontier*, 15.

58. "Articles of Agreement of the Lords Proprietors Concerning Trade," April 10, 1677, CO: 5/286, 124.

59. Hita Salazar to the King, November 10, 1678, AGI-SD 839, Stetson Collection, reel 15.

60. Hita Salazar to the King, November 10, 1678, in response to a royal cedula of November 5, 1677, AGI-SD 839, Stetson Collection, reel 15.

61. Hita Salazar to Barreda, October 31, 1679, AGI-SD 226, Ross Papers, folder 55, no. 41.

62. Hita Salazar to the King, March 8, 1680, AGI-SD 226, Ross Papers, folder 55, no. 41.

63. See entries for July 14, 1677, April 12, 1680, and June 4 and 24, 1680, in Salley, *Journals of Grand Council*, 82–85; Crane, *Southern Frontier*, 19–20.

64. Fr. Francisco Gutierrez de la Vera to Cabrera, May 19, 1681, AGI-SD 226, Ross Papers, folder 57, no. 58.

65. Marquez to the King, December 8, 1680, AGI-SD 839, Ross Papers, folder 56, no. 46.

66. Marquez to the King, September 20, 1681, AGI-SD 226, Ross Papers, folder 89, no. 65.

67. Marquez to the King, January 25, 1682, AGI-SD 226, Ross Papers, folder 59, no. 65.

68. Marquez to the King, January 25, 1682, AGI-SD 226, Ross Papers, folder 59, no. 65.

69. Marquez to the King, September 20, 1681, AGI-SD 226, Ross Papers, folder 59, no. 65.

70. Marquez to the King, September 20, 1681, AGI-SD 226, Ross Papers, folder 59, no. 65.

71. Marquez to the King, September 20, 1681, AGI-SD 226, Ross Papers, folder 59, no. 65.

72. Marquez to the King, January 25, 1682, AGI-SD 226, Ross Papers, folder 59, no. 65.

73. Marquez to the King, January 25, 1682, AGI-SD 226, Ross Papers, folder 59, no. 65.

74. Fr. Martin Lasso to Marquez, December 8, 1681, AGI-SD 226, Ross Papers, folder 59, no. 65.

75. Lasso to Marquez, December 8, 1681, AGI-SD 226, Ross Papers, folder 59, no. 65.

76. Auto, January 2, 1682, AGI-SD, folder 59, no. 65.

77. Auto, January 2, 1682, AGI-SD, folder 59, no. 65.

78. Auto, January 2, 1682, AGI-SD, folder 59, no. 65.

79. Fr. Rodrigo de la Barrera to Marquez, December 8, 1681, AGI-SD 226, Ross Papers, folder 59, no. 65.

80. Marquez to the Viceroy of New Spain, May 19, 1686, AGI-EC 156, P. K. Yonge Library, reel 18; Marquez to the King, July 22, 1686 AGI-SD 61-6-20, Stetson Collection, reel 18.

81. Crane, *Southern Frontier*, 26–35; Bolton, "Spanish Resistance to Carolina Traders," 115–123; Insh, *Scottish Colonial Schemes*, 186–211.

82. Don Faviano de Angelo to the Governor, May 24, 1690, AGI-SD 227A, Ross Papers, folder 62, no. 6, 13–14.

83. Declaration of Acalaque, November 5, 1685, AGI-SD, 839, Ross Papers, folder 88, no. 27, 148–150; Matheos to Cabrera, September 21, 1685, AGI-SD 839, Ross Papers, folder 88, no. 27, 42, 46, 50; Matheos to Cabrera, October 4, 1685, AGI-SD 839, Ross Papers, folder 88, no. 27, 70; Matheos to Cabrera, January 12, 1686, AGI-SD 839, Ross Papers, folder 88, no. 27, 209.

84. Matheos to Cabrera, February 8, 1686, AGI-SD 839, Ross Papers, folder 88, no. 27, 228.

85. Boyd, "Expedition of Marcos Delgado," 26–27.

86. Declaration of Rodriguez Tijnado, March 16, 1685, AGI-SD 839, Ross Papers, folder 88, no. 27, 4–6; Declaration of Niquisaya, March 22, 1685, AGI-SD 839, Ross Papers, folder 2, no. 27, 8–11; Caleb Westbrook to Gov. Joseph West, February 21, 1685, BPRO-SC, 2:1; Worth, *Struggle for Georgia Coast*, 36–46.

87. Lord Cardross and William Dunlop to Peter Colleton, March 27, 1685, in *Scottish Historical Review* 25 (1928): 104.

88. CO: 5/287, 198–202; Crane, *Southern Frontier*, 30.

89. Woodward to John Godfrey, March 21, 1685, Sainsbury, Fortescue, Headlam, and Newton, CSP, 12:19.

90. See CO: 5/287, 140.

91. Westbrook to West, February 21, 1685, BPRO-SC, 2:1.

92. "Declaration of Nicolas, a Christian of Zapala," December 29, 1685, AGI-SD 839, Ross Papers, folder 88, no. 27, 191; Declaration of Elmo Marmi, January 11, 1686, AGI-SD 839, Worth Collection, reel 6, no. 1.

93. As among the Huron, for example. Thwaites, *Jesuit Relations*, 10:222–223.

94. Malatchi's speech to Alexander Heron, December 7, 1746, in Juricek, GT, 149.

95. Emistisiguo's speech in "Governor Wright's Talks with the Creeks," April 14, 1774, in Juricek, *Early American Indian Documents: Georgia and Florida Treaties, 1763–1776* (hereafter GFT), 140.

96. Matheos to Marquez, October 4, 1685, AGI-SD 839, Ross Papers, folder 88, no. 27, 77–79; Matheos to Marquez, January 12, 1686, AGI-SD, folder 88, no. 27, 220–221; Testimony of Pedro de la Vera, December 10, 1688, Marquez Residencia, AGI-EC, 156C, f. 107, P. K. Yonge Library.

97. Fr. Juan Mercado to Matheos, n.d. (c. November, 1685). Enclosure to Matheos's letter to Marquez, November 27, 1685, AGI-SD 839, Ross Papers, folder 88, no. 27, 124.

98. Nairne, *Muskhogean Journals*, 60–61.

99. Matheos to Marquez, October 4, 1685, AGI-SD 839, Ross Papers, folder 88, no. 27, 66; Matheos to Marquez, January 12, 1685, AGI-SD 839, Ross Papers,

folder 88, no. 27, 209, 211; Matheos to Marquez, May 29, 1686, AGI-SD 839, Worth Collection, reel 6, no. 1, f. 628.

100. Matheos to Marquez, September 21, 1685, AGI-SD, Ross Papers, folder 88, no. 27, 42–43; Declarations of Pentocolo and Acalaque, Infidels, November 5, 1685, AGI-SD 839, Ross Papers, folder 88, no. 27, 144–150.

101. Matheos to Cabrera, February 8, 1686, AGI-SD 839, Ross Papers, folder 88, no. 27, 228–234.

102. Matheos to Marquez, May 21, 1686, AGI-SD 839, Worth Collection, reel 6, no. 1, f. 628.

103. Matheos to Marquez, August 21, 1686, AGI-MEX 616, Worth Collection, reel 6, no. 48, 1–4.

104. Matheos to Marquez, January 12, 1686, AGI-SD 839, Ross Papers, folder 88, no. 27, 225.

2. Enemigos

1. Don Diego de Quiroga y Losada to the King, April 1, 1688, AGI-SD 227A, Stetson Collection, reel 19.

2. Crane, *Southern Frontier*, 171–207; Braund, *Deerskins and Duffels*, 32–33; Ford, *Triangular Struggle*, chap. 3.

3. Bartram, *Travels*, 68.

4. Adair, *American Indians*, 39.

5. Quiroga y Losada to the King, September 29, 1689, AGI-SD 227B, Worth Collection, reel 6, no. 34; Enrique Primo de Ribera's orders to build a Fort at Apachicola, October 6, 1689, AGI-SD 234, Worth Collection, reel 6, no. 34, ff. 749–750.

6. De Ribera to Quiroga y Losada, December 30, 1689, AGI-SD 234, Worth Collection, reel 6, no. 34, f. 751.

7. John Stewart to William Dunlop, April 27, 1690, *South Carolina Genealogical Society Magazine* 32.1 (January 1931): 30.

8. For a summary of Angelo's activities, see de Angelo to Quiroga y Losada, April 14 and May 24, 1690, AGI-SD 227A, Ross Papers, folder 62, no. 6, 10–14.

9. Auto, September 18, 1691, AGI-SD 228, Stetson Collection, reel 22.

10. Crane, *Southern Frontier*, 36; Boyd, "Further Considerations," 459; Mason, "Ocmulgee Old Fields," 249; Hann, "Seventeenth-Century Forebears," 77; Worth, "The Lower Creeks," 278–279; Barreda peticion, April 30, 1692, AGI-SD 227B, reel 7; Gov. Laureano de Torres y Ayala to the King, March 11, 1695, AGI-SD 839, Stetson Collection, reel 24.

11. Barreda to Quiroga y Losada, April 30, 1692, AGI-SD 227B, reel 7; Fr. Francisco Gutierrez de Vera to Cabrera, May 19, 1681, AGI-SD 226, Ross Papers, folder 57, no. 58; Auto, Domingo Leturiondo, November 4, 1685, Ross Papers, folder 88, no. 27. Foster, "Cofradia and Compadrazgo."

12. Anonymous, "Indian Village Map" c. 1715; John Barnwell–William Hammerton map of Southeastern North America, c. 1721, in Cumming, *Southeast in Early Maps*, plate 48c; Herman Moll map of Carolina, c. 1729, Crown Collection, University of Georgia Libraries Hargrett Rare Book Room.

13. *Journal of South Carolina Commons House of Assembly* (hereafter *JCHA-SC*) entry for January 13, 1693, and January 14, 1693, in Salley, *JCHA-SC*, 11–12.

14. Barreda to Quiroga y Losada, April 30, 1692, AGI-SD 227B, reel 7.

15. Perdue, *Slavery and Cherokee Society*, 3–18; Richter, "War and Culture," 528–559.

16. On the early attacks, see Barreda peticion, April 30, 1692, AGI-SD 227B, reel 7, f. 895; Torres y Ayala to the King, April 10, 1692, AGI-SD 228, Stetson Collection, reel 22; Testimony of the Junta, November 30, 1694, enclosed in Torres y Ayala to the King, March 11, 1695, AGI-SD 839, Ross Papers, folder 8, no. 39, 13.

17. Testimony before the Junta, November 3, 1694, AGI-SD 839, folder 89, no. 39, 15.

18. Testimony before the Junta, November 3, 1694, AGI-SD 839, folder 89, no. 39, 13, 15, 19.

19. Testimony before the Junta, November 3, 1694, AGI-SD 839, folder 89, no. 39, 14.

20. Steinen, "Ambushes, Raids, and Palisades."

21. Steinen, "Ambushes, Raids, and Palisades," 139; Torres y Ayala to the King, March 11, 1695, AGI-SD 839, Ross Papers, folder 89, no. 39, 2.

22. West to Torres y Ayala, January 25, 1695, AGI-SD 839, Ross Papers, folder 89, no. 39, 20; Torres y Ayala to West, March 3, 1695, AGI-SD 839, Ross Papers, folder 89, no. 39, 22–25; Lords Proprietors of South Carolina to John Archdale, June 28, 1695, CO: 5/289, 28; Archdale to Lords Proprietors of South Carolina, n.d. (c. 1696), Archdale Papers, doc. 11, reel 0821A; Torres y Ayala to Archdale, January 24, 1696, Archdale Papers, doc. 13; Archdale to Torres y Ayala, April 4, 1696, Archdale Papers, doc. 40; Crane, *Southern Frontier*, 38.

23. Archdale to Torres y Ayala, n.d., in "Archdale's Description of Carolina," Salley, *Narratives of Early Carolina*, 301.

24. Barreda's peticion, April 30, 1692; Declaration of Francisco, an Apalachee cacique, March 6, 1691, AGI-SD 227B, reel 7, f. 908.

25. Joaquin de Florencia, "Orders to Promote Good Government," December 26, 1694, in Hann, "Visitations and Revolts," 191; Torres y Ayala to the Viceroy of New Spain, July 20, 1695, AGI-MEX 61-6-21, Stetson Collection, reel 24. On the marriage alliance between the Cowetas and the chief of San Luis de Talimali, see Mercado to Matheos, n.d. (c. November 1685), AGI-SD 839, folder 88, no. 27.

26. Auto, Torres y Ayala, Order for Abandonment of the Apalachicola Fort, September 18, 1691, AGI-SD 228, Stetson Collection, reel 22; Torres y Ayala to the Viceroy, July 20, 1695, AGI-SD 61-6-21, 43, Stetson Collection, reel 24; Entry for July 9, 1712, W. McDowell, *Journal of the Commissioners of the Indian Trade* (hereafter JCIT), 32.

27. Testimony before the Junta, November 3, 1694, AGI-SD 839, Ross Papers, folder 89, no. 39, 15.

28. Manuel Solana to Zúñiga, October 22, 1702, AGI-SD 358, in Boyd, "Further Considerations," 468–469.

29. Mercado to Matheos, n.d. (c. November 1685), AGI-SD 839, folder 88, no. 27.

30. Barcia, *History*, 362.

31. Boyd, *Here They Once Stood*, 20; Don Patricio, Cacique of Ivitachuco, and Don Andres, Cacique of San Luis to the King, February 12, 1699, in Boyd, *Here They Once Stood*, 24; Hann, *Apalachee*, 229–231.

32. "Order from Gov. Don Joseph de Zúñiga," November 5, 1700, in Boyd, *Here They Once Stood*, 31.

33. Auto, February 22, 1701, in Boyd, *Here They Once Stood*, 34.

34. Peckham, *Colonial Wars*, 59.

35. Giraud, *History of French Louisiana* vol. 1; Higginbotham, *Old Mobile*, 15–86.

36. Crane, *Southern Frontier*, 47–70.

37. Auto, August 5, 1701, AGI-SD 858, f. 473, Worth Collection, reel 5, no. 7.

38. Solana to Zúñiga, October 2, 1702, and Francisco Romo de Urisa to Zúñiga, October 23, 1702, AGI-SD 858, both in Boyd, "Further Considerations," 468–472; Worth, *Timucuan Chiefdoms*, 2:144.

39. Boyd, "Further Considerations," 468–472.

40. Romo de Urisa to Zúñiga, October 22, 1702, in Boyd, "Further Considerations," 471–472.

41. Zúñiga to the King, September 30, 1702, AGI-SD 858, Worth Collection, reel 5, no. 8.

42. Entries for August 20 and 26, 1702, Salley, JCHA-SC, 64.

43. Romo de Urisa to the Governor, October 22, 1702, in Boyd, "Further Considerations," 470–472.

44. Solana to Zúñiga, October 22, 1702, in Boyd, "Further Considerations," 470–472.

45. Solana to Zúñiga, October 22, 1702, in Boyd, "Further Considerations," 470–472.

46. Don Patricio de Hinachuba to the Governor, August 30, 1702, in Boyd, *Here They Once Stood*, 38.

47. Solano to Zúñiga, October 22, 1702, in Boyd, "Further Considerations," 469. For the battle's location, see both the "Anonymous Map of Indian Towns in Carolina, c. 1715" in the Crown Collection, University of Georgia, and the Barnwell-Hammerton map, c. 1721, in Cumming, *Southeast in Early Maps*, plate 48c.

48. Entry for September 6, 1703, Salley, JCHA-SC, 103.

49. James Moore to Governor Johnson, April 16, 1704 in Hann, *Apalachee*, 387–389.

50. Moore to Johnson, April 16, 1704, in Hann, *Apalachee*, 387–389.

51. On the raid itself, see Hann, *Apalachee*, 387–389. On the religious affiliation of the remaining Spanish adherents, see LeHarpe, *French in Louisiana*, 44.

52. Worth, *Timucuan Chiefdoms*, 2:145–146; Solana to Zúñiga, June 29, 1704, Royal Officials to the Viceroy, August 18, 1704, and Jose Guzman to the Viceroy, August 22, 1704, all found in Boyd, *Here They Once Stood*, 59–62; Andres Garcia to a Superior, September 3, 1704, AGI-SD 858, Worth Collection, reel 5, no. 7; Viceroy of New Spain to the King, AGI-MEX 61–2–22, 1–24, Spellman Collection, reel 144J; Informe of the Governor, October 6, 1704, AGI-SD 858; Garcia to Zúñiga, June 20, 1705, AGI-SD 858, f. 434, Worth Collection, reel 5, no. 7; Informe of Governor Zúñiga, January 30, 1706, f. 285, Worth Collection, reel 5, no. 8.

53. Crane, *Southern Frontier*, 83; "A Humble Submission of Several Kings, Princes, Generals, etc., to the Crown of England, 1705," in Hayes, *Indian Treaties*, 1–3.

54. Hinderaker, " 'Four Indian Kings.' "

55. On Brims's identity, see Joseph Ramos Escudero to the Conde de Montijo, October 15, 1734, AGI-SD 2591, Worth Collection, reel 3, no. 24.

56. Steinen, "Ambushes, Raids, and Palisades."

57. See Hayes, *Indian Treaties*, 1.

58. Entries for November 25 and December 11, 1706, Salley, JCHA-SC, 9–10 and 21–24, respectively.

59. King to the Viceroy, February 10, 1708, Archivo General de la Nacion Mexico: Historia-Volumen 298, f. 64–65, Spellman Collection, reel 144G.

60. Higginbotham, *Old Mobile*, 310–311.

61. Viceroy of New Spain to the King, February 8, 1714, AGI-MEX 61–1-34, Ross Papers, folder 110, no. 1.

62. Entry for October 27, 1707, Salley, *JCHA-SC*, 10–11.

63. Entry for November 7, 1707, Salley, *JCHA-SC*, 33.

64. Nairne, *Muskhogean Journals*, published in 1988.

65. Nairne to the Lords Proprietors, July 10, 1708, BPRO-SC, 5:194.

66. Nairne, *Muskhogean Journals*, 32–33.

67. Nairne, *Muskhogean Journals*, 34–36.

68. Nairne, *Muskhogean Journals*, 36.

69. Jean-Baptiste le Mayne de Bienville to Louis Phélypaux Ponchartrain August 20, 1709, in Rowland and Sanders, *MPA*, 3:136.

70. Entry for June 22, 1711, *JCHA-SC*, South Carolina Department of Archives and History.

71. Entry for June 22, 1711, *JCHA-SC*, South Carolina Department of Archives and History.

72. Entry for June 22, 1711, *JCHA-SC*, South Carolina Department of Archives and History.

73. Sahlins, *Tribesmen*, 86–90.

74. Crane, *Southern Frontier*, 96.

75. *JCHA-SC* entry for August 6, 1712, in Joseph Barnwell, "Second Tuscarora Expedition," 43.

76. Map insert in Joseph Barnwell, "Second Tuscarora Expedition." For a retrospective account of the second Tuscarora expedition, see King Hagler to Creek Headmen, n.d. (c. 1751), Clinton Papers, 755. Special thanks to Robert Cox for bringing this document to my attention.

77. Barnwell, "Second Tuscarora Expedition," 39.

78. Muller, *Mississippian Political Economy*, chap. 6; Worth, *Timucuan Chiefdoms*, 1:9–11.

79. Nairne, *Muskhogean Journals*, 34; James Axtell, *Natives and Newcomers*, 104–120.

80. Mason, "Ocmulgee Old Fields," 140–180; Waselkov, "Macon Trading House," 190–196; Braley, *Tarver and Little Tarver*, 204–205, 310–322.

81. On Indian "dependency" in the modern world capitalist system, see R. White, *Roots of Dependency*, xiv–xix; Dos Santos, "Structure of Dependence"; Dunaway, "Incorporation as Interactive Process"; Merrell, *Indians' New World*, 49–91.

82. Braund, *Deerskins and Duffels*, 28–39.

83. Entry for June 13, 1711, *JCHA-SC*, South Carolina Department of Archives and History.

84. *JCHA-SC* entry for August 6, 1712, in Joseph Barnwell, "Second Tuscarora Expedition," 43.

85. W. McDowell, *JCIT*, May 4, 1714, 53.

86. W. McDowell, *JCIT*, June 12, 1712, 26.

87. Crane, *Southern Frontier*, 120.

88. Corocoles y Martinez to the King, July 5, 1715, and December 23, 1715, AGI-SD 843, Stetson Collection, reel 35.

89. Corocoles y Martinez to the King, July 5, 1715, and December 23, 1715, AGI-SD 843, Stetson Collection, reel 35.

90. Declarations of Juan Gabriel de Vargas, Joseph Fernandez, and Joseph de

Rojas, January 9–10, 1710, enclosed in Corocoles y Martinez to the King, January 22, 1710, AGI-SD 841, Stetson Collection, reel 34.

91. Spanish soldiers referred to Musgrove as "Chanlacta Maestechanles," which resembles the name Barcia used to describe Musgrove in his 1722 *Ensayo Chronologico.* Declaration of de Rojas, January 9, 1710, AGI-SD 841, Stetson Collection, reel 34.

92. Testimony of de Vargas, January 9, 1710, AGI-SD 841, Stetson Collection, reel 34.

93. Ponchartrain to Bienville, July 9, 1709, Rowland and Sanders, MPA-FD, 3:127.

94. Braund, *Deerskins and Duffels,* 34.

3. A New World Order

1. Corocoles y Martinez to the King, July 5, 1715, AGI-SD 834, f. 4, Stetson Collection, reel 35.

2. W. McDowell, *JCIT,* April 12, 1715, 65; Corocoles y Martinez to the King, July 5, 1715, AGI-SD 843.

3. Corocoles y Martinez to the King, July 5, 1715, AGI-SD 843, f. 5; George Rodd to an employer in London, May 8, 1715, Sainsbury, Fortescue, Headlam, and Newton, CSP, 28:167.

4. Crane, *Southern Frontier,* 162–186; Corkran, *Creek Frontier,* chap. 2; Braund, *Deerskins and Duffels,* 36; Durschlag, "First Creek Resistance," 337–420; Rayson, " 'Great Matter to Tell,' " 248–303; Oatis, "Colonial Complex"; Haan, "Trade Do's Not Flourish"; Ramsey, " 'Something Cloudy' "; Gallay, *Indian Slave Trade,* 315–344.

5. Crane, *Southern Frontier,* 255; John Hann, "St. Augustine's Fallout."

6. Crane, *Southern Frontier,* 187–280; Corkran, *Creek Frontier,* chap. 3; J. McDowell, "Royalizing South Carolina."

7. See Crane, *Southern Frontier,* 255; Corkran, *Creek Frontier,* x.

8. Braund, *Deerskins and Duffels,* 22.

9. Two shrewd minds worth noting: Baron Karl von Klausewitz and Mao Tse-Tung. See *The Macmillan Dictionary of Quotations* (New York: Macmillan, 1989), 596, 589.

10. Crane, *Southern Frontier,* 168–169, 172; and Nathaniel Osborne to the Secretary, May 28, 1715; William Dennis to the Secretary, May 28, 1715; and John Urmston to the Secretary, June 12, 1715, in Society for the Propagation of the Gospel in Foreign Parts, Letterbook Series A (hereafter SPG), 10:99–100, 102, and 82, respectively; William Andrews to the Secretary, April 13, 1717, SPG 13:312. See also Board of Trade to Secretary of State Stanhope, July 19, 1715; William Rhett to the King, August 15, 1715; and Samuel Eveleigh to the Lords Proprietors, October 7, 1715, in BPRO-SC, 6:99, 116, and 118, respectively.

11. Francis Le Jau to the Secretary, May 10, 1715, in Klingberg, *Carolina Chronicle of Le Jau,* 152.

12. Pennington, "South Carolina Indian War," 267.

13. Patrick Mackey to James Oglethorpe, March 29, 1735, Juricek, GT, 50.

14. Thomas Hasell to the Secretary, May 26, 1715, and December 1, 1715, SPG 10:96–97; Eveleigh to Messrs. Boone and Berresford, July, 19, 1715, Sainsbury, Fortescue, Headlam, and Newton, CSP, 28:299; Le Jau to the Secretary, May 21, 1715, August 23, 1715, and March 1716, in Klingberg, *Carolina Chronicle,* 158, 164,

174–175, respectively; "Certificat by Robert Daniel," August 13, 1716, Sainsbury, Fortescue, Headlam, and Newton, CSP, 24:225.

15. Gideon Johnson to the Secretary, December 19, 1715, SPG 11:101.

16. Entry for May 24, 1717, Green, JCHA-SC, vol. 12.

17. Corocoles y Martinez to the King, July 5, 1715, AGI-SD 843, Stetson Collection, reel 35.

18. Salinas Varona to the Governor of Florida, July 24, 1717, in Boyd, "Second and Third Expeditions," 126–127.

19. Varona to Governor of Florida, July 24, 1717, in Boyd, Second and Third Expeditions," 126–127..

20. Varona to Governor of Florida, July 24, 1717, in Boyd, "Second and Third Expeditions," 126–127.

21. Varona to Governor of Florida, July 24, 1717, in Boyd, "Second and Third Expeditions," 126–127.

22. Bienville to Ponchartrain, June 15, 1715; Bienville to Ponchartrain, September 1, 1715, in Rowland and Sanders, MPA, 3:181, 187.

23. Bienville to Ponchartrain, September 1, 1715, in Rowland and Sanders, MPA, 3:187; Penicaut, Fleur de Lys and Calumet, 205.

24. Corocoles y Martinez to Gov. Charles Craven, September 26, 1715, AGI-SD 853, Worth Collection, reel 15, no. 17.

25. D. Bushnell, "Account of Lamhatty"; Corocoles y Martinez to the King, January 22, 1710, including the enclosed testimony of de Vargas and de Rojas, AGI-SD 841, Stetson Collection, reel 34.

26. Crane, Southern Frontier, 182–183; Thomas Broughton to the Lords Proprietors; and Broughton to the Board of Trade, April 28, 1716, BPRO-SC, 6:155–159 and 185.

27. Cheves, letter of George Chicken, "A Letter from Carolina and a Journal of the March of the Carolinians into the Cherokee Mountains, in the Yemassee Indian War, 1715–16," in Letterbook, 330–331, 339.

28. Colonial Office, Journal of Grand Council of South Carolina, 1671–1680 (hereafter SC-CJ), entry for January 25–26, 1727, CO: 5/387, 237–247; "Chicken Journal 1715–1716," 345–350.

29. "Chicken Journal, 1715–16," 346–47.

30. Broughton to the Board of Trade, April 28, 716, BPRO-SC, 6:185.

31. Boyd, "Pena's Expedition," 5.

32. Boyd, "Pena's Expedition," 20.

33. Crane, "Origin of the Name," 339–40. For an early reference to the "Creek" Indians, see entry for December 11, 1706, Salley, JCHA-SC, 21.

34. Charlesworth Glover's 1725 Census, in Salley, Creek Indian Tribes, n.p.

35. Salley, Creek Indian Tribes," 26.

36. Salley, Creek Indian Tribes," 23–24.

37. Salley, Creek Indian Tribes," 26.

38. For some varying perspectives on Southeastern Indian women, see Braund, "Guardians of Tradition," 244; Perdue, Cherokee Women, 65–85.

39. Nairne, Muskhogean Journals, 48.

40. Richard Beresford to the Board of Trade, April 27, 1717, BPRO-SC, 7:18.

41. See W. McDowell, JCIT, March 22, 1717, 169; Joseph Boone to the Board of Trade, April 26, 1717, and Beresford to the Board of Trade, both BPRO-SC, 7:15–21.

42. Entry for May 29, 1717, Green, JCHA-SC, vol. 12.

43. Entry for May 24, 1717, Green, JCHA-SC, vol. 12.

44. Boone to the Board of Trade, April 26, 1717; Beresford to the Board of Trade, April 27, 1717; and Lords Proprietors to the Board of Trade, June 4, 1717, all in BPRO-SC, 7:15, 18, 53, respectively; W. McDowell, JCIT, May 24, 1717, 183; Law to Reclaim Slaves and Horses from Western Indians, December 11, 1717, in Vaughn and Rosen, *Early American Indian Documents*, 204.

45. Varona to Gov. Juan de Ayala Escobar, September 9, 1717, in Boyd, "Second and Third Expeditions," 129; The King to Viceroy Valero, March 13, 1719, Archivo General de la Nacion de Mexico: Historia-Volumen 298, f. 77, Spellman Collection, reel 144G; Barcia, *History*, 360; Diary of Alonso Marques del Toro, Interview with Tickhonabe, March 15, 1738, AGI-SD 2593, Worth Collection, reel 4, no. 1.

46. Auto, Juan Ayala Escobar, April 2, 1717, enclosed in Escobar to the King, April 18, 1717, AGI-SD 843, Worth Collection, reel 4, no. 24, 28–31.

47. Escobar meeting with the Uchise Chiefs, April 4, 1717, AGI-SD 843, Worth Collection, reel 4, no. 24, 43.

48. Escobar and Uchise Chiefs, April 4, 1717, AGI-SD 843, Worth Collection, reel 4, no. 24, 43.

49. Escobar and Uchise Chiefs, April 4, 1717, AGI-SD 843, Worth Collection, reel 4, no. 24, 46.

50. Escobar and Uchise Chiefs, April 4, 1717, AGI-SD 843, Worth Collection, reel 4, no. 24, 48.

51. Escobar and Uchise Chiefs, April 4, 1717, AGI-SD 843, Worth Collection, reel 4, no. 24, 48.

52. Escobar and Uchise Chiefs, April 4, 1717, AGI-SD 843, Worth Collection, reel 4, no. 24, 48.

53. Escobar and Uchise Chiefs, April 4, 1717, AGI-SD 843, Worth Collection, reel 4, no. 24, 56.

54. Escobar and Uchise Chiefs, April 4, 1717, AGI-SD 843, Worth Collection, reel 4, no. 24, 56.

55. Tepaske, *Governorship of Spanish Florida*, chap. 3; A. Bushnell, *Situado y Sabana*; Worth, *Timucuan Chiefdoms*, 1:130–131.

56. Escobar with Uchise Chiefs, April 4, 1717, AGI-SD 843, Worth Collection, reel 4, no. 24, 43.

57. Escobar with Uchise Chiefs, April 4, 1717, AGI-SD 843, Worth Collection, reel 4, no. 24, 59.

58. Escobar with Uchise Chiefs, April 4, 1717, AGI-SD 843, Worth Collection, reel 4, no. 24, 60.

59. Escobar with Uchise Chiefs, April 4, 1717, AGI-SD 843, Worth Collection, reel 4, no. 24, 64.

60. Escobar to the King, April 18, 1717, AGI-SD 843, Worth Collection, reel 4, no. 24, 28–31.

61. Bienville to Ponchartrain, January 2, 1716, Rowland and Sanders, MPA, 3:192–193; Marc-Antoine Hubert to the Council, October 26, 1717, Rowland and Sanders, MPA, 2:250; Daniel Thomas, *Fort Toulouse*, 6–10.

62. Boone to the Board of Trade, June 8, 1717, BPRO-SC, 7:49; W. McDowell, JCIT, June 28, 1717, 192.

63. Entry for May 31, 1717, Green, JCHA-SC, vol. 12.

64. Mary Bosomworth, "Memorial, August 10, 1747," in Juricek, GT, 141.

65. In May, Carolina officials, no doubt in consultation with Musgrove, twice

suggested Pon Pon as the ideal place to negotiate peace. Entry for May 25 and May 31, 1717, Green, *JCHA-SC*, vol. 12.

66. W. McDowell, *JCIT*, June 17, 1717, 188–191.

67. Hudson, *Knights of Spain*, 175–184; Worth, *Struggle for Georgia Coast*, 73, 106, 111, 113.

68. Entry for November 15, 1717, Green, *JCHA-SC*, vol. 11.

69. Boyd, "Second and Third Expeditions," 115–116.

70. Boyd, "Second and Third Expeditions," 119.

71. Boyd, "Second and Third Expeditions," 120.

72. Crane, *Southern Frontier*, 258.

73. Discussed retrospectively in Edmund Atkin's "Talk in the Muculassee Square," September 15, 1759, in Lyttleton Papers, reel 3.

74. Boyd, "Second and Third Expeditions," 121.

75. Boyd, "Second and Third Expeditions," 121.

76. Boyd, "Second and Third Expeditions," 121.

77. Entries for November 6 and 7, 1717, Green, *JCHA-SC*, vol. 11; W. McDowell, *JCIT*, November 9, 1717, 225.

78. The original treaty is not extant. For a recounting of some of the articles, see Thomas Bosomworth's Journal entry for August 4, 1752, in W. McDowell, *Colonial Records of South Carolina: Documents Relating to Indian Affairs, 1750–1754* (hereafter DRIA [1750–54]), 274.

79. Malatchi's speech to Heron, December 7, 1747, Juricek, *GT*, 148; Speech of the Oakfuskee King, June 6, 1767, Juricek, *GFT*, 35.

80. Wood, *Black Majority*, 98–166.

81. Crane, *Southern Frontier*, 47–70; "Law to Appropriate Yamasee Lands," June 13, 1716, in Vaughn and Rosen, *Early American Indian Documents*, 183.

82. Verner Crane rightly recognized the November treaty as an "entering wedge" to peace, but he was unaware of Creek overtures to the Spanish taking place at the same time. Crane, *Southern Frontier*, 259.

83. Declaration of an Infidel Indian on the English in Caveta, December 18, 1717, AGI-SD 843, Stetson Collection, reel 37.

84. Escobar to the King, December 22, 1717, AGI-SD 843, Stetson Collection, reel 37.

85. Barcia, *History*, 360.

86. Barcia, *History*, 360.

87. Barcia, *History*, 361.

88. Barcia, *History*, 361.

89. Barcia, *History*, 363.

90. Barcia, *History*, 364.

91. Barcia, *History*, 365.

92. Barcia, *History*, 365.

93. De Ribera to Escobar, April 28, 1718, AGI-SD 843, Stetson Collection, reel 37.

94. De Ribera to Escobar, April 28, 1718, AGI-SD 843, Stetson Collection, reel 37.

95. De Ribera to Escobar, April 28, 1718, AGI-SD 843, Stetson Collection, reel 37.

96. On the Iroquois Neutrality Policy, see Richter, *Ordeal of the Longhouse*, 190–235; Fenton, *Great Law and Longhouse*, 296–348; Eid, "Ojibwa-Iroquois War"; Wallace, "Origins of Neutrality."

97. Barcia, *History*, 364; Declaration of the Indian Francisco Luis, January 13, 1745 in Gov. Manuel de Montiano to the Director of the Havana Company, February 14, 1745, AGI-SD 863, Worth Collection, reel 14, no. 6.

98. De Ribera to Escobar, April 18, 1718, AGI-SD 843, Stetson Collection, reel 37.

99. See especially Malatchi's speech to Heron, December 7, 1747, in Juricek, *GT*, 148; William Stephens's Report on Malatchi's Talk with Oglethorpe, May 2, 1740, in Juricek, *GT*, 101; Devall Landlord's speech in *South Carolina Gazette*, July 19, 1760.

100. Quoted in Crane, *Southern Frontier*, 261.

4. The Challenge of Triple-Nation Diplomacy

1. De Ribera to Escobar, April 28, 1718, AGI-SD 843, Stetson Collection, reel 37.

2. De Ribera to Escobar, April 28, 1718, AGI-SD 843, Stetson Collection, reel 37.

3. De Ribera to Escobar, April 28, 1718, AGI-SD 843, Stetson Collection, reel 37.

4. De Ribera to Escobar, April 28, 1718, and Antonio de Benavides to the King, September 28, 1718, both in AGI-SD 843, Stetson Collection, reel 37.

5. De Ribera to Escobar, April 27, 1718, AGI-SD 843, Stetson Collection, reel 37.

6. Corkran, *Creek Frontier*, 61.

7. SC-CJ entry for May 26, 1722, CO: 5/425, 301–304.

8. W. McDowell, *JCIT*, July 19, 1718, 310.

9. Helms, "Esoteric Knowledge."

10. Togulky, in Timothy, *Augusta Congress Journal*, 34; Emistisiguo, in Juricek, *GFT*, 35.

11. W. McDowell, *JCIT*, June 13, 1718, 286.

12. SC-CJ entry for August 25, 1721, CO: 5/425, 69–70.

13. SC-CJ entry for June 14, 1722, CO: 5/425, 310.

14. "Message from the Lower House," SC-CJ entry for January 22, 1723, CO: 5/425, 386.

15. Crane, *Southern Frontier*, 265.

16. SC-CJ entry for October 4, 1723, CO: 5/427, 5.

17. John Wood to John Bee, July 30, 1723, BPRO-SC, 10:131.

18. "Letter of Theophilus Hastings," SC-CJ entry for April 15, 1723, added to entry for May 16, 1723, CO: 5/427, 13.

19. "Letter of Theophilus Hastings," SC-CJ entry for April 15, 1723, CO: 5/427, 13.

20. The two Indians were "Istomelogagee" and "Callabachee," both from Cussita. SC-CJ entry for May 16, 1723, CO: 5/427, 13.

21. "Talk" with Ouletta, October 25, 1723, BPRO-SC, 10:175–177.

22. "Talk" with Ouletta, November 15, 1723, BPRO-SC, 10:178–179.

23. "Talk" with Ouletta, October 25, 1723, BPRO-SC, 10:175, 177.

24. "Talk" with Ouletta, October 25, 1723, BPRO-SC, 10:175, 177.

25. "Talk" with Ouletta, October 25, 1723, BPRO-SC, 10:175, 177.

26. "Talk" with Ouletta, October 25, 1723, BPRO-SC, 10:175, 177.

27. "Talk" with Ouletta, October 25, 1723, BPRO-SC, 10:180.

28. Barcia, *History*, 360–361; Miguel Roman de Castilla y Vega to the Viceroy, April 18, 1758, Spellman Collection, reel 144J.

29. Entries for June 5 and 9, 1724, Salley, *JCHA-SC*, 12, 19–20.

30. William Hatton to Francis Nicholson, November 14, 1724, BPRO-SC, 11:270. See also Crane, *Southern Frontier*, 266.

31. "Journal of Tobias Fitch," in Mereness, *Travels*, 178–180.

32. Mereness, *Travels*, 182–183. On Tickhonabe's "son," see Vega's minutes from a meeting with Acmucaiche, April 18, 1758, enclosed in Vega to the Viceroy of New Spain, April 29, 1758, Mexican Archives, Charles Spellman Collection, 144J, f. 21.

33. Mereness, *Travels*, 186.

34. Mereness, *Travels*, 183.

35. Mereness, *Travels*, 183.

36. SC-CJ entry for August 24, 1725, CO: 5/428.

37. Mereness, *Travels*, 194–195.

38. Mereness, *Travels*, 194–195.

39. Saunt, "New Order of Things," 13.

40. Mereness, *Travels*, 194–195.

41. Mereness, *Travels*, 194.

42. Mereness, *Travels*, 209.

43. Mereness, *Travels*,210–211.

44. Mereness, *Travels*, 210.

45. Informe of the Consejo des Indias, March 30, 1727, AGI-SD 837, Stetson Collection, reel 39.

46. Informe of the Consejo, March 30, 1727, AGI-SD 837, Stetson Collection, reel 39.

47. Informe of the Consejo, March 30, 1727; Tobias Fitch to Lt. Gov. Arthur Middleton, August 1, 1726, SC-CJ entry for September 1, 1726, CO: 5/429, 12.

48. SC-CJ entry for April 26–29, 1726, CO: 5/429, 189–196. Fitch reappointed April 29.

49. Fitch to Middleton, August 1, 1726, in SC-CJ entry for October 8, 1726, CO: 5/429, 13.

50. Fitch to Middleton, August 1, 1726, in SC-CJ entry for October 8, 1726, CO: 5/429, 13.

51. Fitch's Talk at Tuckebatchee, September 23, 1726, CO: 5/429, 15–26.

52. SC-CJ entry for January 25–26, 1727, CO: 5/387, 237–247.

53. SC-CJ entry for January 25–26, 1727, CO: 5/387, 247.

54. SC-CJ entry for January 25–26, 1727, CO: 5/387, 247.

55. Crane, *Southern Frontier*, 270; SC-CJ entries for August 2–3 and 31, 1727, CO: 5/429, 2–8, 23–24, respectively.

56. "Glover's Journal," BPRO-SC, 13:82, 99–122.

57. "Glover's Journal," BPRO-SC, 13:87.

58. "Glover's Journal," BPRO-SC, 13:83.

59. "Glover's Journal," BPRO-SC, 13:85–86.

60. "Glover's Journal," BPRO-SC, 13:83–98.

61. "Glover's Journal," BPRO-SC, 13:112–130.

62. "Glover's Journal," BPRO-SC, 13:145.

63. "Glover's Journal," BPRO-SC, 13:152–161.

64. Declaration of Don Juan Jacinto, January 13, 1745, enclosed with Montiano to the Director of the Havana Company, February 14, 1745, AGI-SD 863, Worth Collection, reel 14, no. 6.

65. Declaration of Jacinto, January 13, 1745, AGI-SD 863, Worth Collection, reel 14, no. 6.

66. Crane, *Southern Frontier*, 272; "Glover's Journal," BPRO-SC, 13:162–163.

67. "Glover's Journal," BPRO-SC, 13:164.

68. "Glover's Journal," BPRO-SC, 13:166.

69. Informe of the Consejo, April 26, 1731, AGI-SD 837, Stetson Collection, reel 40.

70. Choctaw factionalism, by way of contrast, descended into civil war. See Galloway, "Choctaw Factionalism," 120–151.

71. "Glover's Journal," BPRO-SC, 13:106.

72. Escobar, April 4, 1717, AGI-SD 843, Worth Collection, reel 4, no. 24.

73. "Glover's Journal," BPRO-SC, 13:126–127.

74. Hudson, *Southeastern Indians*, 175–181, 301, 363; Swanton, "Social Organization," 631–636. For comparison see Evans-Pritchard, *Witchcraft, Oracles, and Magic*.

75. Mereness, *Travels*, 210–211.

76. "Glover's Journal," BPRO-SC, 13:89.

77. SC-CJ entry for February 8, 1722, CO: 5/425, 279.

78. "Glover's Journal," BPRO-SC, 13:130–132.

5. Oglethorpe's Friends—and Enemies

1. *Gentleman's Magazine*, vol. 3, entries for August 1 and 17, 1734, and obituaries, 449–451; *Gentleman's Magazine*, vol. 4, entry for October 30, 1734, 571. The report of Tomochichi's meeting with the King and Queen has been reprinted in Juricek, GT, 21.

2. Escudero to the Conde de Montijo, October 10, 1734, AGI-SD 2591, Worth Collection, reel 3, no. 24.

3. Escudero to the Conde de Montijo, October 15, 1734, AGI-SD 2591, Worth Collection, reel 3, no. 24.

4. Escudero to the Conde de Montijo, October 15, 1734, AGI-SD 2591, Worth Collection, reel 3, no. 24.

5. For an account of Tomochichi's lavish funeral, see the Journal of William Stephens, October 4–6, 1739, in Candler, CRG, 4:428.

6. See Corkran, *Creek Frontier*, chap. 5; Braund, *Deerskins and Duffels*, 38–39; Snapp, *John Stuart*, chap. 1.

7. Crane, *Southern Frontier*, 303–323.

8. Quoted in Ver Steeg, *Narrative*, 45.

9. Perier and de la Chaise to the Directors of the Company of the Indies, April 22, 1729, Rowland and Sanders, MPA, 2:639; Diron d'Artaguette to Maurepas, October 17, 1729, Rowland, Sanders, and Galloway, MPA, 4:20; Perier to Ory, November 15, 1730, Rowland, Sanders, and Galloway, MPA, 4:74–75.

10. *South Carolina Gazette*, June 2, 1732.

11. Thomas Causton to the Trustees, January 17, 1735, Candler, CRG, 20:427.

12. Interview with Samuel Eveleigh, January 3, 1736, in Easterby, JCHA-SC, 154.

13. Wittlemico, Musgrove's "uncle," was an Apalachicola man who lived on Musgrove's land. "Oweeka," also a long-term Carolina resident, was, I suspect, from Apalachicola. See "Message from the Lower House," in SC-CJ entry for January 5, 1722, 219–220, CO: 5/425; SC-CJ entry for March 8, 1722, CO: 5/425, 287–289.

14. Memorial and Representation of Coosaponakeesa, 1754, Juricek, GT, 235.

15. Interview with Eveleigh, January 3, 1736, Easterby, JCHA-SC, 154.

16. Oglethorpe, "A Curious Account of the Indians," c. February 1733, Juricek, GT, 10.

17. Peter Gordon's Journal, in Juricek, GT, 9.

18. Gordon's Journal, in Juricek, GT, 9.

19. Oglethorpe to the Trustees, May 14, 1733, in Lane, *Oglethorpe's Georgia*, 1:16.

20. *South Carolina Gazette*, July 7, 1733.

21. Oglethorpe to the Trustees, February 10, 1733, in Lane, *Oglethorpe's Georgia*, 1:5.

22. Oglethorpe to the Trustees, March 12, 1733, Juricek, GT, 11.

23. Entry for February 14, 1736, in Parker, *Heart of Wesley's Journal*, 8–9.

24. *South Carolina Gazette*, May 12, 1733; "Talks with the Trustees on Regulation," Egmont's Journal, in Juricek, GT, 24.

25. Egmont's Journal, in Juricek, GT, 24.

26. Oglethorpe to the Trustees, March 12, 1733, Juricek, GT, 11.

27. Oglethorpe to the Trustees, February 10, 1733, Lane, *Oglethorpe's Georgia*, 1:5.

28. Possibly the same man known as Oweeka, who had lived on Musgrove's land in South Carolina.

29. "First Conference with the Lower Creeks," *South Carolina Gazette*, June 2, 1733, in Juricek, GT, 13–14.

30. Oglethorpe's first conference with the Lower Creeks, Juricek, GT, 13–14.

31. "Oglethorpe's Treaty with the Lower Creek Indians," *Georgia Historical Quarterly* 4.1 (March 1920): 12–14.

32. Crane, *Southern Frontier*, 299; "Articles of Friendship and Commerce," Easterby, *JCHA-SC* (1736–39), 109.

33. "Oglethorpe's Treaty," *Georgia Historical Quarterly* 4.1 (March 1920): 14.

34. "Oglethorpe's Treaty," *Georgia Historical Quarterly* 4.1 (March 1920): 7.

35. No record indicates that the coastal peoples were visited by any persons from Chattahoochee towns until the 1680s. Occasional references to the Tamas living in the Ocmulgee River region are the only hint that the Guale people had contact with the interior. For the exceptions to this general rule, see Gonzalo Menendez de Canco, Governor of Florida, to Phillip II, King of Spain, June 28, 1600; and the Relation of Governor Ibarra for November–December 1604, in Serrano y Sanz, *Documentos Historicos*, 142–143, 155, 184; "Consejo des Indias," July 28, 1646, AGI-SD 235, Stetson reel 36.

36. The variety of spellings for this town's name suggests that Europeans had a very hard time pronouncing it. Most commonly they inverted the consonant clusters "ch" and "sh." Some examples: Ysachi; Osuche; Uchise; Ousechees; Owsuchees. In French: Ausoches. As to the ethnic identity of that town, independent sources confirm the presence of Tamas and Ocutis, both of which were ancestral to central Georgia. See Claude Delisle, in Kernion, trans., "Documents Concerning the History of the Indians of the Eastern Region of Louisiana," LHQ, v. 8, no. 1 (January, 1925): 37; Deposition of George Coussins, July 19, 1735, Salley, *JCHA-SC*, 120.

37. Galloway, *Choctaw Genesis*, 302–305.

38. First Conference with the Lower Creeks, Juricek, GT, 13; *South Carolina Gazette*, March 24, 1733; Hvidt, *Von Reck's Voyage*, 35.

39. See Hvidt, *Von Reck's Voyage*, 35.

40. Mason, "Ocmulgee Old Fields," 93–120; Braley, *Tarver and Little Tarver*, 129–136, 166–167.

41. "Oglethorpe's Treaty," *Georgia Historical Quarterly* 4.1 (March 1920): 7.

42. Martin and Szuter, "War Zones and Game Sinks"; Krech, *Ecological Indian*, 163; Braund, *Deerskins and Duffels*, 40–80.

43. "Oglethorpe's Treaty," *Georgia Historical Quarterly* 4.1 (March 1920): 7.

44. Oglethorpe to the Trustees, June 9, 1733, Candler, CRG, 20:23–24.

45. Alvaro Lopez de Toledo to Gov. Francisco de Moral Sanchez, June 29, 1734, enclosure in Sanchez to the King, July 29, 1734, AGI-SD 2584, Worth Collection, reel 3, no. 4.

46. Sanchez to the King, July 29, 1734, AGI-SD 2584, Worth Collection, reel 3, no. 4.

47. Antonio Arredondo, Report of the Indians of Florida, November 27, 1736, AGI-SD 2591, Worth Collection, reel 3, no. 35.

48. Entry for December 10, 1736, Easterby, JCHA-SC, 78–151.

49. Salley, SC-CJ, "Obihatchee's Talk with the Lieutenant Governor," July 6, 1736, CO: 5/437, 59–60; *South Carolina Gazette*, July 10, 1736.

50. "Talks with the Lower and Upper Creeks: Second Audience," July 3, 1736, Juricek, GT, 73.

51. Deposition of John Cowdonhead, July 4, 1735, Salley, JCHA-SC, 115.

52. Deposition of John Cowdonhead, July 4, 1735, Salley, JCHA-SC, 115.

53. Mackey to the Trustees, March 23, 1735, Juricek, GT, 46.

54. Mackey to the Trustees, March 23, 1735, Juricek, GT, 46.

55. Moral Sanchez to the King, April 5, 1735, AGI-SD 2591, Worth Collection, reel 3, no. 27.

56. Mackey to the Trustees, March 23, 1735, Juricek, GT, 46.

57. Moral Sanchez to the King, April 5, 1735, AGI-SD 2591, Worth Collection, reel 3, no. 27.

58. Moral Sanchez to the King, May 23, 1735, AGI-SD 2591, Worth Collection, reel 3, no. 27.

59. Mackey to Oglethorpe, March 29, 1735, Juricek, GT, 49.

60. Moral Sanchez to the King, January 10, 1737, including enclosure from Nieto to Moral Sanchez, AGI-SD 2592, Worth Collection, reel 3, no. 41.

61. *South Carolina Gazette*, December 28, 1734.

62. For a discussion of traveling and spiritual power, see O'Brien, *Choctaws in a Revolutionary Age*, 50–69.

63. Tomochichi may have even offended some of the Yamacraws with his heavy handedness. On one occasion a Yamacraw man named Sallote in protest tried to strike Tomochichi's "queen" with a firebrand. Apokutche, a delegate to London, even complained that Tomochichi "makes himself greater than he should be." See Thomas Christie to the Trustees, March 19, 1735, in Lane, *Oglethorpe's Georgia*, 1:136.

64. Mackey to Causton, March 27, 1735, Juricek, GT, 48–49.

65. Mackey to Causton, March 27, 1735, Juricek, GT, 48–49.

66. Causton to Mackey, April 10, 1735, Juricek, GT, 52–53.

67. Causton to the Trustees, June 20, 1735, Juricek, GT, 55–58.

68. Baine, "Myth of the Creek Pictograph."

69. On the migration legend, see Gatschet, *Migration Legend*, 1:214–249 and 2:26–71; Swanton, "Social Organization," 33–75; Knight, "Mississippian Ritual," 22–44.

70. Candler, "Migration Legend," CRG, 20:381–387.

71. Candler, "Migration Legend," CRG, 20:387.

72. Ong, *Orality and Literacy*; Goody, *Logic of Writing*; Goody, *Domestication of*

Savage Mind. For a contrary opinion, see Boone, "Writing and Recording Knowledge."

73. Causton to the Trustees, June 20, 1735, Juricek, GT, 55–58. Apalachicola traditions, by way of contrast, assert Apalachicola primacy and portray the alliance with the Cussitas as one between "friends." See Lower Creek Headmen to Governor Wright and John Stuart, September 18, 1768, Juricek, GFT, 61.

74. For accounts of the war's origins, see Leach, *Arms for Empire*, 206–210; Peckham, *Colonial Wars*, 89.

75. Peckham, *Colonial Wars*, 89.

76. Bolton and Ross, *Debatable Land*, chap. 6; Lanning, *Diplomatic History of Georgia*, 220; J. Wright, *Anglo-Spanish Rivalry*, 90. Quote taken from Sonderegger, "Southern Frontier," 143.

77. Causton to the Trustees, June 20, 1735, Juricek, GT, 57.

78. Mackey to Oglethorpe, March 29, 1735, Juricek, GT, 50–51.

79. Oglethorpe to the Trustees, March 16, 1736, Juricek, GT, 61; *South Carolina Gazette*, May 1, 1736.

80. Quoted in Oglethorpe to the Trustees, March 16, 1736, Juricek, GT, 61. See also *South Carolina Gazette*, May 1, 1736.

81. *South Carolina Gazette*, May 1, 1736; Moral Sanchez to Bienville, April 5, 1736, AGI-SD 2591, Worth Collection, reel 15, no. 15.

82. For accounts of the various attacks, see Governor Moral Sanchez to the King, January 10, 1737, AGI-SD 2591, Worth Collection, reel 3, no. 41; William Stephens's Journal, January 20, 1738, Candler, CRG, 4:69–70; Montiano to Governor Guemes y Horcasitas, July 21, 1738; Montiano to the Viceroy of New Spain, July 22, 1738; Montiano to Maruez de Torrenueva, August 5, 1738. All can be found in *Coleccion de Various Documentos Para La Historia de la Florida y Tierras Adyacentes*, Tomo 1, (London: Trubner y Compania) no. 60 in the Biblioteca Nacional, Madrid. Photocopies in the possession of Dr. John Worth.

83. Thomas Johns's Narrative, December 2, 1736, in Easterby, JCHA-SC, 138–140.

84. Moral Sanchez to the King, October 12, 1735, AGI-SD 2591, Worth Collection, reel 3, no. 25.

85. Moral Sanchez to the King, April 25, 1736, AGI-SD 2591, Worth Collection, reel 3, no. 31. For more on Chislacaliche's intelligence activities, see "Letter from Nieto" enclosed in Moral Sanchez to the King, January 10, 1737, AGI-SD 2591, Worth Collection, reel 3, no. 31.

86. Bienville to Maurepas, February 10, 1736, Rowland and Sanders, MPA, 1:291; Moral Sanchez to Bienville, April 5, 1736, AGI-SD 850, Worth Collection, reel 14, no. 15.

87. Moral Sanchez to the Governor of Louisiana, April 5, 1763, AGI-SD 850, Worth Collection, reel 14, no. 15; Secretary Salmon to Moral Sanchez, January 27, 1738, AGI-SD 850, Worth Collection, reel 14, no. 15; Don Francisco Campo de Arve to the Viceroy of New Spain, September 6, 1739, Documents from the Mexican Archives, Spellman Collection, reel 144G.

88. TePaske, *Governorship of Spanish Florida*, 136.

89. Guemes y Horcasitas to the King, January 18, 1738, AGI-SD 2592, Worth Collection, reel 3, n. 42. For an inventory of trade goods, see Juan Marquez del Toro's diary entry for February 22, 1738, AGI-SD 2593, Worth Collection, reel 4, no. 1.

90. Guemes y Horcasitas to the King, January 18, 1738, AGI-SD 2592, Worth Collection, reel 3, no. 42.

91. Del Toro diary entry for February 18, 1738, Worth Collection, reel 4, no. 1. On Juan Ignacio, see Guemes y Horcasitas to the King, January 18, 1738, AGI-SD 2592, Worth Collection, reel 3, no. 42.

92. See Quilate's reply in del Toro's diary entry for April 14, 1738, Worth Collection, reel 4, no. 1.

93. Del Toro's diary entry for April 14, 1738, Worth Collection, reel 4, no. 1.

94. See "Report of Oglethorpe's Talks with Headmen of Four Lower Creek Towns," October 22, 1738, Juricek, GT, 87; "Minutes of Oglethorpe's Talks with Headmen of Four Lower Creek Towns," Juricek, GT, 88–89.

95. Oglethorpe to Hermann Verelst, June 15, 1739, Juricek, GT, 92–93.

96. "Ranger's Report," in Mereness, Travels, 213–236; Lt. Thomas Eyre's Account, Juricek, GT, 95–96. See also "Oglethorpe's Treaty," Georgia Historical Quarterly 4.1 (March 1920): 6.

97. "Eyre's Account," September 1739, Juricek, GT, 95–96.

98. Journal of William Stephens, November 5, 1739, Candler, CRG, 4:447.

99. Oglethorpe to the Trustees, November 16, 1739, Candler, CRG, 22.2:266; Leach, Arms for Empire, 212.

100. Tooanaway was reported to be in charge of two hundred men. Oglethorpe was expecting four hundred more. Oglethorpe to the Trustees, October 5, 1739, Juricek, GT, 98–99.

101. Montiano to Guemes y Horcasitas and Montiano to the King, January 31, 1740, Montiano, Collections, 32–42.

102. Information provided by none other than Juan Ignacio. Montiano to Guemes y Horcasitas and Montiano to the King, January 31, 1740, Montiano, Collections, 32–42.

103. Anonymous. "Diario de las Noticias a Recidas en el Puerto de Cartagena de Yndias Desde el Prncipio de Junio de 1739," entries for July 17 and July 24, 1742, 132, 143. Original in the Huntington Library.

104. Accounts of the early military encounters during the war of Jenkins's Ear testify to the degree of Chickasaw and Yuchi participation. See "Eyre's Account," September, 1739, Juricek, GT, 94; Montiano to William Bull, March 13, 1739, and Montiano to Oglethorpe, March 13, 1739, in Coleccion de Varios Documentos Para la Historia de la Florida y Tierras Adyacentes (Londres: Trubner and Company, n.d.), vol. 1, f. 232. Original in the Biblioteca National, Madrid. Facsimile copies in the possession of John E. Worth, Randell Research Center of the University of Florida, Pineland FL; Journal of William Stephens, October 22, 1739, in Candler, CRG, 4:436; Oglethorpe to William Stephens, February 1, 1740, Candler, CRG, 22.2:314.

105. Entry for July 6, 1740, Montiano, Collections, 7:56–58.

106. Oglethorpe to William Stephens, September 25, 1741, Juricek, GT, 104; South Carolina Gazette, July 19, 1742.

107. South Carolina Historical Society Collections, 5:84.

108. TePaske, Governorship of Spanish Florida, 214–215.

109. The Stono Rebellion.

110. Montiano to Guemes y Horcasitas, August 19, 1739, Montiano, Collections, 32.

111. For some examples see Montiano to Guemes y Horcasitas, January 31, 1740, and February 23, 1740, Montiano, Collections, 7:32–44.

112. South Carolina Historical Society Collections, 4:41.

113. Kimber, Relation of Late Expedition, 17–19, 23.

114. Kimber, *Relation of Late Expedition*, 34.

115. Oglethorpe to the Trustees, December 29, 1739, Candler, CRG, 22.2:287.

116. Declaration of Francisco Luis, January 13, 1745, AGI-SD 863, Worth Collection, reel 14, no. 6.

6. The Twin

1. The land grant extended to "all the Lands upon the Savannah River as far as the River Ogechee." "Oglethorpe's Second Treaty with the Lower Creeks at Coweta," August 11, 1739, Juricek, GT, 96.

2. Malatchi's speech to Heron, December 7, 1747, Juricek, GT, 148–149.

3. Juricek, GT, 149–151.

4. Stephens's report on Malatchi's talk with Oglethorpe, May 2, 1740, Juricek, GT, 102.

5. Swanton, "Social Organization," 96; Corkran, *Creek Frontier*, 60; Braund, *Deerskins and Duffels*, 203; Reid, *Better Kind of Hatchet*, 19–22.

6. Swanton, "Social Organization," 615–616; Swanton, *Indian Tribes*, 714; Hudson, *Southeastern Indians*, 323, 337; Hultkrantz, *Conceptions of the Soul*, 420, 423.

7. Swanton, "Social Organization," 361.

8. Hudson, *Southeastern Indians*, 171–172.

9. In May 1740 William Stephens described Malatchi as "near thirty" years of age. See report on Malatchi's Talk with Oglethorpe, Juricek, GT, 102.

10. The generational factor is often overlooked by most historians who study Indian dependency. See White, *Roots of Dependency*, for the best economic analyses.

11. Chigelly appears to have been affected personally by the Tugaloo massacre. See Tobias Fitch's talk at Tuckebatchee, September 23, 1726, CO: 5/429, 19–20; Chigelly's talk with Middleton and the Long Warrior of Tunessee, SC-CJ entry for January 25–26, 1727, CO: 5/387, f. 237–47.

12. Nairne, *Muskhogean Journals*, 33.

13. Due to the ambiguous, sometimes contradictory nature of the evidence, I have chosen to use the term "kinsman" with respect to Malatchi since his precise biological relationship to Brims is uncertain. Colonial documents, compiled over a twenty-year span, consistently use the term "son." Not once is the term "nephew" used. But Malatchi and the Bosomworths have left repeated clues that they shared a common clan affiliation, with Mary asserting that they were "relations," an unmistakable reference to clan affiliation.

14. W. McDowell, DRIA (1750–54), 296.

15. Malatchi's speech to Heron, December 7, 1747, Juricek, GT, 148.

16. See Mary Bosomworth's "Memorial, 1747," Juricek, GT, 140–141; Deposition of Joseph Piercey, September 27, 1751, Juricek, GT, 188; W. McDowell, DRIA (1750–54), 270, 275; Malatchi speech to Heron, December 7, 1745, Juricek, GT, 149.

17. For a discussion on "role theory" as it applies to American Indians, see Gearing, *Priests and Warriors*, 55–63, 104.

18. SC-CJ entry for August 16, 1732, CO: 5/434, f. 1.

19. SC-CJ entry for September 6, 1732, CO: 5/434, f. 2.

20. Oglethorpe's first conference with the Lower Creeks, May 18–21, 1733, Juricek, GT, 12.

21. Mackey to Causton, March 27, 1735, Juricek, GT, 48.

22. Talks with the Lower Creeks: First Audience, June 27, 1736, Juricek, *GT*, 68–69.

23. Juricek, *GT*, 69.

24. Stephens's report, Juricek, *GT*, 101–102; A. Willy to Childermas Croft, May 10, 1740; A. Wood to Lt. Gov. William Bull, May 22, 1740, both in BPRO-SC, 20:256, 279.

25. Stephens's report, May 2, 1740, Juricek, *GT*, 101–102.

26. Stephens's report, May 2, 1740, Juricek, *GT*, 101–102.

27. SC-CJ journal entries for June 22 and 23, 1743, CO: 5/442. This was an especially important political contact because Oglethorpe soon left Georgia for good.

28. Adair, *History*, 297; Nairne, *Muskhogean Journals*, 46.

29. Also rendered Hopaii, Hopay, and Opoy.

30. Lankford, "Red and White," 55–56. One specific example, the Mortar of Okchay, who was known earlier in life as Yahatustunuggee (Wolf Warrior), only later emerged as the *otis mico*, a peace chief. See Congress at Pensacola, May 26–28, 1765, Juricek, *GFT*, 261–262.

31. Malatchi's speech to Heron, December 7, 1747, Juricek, *GT*, 150.

32. Malatchi, an *opiya mico*, appears not to have been the only head warrior in Coweta. Nor do *opiya micos* from other towns appear to have monopolized the position of head warrior. See Declaration of Lower Creek Headmen Recognizing Malatchi as their Natural Prince," December 14, 1747, Juricek, *GT*, 155–156; "A List of Creek Indians at Mr. ———'s Landing, September 4, 1749, in SC-CJ, minutes of September 6, 1749, CO: 5/457, f. 618.

33. Adair, *American Indians*, 171.

34. Gatschet, *Migration Legend*, 165; Martin and Mauldin, *Dictionary*, 55.

35. Malatchi never appears to have claimed that he was a "prophet" per se, but on occasion he eludes to his belief that he did possess a certain gift of divination. When speaking before Gov. James Glen concerning the recent plunder of a trade store on the Oconee River, Malatchi exclaimed, "It is true I am no Prophet, but I foretold what would be the consequences of their building a House at the Occonies, and we saw what became of it." See W. McDowell, DRIA (1750–54), 397.

36. See Gearing, *Priests and Warriors*, 55–63.

37. Malatchi's speech to Heron, December 7, 1747, Juricek, *GT*, 150.

38. SC-CJ entry for November 1, 1746, CO: 5/455, f. 175, 89.

39. Ibid.

40. William Stephens and the Assistants of Georgia to Secretary Martin, July 19, 1750, Juricek, *GT*, 199.

41. William Stephens's report on Tomochichi's Land Grant to the Matthewses, December 13, 1737, Juricek, *GT*, 86.

42. Mary's bicultural position both hindered and helped her at various points in her life. On Mary's activities, see Gillespie, "Sexual Politics of Race and Gender; Green, "Mary Musgrove." On the issue of identity manipulation, see Merrell, "Cast of His Countenance."

43. Juricek, *GT*, 79–80, 84.

44. Fischer, "Mary Musgrove: Englishwoman"; Green, "Mary Musgrove," 29–47.

45. Chigelly's talk to Maj. William Horton, n.d., December 4, 1746, Juricek, *GT*, 132.

46. Galphin to Horton, n.d. (c. December 1746), Juricek, GT, 130–131.

47. Malatchi's speech to Heron, December 7, 1747, Juricek, GT, 150.

48. Heron to Andrew Stone, December 8, 1747, Juricek, GT, 154.

49. "Declaration of Lower Creek Nation Recognizing Malatchi as Their Natural Prince," December 14, 1747, Juricek, GT, 155–156.

50. Declaration of the Indian Francisco Luis, January 13, 1745, AGI-SD 863, Worth Collection, reel 14, no. 6; Juan Isidore de Leon to Montiano, May 20, 1745, AGI-SD 863, Worth Collection, reel 14, no. 8; De Leon to Montiano, August 4, 1747, Worth Collection, reel 14, no. 8.

51. See two "deeds," January 4, 1748, Juricek, GT, 157–158.

52. "Deeds," January 4, 1748, Juricek, GT, 157–158.

53. Fischer, "Mary Musgrove Creek: Englishwoman," 217–218.

54. President and the Assistants of Georgia: Further Talks, August 17, 1749, Juricek, GT, 183.

55. "Talks with Creeks," SC-CJ entry for November 1–3, 1746, CO: 5/455, f. 175–179; SC-CJ entry for February 17, 1746, CO: 5/455, 114–115.

56. Malatchi's speech to Heron, December 7, 1747, Juricek, GT, 151.

57. "Lower Creek Recognition of Mary Bosomworth as Princess with Authority to Negotiate over Lands," August 12, 1749, Juricek, GT, 179–180.

58. Governor Vaudreuil to Michel de la Rouillé, February 1, 1750, Rowland, Sanders, and Galloway, MPA, 4:44; Galphin to William Pinckney, November 3, 1750, in W. McDowell, DRIA (1750–54), 4; Harry Parker to Glen, April 16, 1751, in W. McDowell, DRIA (1750–54), 21; Glen to the Board of Trade, October 2, 1750, BPRO-SC, 24:121; Deposition of Adam Bosomworth, October 2, 1750, Juricek, GT, 211.

59. "Confirmation by Malatchi and Other Creek Headmen of Mary Bosomworth as Princess with Authority to Negotiate over Lands, and Confirmation . . . for the Yamacraw Tract," August 2, 1750, Juricek, GT, 202–209.

60. President and the Assistants of Georgia: Talks with Lower Creeks, August 12, 1749 and August 17, 1749, Juricek, GT, 179, 182–183.

61. Talks with Malatchi and Lower Creek Headmen, August 11, 1749, Juricek, GT, 176.

62. President Stephens and the Assistants: Talk with the Ousechees, September 7, 1749, Juricek, GT, 181.

63. W. McDowell, DRIA (1750–54), 305.

64. Discussed retrospectively in Fulgencio Garcia de Solis to the King, July 17, 1754, Mexican documents, Spellman Collection, reel 144J.

65. Galphin to Parker, November 4, 1750, Juricek, GT, 214; "Instructions to Patrick Graham," Juricek, GT, 215.

66. Graham's deed, Juricek, GT, 219–221.

67. Galphin to Pinckney, November 3, 1750; Daniel Clark to Glen, March 26, 1751; Glen to the Committee on Indian Affairs, n.d. (c. 1751); Talk of the Overhills Cherokees, April 9, 1751; Glen to the Upper Creek Nation, March 20, 1752, all in W. McDowell, DRIA (1750–54), 4, 7, 54, 74, 208–212, respectively.

68. Glen to the Cherokee Nation, April 5, 1752, W. McDowell, DRIA (1750–54), 233.

69. Glen to the Upper Creek Nation, April 28, 1752, W. McDowell, DRIA (1750–54), 210.

70. Glen to the Upper Creek Nation, April 28, 1752, W. McDowell, DRIA (1750–54), 210–212.

71. Instructions to Thomas Bosomworth in W. McDowell, DRIA-SC (1750–54), 343–344.

72. W. McDowell, DRIA (1750–54), 344.

73. W. McDowell, DRIA (1750–54), 274.

74. W. McDowell, DRIA (1750–54), 274.

75. W. McDowell, DRIA (1750–54), 275.

76. SC-CJ entry for January 22, 1746, CO: 5/455, f. 14.

77. Acorn Whistler had been suspected of plotting against the English on previous occasions. See Cornelius Cook to Glen, January 10, 1746, and Glen to Cook, n.d., in SC-CJ, entry for January 22, 1746, CO: 5/455, f. 14. See especially Peter Chartier to Glen, in SC-CJ entry for September 4, 1749, CO: 5/457.

78. W. McDowell, DRIA (1750–54), 276. Malatchi's and Acorn Whistler's verbal exchange quoted on p. 278.

79. W. McDowell, DRIA (1750–54), 278.

80. W. McDowell, DRIA (1750–54), 279.

81. W. McDowell, DRIA (1750–54), 282.

82. W. McDowell, DRIA (1750–54), 285.

83. W. McDowell, DRIA (1750–54), 287.

84. W. McDowell, DRIA (1750–54), 287–288.

85. W. McDowell, DRIA (1750–54), 289.

86. W. McDowell, DRIA (1750–54), 290.

87. W. McDowell, DRIA (1750–54), 291–292.

88. W. McDowell, DRIA (1750–54), 311.

89. W. McDowell, DRIA (1750–54), 314–315.

90. W. McDowell, DRIA (1750–54), 315.

91. W. McDowell, DRIA (1750–54), 316.

92. W. McDowell, DRIA (1750–54), 317–318.

93. W. McDowell, DRIA (1750–54), 349.

94. SC-CJ, entry for November 1, 1746, CO: 5/455, 175; W. McDowell, DRIA (1750–54), 305.

95. W. McDowell, DRIA (1750–54), 294.

96. W. McDowell, DRIA (1750–54), 306.

97. W. McDowell, DRIA (1750–54), 304.

98. Tasattee of Hywassee to Glen, November 28, 1752, and Ludovick Grant to Glen, February 8, 1753, both in W. McDowell, DRIA (1750–54), 362–363, 367, respectively.

99. Glen to the Head Men of the Creek Nation, n.d., W. McDowell, DRIA (1750–54), 375.

100. Proceedings of the Council Concerning Indian Affairs, W. McDowell, DRIA (1750–54), 389.

101. Proceedings of the Council, W. McDowell, DRIA (1750–54), 393.

102. Proceedings of the Council, W. McDowell, DRIA (1750–54), 396–397.

103. Proceedings of the Council, W. McDowell, DRIA (1750–54), 398.

104. Proceedings of the Council, W. McDowell, DRIA (1750–54), 405.

105. Proceedings of the Council, W. McDowell, DRIA (1750–54), 406–407.

106. Proceedings of the Council, W. McDowell, DRIA (1750–54), 408.

107. Proceedings of the Council, W. McDowell, DRIA (1750–54), 408, 411.

108. Proceedings of the Council, W. McDowell, DRIA (1750–54), 411.

109. Proceedings of the Council, W. McDowell, DRIA (1750–54), 412.

110. Proceedings of the Council, W. McDowell, DRIA (1750–54), 412.

111. Proceedings of the Council, W. McDowell, DRIA (1750–54), 413.

112. Glen to the Board of Trade, June 25, 1753, BPRO-SC, 25:328.

113. See Malatchi to Glen, June 26, 1753; James Germany to Lachlan McGillavray, July 15, 1753; Red Coat, King of Oakfuskee to Glen, July 26, 1753; and Lachlan McIntosh to Glen, November 2, 1753, all in W. McDowell, DRIA (1750–54), 381.

114. William Little, Talks with Creek Headmen at Augusta, December 15–18, 1755, Juricek, GT, 239.

115. Declaration of Antonio Micono, September 26, 1754, Mexican documents, Spellman Collection, reel 144J.

116. Governor Melchior de Feliu to the Viceroy of New Spain, February 20, 1763, Stetson Collection, reel 7.

117. Atkin to Gov. Henry Ellis, January 25, 1760, Juricek, GT, 308.

118. Provincial Council of Georgia, Talks with the Headmen of Coweta and Cussita, October 10, 1759, Juricek, GT, 300.

119. Louis Billouart, Sieur de Kerlerec to Jean-Baptiste De Machault d'Arnouville, December 18, 1754, Rowland, Sanders, and Galloway, MPA, 5:157.

120. Malatchi to Glen, November 15, 1754, W. McDowell, *Colonial Records of South Carolina: Documents Relating to Indian Affairs, 1750⁴–1765* (hereafter DRIA [1754–65]), 29.

121. Lachlan McGillavray Journal in W. McDowell, DRIA (1754–65), 56–57, 67–68; McIntosh to Glen, August 9, 1755, in W. McDowell, DRIA (1754–65), 72.

122. McGillavray to Glen, February 17, 1756, in W. McDowell, DRIA (1754–65), 103.

123. Braund, *Deerskins and Duffels*, 140–141.

124. Congress with the Lower Creeks at Augusta, November 14, 1768, Juricek, GFT, 72.

125. Sahlins, *Tribesmen*, 6.

7. The Invention of the Creek Nation

1. Treaty of Paris, February 10, 1763, in Israel, *Major Peace Treaties*, 1:305–328. The best discussion of the treaty negotiations can be found in Gipson, *British Empire*, 8:383–411. For a detailed discussion of the "Triple Nation Transfer," as it occurred in Florida, see Gold, *Borderland Empires in Transition*.

2. Bailyn, *Ideological Origins*; Holton, *Forced Founders*, 7. For a more nuanced view, see the introduction of F. Anderson, *Crucible of War*.

3. White, *Middle Ground*, 269–314; Richter, "Native Peoples of North America; Dowd, *War under Heaven*.

4. Hudson refers to Mississippian society as a small, bounded social world. Hudson, *Knights of Spain*, 22. On the decline of Mississippian society and the creation of the historic "tribes," see Merrell, *The Indians' New World*, 92–133; Ethridge and Hudson, "Transformation of the Southeastern Indians"; Galloway on "Confederation, in Forgotten Centuries; Patricia Galloway, "Confederacy as a Solution to Chiefdom Dissolution: Historical Evidence in the Choctaw Case," in Hudson and Tesser, *The Forgotten Centuries*.

5. Adair, *American Indians*, 276.

6. "1732 Treaty of Peace with South Carolina," in Easterby, JCHA-SC, 108–111, duplicated in *Pennsylvania Gazette*, July 17, 1732.

7. See, for example, James Glen's attempts to explain the divisions within the Creek Nation in Glen to the Board of Trade, July 15, 1750, BPRO-SC, 24:66. On the metropolitan use of the term "Creek Nation," see H. Fox to the Duke of

Bedford, November 13, 1750, BPRO-SC, 24:141; Lords to William Pitt, December 24, 1756, BPRO-SC, 27:171; Lords to the King, December 24, 1756, BPRO-SC, 27:172–173; Lyttleton to Pitt, November 4, 1758, BPRO-SC, 28:96; Thomas Boone to the Board of Trade, June 1, 1763, BPRO-SC, 29:334. For an interesting discussion on the politics of naming, see David Thomas, *Skull Wars*, 4–5, 203–206; and Stuckey and Murphy, "By Any Other Name."

8. On Spanish recognition of Ochise-Tallapoosa differences, see Alonso Marques del Toro's journal entry for February 27, 1738, AGI-SD 2592, Worth Collection, reel 3, no. 42; Vega to the Viceroy, April 29, 1758, and Vega to the Viceroy, February 12, 1759, both in Mexican documents, Spellman Collection, reel 144J. On the close relationship between the Apiscas and Tallapoosas, see Meeting with Acmucaiche, April 18, 1758, enclosed with Vega to the Viceroy, April 29, 1758, Mexican documents, Spellman Collection, reel 144J.

9. For examples of French usages, see Vaudreuil to Rouille, June 24, 1750; Kerlerec to Berryer, August 4, 1760; and minutes of the Council with the Choctaws, November 14, 1763. All can be found in Rowland, Sanders, and Galloway, MPA, 5:47, 258–260, 294–301.

10. Ellis to Lyttleton, May 3, 1758, Lyttleton Papers.

11. Willis, "Colonial Conflict," 202–259.

12. This was particularly true in the 1750s. For examples, see Candler, CRG, 7:45, 268, 333, 485, 546, 572. On the effects of Creek mobility on Creek communal architecture, see "Historic Creek Architectural Adaptations to the Deerskin Trade," in Waselkov, *Archaeological Excavations*, 39–76.

13. Atkin to Lyttleton, February 13, 1760, Lyttleton Papers.

14. Atkin to Lyttleton, February 21, 1760, Lyttleton Papers.

15. For a discussion of the formation of the Creeks and Seminoles in Florida, see Weisman, *Unconquered People*, 5–42; Porter, "The Founder"; Doster, *Creek Indians and Their Florida Lands*, 13–66.

16. Saunt, "New Order of Things," chap. 1; Weisman, *Like Beads on a String*, 37–81.

17. Chislacaliche's son went by the name of Phillip, a sure sign that he had been baptized. See de Leon to Montiano, August 4, 1747, AGI-SD 863, Worth Collection, reel 14, no. 8.

18. See minutes from the Junta of Florida, July 9, 1738, Biblioteca Nacional, Madrid. Facsimile in the possession of John Worth.

19. Montiano to the Director of the Havana Company, with enclosures, February 14, 1745, AGI-SD 863, Worth Collection, reel 14, no. 6.

20. Provincial Council of Georgia: Talk with the Cowkeeper of Alachua, September 13, 1757, Juricek, GT, 259.

21. Timothy, *Augusta Congress Journal*, 27.

22. Some Creeks even pleaded with Spanish officials to form new towns south of the St. John's River, under the aegis of Spanish administration. See Juan Joseph Solana's "Relations," entries for November 1758," and "June 26, 1759," in AGI-SD 2584, Worth Collection, reel 3, no. 16.

23. Anonymous to Montiano, November 15, 1749, and Montiano to the King, February 23, 1750, both in AGI-SD 846, Stetson Collection, reel 49.

24. Melchor de Navarette to the Viceroy of New Spain, May 21, 1751, AGI-SD 846, Stetson Collection, reel 49.

25. See testimony of Antonio de Torres, August 1, 1764, Mexican documents, Spellman Collection, reel 144J.

26. On Acmucaiche's activities with the Pensacola garrison and the two Indian towns see, for example, Vega to the Viceroy, April 18, 1758, and Vega to the Viceroy, February 12, 1759, in Mexican documents, Spellman Collection, reel 144J.

27. W. McDowell, DRIA (1750–54), 275, 289; Stephens and the Assistants to Secretary Martyn, July 29, 1750, GT, 201.

28. See Journal of Thomas Bosomworth, 280–291.

29. Confirmation Deeds for the Yamacraw Tract and the Three Islands, and Malatchi as "Prince," August 2, 1750, GT, 204, 206–207, 209–210; Deposition of Adam Bosomworth, October 2, 1750, GT, 211.

30. W. McDowell, DRIA (1750–54), 282.

31. Del Toro diary entry for April 15, 1738, AGI-SD 2593, Worth Collection, reel 4, no. 1.

32. Glen to Lyttleton, January 23, 1758, Lyttleton Papers.

33. Acorn Whistler's Talk to Glen, c. April 1, 1752, W. McDowell, DRIA (1750–54), 229.

34. Talks with the Upper Creeks, July 7, 1759, in Atkin to Lyttleton, November 30, 1759, Lyttleton Papers.

35. Bartram, *Travels*, 366.

36. Speech of the Long Warrior of Tunnessee to Arthur Middleton, entry for January 25, 1727, SC-CJ, CO: 5/387, 238.

37. Bartram, *Travels*, 366.

38. Swanton, *Early History*, 215.

39. By mid-century the term "Miscogas" begins to appear in the English documents. See Atkin's journal entry for Saturday, October 27, 1759, Lyttleton Papers; *South Carolina Gazette*, June 5, 1760; Talk with the Wolf of Muccalassee, November 16, 1759, Lyttleton Papers.

40. Weisman, "Archaeological Perspectives."

41. Crane, *Southern Frontier*, 260.

42. On Atkin's superintendency, see Jacobs, *Indians of Southern Colonial Frontier*, xv–xxxvi; Alden, "Albany Congress."

43. On the secret British southern strategy, see Pitt to Lyttleton, January 27, 1758; Pitt to Lyttleton, March 7, 1758; and Maj. Gen. Jeffrey Amherst to Lyttleton, January 4, 1759, all in Lyttleton Papers, Letterbook A, pp. 1–3, 53–63. (Note: At the time I conducted research at the Clements Library the Lyttleton letterbooks had yet to be catalogued. "Letterbook A" is simply the designation that the curator of manuscripts and I assigned to it, for the sake of convenience.)

44. Lyttleton to Adm. Edward Boscawen, August 22, 1758; Lyttleton to Amherst, February 7, 1759, all in Lyttleton Letterbook A, 22–23.

45. Jacobs, *Indians of Southern Colonial Frontier*, 62.

46. On Atkin's denial in Tuckebatchee, see Atkin's Conference with the Tuckebatchee *Mico*, July 24, 1759, Lyttleton Papers. For Atkin's cryptic remarks disparaging to metropolitan and colonial officials, see Atkin to Lyttleton, November 30, 1759, Lyttleton Papers.

47. Escudero to Vega, July 6, 1759, Mexican Documents, Spellman Collection, reel 144J, 59–63. Escudero not only could speak Spanish, but he was literate.

48. Escudero to Vega, July 6, 1759, Mexican Documents, Spellman Collection, reel 144J, 59–63.

49. Atkin to Lyttleton, November 30, 1759, Lyttleton Papers.

50. Atkin to Lyttleton, June 17, 1759, Lyttleton Papers.

51. Atkin's Conference with the Tuckebatchey *Mico*, July 24, 1759, Lyttleton Papers.

52. Vega to the Viceroy, April 18, 1758, Mexican Documents, Spellman Collection, reel 144J, f. 21–24; Declaration of the Junta at Pensacola, December 28, 1758, Mexican Documents, Spellman Collection, reel 144J, 39–42.

53. Atkin's Conference with the Tuckebatchey *Mico*, July 24, 1759, Lyttleton Papers.

54. Atkin's Conference with the Tuckebatchey *Mico*, July 24, 1759, Lyttleton Papers

55. Atkin's Speech at the Door of the Eneah *Mico*, September 29, 1759, Lyttleton Papers.

56. Atkin to Lyttleton, November 30, 1759, Lyttleton Papers.

57. Red Coat King to Glen, July 26, 1753; McIntosh to Glen, July 24, 1753; Grant to Glen, February 8, 1754; Malatchi to Glen, May 12, 1754; McGillavray to Glen, April 14, 1754; McIntosh to Glen, April 3, 1754; and Malatchi to Glen, May 7, 1754; all in W. McDowell, DRIA (1750–54), 474, 504, 507, respectively. See also Atkin to Lyttleton, October 28, 1759; Ellis to Lyttleton, February 5, 1760, Lyttleton Papers.

58. Cherokee contact initiated with the commander of the Alabama fort in August 1753. See Rowland, Sanders, and Galloway, MPA, 5:144.

59. For a good summary of these events, see Alden, *John Stuart*, 52–61. For an account of that meeting, see Ray Demere's Indian Intelligence Report, November 25, 1756, Loudoun Papers, box 53, folder 2279.

60. On the Briar Creek Affair and Pepper's agency, see James Germany to Messrs. Rae & Barksdale, July 10, 1756, Lyttleton Papers; Depositions of Jacob Pauls and William Carr, and of Peter Elliot, September 10, 1756, enclosures in White Outerbridge to Lyttleton, September 11, 1756, Lyttleton Papers; Lyttleton to the Board of Trade, August 11, 1756, BPRO-SC, 27:137; Outerbridge to Lyttlelton, October 22, 1756, W. McDowell, DRIA (1754–65), 210; Lyttleton to the Board of Trade, August 11, 1756, and Lyttleton to the Board of Trade, October 17, 1756, both in BPRO-SC, 27:137, 154–155, respectively.

61. Paul Demere to Lyttleton, May 2, 1759; Same to Same, May 12, 1759; Same to Same, May 15, 1759; W. McDowell, DRIA (1754–65), 492–493.

62. Atkin's Interview with Billy Germany, August 20, 1759, Lyttleton Papers.

63. Atkin to Lyttleton, November 30, 1759, Lyttleton Papers.

64. On the Cherokee war, see Alden, *John Stuart*, chaps. 5–6; Corkran, *Cherokee Frontier*, 191–254.

65. *South Carolina Gazette*, January 5, 1760.

66. For some varying intelligence, see Atkin's Interview with Billy Germany, August 20, 1759; and Atkin's Talk at the Door of the Enyhah *Mico*'s House," September 29, 1759, both Lyttleton Papers.

67. Ultimately, colonial officials believed that the British Army's punitive measures against the Cherokees played a significant role in mitigating Creek hostility. For the trader's report, see *South Carolina Gazette*, March 29, 1760. On the effects of the British military campaign, see Lyttleton to Knox, June 28, 1761, Knox Papers.

68. Outerbridge to Lyttleton, February 6, 1760; Outerbridge to Lyttleton, February 9, 1760, Lyttleton Papers.

69. *South Carolina Gazette*, May 17, 1760, and Provincial Council of Georgia: Talks with a Lower Creek War Party, April 14, 1760, Juricek, GT, 313–314; Pro-

vincial Council of Georgia: Talk with Chehaw Emissaries, November 8, 1760, Juricek, GT, 336–337.

70. *South Carolina Gazette*, May 31, 1760 and June 21, 1760.

71. *South Carolina Gazette*, June 21, 1760.

72. *South Carolina Gazette*, June 21, 1760, and June 28, 1760. On the Creek reaction, see *South Carolina Gazette*, May 31 and June 7, 1760.

73. See the talks of the Wolf and Devall's Landlord in *South Carolina Gazette*, July 19, 1760.

74. Provincial Council of Georgia: Salechi's Report, June 28, 1760, Juricek, GT, 313–314; *South Carolina Gazette*, August 9, 1760.

75. Adair, *American Indians*, 189.

76. *South Carolina Gazette*, March 22, 1760.

77. Provincial Council of Georgia, Talk with a Delegation of Lower Creeks, May 20, 1760, Juricek, GT, 317–319.

78. *South Carolina Gazette*, July 19, 1760.

79. Atkin to Lyttleton, September 21, 1759, Lyttleton Papers.

80. Atkin to Lyttleton, September 21, 1759, Lyttleton Papers.

81. Atkin to Lyttleton, September 21, 1759, Lyttleton Papers.

82. Talk of Skiagusta of Kehowee and the Good Warrior of Estato to Glen, April 15, 1752, W. McDowell, DRIA (1750–54), 247.

83. Fried, *Evolution of Political Society*, 170.

84. Sahlins, *Tribesmen*, 81–82.

85. John Pettycrow to Glen, December 1, 1754, W. McDowell, DRIA (1754–60), 30.

86. On the Briar Creek Affair, see Germany to Rae & Barksdale, July 10, 1756, Lyttleton Papers; Depositions of Pauls and Carr, and Elliot, September 10, 1756, in Outerbridge to Lyttleton, September 11, 1756, Lyttleton Papers.

87. Reynolds to Lyttleton, November 26, 1756, and Outerbridge to Lyttleton, October 22, 1756, W. McDowell, DRIA (1754–65), 210; Lyttleton to the Board of Trade, October 17, 1756, BPRO-SC, 27:137, 154–155.

88. Pepper to Lyttleton, November 18, 1756; Pepper to Lyttleton, November 30, 1756; Pepper to Lyttleton, December 21, 1756; Pepper to Lyttleton, April 25, 1757, all in W. McDowell, DRIA (1754–65), 254, 295, 298, 367 respectively.

89. Juricek, GT, 231.

90. Stumpe's speech in Provincial Council of Georgia: Conference with Upper and Lower Creeks, November 3, 1759, Juricek, GT, 267.

91. Gov. Ellis's Treaty with the Upper and Lower Creeks, November 3, 1757, Juricek, GT, 270–272.

92. Creek Cession Declarations, April 22 and May 1, 1758, Juricek, GT, 277–279.

93. Provincial Council of Georgia: Conference with the Upper and Lower Creeks, October 25, 1757, Juricek, GT, 267.

94. Stuart and Governor Johnstone's Reply to Upper Creek Talk of July 22, 1764, Juricek, GFT, 226; Capt. Robert Mackinnen's Conference with and Grant from the Wolf King, et al, September 20, 1764, Juricek, GFT, 223; Upper Creek "Great Talk" to Stuart and Wright, May 20, 1764, Juricek, GFT, 213.

95. Atkin's Talk in Tuckebatchee Square, July 9, 1759, Lyttleton Papers.

96. Atkin to Lyttleton, September 21, 1759, Lyttleton Papers.

97. Atkin to Lyttleton, November 30, 1759, Lyttleton Papers.

98. Atkin to Lyttleton, November 30, 1759, Lyttleton Papers.

99. *South Carolina Gazette*, May 30, 1761, and September 18, 1762.

100. *South Carolina Gazette*, May 15 and 29, 1762, and September 18, 1762.

101. *South Carolina Gazette*, October 23, 1762.

102. Governor Feliu to the Viceroy, February 20, 1763, AGI-SD 2542, Stetson Collection, reel 52.

103. *South Carolina Gazette*, September 24, 1763.

104. Creek warriors were reported to have waved their tomahawks over the British soldiers' heads at Pensacola. *South Carolina Gazette*, October 22, 1763. On attempts to "fix" boundaries, see Timothy, *Augusta Congress Journal*, 6–7.

105. Stuart was commissioned September 12, 1763. Enclosed in Stuart to Gage, December 31, 1763, Gage Papers, American Correspondence.

106. Stuart to Gage with enclosures, April 11, 1764, Gage Papers.

107. See Talks with the Representatives of the Five Indian Nations, November 3–8, 1763, in Timothy, *Augusta Congress Journal*, 20–38.

108. Lower Creek Talk of September 16, 1763, Timothy, *Augusta Congress Journal*, 12. See also the Gun Merchant's talk to Mr. Colbert, September 27, 1763, in Timothy, *Augusta Congress Journal*, 21.

109. Proclamation of 1763, in Greene, *Colonies to Nation*, 17.

110. Timothy, *Augusta Congress Journal*, 16.

111. Timothy, *Augusta Congress Journal*, 40.

112. Timothy, *Augusta Congress Journal*, 31, 41. On go-betweens on the Anglo-Indian frontier, see Merrell, *Into the American Woods*, 19–41, 54–105.

113. Timothy, *Augusta Congress Journal*, 41.

Epilogue

1. Timothy, *Augusta Congress Journal*, 41.

2. Upper Creek Reply to Stuart, c. mid-February, 1764, Juricek, GFT, 11.

3. Upper Creek Reply to Stuart, c. mid-February, 1764, Juricek, GFT, 42, 21.

4. Elick's speech to Pensacola Congress, May 27, 1765, Juricek, GFT, 262; Trade Conference of 1767, John Stuart and the Lower and Upper Creeks, Mortar's Speech, June 6, 1767, Juricek, GFT, 34.

5. See, for example, the bestowal of string beads at the second Pensacola Congress of 1771. Proceedings of the Second Pensacola Congress with the Upper Creeks, October 29–31, 1771, Juricek, GFT, 387–401.

6. Summarized in Saunt, "New Order of Things," 96–100; Adair, *American Indians*, 286; Bartram, *Travels*, 194.

7. On Panton, Leslie, and Company's activities, see Coker and Watson, *Indian Traders*; Braund, *Deerskins and Duffels*, 164–188; Ethridge, "Contest for Land," 136.

8. For some different perspectives on the Red Stick War, see Martin, *Sacred Revolt*, 171–182; Saunt, *New Order of Things*, 249–279; Ethridge, "Contest for Land," 414–430.

9. Treaty of Fort Jackson, in Israel, *Modern Peace Treaties*, 1:693.

10. Saunt, "A New Order of Things," 574.

11. Summarized in Green, *Politics of Indian Removal*, 30.

12. Braund, *Deerskins and Duffels*, 30.

13. McGillavray to Alejandro O'Neill, January 1, 1784, in Caughey, *McGillavray of the Creeks*, 66.

14. McGillavray to Baron de Carondolet, September 2, 1792, in Caughey, *McGillavray of the Creeks*, 335–337.

15. Swanton, "Social Organization," 323.

16. Braund, *Deerskins and Duffels*, 170–171.

17. Swanton, "Social Organization," 324.

18. Green, *Politics of Indian Removal*, 37.

19. For a good example of the persistence of traditional Southeastern Indian culture, see Carson, *Searching for Bright Path*.

20. Swanton, "Social Organization," 308–309.

21. Debo, *Road to Disappearance*, 142–176; Debo, *And Still the Waters Run*, 290, 292–296.

22. Swanton, "Social Organization," 307–308.

Bibliography

Unpublished Sources

Anonymous. Diario de las Noticias a Recidas en el Puerto de Cartagena de Yndias desde el Principio de Junio de 1739. Quoted by permission of the Huntington Library, San Marino CA.

Archdale, John. Papers. South Carolina Department of Archives and History, Columbia. Microfilm.

Archivo General de las Indias. Audiencia of Mexico. Stetson Manuscript Collection, P. K. Yonge Library of Florida History, University of Florida, Gainesville. Microfilm.

Archivo General de las Indias. Audiencia of Santo Domingo. Stetson Manuscript Collection, P. K. Yonge Library of Florida History, University of Florida, Gainesville. Microfilm.

Archivo General de las Indias. Escribanías de Camará. Residencia Series of the Florida Governors. P. K. Yonge Library of Florida History, University of Florida, Gainesville. Microfilm.

Campbell, John, Earl of Loudoun. Papers. Quoted by permission of the Huntington Library, San Marino CA.

Clinton, George. Papers. William L. Clements Library, University of Michigan, Ann Arbor.

Conner, Jeannette Thurber. Manuscripts Collection. Manuscripts from the Archivo General de las Indias, Seville. P. K. Yonge Library of Florida History, University of Florida, Gainesville. Microfilm.

French, Christopher. *Journal of an Expedition to South Carolina, December 22, 1760–November 14, 1761.* South Carolina Department of Archives and History, Columbia. #P900109.

Gage, General Thomas. Papers. Originals in the William L. Clements Library, University of Michigan, Ann Arbor.

Great Britain. Public Records Office. Kew Colonial Office. Original Papers. Series 5. Microfilm.

Green, Ruth S., and John S. Green, eds. *Journal of the Commons House of Assembly, 1707–1721*. South Carolina Department of Archives and History, Columbia. Transcripts.

Knox, William. Papers. Originals in the William L. Clements Library, University of Michigan, Ann Arbor. Microfilm. 3 reels.

Lyttleton, Governor William Henry. Papers. Originals in the William L. Clements Library, University of Michigan, Ann Arbor. Microfilm.

Ross, Mary. Papers (ac. 73–163). Georgia Department of Archives and History, Atlanta. Typescripts. Quoted courtesy of the Georgia Archives.

Sainsbury, W. Noel, transcriber. *Records in the British Public Record Office Relating to South Carolina, 1663–1782*. 36 vols. Microfilm.

Society for the Propagation of the Gospel in Foreign Parts (SPG). Letter-book Series A. Quoted by permission of the Huntington Library, San Marino CA. Microfilm.

Spellman, Charles. Manuscripts Collection. Documents from the Archivo General de la Nacion de Mexico, Historia-Volumen 298. P. K. Yonge Library of Florida History, University of Florida, Gainesville. Microfilm.

Stetson Manuscript Collection, P. K. Yonge Library of Florida History, University of Florida, Gainesville. Microfilm.

Worth, John. Manuscripts Collection. Documents from the Archivo General de las Indias, Seville, and the Biblioteca Nacionale, Madrid. Randell Research Center, Pineland FL. Microfilm and Photocopies.

Articles, Books, Dissertations, and Theses

Adair, James. *The History of the American Indians*. Ed. Samuel Cole Williams. 1775. Reprint, New York: Promontory, 1986.

Adelman, Jeremy, and Stephen Aron. "From Borderlands to Borders: Empires, Nation-States, and the Peoples in between in North American History." "Forum" essay in *American Historical Review* 104, no. 3 (June 1999): 815–841.

Alden, John. "The Albany Congress and the Creation of the Indian Superintendencies." *Mississippi Valley Historical Review* 27, no. 2 (September 1940): 193–210.

———. *John Stuart and the Colonial Southern Frontier: A Study of Indian Relations, War, Trade, and Land Problems in the Southern Wilderness, 1754–1775*. Ann Arbor: University of Michigan Press, 1944.

Anderson, Benedict. *Imagined Communities: Reflections on the Origin and Spread of Nationalism*. London: Verso, 1983.

Anderson, David. *The Savannah River Chiefdoms: Political Change in the Late Prehistoric Southeast*. Tuscaloosa: University of Alabama Press, 1994.

Anderson, Fred. *The Crucible of War: The Seven Years' War and the Fate of Empire in British North America, 1754–1766*. New York: Knopf, 2000.

Anderson, Gary Clayton. *Kinsmen of Another Kind: Dakota-White Relations in the Upper Mississippi Valley, 1650–1862*. Lincoln: University of Nebraska Press, 1984.

Aquila, Richard. *The Iroquois Restoration: Iroquois Diplomacy on the Colonial Frontier, 1701–1754*. Detroit: Wayne State University Press, 1983.

Arnade, Charles. "Cattle Raising in Spanish Florida, 1513–1763." *Agricultural History* 35 (1961): 116–124.

Aron, Stephen. *How the West Was Lost: The Transformation of Kentucky from Daniel Boone to Henry Clay*. Baltimore: Johns Hopkins University Press, 1996.

Arredondo, Antonio de. *Historical Proof of Spain's Title to Georgia*. Trans. and ed. Herbert Bolton. Berkeley: University of California Press, 1925.

Axtell, James. *Natives and Newcomers: The Cultural Origins of North America*. Oxford: Oxford University Press, 2001.

———. *The Indians' New South: Cultural Change in the Colonial Southeast*. Baton Rouge: Louisiana State University Press, 1997.

———. *The Invasion Within: The Contest of Cultures in Colonial North America*. Oxford: Oxford University Press, 1985.

———. *The European and the Indian: Essays in the Ethnohistory of Colonial North America*. Oxford: Oxford University Press, 1981.

Bailyn, Bernard. *The Ideological Origins of the American Revolution*. Cambridge: Beacon, 1967.

Baine, Rodney. "Note and Document: The Myth of the Creek Pictograph." *Atlanta History* 32 (1988): 43–52.

Barcia, Andres Gonzales de. *Chronological History of the Continent of Florida*. Trans. Anthony Kerrigan. Gainesville: University of Florida Press, 1951.

Barker, Eirlys. " 'Much Blood and Treasure': South Carolina's Indian Traders, 1670–1755." Ph.D. diss., College of William and Mary, 1993.

Barnwell, John. "Journal of John Barnwell." *Virginia Magazine of History and Biography* 6 (April–July 1898): 391–402.

Barnwell, Joseph. "The Second Tuscarora Expedition." *South Carolina Genealogical and Historical Magazine* 9 (1908): 33–48.

Barsh, Russel. "The Nature and Spirit of North American Political Systems." *American Indian Quarterly* 10, no. 3 (summer 1986): 196.

Barth, Frederick, ed. *Ethnic Groups and Boundaries: The Social Organization of Cultural Difference*. Boston: Little Brown, 1969. 9–38.

Barthes, Roland. *Mythologies*. Trans. Annette Lauers. New York: Hill and Wang, 1972.

Bartram, William. *The Travels of William Bartram*. Ed. Mark Van Doren. New York: Dover, 1928.

Beck, Robin A. "The Burke Phase: Late Prehistoric Settlements in the Upper Catawba River Valley, North Carolina." Master's thesis, University of Alabama, 1997.

Bell, Amelia W. "The Kashita Myth." *Anthropology Tomorrow* 12, no. 1 (spring 1979): 46–63.

Bloch, Marc. *The Historian's Craft*. Trans. Peter Putnam. New York: Knopf, 1953.

Bolton, Herbert. "Spanish Resistance to the Carolina Traders in Western Georgia, 1680–1704." *Georgia Historical Quarterly* 9, no. 2 (June 1925): 115–130.

Bolton, Herbert, and Mary L. Ross. *The Debatable Land: A Sketch of the Anglo-Spanish Contest for the Georgia Country*. Berkeley: University of California Press, 1925.

Bond, Richmond. *Queen Anne's American Kings*. Oxford: Clarendon, 1952.

Boone, Elizabeth Hill. "Writing and Recording Knowledge." In *Writing without Words: Alternative Literacies in Mesoamerica and the Andes*, ed. Elizabeth Hill and Walter Mignolo, 1–26. Durham: Duke University Press, 1994.

Boone, Elizabeth Hill, and Walter Mignolo, eds. *Writing without Words: Alternative Literacies in Mesoamerica and the Andes*. Durham: Duke University Press, 1994.

Bossu, Jean-Bernard. *Travels in the Interior of North America, 1751–1762*. Trans. and ed. Seymour Feiler. Norman: University of Oklahoma Press, 1962.

Boyd, Mark. "Diego Pena's Expedition to Apalachee and Apalachicolo in 1716." *Florida Historical Quarterly* 28 (1949): 1–27.

———. "Documents Describing the Second and Third Expeditions of Lieutenant Diego Pena to Apalachee and Apalachicolo in 1717 and 1718." *Florida Historical Quarterly* 31, no. 1 (July 1952): 109–139.

———. "Further Considerations of the Apalachee Missions." *The Americas* 9, no. 4 (April 1953): 459–479.

Boyd, Mark, trans. and ed. "The Expedition of Marcos Delgado from Apalachee to the Upper Creek Country in 1686." *Florida Historical Quarterly* 16 (1937): 2–31.

———. "The Siege of Saint Augustine by Governor Moore of South Carolina in 1702 as Reported to the King of Spain by Don Joseph Zuniga y Zerda, Governor of Florida." *Florida Historical Quarterly* 26, no. 4 (1948): 345–352.

Boyd, Mark, Hale G. Smith, and John G. Griffin. *Here They Once Stood: The Tragic End of the Apalachee Missions*. Gainesville: University Press of Florida, 1951.

Braley, Chad. *Historic Indian Period Archaeology of the Georgia Coastal Plain*. Report no. 34. Athens: University of Georgia Laboratory of Archaeology, 1995.

Braley, Chad, principal investigator. *Archaeological Investigation of the Tarver (9J06) and Little Tarver (9J0198) Sites, Jones County, Georgia*. Contract no. EMW-95-C-4865. Southeastern Archaeological Services, August 13, 1997.

Braund, Kathryn. *Deerskins and Duffels: The Creek Indian Trade with Anglo-America*. Lincoln: University of Nebraska Press, 1993.

———. "Guardians of Tradition and Handmaidens to Change: Women's Roles in Creek Economic and Social Life in the Eighteenth Century." *American Indian Quarterly* 14 (1990): 329–358.

Brooks, A. M. *The Unwritten History of Old St. Augustine*. St. Augustine: The Record, 1909.

Brown, Ian. "The Calumet Ceremony in Eastern North America." *American Antiquity* 54 (1989): 311–331.

Bushman, Richard. *The Refinement of America: Persons, Houses, and Cities*. New York: Knopf, 1992.

Bushnell, Amy Turner. *Situado y Sabana: Spain's Support System for the Presidio and Mission Provinces of Florida*. Anthropological Papers of the American Museum of Natural History, no. 74. Athens: University of Georgia Press, 1994.

Bushnell, David I., ed. "The Account of Lamhatty." *American Anthropologist* 10 (1908): 568–574.

Calderon, Gabriel Diaz Vara, Bishop of Cuba. *A Seventeenth Century Letter of Gabriel Diaz Vara Calderon, Bishop of Cuba, Describing the Indians and Indian Missions of Florida*. Trans. Lucy Wenhold. Smithsonian Miscellaneous Collections, vol. 95, no. 16. Washington DC: Smithsonian, 1936.

Caldwell, Joseph R. "Palachacolas Town, Hampton County, South Carolina." *Journal of the Washington Academy of Sciences* 38, no. 10 (1948): 321–324.

Calloway, Colin. *New Worlds for All: Indians, Europeans, and the Remaking of Early America*. Baltimore: Johns Hopkins University Press, 1997.

Calmes, Alan. "Indian Cultural Traditions and European Conquest of the Georgia–South Carolina Coastal Plain, 3000 B.C. to 1733 A.D.: A Combined Archaeological and Historical Investigation." Ph.D. diss., University of South Carolina, 1968.

Campbell, Janis. "The Social and Demographic Effects of Creek Removal." Ph.D. diss., University of Oklahoma, 1997.

Candler, Allen D., Kenneth Coleman, and Milton Ready, eds. *The Colonial Records of the State of Georgia*. Vols. 1–26. Atlanta: C. P. Byrd, 1904–1916.

Canny, Nicholas, ed. *The Oxford History of the British Empire: British Overseas Enterprise to the Close of the Seventeenth Century*. Oxford: Oxford University Press, 1998.

Carson, James Taylor. *Searching for the Bright Path: The Mississippi Choctaws from Prehistory to Removal*. Lincoln: University of Nebraska Press, 1999.

Cashin, Edward. *Governor Henry Ellis and the Southern Colonial Frontier*. Athens: University of Georgia Press, 1994.

————. *Lachlan McGillavray: Indian Trader*. Athens: University of Georgia Press, 1992.

Caughey, John W. *McGillavray of the Creeks*. Norman: University of Oklahoma Press, 1938.

Chadhuri, Jean, and Joyotpaul Chadhuri. *A Sacred Path*. Los Angeles: UCLA American Indian Studies Center, 2001.

Cheves, Langdon, ed. *Letterbook of the City of Charleston*. City of Charleston, 1894.

————. *The Shaftesbury Papers*. 1897. Reprint, Columbia: South Carolina Historical Society Publications, 2000.

Clausewitz, Karl von. *War, Politics, and Power*. Trans. and ed. Edward M. Collins. Chicago: Gateway, 1962.

Clayton, Lawrence, Vernon J. Knight, and Edward Moore, eds. *The De Soto Chronicles: The Expedition of Hernando De Soto to North America in 1539–1543*. 2 vols. Tuscaloosa: University of Alabama Press, 1993.

Clinton, Catherine, and Michele Gillespie. *The Devil's Lane: Sex and Race in the Early South*. Oxford: Oxford University Press, 1997.

Coclanis, Peter. *The Shadow of a Dream: Economic Life and Death in the South Carolina Low Country, 1670–1920*. New York: Oxford University Press, 1989.

Coker, William S., and Thomas D. Watson. *Indian Traders of the Southeastern Spanish Borderlands: Panton, Leslie, and Company and John Forbes and Company, 1783–1847*. Gainesville: University Press of Florida, 1985.

Coleman, Kenneth, and Joseph Ready, eds. *The Colonial Records of Georgia*. Vols. 27–32. Athens: University of Georgia Press, 1977–1989. (Vols. 33–39 currently in typescript at the Georgia Department of Archives and History, Atlanta.)

Corkran, David. *The Cherokee Frontier: Conflict and Survival, 1740–1762*. Norman: University of Oklahoma Press, 1962.

————. *The Creek Frontier, 1540–1783*. Norman: University of Oklahoma Press, 1967.

Cotteril, R. S. *The Southern Indians: The Story of the Five Civilized Tribes before Removal*. Norman: University of Oklahoma Press, 1953.

Crane, Verner. "An Historical Note on the Westo Indians." *American Anthropologist* 20 (1918): 331–337.

————. "The Origin of the Name of the Creek Indians." *Mississippi Valley Historical Review* 5, no. 3 (1913): 339–342.

————. *The Southern Frontier*. 1928. Reprint, New York: Norton, 1981.

Crosby, Alfred. "Virgin Soil Epidemics as a Factor in the Aboriginal Depopulation in America." *William and Mary Quarterly* 3d. ser., 33 (1976): 289–299.

Cumming, William P. *The Southeast in Early Maps*. 3rd. ed. Ed. Louis DeVorsey. Chapel Hill: University of North Carolina Press, 1998.

Debo, Angie. *And Still the Waters Run: The Betrayal of the Five Civilized Tribes*. Princeton: Princeton University Press, 1968.

———. *The Road to Disappearance: A History of the Creek Indians.* Norman: University of Oklahoma Press, 1941.

Deloria, Vine Jr. *Custer Died for Your Sins: An Indian Manifesto.* New York: Avon, 1969.

Deloria, Vine Jr., and David E. Wilkins. *Tribes, Treaties, and Constitutional Tribulations.* Austin: University of Texas Press, 1999.

Dennis, Matthew. *Cultivating a Landscape of Peace: Iroquois-European Encounters in Seventeenth-Century America.* Ithaca NY: Cornell University Press, 1993.

DePratter, Chester B. "Late Prehistoric and Early Historic Chiefdoms in the Southeastern United States." Ph.D. diss., University of Georgia, 1983.

Dobyns, Henry. *Their Number Become Thinned: Native American Population Dynamics in Eastern North America.* Knoxville: University of Tennessee Press, 1983.

Dos Santos, Theotonio. "The Structure of Dependence." *American Economic Review* 60 (May 1970): 231–236.

Doster, James. *The Creek Indians and Their Florida Lands.* Vol. 1. New York: Garland, 1974.

Dowd, Gregory Evans. *A Spirited Resistance: The North American Indian Struggle for Unity, 1745–1815.* Baltimore: Johns Hopkins University Press, 1992.

———. *War under Heaven: Pontiac, the Indian Nations, and the British Empire.* Baltimore: Johns Hopkins University Press, 2002.

Dunaway, Wilma. "Incorporation as an Interactive Process: Cherokee Resistance to Expansion of the Capitalist World System." *Sociological Inquiry* 66, no. 4 (November 1996): 455–470.

Durkheim, Emile, and Marcel Mauss. *Primitive Classification.* Trans. Rodney Needham. Chicago: University of Chicago Press, 1963.

Durschlag, Richard. "The First Creek Resistance: Transformations in Creek Indian Existence and the Yamassee War." Ph.D. diss., Duke University, 1995.

Earle, Timothy, ed. *Chiefdoms: Power, Economy, and Ideology.* Cambridge: Cambridge University Press, 1991.

Easterby, J. H., ed. *Colonial Records of South Carolina, Journal of the Commons House of Assembly, 1736–1750.* Vols. 1–9. Columbia: State, 1962.

Eid, Leroy. "The Ojibwa-Iroquois War: The War the Five Nations Did Not Win." *Ethnohistory* 26, no. 4 (1979): 279–324.

Eliades, David. "Indian Policy of Colonial South Carolina, 1670–1783." Ph.D. diss., University of South Carolina, 1981.

Elliot, J. H. *Imperial Spain, 1496–1716.* London: Penguin, 1963.

Engels, Frederick. *The Origin of the Family, Private Property, and the State.* 1884. Reprint, London: Penguin, 1986.

Ethridge, Robbie. "A Contest for Land: The Creek Indians on the Southern Frontier, 1796–1816." Ph.D. diss., University of Georgia, 1996.

Ethridge, Robbie, and Charles Hudson. "The Early Historic Transformation of the Southeastern Indians," in Patricia Beaver and Carole Hill,
eds., *Cultural Diversity in the U.S. South: Anthropological Contributions
to a Region in Transition*. Proceedings of the Southern Anthropological
Society, no. 31. Athens: University of Georgia Press, 1998. 34–50.

Evans-Pritchard, E. E. *The Nuer*. London: Clarendon, 1940.

———. *Witchcraft, Oracles, and Magic among the Azande*. Oxford: Clarendon, 1977.

Fabel, Robin. "St. Marks, Apalachee, and the Creeks." *Gulf Coast Historical Review* 1, no. 2 (spring 1986): 4–22.

Fabel, Robin, and Robert Rea, eds. "Lieutenant Thomas Campbell's So-
journ among the Creeks: November 1764–May 1765." *Alabama Historical Quarterly* 36 (summer 1974): 97–111.

Fairbanks, Charles. "The Function of Black Drink among the Creeks." In
Black Drink: A Native American Tea, ed. Charles M. Hudson, 120–149.
Athens: University of Georgia, 1979.

Feest, Christian R. "Creek Towns in 1725." *Ethnologische Zeitscrift* 1
(1974): 161–175.

Fenton, William. *The Great Law and the Longhouse: A Political History of the
Iroquois Confederacy*. Norman: University of Oklahoma Press, 1998.

Ferguson, Niall, ed. *Virtual History: Alternatives and Counterfactuals*. New
York: Basic, 1997.

Fischer, David Hackett. *Albion's Seed: Four British Folkways in America*.
Oxford: Oxford University Press, 1989.

Fischer, Doris. "Mary Musgrove: Creek Englishwoman." Ph.D. diss.,
Emory University, 1990.

Ford, Lawrence C. *The Triangular Struggle for Spanish Pensacola, 1689–
1739*. Washington DC: Catholic University Press, 1939.

Foret, Michael J. "On the Marchlands of Empire: Trade, Diplomacy, and
War on the Southeastern Frontier." Ph.D. diss., College of William and
Mary, 1990.

Foster, George M. "Cofradia and Compadrazgo in Spain and Spanish
America." *Southwestern Journal of Anthropology* 9, no. 1 (1953): 1–28.

Freud, Sigmund. *Totem and Taboo: Some Points of Agreement between the
Mental Lives of Savages and Neurotics*. London: Routledge, 1950.

Fried, Morton. *The Evolution of Political Society: An Essay in Political Anthropology*. New York: Random House, 1967.

———. *The Notion of Tribe*. Menlo Park CA: Cummings, 1975.

Gallay, Allan. *The Formation of a Planter Elite: Jonathan Bryan and the Southern Colonial Frontier*. Athens: University of Georgia Press, 1989.

———. *The Indian Slave Trade: The Rise of the English Empire in the American
South, 1670–1717*. New Haven: Yale University Press, 2002.

Galloway, Patricia. "Choctaw Factionalism and Civil War, 1746–1750."
In *The Choctaw before Removal*, ed. C. K. Reeves, 120–156. Jackson: University Press of Mississippi, 1985.

———. *Choctaw Genesis, 1500–1700*. Lincoln: University of Nebraska Press, 1995.

———. "Colonial Period Transformations in the Mississippi Valley: Disintegration, Alliance, Confederation, Playoff." In *The Transformation of the Southeastern Indians, 1540–1760*, ed. Robbie Ethridge and Charles Hudson, 225–248. Jackson: University Press of Mississippi, 2002.

———. "Confederacy as a Solution to Chiefdom Dissolution: Historical Evidence in the Choctaw Case." In *The Forgotten Centuries: Indians and Europeans in the American South, 1521–1704*, ed. Charles Hudson and Carmen Tesser, 393–420. Athens: University of Georgia Press, 1994.

Galloway, Patricia, ed. *The Southeastern Ceremonial Complex: Artifacts and Analysis, The Cottonlandia Conference*. Lincoln: University of Nebraska Press, 1989.

———. *The Hernando De Soto Expedition: History, Historiography, and "Discovery" in the Southeast*. Lincoln: University of Nebraska Press, 1997.

Garrat, John. *The Four Indian Kings*. Ottawa: Public Archives of Canada, 1985.

Gatschet, Albert. *A Migration Legend of the Creek Indians: With a Linguistic, Historic, and Ethnographic Introduction*. Vols. 1–2. New York: Kraus Reprint, 1969.

Gearing, Fred. *Priests and Warriors: Social Structures for Cherokee Politics in the Eighteenth Century*. American Anthropological Association Memoir 93, Menosha WI, 1962.

Georgia Historical Society. *Collections* Vol. 7. Savannah: Georgia Historical Society, 1909.

Gillespie, Michele. "The Sexual Politics of Race and Gender: Mary Musgrove and the Georgia Trustees." In *The Devil's Lane: Sex and Race in the Early South*, ed. Catherine Clinton and Michele Gillespie, 187–204. Oxford: Oxford University Press, 1997.

Gipson, Lawrence Henry. *The British Empire before the American Revolution*. 13 vols. New York: Knopf, 1967.

Giraud, Marcel. *A History of French Louisiana*. 3 vols. Trans. Joseph Lambert. Baton Rouge: Louisiana State University Press, 1974.

Gluckman, Max, and Fred Eggan, eds. *Political Systems and the Distribution of Power*. London: Travistock, 1965.

Gold, Robert L. *Borderland Empires in Transition: The Triple-Nation Transfer of Florida*. Edwardsville IL: Southern Illinois Press, 1969.

Goody, Jack. *The Domestication of the Savage Mind*. Cambridge: Cambridge University Press, 1977.

———. *The Logic of Writing and the Organization of Society*. Cambridge: Cambridge University Press, 1986.

Gramsci, Antonio. *Prison Notebooks*. 2 vols. Ed. and Trans. Joseph A. Buttigieg and Antonio Callari. New York: Columbia University Press, 1975.

Green, Donald. *The Creek People*. Phoenix: Indian Tribal Series, 1973.

Green, Michael. "Mary Musgrove: Creating a New World." In *Sifters: Native American Women's Lives*, ed. Theda Perdue, 29–47. Oxford: Oxford University Press, 2001.

———. *The Politics of Indian Removal: Creek Government and Society in Crisis*. Lincoln: University of Nebraska Press, 1982.

Greene, Jack P., ed. *Colonies to Nation, 1763–1789: A Documentary History of the American Revolution*. New York: W. W. Norton, 1975.

Haan, Richard L. " 'The Trade Do's Not Flourish as Formerly': The Ecological Origins of the Yamasee War of 1715." *Ethnohistory* 28 (fall 1982): 341–358.

Haas, Mary. "Creek Inter-Town Relations." *American Anthropologist* 42, no. 3 (1940): 479–489.

Hahn, Steven. "The Invention of the Creek Nation." Ph.D. diss., Emory University, 2000.

Halley, David. *Ocmulgee Archaeology*. Athens: University of Georgia Press, 1994.

———. "Platform Mound Construction and the Instability of Mississippian Chiefdoms." In *Political Structure and Change in the Prehistoric Southeastern United States*, ed. John Scarry, chap. 6. Gainesville: University Press of Florida, 1996.

Hann, John. *Apalachee: The Land between the Rivers*. Gainesville: University Press of Florida, 1988.

———. *A History of the Timucua Indians and Missions*. Gainesville: University Press of Florida, 1996.

———. "Late Seventeenth-Century Forebears of the Lower Creeks and Seminoles." *Southeastern Archaeology* 15, no. 1 (September 1996): 66–80.

———. "St. Augustine's Fallout from the Yamassee War." *Florida Historical Quarterly* 68 (October 1989): 180–200.

———. "Florida's Terra Incognita: West Florida's Natives in the Sixteenth and Seventeenth Century." *The Florida Anthropologist* 41, no. 1 (1988): 61–107.

Hann, John, trans. "Translation of Governor Robolledo's 1657 Visitation of Three Florida Provinces and Related Documents." *Florida Archaeology* 2 (1986): 81–137.

———. "Visitations and Revolts in Florida, 1656–1695." *Florida Archaeology* 7 (1993): 1–296.

Harris, Walter. *Here the Creeks Sat Down*. Macon GA: J. W. Burke, 1958.

Hatch, James, ed. *Mississippian Communities and Households*. Tuscaloosa: University of Alabama Press, 1995.

Hayes, Louise, ed. *Indian Treaties, Cessions of Land in Georgia, 1705–1837*. (Atlanta: W.P.A. Project no. 7158, 1941).

Helms, Mary. "Esoteric Knowledge, Geographical Distance, and the Elaboration of Leadership Status: Dynamics of Resource Control." In *Profiles in Cultural Evolution: Papers From a Conference in Honor of*

Elman R. Service, ed. Terry Rambo and Kathleen Gillogly, 333–350. Ann Arbor: University of Michigan Press, 1991.

Henige, David. "Life after Death: The Posthumous Aggrandizement of Coosa." *Georgia Historical Quarterly* 4 (winter 1994): 687–715.

Hewitt, J. N. B. *Notes on the Creek Indians*. Ed. John Swanton. Smithsonian Institution Bureau of American Ethnology Bulletin 123. Anthropological Papers, no. 10.

Higginbotham, Jay. *Old Mobile: Fort Louis de la Louisiane, 1702–1711*. Mobile: Museum of the City of Mobile, 1977.

Hinderaker, Eric. *Elusive Empires: Constructing Colonialism in the Ohio Valley, 1673–1800*. Cambridge: Cambridge University Press, 1997.

———. "The 'Four Indian Kings' and the Imaginative Construction of the First British Empire." *William and Mary Quarterly*, 3d. ser., 53.3 (July 1996): 487–526.

Hirschmann, Albert. *The Passions and the Interests: Political Arguments for Capitalism before Its Triumph*. Princeton: Princeton University Press, 1977.

Hobsbawm, Eric, and Terence Ranger, eds. *The Invention of Tradition*. Cambridge: Cambridge University Press, 1983.

Hoffman, Kathleen. "The Archaeology of the Convento de San Francisco." In *The Spanish Missions of La Florida, 1993*, ed. Bonnie McEwan, 62–86. Gainesville: University Press of Florida, 1993.

Hoffman, Paul. "Did Coosa Decline between 1541 and 1560?" *The Florida Anthropologist* 50, no. 1 (March 1997): 25–29.

Hoffman, Ron, Mechal Sobel, and Fredrika Teute. *Through a Glass Darkly: Reflections on Personal Identity in Early America*. Chapel Hill: University of North Carolina Press, 1997.

Holmes, Geoffrey. *British Politics in the Age of Anne*. 2d ed. London: Hambledon, 1987.

Holton, Woody. *Forced Founders: Indians, Debtors, and Slaves and the Making of the American Revolution in Virginia*. Chapel Hill: University of North Carolina Press, 1999.

Hoxie, Frederick, ed. *Encyclopedia of North American Indians: Native American History, Culture, and Life from Paleo-Indians to the Present*. New York: Houghton Mifflin, 1996.

Hudson, Charles. *Black Drink: A Native American Tea*. Athens: University of Georgia Press, 1979.

———. *The Juan Pardo Expeditions: Exploration of the Carolinas and Tennessee, 1566–1568*. Washington DC: Smithsonian Institution Press, 1990.

———. *Knights of Spain, Warriors of the Sun: Hernando de Soto and the South's Ancient Chiefdoms*. Athens: University of Georgia Press, 1997.

———. *The Southeastern Indians*. Knoxville: University of Tennessee Press, 1976.

————. "A Spanish-Coosa Alliance in Sixteenth-Century North Georgia." *Georgia Historical Quarterly* 72, no. 4 (winter 1988): 599–626.

Hudson, Charles, ed. *Black Drink: A Native American Tea.* Athens: University of Georgia Press, 1979.

Hudson, Charles, and Carmen Tesser, eds. *The Forgotten Centuries: Indians and Europeans in the American South, 1521–1704.* Athens: University of Georgia Press, 1994.

Hukler, Gerralt, and Bruce Mannhiem, eds. *The Politics of Anthropology: From Colonialism and Sexism toward a View from Below.* The Hague: Mouton, 1979.

Hultkrantz, Ake. *Conceptions of the Soul among North American Indians.* Monograph Series, no. 1. Stockholm: Ethnographical Museum of Sweden, 1953.

Hvidt, Kristian, ed. *Von Reck's Voyage: Drawings and Journal of Philip Georg Friedrich von Reck.* Savannah: Beehive, 1990.

Insh, George Pratt. *Scottish Colonial Schemes, 1620–1686.* Glasgow: Maclehouse, Jackson, 1922.

Irving, Leonard A. *Spanish Approach to Pensacola, 1689–1693.* Albuquerque: Quivira Society, 1939.

Israel, Fred L., ed. *Major Peace Treaties of Modern History, 1648–1967.* 5 vols. New York: Chelsea House, 1967.

Jacobs, Wilbur, ed. *Indians of the Southern Colonial Frontier: The Edmund Atkin Report and Plan of 1755.* Columbia: University of South Carolina Press, 1950.

Jennings, Francis. *The Ambiguous Iroquois Empire: The Covenant Chain Confederation of Indian Tribes with English Colonies from Its Beginnings to the Lancaster Treaty of 1744.* New York: Norton, 1984.

Jennings, Francis, and William Fenton, eds. *The History and Culture of Iroquois Diplomacy: An Interdisciplinary Guide to the Treaties of the Six Nations and Their League.* Syracuse: Syracuse University Press, 1985.

————. *Empire of Fortune: Crowns, Colonies, and Tribes in the Seven Years War in America.* New York: Norton, 1988.

Johnson, Allen, and Timothy Earle. *The Evolution of Human Societies: From Foraging Group to Agrarian State.* Stanford: Stanford University Press, 1987.

Johnson, J. G. "The Spaniards in Northern Georgia During the Sixteenth Century." *Georgia Historical Quarterly* 9, no. 2 (June 1925): 159–167.

————. "The Yamassee Revolt of 1597 and the Destruction of the Georgia Missions." *Georgia Historical Quarterly* 9, no. 1 (1925): 44–53.

Juricek, John T., ed. *Early American Indian Documents: Treaties and Laws, 1607–1789.* Vol. 11, *Georgia Treaties, 1733–1763.* Frederick MD: University Publications of America, 1989.

————. *Early American Indian Documents: Treaties and Laws, 1607–1789. Vol. 12, Georgia and Florida Treaties, 1763–1776.* Frederick MD: University Publications of America, 2002.

Kan, Sergei. *Symbolic Immortality: The Tlingit Potlatch in the Nineteenth Century*. Washington DC: Smithsonian Institution Press, 1989.

Kaviraj, Sudipta. "The Imaginary Institution of India." *Subaltern Studies* 7. Delhi: Oxford University Press, 1992.

Kelton, Paul. "The Great Southeastern Smallpox Epidemic, 1696–1700: The Region's First Major Epidemic?" In *The Transformation of the Southeastern Indians, 1540–1760*, ed. Robbie Ethridge and Charles Hudson, 21–37. Jackson: University Press of Mississippi, 2002.

Kernion, George C. H., ed. and trans. "Documents Concerning the History of the Indians of the Eastern Region of Louisiana." *Louisiana Historical Quarterly* 8, no. 1 (January 1925): 28–40.

Keyes, Greg. "Myth and Social History in the Early Southeast." In *Perspectives on the Southeast: Linguistics, Archaeology, and Ethnohistory*, Southern Anthropological Society Proceedings 27, ed. Patricia Kwatchka, 106–125. Athens: University of Georgia Press, 1994.

Kimber, Edward. *A Relation or Journal of a Late Expedition to the Gates of St. Augustine on Florida*. 1744. Reprint, Boston: Charles Goodspeed, 1935.

Klein, Rachel N. *Unification of a Slave State: The Rise of the Planter Class in the South Carolina Backcountry, 1760–1808*. Chapel Hill: University of North Carolina Press, 1990.

Klingberg, Frank, ed. *The Carolina Chronicle of Dr. Francis LeJau*. Berkeley: University of California Press, 1956.

Knauft, Bruce. *From Primitive to Postcolonial in Melanesia and Anthropology*. Ann Arbor: University of Michigan Press, 1999.

Knight, Vernon J. "The Formation of the Creeks." In *The Forgotten Centuries: Indians and Europeans in the American South, 1521–1704*, ed. Charles Hudson and Carmen Tesser, 373–392. Athens: University of Georgia Press, 1994.

———. "Mississippian Ritual." Ph.D. diss., University of Florida, 1981.

———. "Symbolism of Mississippian Mounds." In *Powhatan's Mantle: Indians in the Colonial Southeast*, ed. Peter Wood, Gregory A. Waselkov, and M. Thomas Hatley, 279–291. Lincoln: University of Nebraska Press, 1989.

———. *Tuckabatchee: Archaeological Investigations at an Historic Creek Town, Elmore County, Alabama*. Report of Investigations 45. Tuscaloosa: University of Alabama Office of Archaeological Research, 1985.

Knight, Vernon, and Marvin T. Smith. "Big Tallassee: A Contribution to Upper Creek Site Archaeology." In *Early Georgia* 8, nos. 1–2 (1980): 59–74.

Kowaleski, Stephen, and James Hatch. "The Sixteenth-Century Expansion of Settlement in the Upper Oconee Watershed, Georgia." *Southeastern Archaeology* 10, no. 1 (1991): 1–17.

Krech, Shepard III. *The Ecological Indian: Myth and History*. New York: W. W. Norton, 1999.

Kugel, Rebecca. *To Be the Main Leaders of Our People: A History of Minnesota*

Ojibwe Politics, 1825–1898. East Lansing: Michigan State University Press, 1998.

Kwatchka, Patricia, ed. *Perspectives on the Southeast: Linguistics, Archaeology, and Ethnohistory*. Southern Anthropological Proceedings no. 22. Athens: University of Georgia Press, 1994.

Lamar, Howard, and Leonard Thompson, eds. *The Frontier in History: North America and Southern Africa Compared*. New Haven: Yale University Press, 1981.

Landers, Jane. *Black Society in Spanish Florida*. Urbana: University of Illinois Press, 1999.

Lane, Mills, ed. *General Oglethorpe's Georgia: Colonial Letters, 1733–1743*. 2 vols. Savannah: Beehive, 1975.

Lankford, George. "Red and White: Some Reflections on Southeastern Symbolism." *Southern Folklore* 50 (1993): 54–80.

Lanning, John Tate. *The Diplomatic History of Georgia: A Study of the Epoch of Jenkins' Ear*. Chapel Hill: University of North Carolina Press, 1936.

Larsen, Clark S., ed. *The Archaeology of Mission Santa Catalina de Guale: Two Biocultural Interpretations of a Population in Transition*. New York: Anthropological Papers of the American Museum of Natural History, 1990.

Leach, Douglas E. *Arms for Empire: A Military History of the British Colonies in North America, 1607–1763*. New York: Macmillan, 1973.

LeHarpe, Bernard. *The Historical Journal of the Establishment of the French in Louisiana*. Ed. Glenn R. Conrad. Trans. Joan Cain and Virginia Koenig. Lafayette LA: University of Southwest Louisiana Press, 1971.

Lemon, James T. *The Best Poor Man's Country: A Geographical Study of Early Pennsylvania*. Baltimore: Johns Hopkins University Press, 1972.

Lévi-Strauss, Claude. *Structural Anthropology*. London: Penguin, 1963.

———. *Totemism*. Trans. Rodney Needham. Boston: Beacon, 1963.

———. *The Savage Mind*. Chicago: University of Chicago Press, 1962.

Lipscomb, Terry. *Colonial Records of South Carolina: Journal of the Commons House of Assembly, 1752–1755*. Vols. 12–13. Columbia: University of South Carolina Press, 1983.

Lolly, Terry L. "Ethnohistory and Archeology: A Map Method for Locating Historic Upper Creek Indian Towns and Villages." *Journal of Alabama Archaeology* 42, no. 1 (June 1996): 1–92.

Lowie, Robert. *The Origin of the State*. New York: Harcourt Brace, 1927.

Malinowski, Bronislaw. *Magic, Science, and Religion and Other Essays*. Ed. Robert Redfield. Glencoe IL: Free Press, 1948.

Marshall, P. J., ed. *Oxford History of the British Empire. Vol. 2, The Eighteenth Century*. Oxford: Oxford University Press, 1998.

Martin, Jack B., and Margaret McKane Mauldin. *A Dictionary of Creek/Muskogee*. Lincoln: University of Nebraska Press, 2000.

Martin, Joel. "Rebalancing the World in the Contradictions of History: Creek/Muskogee." In *Native Religions and Cultures of North America:*

Anthropology of the Sacred, ed. Lawrence E. Sullivan, 85–103. New York: Continuum, 2000.

———. *Sacred Revolt: The Muskogees' Struggle for a New World*. Boston: Beacon, 1991.

Martin, Paul S., and Christine R. Szuter. "War Zones and Game Sinks in Lewis and Clark's West." *Conservation Biology* 12, no. 1 (February 1999): 36–45.

Mason, Carol. "Eighteenth-Century Culture Change among the Lower Creeks." *Florida Anthropologist* 16 (September 1963): 65–80.

———. "Archaeology of Ocmulgee Old Fields, Macon, Georgia." Ph.D. diss., University of Michigan, 1963.

McConnell, Michael N. *A Country Between: The Upper Ohio Valley and Its Peoples, 1724–1774*. Lincoln: University of Nebraska Press, 1992.

McCusker, John, and Russell Menard. *The Economy of British America, 1607–1789*. Chapel Hill: University of North Carolina Press, 1985.

McDowell, Jon Alexander. "Royalizing South Carolina: The Revolution of 1719." Ph.D. diss., University of South Carolina, 1991.

McDowell, W. L., ed. *Colonial Records of South Carolina: Journal of the Commissioners of the Indian Trade, September 20, 1710–August 29, 1718*. Columbia SC: State Printing, 1955.

———. *Colonial Records of South Carolina: Documents Relating to Indian Affairs, 1750–1754*. Columbia SC: State Printing, 1958.

———. *Colonial Records of South Carolina: Documents Relating to Indian Affairs, 1754–1765*. Columbia SC: State Printing, 1970.

McEwan, Bonnie, ed. *Indians of the Greater Southeast: Historical Archaeology and Ethnohistory*. Gainesville: University Press of Florida, 2000.

———. *The Spanish Missions of La Florida*. Gainesville: University Press of Florida, 1993.

McIlwaine, H. R., ed. *Journal of the House of Burgesses of Virginia, 1619–1658/59*. Richmond: Colonial, 1915.

Menard, Russel. "From Servants to Slaves: The Transformation of the Chesapeake Labor System." *Southern Studies* 16 (1977): 355–390.

Mereness, Newton, ed. *Travels in the American Colonies*. New York: Macmillan, 1916.

Meriwether, Robert. *The Expansion of South Carolina, 1729–1765*. Kingsport TN: Southern, 1940.

Merrell, James H. "The Cast of His Countenance: Reading Andrew Montour." In *Through a Glass Darkly: Reflections on Personal Identity in Early America*, ed. Ron Hoffman, Mechal Sobel, and Fredrika Teute. Chapel Hill: University of North Carolina Press, 1997.

———. *The Indians' New World: Catawbas and Their Neighbors from European Contact through the Era of Removal*. New York: Norton, 1989.

———. *Into the American Woods: Negotiators on the Pennsylvania Frontier*. New York: Norton, 1999.

Milanich, Jerald, and William Sturtevant, eds. *Francisco Pareja's 1613*

Confessionario: A Documentary Source for Timucuan Ethnography. Trans. Emilio Moran. Tallahassee: Florida Division of Archives, History, and Records Management, 1972.

Montiano, Don Manuel de. *Collections of the Georgia Historical Society: Letters of Montiano, Siege of St. Augustine*. Vol. 7, pt. 1. Savannah: Georgia Historical Society, 1909.

Moore, John Alexander. "Royalizing South Carolina: The Revolution of 1719." Ph.D. diss., University of South Carolina, 1991.

Moore, John H. "Mvskoke Personal Names." *Names* 43, no. 3 (September 1995): 187–212.

Morgan, Edmund S. *American Slavery, American Freedom: The Ordeal of Colonial Virginia*. New York: Norton, 1975.

Morgan, Kenneth. "The Organization of the Colonial Rice Trade." *William and Mary Quarterly* 3d. ser., no. 52 (1995): 433–452.

Morris, Michael. "The Bringing of Wonder: The Effect of European Trade on the Indians of the Southern Backcountry, 1700–1783." Ph.D. diss., Auburn University, 1993.

Muller, Jon. *Mississippian Political Economy*. New York: Plenum, 1997.

Nairne, Thomas. *Nairne's Muskhogean Journals: The 1708 Expedition to the Mississippi River*. Ed. Alexander Moore. Jackson: University Press of Mississippi, 1988.

Oatis, Steven. "A Colonial Complex: Indians and Imperialists in the Yamasee War." Ph.D diss., Emory University, 1999.

O'Brien, Greg. *Choctaws in a Revolutionary Age, 1750-1830* (Lincoln: University of Nebraska Press, 2002).

Olsberg, R. Nicholas, ed. *Colonial Records of South Carolina: Journal of the Commons House of Assembly, 1750–1751*. Vol. 10. Columbia: University of South Carolina Press, 1975.

Ong, Walter. *Orality and Literacy: the Technologizing of the Word*. London: Methuen, 1982.

Opler, Morris E. "The Creek 'Town' and the Problem of Creek Indian Political Reorganization." In *Human Problems in Technological Change: A Casebook*, ed. Edward Spicer, 165–180. New York: Russel Sage Foundation, 1952.

———. "Report on the History and Contemporary State of Aspects of Creek Social Organization." *Papers in Anthropology* 13, no. 1 (spring 1972): 30–75.

Pargellis, Stanley. *Lord Loudon in North America*. New Haven: Yale University Press, 1933.

Parker, Percy Livingstone, ed. *The Heart of John Wesley's Journal*. New York: Fleming H. Revell, n.d.

Pauketat, Timothy. *The Ascent of Chiefs: Cahokia and Mississippian Politics in Native North America*. Tuscaloosa: University of Alabama Press, 1994.

———. "Specialization, Political Symbols, and the Crafty Elite of Cahokia." *Southeastern Archaeology* 16, no. 1 (summer 1997): 1–16.

Peckham, Howard. *The Colonial Wars, 1689–1762*. Chicago: University of Chicago Press, 1964.

Penicaut, Andre. *Fleur de Lys and Calumet: Being the Penicaut Narrative of French Adventure in Louisiana*. Trans. Richebourg Gaillard McWilliams. Baton Rouge: Louisiana State University Press, 1953.

Pennington, Edgar Legare. "The South Carolina Indian War of 1715 as Seen by the Clergymen." *South Carolina Genealogical and Historical Magazine* 32, no. 4 (October 1931): 251–269.

Perdue, Theda. *Sifters: Native American Women's Lives*. Oxford: Oxford University Press, 2001.

———. *Cherokee Women: Gender and Culture Change, 1700–1835*. Lincoln: University of Nebraska Press, 1998.

———. *Slavery and the Evolution of Cherokee Society, 1540–1866*. Knoxville: University of Tennessee Press, 1979.

Piker, Joshua. "The Fanni Micos of Oakfuskee: The Role of A Creek Town in Eighteenth-Century Inter- and Intra-Cultural Diplomacy." Paper Presented at the American Society for Ethnohistory Annual Meeting, Portland, Oregon, 1996.

———. " 'Peculiarly Connected': The Creek Town of Oakfuskee and the Study of Colonial American Communities." Ph.D. diss., Cornell University, 1998.

———. " 'White and Clean' and Contested: Creek Towns and Trading Paths in the Aftermath of the Seven Years' War." *Ethnohistory* 50.2 (spring 2003): 315–347.

Porter, Kenneth. "The Founder of the 'Seminole Nation': Secoffee or Cowkeeper." *Florida Historical Quarterly* 27 (1948–49): 362–84.

Price, Catherine. *The Oglala People: A Political History, 1841–1879*. Lincoln: University of Nebraska Press, 1996.

Priestley, Herbert I. *Tristan de Luna: Conquistador of the Old South*. Glendale CA: Arthur H. Clark, 1936.

Priestley, Herbert I., trans. and ed. *The Luna Papers: Documents Relating to the Expedition of Don Tristan de Luna y Arellano for the Conquest of La Florida in 1559–1661*. 3 vols. Deland FL: Florida State Historical Society, 1928.

Radcliffe-Brown, H. R. *Structure and Function in Primitive Society*. Glencoe IL: Free Press, 1953.

Rambo, Terry, and Kathleen Gillogly, eds. *Profiles in Cultural Evolution: Papers from a Conference in Honor of Elman R. Service*. Ann Arbor: University of Michigan Press, 1991.

Ramenofsky, Ann. *Vectors of Death: The Archaeology of European Contact*. Albuquerque: University of New Mexico Press, 1987.

Ramsey, William. " 'Something Cloudy in Their Looks': The Origins of the Yamasee War." *Journal of American History* 90.1 (June 2003): 1–68.

Rayson, David Timothy. "'A Great Matter to Tell': Indians, Europeans, and Africans from the Mississippian Era through the Yamassee War in the North American Southeast." Ph.D. diss., University of Minnesota, 1996.

Reding, Katherine, ed. and trans. "Plans for the Colonization and Defense of Apalache, 1675." *Georgia Historical Quarterly* 9, no. 2 (June 1925): 169–174.

Redmond, Elsa, ed. *Chiefdoms and Chieftaincy in the Americas.* Gainesville: University Press of Florida, 1999.

Reeves, Carolyn, ed. *The Choctaw before Removal.* Jackson: University Press of Mississippi, 1985.

Reid, John Phillip. *A Better Kind of Hatchet: Law, Trade, and Diplomacy in the Cherokee Nation during the Early Years of European Contact.* University Park: Pennsylvania State University Press, 1976.

Richter, Daniel. *Facing East from Indian Country: A Native History of Early America.* Cambridge: Harvard University Press, 2001.

———. "Native Peoples of North America and the Eighteenth-Century Empire." In *Oxford History of the British Empire*, ed. P. J. Marshall, Vol. 2: *The Eighteenth Century*, 347–371. Oxford: Oxford University Press, 1998.

———. *The Ordeal of the Longhouse: The Peoples of the Iroquois League in the Era of European Colonization.* Chapel Hill: University of North Carolina Press, 1992.

———. "War and Culture: The Iroquois Experience." *William and Mary Quarterly* 40, no. 3 (1983): 528–559.

Richter, Daniel, and James Merrell, eds. *Beyond the Covenant Chain: The Iroquois and Their Neighbors in Indian North America, 1600–1800.* Syracuse NY: Syracuse University Press, 1987.

Robertson, James, trans. "Account by a Gentleman from Elvas." In *The DeSoto Chronicles: The Expedition of Hernando De Soto to North America in 1539–1543*, vol. 1, ed. Lawrence Clayton, Vernon J. Knight, and Edward Moore, (need page nos.). Tuscaloosa: University of Alabama Press, 1993.

Rollings, Willard. *The Osage: An Ethnohistorical Study of Hegemony on the Prairie Plains.* Columbia: University of Missouri Press, 1992.

Ross, Mary L. "The French on the Savannah, 1605." *Georgia Historical Quarterly* 8, no. 3 (September 1924): 167–190.

Rowland, Dunbar, and A. G. Sanders, eds. *Mississippi Provincial Archives —French Dominion.* Vols. 1–3. Jackson: Mississippi Department of Archives and History, 1927.

Rowland, Dunbar, A. G. Sanders, and Patricia Galloway, eds. and trans. *Mississippi Provincial Archives—French Dominion.* Vols. 4–5. Baton Rouge: Louisiana State University Press, 1984.

Sahlins, Marshal. *Islands of History.* Chicago: University of Chicago Press, 1985.

————. *Tribesmen.* Englewood Cliffs NJ: Prentice-Hall, 1968.

Sainsbury, Noel. *Great Britain Public Record Office, Calendar of State Papers, Colonial Series.* Vol. 7. London: 1860–.

Sainsbury, Noel, J. W. Fortescue, Cecil Hedlam, and A. P. Newton. *Great Britain Public Record Office, Calendar of State Papers, Colonial Series.* 38 volumes. London: 1860–1919.

Salley, A. S. "The Creek Indian Tribes in 1725: Charlesworth Glover's Account of the Indian Tribes of March 15, 1725." *South Carolina Genealogical and Historical Quarterly* 32, no. 2 (April 1931): 241–242.

Salley, A. S., ed. *Journal of Colonel John Herbert, October 17, 1727 to March 19, 1728.* Columbia: State Printing, 1936.

————. *Journal of the South Carolina Commons House of Assembly, 1692–1726.* 16 vols. Columbia: State Printing, 1907–1945.

————. *Journal of the South Carolina Commons House of Assembly, 1736–1739.* Columbia: State Printing, 1947.

————. *Journal of the Grand Council of South Carolina, 1671–1680.* Columbia: State Printing, 1907.

————. *Narratives of Early Carolina, 1650–1708.* New York: Scribner's Sons, 1911.

Saunders, William, ed. *Colonial Records of North Carolina.* Raleigh: P. M. Hale, 1886.

Saunt, Claudio M. " 'The English Has Now a Mind to Make Slaves of Them All': Creeks, Seminoles, and the Problem of Slavery." *American Indian Quarterly* 22 (winter–spring 1998): 157–181.

————. " 'A New Order of Things': Creeks and Seminoles in the Deep South Interior, 1733–1816." Ph.D. diss., Duke University, 1996.

————. *A New Order of Things: Property, Power, and the Transformation of the Creek Indians, 1733–1816.* Oxford: Oxford University Press, 1999.

Scarry, John. "The Nature of Mississippian Societies." In *Political Structure and Change in the Prehistoric Southeastern United States*, ed. John Scarry, chap. 2. Gainesville: University Press of Florida, 1996.

Schell, Frank, Vernon Knight, and Gail Schell. *Cemochechobee: Archaeology of a Mississippian Ceremonial Center on the Chattahoochee River.* Gainesville: University Press of Florida, 1981.

Serrano y Sanz, Manuel. *Documentos Historicos de la Florida y la Luisiana, Siglos 16 al 18.* Madrid: V. Suarez, 1912.

Service, Elman R. *Primitive Social Organization: An Evolutionary Perspective.* New York: Random House, 1962.

————. *Origins of the State and Civilization.* New York: W. W. Norton, 1975.

Shannon, Timothy. "Dressing for Success on the Mohawk Frontier: Hendrick, William Johnson, and the Indian Fashion." *William and Mary Quarterly* 53, no. 1 (January 1996): 13–42.

Shoemaker, Nancy. "An Alliance between Men: Gender Metaphors in

Eighteenth-Century American Indian Diplomacy East of the Mississippi." *Ethnohistory* 46.2 (spring 1999): 239–263.

Simpson, D. P., ed. *Cassell's Latin Dictionary.* New York: Macmillan, 1959.

Smith, Alan G. R. *The Emergence of a Nation State: The Commonwealth of England, 1529–1660.* Foundations of Modern Britain Series. Gen. ed., Geoffrey Holmes. London: Longman, 1984.

Smith, Marvin T. "Aboriginal Population Movements in the Postcontact Southeast." In *Transformation of the Southeastern Indians 1540–1670,* ed. Robbie Ethridge and Charles Hudson, 3–20. Jackson: University Press of Mississippi, 2002.

———. *Archaeology of Aboriginal Culture Change in the Interior Southeast: Depopulation during the Early Historic Period.* Gainesville: University of Florida Press, 1987.

———. *Coosa: The Rise and Fall of a Mississippian Chiefdom.* Gainesville: University of Florida Press, 2000.

Smith, Todd Foster. "On the Convergence of Empire: The Caddo Indian Confederacies, 1542–1835." Ph.D. diss., Tulane University, 1989.

Snapp, J. Russel. *John Stuart and the Struggle for Empire on the Southern Frontier.* Baton Rouge: Louisiana State University Press, 1996.

Snell, David R. "Indian Slavery in Colonial South Carolina." Ph.D. diss., University of Alabama, 1972.

Sonderegger, Richard Paul. "The Southern Frontier from the Founding of Georgia to the End of King George's War." Ph.D. diss., University of Michigan, 1964.

South Carolina Historical Society. *Collections,* vol. 5. Charleston: South Carolina Historical Society, 1897.

Speck, Frank. "Some Comparative Traits of the Maskogian Languages." *American Anthropologist* 9 (1907): 470–483.

———. *Ethnology of the Yuchi Indians.* Anthropological Publications of the University of Pennsylvania Museum. Vol. 1, no. 1. Atlantic Highlands NJ: Humanities Press, 1909.

———. *The Creek Indians of Taskigi Town.* Millwood NY: Kraus Reprint, 1974.

Spivak, Gayatri C. "The Rani of Sirmur: An Essay on Reading the Archives." *History and Theory* 24, no. 3 (1985): 247–272.

Spoehr, Alexander. "Changing Kinship Systems: A Study in the Acculturation of the Creeks, Cherokee, and Choctaw." *Anthropological Series, Field Museum of Natural History* 33, no. 4 (January 1947): 159–233.

———. "Brief Communication: Creek Inter-Town Relations." *American Anthropologist* 43 (1941): 133–134.

Steinen, Karl T. "Ambushes, Raids, and Palisades: Mississippian Warfare in the Interior Southeast." *Southeastern Archaeology* 11, no. 2 (winter 1992): 132–139.

Steoponaitis, Vin. "Contrasting Patterns of Mississippian Development." In *Chiefdoms: Power, Economy, and Ideology*, ed. Timothy Earle, 193–228. Cambridge: Cambridge University Press, 1997.

Stiggins, George. *Creek Indian History: A Historical Narrative of the Genealogy, Traditions, and Downfall of the Ispocoga or Creek Indian tribe of Indians*. Intro. and notes by William S. Wyman. Birmingham AL: Birmingham Library Press, 1989.

Stuckey, Mary E., and John M. Murphy. "By Any Other Name: Rhetorical Colonialism in North America." *American Indian Culture and Research Journal* 25.4 (2001): 73–98.

Sturtevant, William. *The Missions of Spanish Florida: Spanish Borderlands Sourcebooks*. Vol. 23. New York: Garland, 1991.

Sullivan, Faye Ann. "The Georgia Frontier, 1754–1775." Master's thesis, Florida State University, 1975.

Sullivan, Lawrence E. *Native Religions and Cultures of North America: Anthropology of the Sacred*. New York: Continuum, 2000.

Swagerty, William Royce Jr. "Beyond Bimini: Indian Responses to European Incursions in the Spanish Borderlands, 1513–1600." Ph.D. diss., University of California at Santa Barbara, 1981.

Swanton, John R. "Animal Stories from the Indians of the Muskhogean Stock." *Journal of American Folklore* 26, no. 101 (July–September 1913): 193–218.

————. *Indian Tribes of the Southeastern United States*. U.S. Bureau of American Ethnology Bulletin no. 137. Washington DC: Government Printing Office, 1946.

————. "Social Organization and Social Usages of the Creek Confederacy." *42nd Annual Report of the Bureau of American Ethnology*. Washington DC: Government Printing Office, 1928.

————. *Early History of the Creek Indians and their Neighbors*. U.S. Bureau of American Ethnography Bulletin no. 103. Washington DC: Government Printing Office, 1922.

————. *Myths and Tales of the Southeastern Indians*. 1929. Reprint, Norman: University of Oklahoma Press, 1995.

Swartz, Marc., ed. *Local Level Politics: Social and Cultural Perspectives*. Chicago: Aldine, 1968.

Swartz, Marc, Victor Turner, and Arthur Tuden, eds. *Political Anthropology*. Chicago: Aldine, 1966.

Talbot, Francis Xavier, S.J. *Saint among the Hurons: The Life of Jean de Brebeuf*. New York: Harper & Brothers, 1949.

Tepaske, John Jay. *The Governorship of Spanish Florida, 1700–1763*. Durham NC: Duke University Press, 1964.

Thomas, Daniel H. *Fort Toulouse: The French Outpost at the Alabamas on the Coosa*. With an introduction by Gregory Waselkov. Tuscaloosa: University of Alabama Press, 1989.

Thomas, David H. *Skull Wars: Kennewick Man, Archaeology, and the Battle for Native American Identity*. New York: Basic, 2000.

Thomas, David H., ed. *Columbian Consequences: Archaeological and Historical Perspectives on the Spanish Borderlands East*. Vol. 2. Washington DC: Smithsonian Institution Press, 1990.

Thrower, Norman. *Maps & Civilization: Cartography in Culture and Society*. Chicago: University of Chicago Press, 1972.

Thwaites, Reuben G., ed. *The Jesuit Relations and Allied Documents: Travels and Explorations of the Jesuit Missionaries in New France, 1610–1791*. 73 vols. Cleveland: Burrows Brothers, 1899.

Timothy, Peter. *Journal of the Congress of the Four Southern Governors and the Superintendent of that District with the Five Nations of Indians at Augusta, 1763*. Charles Town SC: 1764.

Tooker, Elizabeth. "Clans and Moieties in North America." *Current Anthropology* 12 (1971): 357–76.

Tooker, E., and Morton Fried, eds. *The Development of Political Organization in Native North America*. Washington DC: Proceedings of the American Ethnological Society, 1983.

Tuggle, W. O. *Shem, Ham, and Japeth: The Papers of W. O. Tuggle*. Ed. Eugene Current-Garcia. Athens: University of Georgia Press, 1984.

Turner, Victor. *Schism and Continuity in an African Society: A Study of Ndembu Village Life*. Manchester: University of Manchester Press, 1957.

———. *Dramas, Fields, and Metaphors: Symbolic Action in Human Society*. Cornell: Cornell University Press, 1974.

Usner, Daniel. *Indians, Settlers, and Slaves in a Frontier Exchange Economy: The Lower Mississippi Valley before 1783*. Chapel Hill: University of North Carolina Press, 1992.

Vaughn, Alden, and Deborah Rosen, eds. *Early American Indian Documents: Treaties and Laws, 1607–1789*. Vol. 16, *Carolina and Georgia Laws*. Frederick MD: University Publications of America, 1998.

Ver Steeg, Clarence, ed. *A True and Historical Narrative of the Colony of Georgia, by Pat. Tailfer and Others, with Comments by the Earl of Egmont*. Athens: University of Georgia Press, 1960.

Wallace, Anthony F. C. "Origins of Iroquois Neutrality: The Grand Settlement of 1701." *Pennsylvania History* 24, no. 3 (July 1957): 223–235.

Waselkov, Gregory. "Seventeenth-Century Trade in the Colonial Southeast." *Southeastern Archaeology* 2, no. 8 (winter 1989): 117–133.

———. *Archaeological Excavations at the Early Historic Creek Indian Town of Fusihatchee (Phase I, 1988–1989)*. A Report to the National Science Foundation, Grant no. BNS-8718934 (May 1990).

———. "Historic Creek Indian Responses to European Trade and the Rise of Political Factions." In *Ethnohistory and Archaeology: Approaches to Postcontact Change in the Americas*, ed. J. Daniel Rogers, 123–131. New York: Plenum, 1993.

———. "The Macon Trading House and Early Indian-European Contact in the Colonial Southeast." In *Ocmulgee Archaeology, 1936–1986*, ed. David Halley, 190–196. Athens: University of Georgia Press, 1994.

Waselkov, Gregory, and Kathryn Braund, eds. *William Bartram on the Southeastern Indians.* Lincoln: University of Nebraska Press, 1995.

Waselkov, Gregory, and John W. Cottier. "European Perceptions of Eastern Muskogean Ethnicity." In *Proceedings of the Tenth Meeting of the French Colonial Historical Society, 1984,* ed. P. P. Boucher, 23–33. Frederick MD: University Press of America, 1984.

Weber, David. *The Spanish Frontier in North America.* New Haven: Yale University Press, 1992.

Weber, Mabel, ed. "Journall, Capt. Dunlop's Voyage to the Southward, 1687." *South Carolina Historical and Genealogical Magazine* 30, no. 3 (July 1929): 127–133.

Weiner, Margaret. *Visible and Invisible Realms: Power, Magic, and Colonial Conquest of Bali.* Chicago: University of Chicago Press, 1995.

Weisman, Brent. "Archaeological Perspectives on Seminole Ethnogenesis." In *Indians of the Greater Southeast: Historical Archaeology and Ethnohistory,* ed. Bonnie McEwan, 299–315. Gainesville: University Press of Florida, 2000.

———. *Like Beads on a String: A Culture History of the Seminole Indians in Northern Peninsular Florida.* Tuscaloosa: University of Alabama Press, 1989.

———. *Unconquered People: Florida's Seminole and Miccosukee Indians.* Gainesville: University Press of Florida, 1999.

White, Christine. "Opothleyahola: Factionalism and Creek Politics." Ph.D. diss., Texas Christian University, 1986.

White, Richard. *The Middle Ground: Indians, Empires, and Republics in the Great Lakes Region, 1650–1815.* Cambridge: Cambridge University Press, 1991.

———. *The Roots of Dependency: Subsistence, Environment, and Social Change among the Choctaws, Pawnees, and Navajos.* Lincoln: University of Nebraska Press, 1983.

Wickman, Patricia R. *The Tree that Bends: Discourse, Power, and the Survival of the Maskoki People.* Tuscaloosa: University of Alabama Press, 1999.

Widmer, Randolph. "The Structure of Southeastern Chiefdoms." In *The Forgotten Centuries: Indians and Europeans in the American South, 1521–1704,* ed. Charles Hudson and Carmen Tesser, 125–155. Athens: University of Georgia Press, 1994.

Wilder, Effie Leland. *Henry Woodward: Forgotten Man of American History.* South Carolina State Archives. No Date.

Willis, William. "Colonial Conflict and the Cherokee Indians, 1710–1760." Ph.D. diss., Columbia University, 1955.

———. "Patrilineal Institutions in Southeastern North America." *Ethnohistory* 10 (1963): 250–269.

Wilson, Samuel M., and Daniel Rodgers, eds. *Ethnohistory and Archaeology: Approaches to Postcontact Change in the Americas.* New York: Plenum, 1993.

Wood, Peter. *Black Majority: Negroes in Colonial South Carolina from 1670 through the Stone Rebellion*. New York: Knopf, 1974.

Woodward, Henry. "A Faithfull Relation of My Westoe Voyage, 1674." In *Narratives of Early Carolina*, ed. A. S. Salley, 130–131, *Narratives of Early Carolina, 1650–1708*. New York: Scribner's Sons, 1911.

Woodward, Thomas S. *Woodward's Reminisces of the Creek, or Muscogee Indians: Contained in Letters to Friends from Georgia and Alabama*. Mobile AL: Southern University Press, 1965.

Worth, John E. "The Lower Creeks: Origins and Early History." In *Indians of the Greater Southeast: Historical Archaeology and Ethnohistory*, ed. Bonnie McEwan, 265–298. Gainesville: University Press of Florida, 2000.

———. "Prelude to Abandonment: The Interior Provinces of Early Seventeenth-Century Georgia." *Early Georgia* 21 (1993): 24–58.

———. *Struggle for the Georgia Coast: An Eighteenth-Century Spanish Retrospective on Guale and Mocama*. American Museum of Natural History Anthropological Papers, no. 75. Athens: University of Georgia Press, 1995.

———. *The Timucuan Chiefdoms of Florida*. 2 vols. Gainesville: University of Florida Press, 1998.

Worth, John E., trans. "Account by Rodrigo Rangel." In *The DeSoto Chronicles: The Expedition of Hernando De Soto to North America in 1539–1543*, vol. 1, ed. Lawrence Clayton, Vernon J. Knight, and Edward Moore, 284–294. Tuscaloosa: University of Alabama Press, 1993.

———. "Account by Luys Hernandez de Biedma." In *The DeSoto Chronicles: The Expedition of Hernando De Soto to North America in 1539–1543*, vol. 1, ed. Lawrence Clayton, Vernon J. Knight, and Edward Moore, need page no. Tuscaloosa: University of Alabama Press, 1993.

Wright, Amos. "Upper Alabama River Historic Indian Towns and Their Inhabitants." *Journal of Alabama Archaeology* 24, no. 2 (1978): 102–117.

Wright, J. Leitch. *Creeks and Seminoles*. Lincoln: University of Nebraska Press, 1986.

———. *Anglo-Spanish Rivalry in North America*. Athens: University of Georgia Press, 1971.

Young, Biloine Whiting, and Melvin Fowler, *Cahokia: The Great Native American Metropolis* (Urbana: University of Illinois Press, 2000).

Index

Cherokee Women
Gender and Culture Change, 1700–1835
By Theda Perdue

The Brainerd Journal
A Mission to the Cherokees, 1817–1823
Edited and introduced by Joyce B. Phillips
and Paul Gary Phillips

The Cherokees
A Population History
By Russell Thornton

Buffalo Tiger
A Life in the Everglades
By Buffalo Tiger and Harry A. Kersey Jr.

American Indians in the Lower Mississippi Valley
Social and Economic Histories
By Daniel H. Usner Jr.

Powhatan's Mantle
Indians in the Colonial Southeast
Edited by Peter H. Wood, Gregory A. Waselkov,
and M. Thomas Hatley

Creeks and Seminoles
The Destruction and Regeneration
of the Muscogulge People
By J. Leitch Wright Jr.